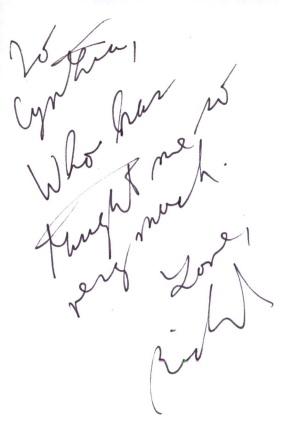

To Cynthia,
Who has
taught me so
very much.
Love,
Richard

BREAKTHROUGH

**Recent Titles in
War, Technology, and History**

BREAKTHROUGH

The Gorlice-Tarnow Campaign, 1915

Richard L. DiNardo

War, Technology, and History
Robert Citino, Series Editor

 PRAEGER

AN IMPRINT OF ABC-CLIO, LLC
Santa Barbara, California • Denver, Colorado • Oxford, England

Library of Congress Cataloging-in-Publication Data
DiNardo, R. L.
    Breakthrough: the Gorlice-Tarnow campaign, 1915 / Richard L. DiNardo.
      p. cm. — (War, technology, and history)
    Includes bibliographical references and index.
    ISBN 978-0-275-99110-4 (alk. paper) — ISBN 978-0-313-08183-5 (ebook)
1. Gorlice-Tarnow, Battle of, Poland, 1915.   I. Title.
    D557.G6D56   2010
    940.4'25—dc22   2010002194

ISBN: 978-0-275-99110-4
EISBN: 978-0-313-08183-5

14   13   12   11   10   1   2   3   4   5

This book is also available on the World Wide Web as an eBook.
Visit www.abc-clio.com for details.

Praeger
An Imprint of ABC-CLIO, LLC

ABC-CLIO, LLC
130 Cremona Drive, P.O. Box 1911
Santa Barbara, California 93116-1911

This book is printed on acid-free paper ∞

Manufactured in the United States of America

To the memory of my *Doktorvater,*
Professor David Syrett (1939–2004)
scholar, teacher, mentor, friend

Contents

A photo essay follows page 68

Maps

Series Foreword

Military historians can be a contentious, feisty lot. There is little upon which they agree. The importance of attrition vs. maneuver, the relative qualities of "deep battle" and "Blitzkrieg," the command abilities of Patton and Montgomery: put two military historians in a room and you'll likely get three opinions on any of these questions. And yet, there is one thing that unites military historians across the spectrum. Virtually everyone within the field recognizes the crucial role that technology has played in the development of the military art. Indeed, this is almost axiomatic: the very first man who picked up a club against his neighbor was wielding "technology" of a sort. The outcome of wars hasbeen profoundly affected by the technological context in which they were fought. From spoke-wheeled chariots to the M1A1 tank, from blades of Toledo steel to the AK-47, from primitive "bombards" to the MOAB ("mother of all bombs"), the problem of technology has stood at the forefront of military history.

Beyond that unifying proposition, however, problems can still arise in analyzing the precise role of technology. Consider for a moment the impact of the Industrial Revolution. Just as it transformed society, economy, and culture, it changed the appearance of war beyond all recognition. It was the age of the mass army, "railroads and rifles," and the telegraph. The growth of industry allowed military forces to grow to unheard-of size. In 1757, Frederick the Great triumphed over the French at Rossbach with an army that totaled 22,000 men; at Königgrätz in 1866, well over 400,000 men would be contesting the issue, and Austrian casualties alone, some 44,000 men, would be precisely twice as large as Frederick's victorious host at Rossbach. The railroad allowed these hordes to move, quite literally, twenty-four hours per day, and the problem of the slow-moving supply column that had bedeviled military operations from time out of mind seemed to have been solved. Moreover, the introduction of the telegraph meant that armies could be kept on a tight leash, even by commanders hundreds of miles away.

For each advantage of the new technology, however, there was a corresponding difficulty. It was soon clear that commanding and controlling the mass army was a huge, even insurmountable, problem. It is generally agreed that Napoleon I had serious problems in this area in 1812, and that he was at his best with armies that totaled 85,000 men or less. It was foolish to expect an army of several hundred thousand men to maneuver nimbly across the countryside, wheel like a company, and whack the opponent a surprise blow in the flank. In fact, getting them to maneuver at all was a stretch. The telegraph was a modern marvel, true, but the vision it offered of total control of far-flung operations turned out to be a mirage. Tied to a static system of poles and wires, it was far more useful to the defender than to the attacker, and it was nearly useless in any kind of mobile campaign. The mass army, then, was a huge body with a small brain, and had a very difficult time doing much more than marching straight ahead and crashing into whatever happened to be in front of it.

At that point, a mutual slaughter began. The other great technological advance of the era was introduction of new firearms—the rifled musket, or simply "rifle." It dramatically improved the range and firepower of infantry and the 1860's would see another breakthrough, the breech-loader, which greatly increased rate of fire. With long-range rifles now in the hands of the defenders, assault columns could theoretically be shot to pieces long before they struck home. In place of the old-style assault, there now arose the firefight, with extended skirmish lines on both sides replacing the formations of line and column. It was an "open order revolution," the logical culmination of tactical developments since the French Revolution. Open order tactics, however, rarely allowed enough concentration of fighting power for a successful assault. Both sides lined up and fired. There were casualties, enormous casualties, often for little gain. It was the great conundrum of the era. Clearly, technology was not so much a solution to a problem on the 19th century battlefield; it was more like the problem itself.

These are the issues that will form the heart of Praeger's new War, Technology, and History series. Books in the series will focus on the crucial relationship between warmaking and technological advance in the past 200 years. During that period, new machines like the rifle, the railroad, and the telegraph (in the 19th century) and the machine gun, the airplane, and the tank (in the 20th) have transformed the face of war. In the young 21st century, the U.S. Army has been emphasizing the ways in which information technology can have an even more radical transformative impact. Historically, armies that have managed to integrate these new technologies have found corresponding success on the battlefield, and their victories have as often as not come at the expense of those who have failed to ground their warmaking doctrine squarely in the available technology. The question is, therefore, much wider than a simple list of technical "specs" for various weapons. Books in the series will link technology and doctrine—that is, the weapons and the manner in which they were employed on actual battlefields of the day. The series is intended for a wide readership, from buffs and wargamers to scholars and "operators"—military officers and policymakers.

It is hard to argue with the notion that technological change has held the key to understanding military history, and in our contemporary era of information management and smart weaponry, technology continues to change the face of battle. Questions remain, however. Is technology our master or our servant? Are there limits to its usefulness? Does it alter the nature of war, or is war based on timeless, unchanging principles? These are a few of the themes to be explored by the authors—recognized experts all—in this new series. It presents no party line or previously agreed-upon point of view. Nor does it offer any simple answers to any of these questions. Welcome to War, Technology, and History.

—Robert M. Citino

Acknowledgments

Although writing a book is a solitary activity, it is also the result of the efforts of many other people. I benefited greatly from the assistance of many friends and colleagues. Prime among them is Robert Citino. Rob was one of those who urged me most strongly to undertake this endeavor. I also profited from his extensive commentary on the manuscript, and he made the maps. Another old friend, Dennis Showalter, also read the manuscript and provided useful comments. More importantly, in our various conversations I always benefited from his shrewd insights on the German army. He also served as a good sounding board and directed me to a number of useful sources. Bruce Gudmundsson rendered invaluable aid. He was incredibly generous with materials from his own capacious library on the army of the *Kaiserreich* and also provided comments on the manuscript. Finally, my old friend Graydon "Jack" Tunstall Jr. gave me copies of a great many documents he had obtained from the Austrian military archives in Vienna, saving me a great deal of time and money. He also provided good insights on the Austro–Hungarian army. I would also like to express my gratitude to the staff of the Alfred M. Gray Research Center at the Marine Corps Base, Quantico, Virginia, for all the help they provided in obtaining materials via interlibrary loan. Ms. Rachel Kingcade also did yeoman's work in tracking down some rather obscure sources. Also deserving thanks is the staff of the Military History Institute at Carlisle, Pennsylvania. Thanks also go to the New York Military Affairs Symposium (NYMAS). There, I gave a presentation on the project to NYMAS, and the questions and feedback proved most helpful. I am most grateful for the generous support of the Marine Corps University Foundation, which helped cover the expenses incurred on several research trips to Germany. My friends and colleagues at the Marine Corps

Command and Staff College, also located at the Marine Corps Base at Quantico, were always there with help and support. Finally, I would like to express my thanks to Dr. Charles D. McKenna, the dean of the college; Colonel Raymond C. Damm Jr., USMC, the director of the college; and Major General Donald R. Gardner, USMC, retired, president emeritus of Marine Corps University. Dr. McKenna and Colonel Damm strongly endorsed, and General Gardner approved, my request for a six-month sabbatical, which allowed me the time to complete the manuscript.

I also owe thanks to a number of people on the other side of the Atlantic. Dr. Lothar Saupe and Frau Brigitte Jacobi at the Bavarian Kriegsarchiv in Munich were most helpful in locating the records of the Bavarian units involved in the campaign. As always, thanks are owed to Dr. Christian Harder and the staff at the Bundesarchiv–Militärarchiv. In particular, Frau Helga Waibel was most attentive to my requests for documents and showed unmatched tolerance in putting up with my haltingly spoken German. Research trips to Freiburg were made all the more pleasant by Jürgen Förster, Klaus Maier, Horst Boog, Detlef and Johanna Vogel, and Roland and Annie Foerster, my friends there. Days of eyestrain at the archives were more than offset by wonderful meals and pleasant excursions into the beautiful German countryside.

I also want to give thanks to my friends for all of the support they have shown over the years, especially Al, Kathy, Jay, Pat, Martin, Karl, Karen, Sheila and Irving. I was also fortunate to have marvelous teachers, two of whom in particular stand out. Cynthia Whittaker, my old teacher and friend of over 30 years, is still one of the great influences in my life. David Syrett exemplified the meaning of the German term *Doktorvater,* or "mentor." He was a great and wonderful teacher; his death at the early age of 65 was a terrible shock to all of us who were privileged to study with him. This book is dedicated to his memory.

I am fortunate in having the love and support of two families. My parents Louis and Ann DiNardo have always been supportive of my choice of career, however unusual it may have seemed. Thanks also to Robert and Jerry, my brothers; their wives, JoAnn and Vinece; Michael and Thomas, my nephews; plus Ann Marie Hardgrove, my niece; and her husband, Brian, for their support. The Moxley clan of Baltimore, Maryland, has been most supportive, especially Eileen Moxley Farmer, her husband, David, and their girls, Alison and Amanda, who think their new uncle is pretty cool even if he is a tad strange. To me, of course, the most important member of the Moxley family is Rita, my dear wife, whose saintly patience was invaluable to me in completing this work.

Although a great many people have been mentioned, I alone am responsible for any errors or omissions in this book.

Introduction

Here all Central Europe tore itself to pieces and expired in agony, to rise again, unrecognizable.

—Winston Churchill[1]

For many people, especially in the English-speaking world, World War I in the east remains, to use Winston Churchill's phrase, "the unknown war." Over the past two decades, there has been a resurgence of interest in the Great War. Not surprisingly, however, most of this attention has been focused on the western front. This bias is clearly illustrated in the coverage devoted to major commanders and battles. Bookshelves fairly groan with works on Douglas Haig, Helmuth von Moltke the Younger, Erich Ludendorff, and Ferdinand Foch, or on operations such as the opening campaign in the west in 1914, Verdun, and the British 1917 campaign in Flanders.[2]

In contrast to such a cornucopia of literature, the student of the eastern front in World War I has comparatively scant pickings from which to choose. Only one major study has focused on the eastern front in general, and that work is now over 30 years old.[3] Some recent works, most notably those of Holger Herwig and Hugh Strachan, have dealt with the eastern front within the broader context of the war in general.[4] Thanks to the efforts of Graydon Tunstall Jr., the Austro–Hungarian part of the war in 1914 and early 1915 has been well covered. In addition, Feldmarschall Franz Baron Conrad von Hötzendorf, the Austro–Hungarian chief of the general staff, was also the subject of a brief study in English.[5]

On the German side of the front, about the only major event that has been covered in any depth was Tannenberg. The minor but interesting seizure of the

Baltic Islands has also received some recent attention.[6] Beyond that, there has been a notable dearth of interest in events on the German part of eastern front, especially during the years 1915–1916.

The intent of this work is to fill in part of that gap by looking at the German–Austro–Hungarian offensive against the Russians at Gorlice–Tarnow in May 1915. This particular operation is of interest to us for several reasons. First, this was the first of the successful breakthrough battles after the onset of trench warfare. The Germans and Austro–Hungarians were able to restore a degree of mobility to warfare in the east that would be missing in the west for at least another two years. This would largely be done by artillery crushing the Russian defenses rather than by any major change in infantry tactics.

Another interesting aspect of the offensive, in a tactical sense, was the use of infantry in exploiting a breakthrough. Although cavalry did get involved in the latter stages of the offensive, especially for the Austro–Hungarians, it played no real role in either creating the breakthrough or exploiting the gap. This study will attempt to provide some explanations as to why this was the case.

World War I was the first coalition war involving Germany since Prussia's participation in the Napoleonic Wars.[7] At Gorlice–Tarnow for the first time in World War I, German and Austro–Hungarian forces operated together on a major scale. How this was done is a major focus of this study. It also includes the political disagreements between Germany and Austria–Hungary over what to do with the Polish territory they now owned.

The success of the operation under consideration here was due in no small part to the German command team in charge of the offensive. Colonel Hans von Seeckt, the chief of staff, is well known to students of the interwar period and those familiar with the works of James Corum.[8] Less well known is *Generaloberst* (later *Generalfeldmarschall*) August von Mackensen, the person who actually commanded the German and Austro–Hungarian forces.[9] Although Mackensen is the subject of a recent biography in German, that book is not overly concerned with his military exploits. In the English-speaking world, Mackensen remains a relatively obscure figure, like so many other German commanders and staff officers more associated with the eastern than the western front.[10] It is one of the goals of this study to introduce the reader to a number of commanders who have remained fairly unknown, even to students of the war.

The duo of Mackensen and Seeckt raises a couple of other issues that this work addresses. The first concerns the relationship between the two men. The conventional wisdom holds that in World War I, the commander was really a front man for his chief of staff, who did all of the thinking. This certainly applies to Seeckt as well as to the better-known duumvirate of Erich Ludendorff and Paul von Hindenburg and the lesser-known pair of Crown Prince Rupprecht of Bavaria and his chief of staff, Hermann von Kuhl.[11] How true is this image?

The second issue raised by the Mackensen–Seeckt combination concerns the politics of the German High Command (*Oberste Heeres Leitung,* or OHL) and imperial Germany itself. Did Colonel-General Erich von Falkenhayn, the head of OHL, view the Mackensen–Seeckt partnership simply as a useful tool for the prosecution of the war or as a possible counterweight against the increasingly influential and powerful combination of Hindenburg and Ludendorff? At least Seeckt seemed to think so.[12]

In total, this examination of Gorlice–Tarnow should provide the reader with a look at a campaign illustrating the kaleidoscopic complexity of World War I at the strategic, operational, and tactical levels. Given the relative paucity of writing on the eastern front in World War I, even the informed reader should find much new material here. If the student of World War I comes away with a better understanding of the war in general and the eastern front in particular, then this work will certainly have served its purpose. The same is true for those whose interest in German history extends to the imperial era. The Gorlice–Tarnow campaign provides an excellent prism through which we can examine the strengths and weaknesses of the *Kaiserreich* at war.

The area over which the Gorlice–Tarnow campaign was conducted has undergone a great many political changes since 1915. Thus, any number of localities in this area have gone through a bewildering number of name changes. The city of Lemberg, for example, can be spelled as Lemberg, Lvov, Lwow, or Lviv. For the sake of simplicity, place names are rendered here as they were in 1915.

Having set some ground rules, let us now embark on our study. This is best done by a quick retelling of affairs in the east in 1914, thus allowing us to get a proper picture of the strategic setting in which the campaign took place.

Chapter 1
The Strategic Setting

> In my opinion, the whole European War depends on the outcome of the struggle between Germany and France, and so the fate of Austria will not be decided on the Bug, but ultimately on the Seine.
>> —Generaloberst Helmuth von Moltke, February 10, 1913[1]

> Visited Generaloberst v. Moltke who is ill in the Prefecture. I found him a broken man, both mentally and physically.
>> —Admiral Georg Alexander von Müller, October 27, 1914[2]

World War I was paradoxical at many levels. Certainly all of the great powers took it as a given that a war would break out eventually. The policymakers of the great powers, however, made their respective decisions to go to war in 1914 for a wide variety of reasons.[3] The great irony was that although all of the powers expected that a war would occur sooner or later, very little thought was given by the great powers prior to 1914 as to what they hoped to accomplish by war. Thus war aims were developed with a degree of clarity only during the war.[4]

The war was even more paradoxical for the military establishments of Europe. Recent scholarship has shown that, at least in Germany and perhaps Russia, the war that was anticipated was not going to be short.[5] Nevertheless, all the major belligerents except Britain went to war in 1914 with war plans that aimed at delivering knockout blows to their principal opponents.

Consequently all of the initial campaigns brought results that were not anticipated by the respective war plans of the great powers. The Germans executed the Schlieffen Plan or, to put it more accurately, the Schlieffen–Moltke Plan, while the French put Plan XVII into effect. Over the late summer of 1914, the

Germans smashed their way across Belgium and into France all the way to the Marne River. Meanwhile, the French launched a series of ill-considered attacks into Lorraine against well-prepared German defenses.[6]

Maintaining his composure, Marshal Joseph Joffre, the French commander, made clever use of the French fortress system along the Franco-German border to screen redeployments of the available French field forces. Creating a new army, the Sixth, Joffre used that, plus the Paris garrison and the British Expeditionary Force, to strike the German right wing and drive it away from Paris. The attack succeeded, forcing the Germans to retreat in what became popularly known as "the miracle of the Marne." Thwarted in their original plans, both sides tried to get around each other's flank, an abortive effort that came to be called "the race to the sea." By the end of 1914, neither the German nor the French war plans had produced victory, with immense casualties on both sides.[7] Although the Germans were now in control of almost all of Belgium and northern France, the victory they sought by the Schlieffen–Moltke plan had eluded them. A continuous front now existed from the English Channel to the Swiss border.

The eastern front in 1914 also yielded a set of mixed results. To gain a better understanding of the results of these campaigns and thus a clear context for the events under consideration in this study, a short review of military relations between Germany and Austria–Hungary is required. Forged after the Congress of Berlin, the Dual Alliance called for the two monarchies to act in concert if attacked by Russia and to remain neutral if attacked by another country.[8] Given these circumstances, Generalfeldmarschall Helmuth Graf von Moltke, the chief of the German general staff, developed a German war plan predicated on having to fight a two-front war against France and Russia. The German posture in the west would be defensive. Moltke would await the French attack and perhaps go over to the counteroffensive later. The German and Austro–Hungarian armies would launch a joint offensive against Russia, aimed at Russian Poland. Given that such a war plan demanded close cooperation between the German and Austro–Hungarian armies, Moltke maintained relatively close contact with his Austrian counterpart, Feldmarschall Friedrich Baron von Beck-Rzikowsky. Any changes that were made in German war plans for the east were passed on to the Austro–Hungarians.[9]

This basic orientation continued during the brief tenure of Moltke successor, Generaloberst Alfred von Waldersee. Matters changed, however, with the advent of Generaloberst Alfred von Schlieffen as chief of the German general staff. Schlieffen reoriented Germany's strategic posture toward the west for a variety of reasons. These included a French Army becoming increasingly powerful and offensive-minded; worries about the Russians retreating into the vastness of the Russian hinterlands, leading to an open-ended campaign into the Russian interior; and concerns that Germany would not be able to withstand the strains of a prolonged two-front war.[10]

Schlieffen's redirection of German strategy toward France and Belgium had profound effects on the Austro-German alliance. During Moltke's tenure, contact with the Austro–Hungarian general staff was maintained with regularity. Under Schlieffen, relations between the German and Austro–Hungarian general staffs virtually ceased entirely. During Schlieffen's decade-long tenure, contacts between Schlieffen and Beck were limited to only the most perfunctory forms.[11]

Matters for the Germans were made worse by the nearly complete divorce between foreign policy and military strategy. To be sure, relations between Bismarck and Moltke were not always sweetness and light. Bismarck, for example, kept the existence of the Reinsurance Treaty with Russia from Moltke until circumstances forced him to reveal it to Moltke. For his part, Moltke had already commented to his Austrian colleague Beck that Germany's strategy did not depend upon Germany's foreign ministry.[12]

With the departure of Bismarck and Moltke, however, foreign policy and military strategy in regard to Austria–Hungary rapidly moved in opposite directions. As noted previously, the focus of Schlieffen's strategic thinking shifted westward against France. At the same time Germany, particularly in the person of Emperor Wilhelm II, made promises to aid Austria–Hungary "almost to the point of irresponsibility."[13]

Consequently the relationship between the German and Austro–Hungarian general staffs, especially the chiefs, oscillated between indifference and disingenuousness. As noted previously, contacts between Schlieffen and Beck had been reduced to only the most token or ceremonial. Matters improved from this rather low baseline with Wilhelm's appointment of Generaloberst Helmuth von Moltke, a nephew of the victor of 1866 and 1870, as Schlieffen's successor in 1906. This coincided with the appointment of Feldmarschalleutnant Franz Baron Conrad von Hötzendorf as Chief of the Austro–Hungarian general staff.[14]

Moltke met with Conrad and corresponded with him on a regular basis, beginning with their first meeting in May 1907 in Berlin. The character of the communications on both sides, however, can be described as less than honest. The Austro–Hungarians, for example, while roughly aware of the general outlines of the Schlieffen Plan, remained ignorant of the full extent of the deployments required by the German Army to carry it out. At the same time, however, Moltke did give written assurances to Conrad that the German Army would act in concert with the Austro–Hungarian Army in an offensive into Russian Poland. The most notable of these assurances was a letter of March 19, 1909, in which Moltke promised Conrad that 45 German divisions would undertake an offensive on the Narew River in support of an Austro–Hungarian offensive between the Bug and Vistula Rivers. After that, however, Moltke generally refused to provide any information to Conrad as to the size of the forces Germany would commit to the eastern front. Despite the indications of Germany's western focus—particularly a letter of February 10, 1913, in which Moltke told Conrad that Austria's fate would be settled on the Seine and not the Bug, Conrad would continue to regard Moltke's 1909 promise as a binding commitment.[15]

For their part, the Austrians were not about to be outdone in being disingenuous. The most notable example of this concerned the Redl affair. The Russian Intelligence Bureau in Warsaw had discovered that Colonel Alfred Redl, an Austrian officer who had served on the intelligence section of the Austro–Hungarian general staff, was a homosexual. Using this as leverage, the Russians were able to blackmail Redl, who gave them a great deal of information, including Austrian mobilization plans against both Russia and Serbia as well as correspondence between Conrad and Moltke. Eventually exposed, Redl was arrested in a Vienna hotel on May 24, 1913. Having been informed of Redl's arrest while at dinner, Conrad ordered that he be questioned for several hours and then left alone in the room with a pistol. Taking the not so subtle hint, Redl shot himself early on the morning of May 25, 1913.[16]

The Austrians immediately moved to cover up the Redl affair, but Conrad's attempt to keep the matter out of the press misfired. The Austrian War Ministry had to acknowledge that Redl was a homosexual and that he had betrayed secrets to foreign agents. The Germans wanted to ascertain the extent of Redl's activities, but any questions they raised about that received evasive answers from the Austrians. Conrad's contribution to this was to give Moltke a lame assurance that Redl could not have betrayed "the whole of their private correspondence."[17]

The other issue where the Austrians were less than forthcoming with the Germans concerned Austria–Hungary's own war plans. The general expectation on the part of the Germans was that Russia would be the focus of Austrian planning. From the Bosnian crisis of 1908 on, however, Conrad began to regard Serbia as the principal threat to Austria–Hungary. Moltke did caution Conrad not to undertake any major action against Serbia until the Russian threat had been eliminated. In addition Austria–Hungary also had to be concerned about the prospect of war with Italy, thus necessitating another plan for that contingency.[18] Moltke, however, fully expected that Austria–Hungary would make its major effort against Russia in the event of a war.

The fruit of this dual dishonesty was that when war began in 1914, both Germany and Austria–Hungary presented each other with several unpleasant surprises. Karl von Kageneck, the German military attaché in Vienna, wrote to Moltke's then deputy Georg von Waldersee and urged him (and presumably Moltke) to "play with absolutely open cards in order that we follow the lessons of all coalition wars."[19] Such fine sentiments, however, were more than a day late and a dollar short. The first unpleasant surprise was the confused nature of the Austro–Hungarian deployment, leading Kaganeck to point out to both Conrad and Austro–Hungarian emperor Francis Joseph that Serbia must remain a secondary theater. Moltke delivered Germany's first unpleasant surprise when he replied in platitudes that were both vague and negative in regard to Conrad's request, of August 3, 1914, for a German offensive against Russian Poland. Moltke compounded this when he gave Count Josef Stürgkh, Austria–Hungary's military representative at German headquarters, the full scope of and details of the Schlieffen–Moltke Plan.[20]

The opening campaign in the east ended up as a fine example of "parallel war," in which Germany and Austria–Hungary fought against Russia at the same time, but without a common plan or in concert, beyond a joint manifesto to be issued to the population of Russian Poland.[21] The Germans, rather surprised by the speed of Russia's mobilization, were caught somewhat flat-footed by the offensive of the Russian Northwest Front's 1st and 2nd Armies into East Prussia. The defense of East Prussia was entrusted to the German Eighth Army, commanded by Generaloberst Maximilian von Prittwitz. Composed of the I, I Reserve, XVII, and XX Corps, the Eighth Army had six infantry and three reserve divisions and a cavalry division, totaling 120,000 men.[22] Defending East Prussia in and of itself was difficult enough, given the size of the invading Russian armies. Matters for the Germans were made worse as Prittwitz exercised almost no control over his corps commanders.

The result was that Prittwitz left the conduct of his initial attack against General Pavel Rennenkamf's Russian 1st Army at Gumbinnen to the obstreperous General der Infanterie Hermann von François, commander of the I Corps. François's move would be supported by an attack into what the I Corps commander presumed to be the Russian left flank by the XVII Corps, commanded by the aggressive General der Kavallerie August von Mackensen. The XVII Corps attack, made on August 20, 1914, under conditions of complete ignorance of the Russian tactical dispositions, ended with Mackensen and his staff, after suffering about 8,000 casualties, being borne off the field among a stream of fugitives retreating to the Rominte River.[23]

The troubling tenor of communications from East Prussia resulted in Moltke relieving both Prittwitz and Georg von Waldersee, his chief of staff. They were replaced by Generaloberst Paul von Hindenburg, with the ambitious Generalmajor Erich Ludendorff as his chief of staff.[24] Arriving at Eighth Army headquarters in the evening of August 23, the new team quickly fell into executing a plan initially formulated by Prittwitz, Waldersee, and Max Hoffmann, one of their principal staff officers.[25] Redeploying the I, XVII, and I Reserve Corps by a combination of railroads and hard marching, the German Eighth Army was able to place strong forces on both flanks of the Russian 2nd Army, advancing from the south toward a projected linkup with the Russian 1st Army, presumed to still be advancing west after its victory at Gumbinnen.[26]

The ensuing German attack on August 27, aided by some fortuitous if unplanned delays in deployment on the August 26 that let the Russians advance deeper into the German trap, succeeded in crushing both flanks of the Russian 2nd Army. By the beginning of September 1914, the Germans had won the first great victory of the war at Tannenberg. The Russian 2nd Army had been destroyed. General Alexander Samsonov, the army's commander, committed suicide on August 29. Close to 100,000 prisoners were taken, with Mackensen's corps garnering the lion's share. The victory also produced Germany's first two popular heroes, Hindenburg and Ludendorff.[27]

At the other end of the eastern front, the course of operations proceeded in a manner that was, to put it mildly, less than favorable to Austria–Hungary. The first unpleasant surprise Conrad handed to his German allies was his decision to direct the Austro–Hungarian Second Army toward Serbia, which he tried to justify to Moltke in his message of August 3, 1914. Conrad subsequently changed his mind, but with Austro–Hungarian mobilization already under way, his decision, compounded by the failure to employ fully the railroad resources available, reduced the Austro–Hungarian deployment in Galicia against Russia to a confused shambles.[28]

The result of this confusion was defeat for the Austro–Hungarian Army on two fronts. In the south, the Austro–Hungarian forces, the Fifth and Sixth Armies, faced the Serbian forces under the command of Field Marshal Radomir Putnik. The elderly Serbian commander had been vacationing at Bad Gleichenberg in July 1914 and was detained by the Hungarian authorities as he returned to Belgrade via Budapest. Putnik was released, however, at the behest of Francis Joseph.[29]

The Austro–Hungarians soon had cause to regret that bit of noblesse oblige. The Austro–Hungarian Fifth and Sixth Armies were under the command of Feldmarschalleutnant Oskar Potiorek, the commander of the Sixth Army. Potiorek, appointed to command by Conrad on August 7, was a singularly bad choice. He had never commanded any unit of division size or larger. Equally unsettling was the fact that Potiorek had been in charge of the security arrangements in Sarajevo for the ill-fated visit of Archduke Franz Ferdinand and his wife on June 28, 1914, and was still somewhat affected by the experience.

Potiorek began his attack across the Drina River into Serbia on August 12 with a total of about 460,000 men, supported by 500 guns. A large number of Potiorek's men, however, were poorly trained reservists. Putnik's total force was about 400,000 men, some of whom had to be detailed to the border with Montenegro. Almost half of Putnik's men, however, were battle-tested veterans from the Balkan Wars, armed with the latest small arms from Germany and 328 artillery pieces of French manufacture.[30]

Four days after Potiorek's force crossed the Drina and the Save Rivers, Putnik unleashed his counterattack. By the end of August all Austro–Hungarian forces had been driven back over the Drina and the Save back to their starting positions. Undeterred by one thrashing, Potiorek decided to try conclusions with Putnik again, this time with a night attack across the Drina, an idea that exhibited more daring than sound military judgment. Potiorek's attack headed into the teeth of a well-posted Serbian defense, and failed with lamentable results.

By mid-September 1914 the second Austro–Hungarian invasion had failed. Putnik attempted to follow up this success with his own invasion of Hungary, but Potiorek was able to put together enough of a defense to drive the Serbian forces back into Serbian territory. Austro–Hungarian casualties had come to over 20,000, with thousands more suffering from various diseases. Austria–Hungary had paid a high price for Conrad's admitted desire to "slap Serbia."[31]

As bad as things went for Austria–Hungary on the Serbian front, far worse was to befall the dual monarchy on the eastern front against Russia. The Austro–Hungarian war plan had called for the Austro–Hungarians to mobilize and deploy the First, Second, Third, and Fourth Armies, plus Army Groups Kövess and Kummer against Russia. Owing to Conrad's whipsawing the Austro–Hungarian Second Army first to Serbia and then back to Galicia, the Austro–Hungarian deployment against Russia would be incomplete and piecemeal.[32]

Aggressive by nature and believing that an offensive, even with inferior forces, would keep the Russians off balance, Conrad decided to undertake an offensive before the Second Army's arrival. By sending his cavalry off on a strategic reconnaissance/raid that accomplished little except the massive consumption of horseflesh, Conrad had effectively blinded his main striking force, the First and Fourth Armies. The Austro–Hungarians thus marched toward Russian territory with neither an idea as to what they were to accomplish nor any clue as to what the Russians were up to. In addition, Conrad was well aware when he ordered the offensive that no German help would be forthcoming for the immediate future.[33]

The Russians, for their part, were just as ignorant of Austro–Hungarian dispositions and intentions. Their one advantage was that the Russian Southwest Front, commanded by General Nicholas Ivanov, was able to mobilize most of the divisions of the 3rd, 4th, 5th, and 8th Armies without much difficulty. Ivanov, a cautious commander even in the best circumstances, was prodded into an offensive by Grand Duke Nicholas, the Russian supreme commander, acting in response to French pleas for assistance.[34]

The result was that in a series of sometimes confused actions near the frontier between Austria–Hungary and Russia east of the San River, the Russians were able to defeat the Austro–Hungarians. The culmination of these frontier battles was at Rava Russka, fought mostly on September 8, 1914. By September 11, 1914, Conrad, now fully aware of the magnitude of his defeats and the Russian intentions to destroy his remaining forces, ordered his armies back to the San. Lemberg, the capital of Austrian Galicia and the nexus of the road and rail net in the area, was abandoned. Conrad's headquarters (*Armeeoberkommando,* or AOK) were evacuated from its location, the fortress of Przemysl, which was left garrisoned to withstand a siege. Austro–Hungarian casualties amounted to about 350,000 in total. Among them was Conrad's son Herbert, killed at Rava Russka on September 8.[35]

Conrad's reaction to this catalog of disasters was typical. He sacked a number of generals for deficiencies real and imagined, although Conrad admitted, in a rare moment of candor, that were Franz Ferdinand still alive, the late Archduke would have had Conrad shot. His second reaction was to call on the Germans for assistance, calls that grew more insistent during the first half of September 1914. His next reaction was bitterness when the Germans told him no help was forthcoming, at least through the first half of September. With the German Eighth still engaged in driving the Russian 1st Army from East Prussian soil, Wilhelm informed Stürgkh that the destruction of two Russian armies was the most help the Austro–Hungarians had any right to expect.[36]

After the conclusion of the First Masurian Lakes campaign in mid-September, the Germans shifted forces to help the Austro–Hungarians. A new force created from parts of the German Eighth Army and forces drawn from the western front was designated as the German Ninth Army and placed under Hindenburg and Ludendorff. The question now was how this force would be used.[37]

Whereas the situation in the east demanded closer cooperation with the Austro–Hungarian Army, actual practice was another matter. To begin with, the decision to create the German Ninth Army was made by Generalleutnant Erich von Falkenhayn, who had been named on September 14, 1914, as the replacement for Moltke, who had broken down completely by this time. The problem was that none of this had been communicated to Conrad, who had to piece together the goings on at German headquarters (*Oberste Heeresleitung* or OHL) from bits of information gleaned from various sources.[38]

Matters were not any better at the high operational levels of command. Relations between the Germans and Austro–Hungarians were more contentious than cordial. On September 18, Ludendorff met Conrad at Neu Sandec to discuss the situation. Conrad lectured Ludendorff about Germany's failure to live up to its prewar promises. Ludendorff, while informing Conrad that the amount of German help coming was not exactly what Conrad desired, told him that help was coming nonetheless.[39]

Recriminations notwithstanding, the two agreed to undertake a combined offensive into Poland. The German Ninth Army, extending Conrad's left, would attack to the northeast from its assembly in Upper Silesia. Four Austro–Hungarian armies with almost 500,000 men and 1,600 guns would attack at the same time. The objective of the German Ninth Army was Ivangorod. The Austro–Hungarian objective was the crossing of the Vistula, Wisloka, and San Rivers. This would outflank the Russian forces in the foothills of the Carpathian Mountains and relieve the besieged fortress of Przemysl and its 100,000-man garrison. Three days later, however, Ludendorff refused to meet with Austro–Hungarian officers to coordinate the impending offensive into Poland.[40]

Despite such high-handed behavior, the assembly of the German Ninth Army, consisting of the Guard Reserve and the XI, XVII, XX, and Landwehr Corps (12 infantry divisions), plus a reinforced cavalry division, proceeded according to schedule and completed its deployment by September 29, 1914.[41] Commencing on September 30, 1914, the Central Powers' offensive made some progress initially, as it happily coincided with a Russian operational pause. On the German Ninth Army's right flank, the XI Corps was able to overcome the Russian defenses at Opatow on October 5, while Mackensen's XVII Corps occupied Radom. On the Ninth Army's right, the Austro–Hungarian First Army made advances as well.[42]

These successes, although they did allow the Austro–Hungarians to relieve Przemysl on October 9, were largely illusory. The poor state of the roads in Poland and Russian preplanned retreats dashed hopes that the Russians could be brought to battle west of the Vistula. Effectively evading the offensive, the Russians were able to fall back on the fortress of Ivangorod while completing the formation of a new 2nd Army at Warsaw. The Germans took only 4,000 prisoners, 35 guns, and a number of machine guns.[43] Hindenburg and Ludendorff then decided to send Mackensen with an ad hoc force consisting of the XVII Corps, Corps Frommel (the 8th Cavalry Division, 35th Reserve Division, and 18th *Landwehr* Division), and later the XX Corps, toward Warsaw.[44]

Starting out on October 9, Mackensen's force made good progress on October 9 and 10, and Mackensen expected to start his attack on the October 11. The attack made little headway, and with good reason. By that time Grand Duke Nicholas, the Russian commander in chief, had completed the reconstitution of the 2nd Army. The Grand Duke planned to launch a major attack from Warsaw against the German Ninth Army's left flank while his other forces held the Vistula River line around Ivangorod, a concept Hindenburg thought quite good.[45] By October 13, Mackensen, through a combination of accurate aerial reconnaissance and information provided by a timely document captured on October 10, was convinced that he was up against a superior enemy force.

By mid-October the momentum of the offensive had broken down completely. Although Hindenburg and Ludendorff had been able to sideslip forces from Ivangorod leftward while the Austro–Hungarian First Army took over the Ivangorod sector, Mackensen's forces before Warsaw were still in a precarious position. Further south, the Austro–Hungarian garrison stoutly defended Przemysl, which was besieged by the Russian 3rd Army. After driving off an effort to storm the fortress by the Russian 3rd Army in early October, the Austro–Hungarian advance forced the Russians to lift the siege. By mid-October, Conrad's forces had relieved Przemysl sufficiently that a large part of the civilian population and 15,000 wounded soldiers could be evacuated. Conrad himself expected to relocate AOK back to the fortress. All attempts to cross the San, however, foundered on the Russian defenses.[46]

Although the attempted Russian counterattack often got in its own way, sufficient progress was made that Russian cavalry crossed the Bzura at Sochaczew on October 17. This move threatened Mackensen's left flank and caused both Hindenburg and Ludendorff considerable worry as well. On October 20, Mackensen received orders to retreat to the southwest toward Rava Russka.

Hindenburg and Ludendorff also turned down flat a proposal from Conrad to let the Russians cross the Vistula and then attack the Russian forces when the Russians had the river at their backs. The Germans thought Conrad's idea clever but too daring and probably beyond the capabilities of the forces at Conrad's disposal.[47]

With the Germans recoiling from Warsaw, the Russians went back over to the offensive in Galicia. This drove the Austro–Hungarians into retreat, falling back into the Carpathian Mountains. Przemysl was once again abandoned to a Russian siege. By the end of October, the Austro–Hungarians were back even beyond where they had started their offensive. The Austro–Hungarians were able to stop the Russian attack with a successful counterattack at Limanova–Lapanow and to halt the Russian offensive in the Carpathians.[48]

As fall headed into winter, the focus of action on the eastern front shifted back to the north. After a meeting between Falkenhayn, Ludendorff, and Conrad's representative Lieutenant Colonel Rudolf Kundmann in Berlin on October 30, 1914, an important change was made in the German command structure. The Kaiser (nominally) appointed Hindenburg (now Generalfeldmarschall) the commander in chief of all German forces in the east (*Oberbefehlshaber Ost*, or Ober Ost) on November 1, 1914. Ludendorff, now Generalleutnant, would continue as Hindenburg's chief of staff. Mackensen would become the new commander of the German Ninth Army.[49] An attempt to create a unified German–Austro–Hungarian command structure foundered on Conrad's opposition and is discussed in the next chapter.

Exactly who created Ober Ost is something of a mystery. All of the writings of anyone who may have had some involvement in this decision tend to treat it in a rather strange way. Falkenhayn, for example, simply referred to the "new commander in chief of the German forces in the east" without ever discussing how the arrangement was arrived at. The German official history simply states that the Kaiser appointed Hindenburg as head of Ober Ost, a tack Ludendorff also followed in his memoirs. Wilhelm II still figured prominently in the appointment of civilian and military officials at the top in this period of the war. Indeed, although the Kaiser replaced Falkenhayn as war minister with Generalleutnant Adolph Wild von Hohenborn, Wilhelm's support was critical to sustaining Falkenhayn against the latter's enemies early in Falkenhayn's tenure as the head of OHL.[50] Filling operational level posts, however, was another matter. In this case it is unlikely that the Kaiser played any role other than issuing the order appointing Hindenburg, an act that was more symbolic than real.[51]

Given the available evidence, it would seem that the decision to place all German forces in the east under *Ober Ost* was most likely Falkenhayn's. Since large German forces were moving from the west to the east, some sort of coordinating authority in the east was necessary to determine the best place for the incoming forces. This was impossible for Falkenhayn, who at that time was totally absorbed in preparations for the last German attempts to bring about a decision in the west in 1914. Finally, the creation of the German Ninth Army demanded a higher headquarters to plan and coordinate the operations of both the German Eighth and Ninth Armies, a role Hindenburg had already filled, at least informally, throughout the early fall of 1914. That situation was going to get even more complex as the German Tenth Army was also being formed. In a sense then, Falkenhayn's creation of Ober Ost simply formalized an arrangement that was already in place.[52]

Once the new command arrangements were in hand, the final campaign on the eastern front in 1914 was launched. The main effort would be made by Mackensen's Ninth Army, once the army had completed its railroad-facilitated deployment through Silesia to its assembly area between Posen and Thorn.[53] The target of the attack would be the city of Lodz, an important communications hub for the Russians and the center of the textile industry in Russian Poland. Securing the city would afford the Germans good billeting areas for the troops in the face of the rapidly oncoming winter.[54]

Launched on November 11, 1914, the Lodz campaign turned into a month-long duel, marked by some of the most interesting cut-and-thrust moves made by both sides in the war. After scoring some successes on November 14–15, including the taking of 20,000 prisoners, the Ninth Army approached Lodz, only to run into a stout Russian defense. Still capable of making operational moves by rail at that time, the Russians were able to rapidly build up a powerful counterattack force at Lodz. Forced back on the defensive, Mackensen ordered a retreat back to the Bzura River, informing Ober Ost later.[55]

Reinforced by troops from the western front, Mackensen was able to go back over to the offensive on December 1. By December 6, 1914, Lodz was in German hands for good. The victorious Lodz campaign had two important results. The first was that Germany had gained a fairly good chunk of Russian Poland. The second was that the Lodz campaign won for Mackensen a place in the pantheon of German heroes, right behind the massive figure (both figuratively and literally) of Hindenburg.[56]

The campaigns of 1914 in the east revealed the strengths and weaknesses of the Central Powers at war. Excellent German staff work and training, guided by Hindenburg's steady hand, eventually yielded great results at Tannenberg. The strategic and operational use of the railroads could also contribute to success, as clearly shown first at Tannenberg and then later in the rapid redeployment of Mackensen's Ninth Army to Silesia for the Lodz campaign. The Germans were able to employ aerial reconnaissance to good use, and the information provided by that means may have saved Mackensen from a potential disaster before Warsaw.[57]

The eastern campaigns showed shortcomings in the German Army as well. The most notable of these concerned operational mobility. Although the railroad, as noted above, could confer operational mobility on an army, sustaining an advance over a long distance was difficult to say the least. Whereas Tannenberg showed that relatively rapid moves could be made overland if the distances to be covered were short, more distant objectives were difficult to attain. The clearest example of this was the overly ambitious and ultimately abortive offensive of Hindenburg and Ludendorff against Warsaw, Ludendorff's claims of successfully buying time notwithstanding.[58]

Another concern was coalition warfare. Germany and Austria–Hungary had gone to war as allies, but in the event ended up waging "parallel war" for much of 1914. After the first months of 1914, the two powers were able to cooperate, but in a very uneven manner. This was exemplified by Ludendorff's meeting with Conrad at Neu Sandec on September 18, 1914, followed by the his refusal to meet with Conrad's representatives three days later. This would have to change if Germany and Austria–Hungary were to fight effectively as allies and was made all the more urgent by the precarious situation Austria–Hungary was in by the end of 1914.[59]

Nonetheless, something had to be done. The short war that everyone had planned for had failed. The long war that some had expected and all had dreaded, but for which none had prepared, was now a grim reality.[60] Decisions, both political and military, had to be made and made quickly. Those decisions are discussed in the next chapter.

Chapter 2

Strategic Decisions and Coalition Warfare

Przemysl is only besieged and the investing troops have been repulsed repeatedly with heavy losses. The Carpathian range is held essentially by our detachments.

—Franz Conrad von Hötzendorf, December 14, 1914[1]

I was able on this occasion to become acquainted with the ideas of Conrad. He is an educated officer, but no great man.

—Erich Ludendorff, January 2, 1915[2]

Galicia is lost to the Austrians without hope of redemption and Przemysl will fall by the end of this month, without the Russians even having to attack—lack of food.

—Max Hoffmann, March 6, 1915[3]

As the final battles of 1914 sputtered out in France and on the eastern front, it was abundantly clear that both sides were faced with profound strategic choices. For the Entente Powers, the choice was between attacking on the western front or undertaking an operation based on one of the possibilities created by France's control of the Mediterranean.

For the Central Powers, their inability to project power (beyond the activities of commerce raiders and u-boats) outside of continental Europe made the choice relatively simple for Germany and Austria–Hungary. For Germany, the choice was between making the main effort on the eastern front or the western front. Austria–Hungary's set of options was between the eastern front, dealing with Russia and the southern front, where Austria–Hungary and Serbia continued their bloody standoff. Within these theoretically simple choices, however, all manner of complexities and dangers abounded.

To master these problems, close cooperation between Germany and Austria–Hungary was required. The outcome of this effort, or even the degree of cooperation achieved, would depend to a great degree on the personal relationship between the respective military chiefs of Germany and Austria–Hungary.

The chief of the German general staff and head of OHL in 1915 was General der Infanterie Erich von Falkenhayn. Born on November 11, 1861, Falkenhayn hailed from an old West Prussian aristocratic family whose roots went back to 14th-century Thuringia. His large family (he was the sixth of seven children) also had a tradition of military service. His grandfather and several of his brothers served in the army, and his older brother Eugen rose to the rank of General der Kavallerie.[4]

After receiving the normal education for a youth seeking to enter the army, Falkenhayn was commissioned as a lieutenant of infantry on April 17, 1880. Over the next 30 years, Falkenhayn followed an unusual career path for a German officer. After graduating from the Kriegsakademie in 1890, he spent a short time as an instructor to the Chilean Army and much time as a field-grade officer in China; he also served on the staff of the expeditionary corps sent by Germany as part of the international force assembled to crush the Boxer Rebellion. After his return to Germany, he was promoted to colonel in 1908, shortly after which he was appointed commander of the Fourth Guards Infantry Regiment. Falkenhayn was promoted to Generalmajor on April 22, 1912.

Falkenhayn's service in China had brought him to the notice of Wilhelm II as well as of the kaiser's brother Prince Heinrich. Both were impressed with Falkenhayn's energetic and youthful appearance and manner. The kaiser surprised a great many people when he appointed Falkenhayn as Prussian war minister on July 7, 1913, given that Falkenhayn was still at the relatively junior rank of Generalmajor. To remedy this, Wilhelm II quickly advanced Falkenhayn to Generalleutnant, a rank more commensurate with his new position.[5]

Falkenhayn had only a brief tenure as Prussian war minister, during which he took a fairly conservative line on a variety of issues. Falkenhayn fought to retain the emperor's prerogatives vis-à-vis the military and to keep the influence of the Reichstag on military policy and behavior to a minimum. The most notable example of this was the Zabern affair. After a junior officer posted in Zabern, located in Alsace, described the local population in disparaging terms to his men, riots broke out among the Alsatian population. The army promptly began rounding up protesters—an action approved by Falkenhayn but severely criticized in the Reichstag, especially by the Social Democrats. On matters more germane to the conduct of war, Falkenhayn took the traditional approach, emphasizing the quality of the individual soldier over quantity. He did, however, authorize an increase in artillery ammunition from 1,200 to 1,500 shells per gun. These levels, however, had not been achieved by the outbreak of the war.

In the July crisis leading up to the start of the war, Falkenhayn was among those who urged that Germany take the plunge into war.[6]

After Moltke's physical and mental breakdown during the Marne campaign, Wilhelm appointed Falkenhayn as chief of the general staff and head of OHL. This appointment came as something of a surprise to many. Falkenhayn was still a Generalleutnant, and a rather junior one at that. Just as in the case of Falkenhayn's appointment as war minister, Wilhelm had passed over a good many generals who were far more senior to make Falkenhayn Moltke's successor. Given the all too recent breakdown of Moltke, the kaiser may have believed that a younger man would be better suited to the position and the strains that went with it. Certainly Wilhelm had been impressed with Falkenhayn's energy and had had the opportunity to observe Falkenhayn closely, both during Falkenhayn's tenure as Prussian war minister and during the 1914 summer campaign, when Falkenhayn traveled with imperial headquarters.[7] A stern-looking man with a piercing stare and a crew cut that would make a Marine proud, Falkenhayn never evoked indifference. His contemporaries either admired or hated him.

Although Falkenhayn was now both the head of OHL and war minister, he was in a difficult situation. Since he was still a relatively junior general officer, it would be difficult for him to impose his will on generals who were considerably senior to him. In any case, Falkenhayn did not enjoy the full trust and confidence of the general staff. Matters were made more difficult when, for a variety of reasons, he had to relinquish the position of war minister. To alleviate these problems to a degree, Falkenhayn was able to get the kaiser to name one of his few close associates, Wild, as war minister. The issue of rank was partially resolved by Falkenhayn's promotion to General der Infanterie the same day he gave up the position of war minister to Wild.[8]

Falkenhayn's penchant for making enemies allowed Wilhelm II to play a critical role for one of the few times in the war. There were any number of people between Spa, Berlin, and Ober Ost who wanted Falkenhayn's chair. Chief among these was the whole of Ober Ost, who had their own ideas on how the war should be run and the strategy that needed to be adopted. Ludendorff, in a classic example of the pot calling the kettle black, derided Falkenhayn as a gambler in a letter to the deposed Moltke. The kaiser, however, was not to be budged. He stood steadfastly by Falkenhayn when the latter was most vulnerable early in his tenure in the second OHL, after the bloody denouement to the 1914 campaign in the west at Ypres. Consequently, all Hoffmann could do in 1915 was to complain constantly about Falkenhayn's sway over the kaiser, going so far as to write, on May 30, 1915, that "his majesty does not love us" (an odd turn of phrase, to say the least).[9] Although the kaiser played a critical role in sustaining Falkenhayn against his enemies, influencing broad decisions on strategic issues was another matter. The man who would make those decisions would be Erich von Falkenhayn.[10]

Falkenhayn's Austro–Hungarian counterpart was the ever-controversial Franz Baron Conrad von Hötzendorf. Born on November 11, 1852, Conrad hailed from a military family. His father, Franz Xaver Conrad von Hötzendorf, had served in the late Napoleonic Wars, fighting at Leipzig in October 1813. He then served as a cavalry officer in various assignments until he was disabled in an accident while leading his hussar regiment against revolutionaries in 1848.[11]

Having entered the Theresa Military Academy at Wiener Neustadt in 1867, Conrad graduated in 1871; he was commissioned as an infantry lieutenant and then posted to the 11th Field Jäger Battalion. Over the ensuing 43 years, Conrad enjoyed a steady ascent to the highest levels of the Austro–Hungarian Army. He made his name most notably as an instructor at the Austro–Hungarian War College and as a very innovative division commander on the Italian frontier. Conrad also attained a considerable reputation as a military writer and theoretician, a field of endeavor that was much admired generally in the Austro–Hungarian Army. He also developed a number of officers who were intensely loyal to him, especially those who were his former students, a number of whom eventually became general officers.[12]

Conrad was appointed chief of the Austro–Hungarian general staff on November 18, 1906, a position he would hold—with the exception of a short hiatus between 1911 and 1913—until he was removed from the position early in 1917 by Emperor Karl, who had succeeded Francis Joseph after the death of the latter on November 21, 1916. During his tenure as chief of the general staff, Conrad was an ardent proponent of war against what he perceived as the rising threat of Serbia.[13] In 1914, Conrad's desire in this regard was fulfilled, although he also got war with Russia as part of the bargain.

Conrad's relationship with a succession of German counterparts might be described as rocky. Contact with Schlieffen, as noted in the previous chapter, was perfunctory at best. Although Conrad got along better with Moltke, their relationship was marked at times by a mutual lack of candor. Conrad ensured that his relationship with Falkenhayn got off to a bad start. After effectively replacing Moltke, Falkenhayn invited Conrad to come to Berlin in late October 1914 for a meeting. The objective was to determine how to proceed in the coming fall 1914 campaign in the east. Conrad did not attend and instead sent Lieutenant Colonel Rudolf Kundmann, one of his aides, to represent him. Although the meeting was conducted with the customary pleasantries, sending Kundmann amounted to a foolish and petty snub on Conrad's part, which certainly did not augur well for the future.[14]

Conrad's style of conducting business was also quite different from that of Falkenhayn. Conrad, his initial snub of Falkenhayn notwithstanding, actually preferred face-to-face meetings. Once the meeting was over, Conrad would follow up with a lengthy written memorandum. In contrast, Falkenhayn generally disliked personal meetings, which he thought too time-consuming, an understandable attitude given the amount of traveling that Falkenhayn had to do, shuttling between Berlin and OHL headquarters on the western front, then located at Meziéres. Falkenhayn generally preferred to use the telephone, a device with which Conrad never felt comfortable. Eventually, at the beginning of May 1915, Falkenhayn established a headquarters for OHL on the eastern front at Pless, about an hour's drive from Conrad's headquarters at Teschen.[15]

Conrad and Falkenhayn also had very different styles of writing. Conrad's memoranda and messages were written in a kind of florid, 19th-century style. Falkenhayn, on the other hand, ever the Prussian, wrote with a short, clipped tone, terse almost to the point of being brusque.[16] Ultimately, one might say that Conrad, in many ways, was a man of the 19th century, while Falkenhayn was more a man of the 20th.

The two men also presented very different appearances physically. Falkenhayn was taller than Conrad and would come into to Teschen fresh from a high-speed auto trip, sporting goggles, a scarf, and a cigar, probably with a good coating of dust from the road, bounding out of the car and exuding a good deal more vigor than Conrad, who was almost a decade older. In contrast, Conrad, always wearing an immaculate uniform, appeared, according to August von Cramon, the German liaison officer attached to AOK, "small and delicate, almost feminine." A greater contrast in simple appearance would be hard to find.[17]

Conrad also found other ways to irritate the Germans. Initially, AOK was established at Przemysl. The course of events in the summer and fall of 1914 mandated several changes of location. After the second Austro–Hungarian retreat from Przemysl and the loss of Lemberg, Conrad established AOK at Teschen. Once ensconced there, Conrad and his staff enjoyed a rather luxurious existence, with officers living in villas, often accompanied by their wives. Although Conrad himself was abstemious in terms of consuming food and drink, love was another matter. On January 20, 1915, he was visited at Teschen by the beautiful Gina von Reininghaus, his mistress. Conrad was a widower, but Gina was married to Austrian hotel magnate Hans von Reininghaus. Gina's visits, plus the frequent appearance of the wives and mistresses of other officers, was more than a little off-putting to the German officers at AOK, such as Kaganeck, a straitlaced Badenese Catholic.[18] More professionally, German officers complained that AOK was too far removed from conditions at the front and exercised no control over the front-line commanders.[19]

Regardless of the differences between Falkenhayn and Conrad in personality, style, and outlook, decisions had to be made. Diplomatically, the major issue facing the Central Powers concerned Italy, Romania, and Bulgaria. Italy's declaration of neutrality in 1914 was taken by the Germans in two ways. Their first reaction was to take it as a gross breach of trust, a feeling that grew after the miscarriage of the Schlieffen Plan.[20] The second reaction was to regard Italy's behavior as a prelude to a decision to join the Entente Powers.

Romania was also a delicate situation. Like Italy, Romania made territorial demands on the dual monarchy. Romania, however, might be persuaded to join the Central Powers, depending on the military situation. Military failure, especially in the east, however, could embolden Romania to enter the war against the Central Powers. Conversely, signal military success against the Entente could entice Romania to join the Central Powers, with the expectation that Romania would seek territorial expansion at Serbia's expense. At the very minimum, the Central Powers sought to maintain Italian and Romanian neutrality while bringing Bulgaria into the war on their side. Certainly the acquisition of Bulgaria as an ally was a prerequisite for the renewal of an offensive against Serbia.[21]

Militarily, matters were made difficult by the differing priorities of Germany and Austria–Hungary. Falkenhayn was convinced that the western front needed to be the focus of Germany's military efforts. Ultimate victory in the war could be secured only with the complete defeat of France, Britain, or both. Of the two western powers, Falkenhayn regarded Britain as the more dangerous; thus the defeat of Britain would be his principal aim. This was one of the few areas of agreement between Falkenhayn and Admiral Alfred von Tirpitz.[22]

Falkenhayn's ideas about Germany's strategic priorities were not shared by a number of his military contemporaries. These men, not an organized cabal but rather a group of officers who shared a climate of opinion, were of the belief that if Germany was to attain a separate peace with one of the Entente Powers, the Entente member in question would be Russia. Even here there were nuances. The principal "easterners" were concentrated in Ober Ost. Although Ober Ost as a whole wanted the east to be the focus of major operations, there were differences as to the ultimate goal. In his letters to Moltke throughout early 1915, Ludendorff mentioned the possibility of attaining tactical successes early on and later trapping the Russian Army in a giant encirclement, but nothing more than that. Hoffmann confided to his diary that a separate peace with Russia might be possible, but only in the aftermath of the overthrow of the tsarist regime. From his perch as chief of staff to the German Sixth Army in France, Seeckt likewise believed that obtaining a separate peace with Russia was possible. OHL's own intelligence estimate noted the despondency and poor morale of the Russian population.[23]

To discuss the diplomatic and military matters described above, a series of meetings was held in late 1914 and early 1915. The first meeting, held in Breslau on December 2, 1914, was the first face-to-face meeting between Conrad and Falkenhayn. It amounted to little more than an opportunity to get acquainted. At their second meeting, in Oppeln on December 19, when Falkenhayn announced the intention to create what would be in effect a strategic reserve of a size yet to be determined, strategic differences emerged immediately. Falkenhayn stated that the western front should be the top priority for the Central Powers, while Conrad declared that Russia was the main enemy, so nothing was decided.[24]

Two weeks later, a larger conference was held in Berlin on New Years' Day, 1915. The conferees included Falkenhayn, Conrad, Ludendorff, and the kaiser.

While the employment of the German strategic reserve, yet to be formed, was the principal topic, there were two other pressing matters. The first concerned the situation at Przemysl and the attempt to relieve the besieged fortress. The garrison of 120,000 men could not hold out for more than a few months. Equally problematic was whether or not the Austro–Hungarian front in the Carpathians could hold. A Russian breakthrough would put the Russian armies in the Hungarian plain, a mortal wound to the dual monarchy.[25]

Conrad wanted to launch an attack against the Russians in the Carpathians and desired German assistance in two ways. The first would be an offensive out of East Prussia, a move that fit in quite well with Ober Ost's ideas. The second was direct German aid in the form of units sent directly to the Carpathian front. After some hemming and hawing plus a telephone conversation with Ober Ost, Falkenhayn agreed to send German troops to the Carpathians.[26] This would ultimately take the form of the Süd Army, a formation that contained both German and Austro–Hungarian units, commanded by General der Infanterie Alexander von Linsingen. On the southern flank of the German Ninth Army, Army Detachment Woyrsch, another formation containing both German and Austro–Hungarian units, was inserted under the command of Generaloberst Remus von Woyrsch.[27]

To break up what he regarded as a nest of personal enemies, Falkenhayn sought to have Ludendorff assigned as Linsingen's chief of staff. Ludendorff protested to the kaiser's military cabinet and requested relief from this assignment and to be posted as a division commander instead. Hindenburg went so far as to threaten resignation, an amazingly high-handed stunt, even for a German field marshal. Wilhelm II was sufficiently outraged to speak darkly of Hindenburg as the "new Wallenstein," referring to the general from the Thirty Years' War who was as known for his untrustworthiness as for his ability. Ultimately, Hindenburg's massive prestige won out, backed by some elements at the kaiser's court, and Ludendorff's appointment was canceled. General der Infanterie Paulus Alfred Wilhelm von Stolzmann was inserted into the position in Ludendorff's place.[28]

To facilitate communications between AOK and OHL, Colonel (later Generalmajor) August von Cramon was assigned as OHL's representative to Teschen on January 30, 1915. Born on April 7, 1861, Cramon was commissioned as a lieutenant on February 13, 1883. Eventually, he reached the rank of lieutenant colonel on January 27, 1910, and was later appointed commander of the Guard Cuirassier Regiment. Promoted to colonel on January 1, 1912, he was serving as chief of staff for the VIII Corps when war broke out. On October 21, 1914, Cramon was appointed commander of the 3rd Cavalry Brigade. After a short tenure as brigade commander in the Champagne region of France in the autumn of 1914, Cramon was assigned to AOK in Teschen.[29]

Cramon's task was to represent Falkenhayn's views to Conrad. He would also keep OHL informed of the conduct of Austro–Hungarian operations and was to report especially on any Austro–Hungarian measures that would be contrary to German interests. The job was not an easy one; it required Cramon to gain and then maintain the trust of both Falkenhayn and Conrad. Cramon was assisted by a small group of officers, including Kaganeck, who split time between Teschen and Vienna in his role as military attaché, and Cramon's nephew, Captain Fritz von Rothkirch, who served as intelligence officer. Later on, Rothkirch moved on to another assignment and was replaced by Paul Fleck.[30]

Cramon's appointment proved to be a major advantage for OHL. He was able to get access regularly to Conrad, but more commonly Cramon worked with Feldmarschalleutnant Anton Hoefer, Conrad's chief of staff. Cramon was also apparently able to develop a good relationship with Colonel Oskar Hranilovic, Conrad's chief intelligence officer. In the still extant messages Cramon sent to OHL's operations section and to Falkenhayn, he was able to insert very detailed information on Russian troop movements and order of battle. The level of detail provided by Cramon indicated that he had excellent sources within AOK's intelligence section. Cramon was also in touch, probably via Kaganeck, with Germany's military attachés in Romania and Bulgaria and regularly passed on information from them to OHL.[31]

The kind of effective representation provided by Cramon at AOK was not really duplicated on the Austro–Hungarian side. Conrad's man at OHL was Feldmarschalleutnant Josef Stürgkh. Although Stürgkh saw his job at OHL in terms very similar to Cramon's at AOK, the available record would seem to indicate that Stürgkh never developed the kind of contacts on the OHL staff that Cramon enjoyed at AOK.[32]

While these steps were being undertaken, Conrad prepared his offensive to relieve Przemysl. His major punch would be delivered by the Austro–Hungarian Third Army, whose attack would be aimed at Dukla Pass, the shortest route to Przemysl. Attacks would also be launched all along the front, most notably in the south by Karl Baron von Pflanzer-Baltin's Austro–Hungarian Seventh Army. The Austro–Hungarian effort would be supported by a limited attack by Mackensen's German Ninth Army, marked by heavy artillery preparation, toward Warsaw.[33]

Conrad's plans, however, were based on a weak foundation. For the Carpathian offensive, Conrad had amassed about 175,000 troops, but they were supported by only about 1,000 guns. He was also asking his troops to attack through some of the harshest terrain in Europe, in freezing cold and with the Russians objecting every step of the way.

The offensive began on January 23, 1915. The troops were trying to slog their way though the Carpathians in temperatures as low as minus 13 degrees Fahrenheit. Ludendorff confided to Moltke that he expected Austro–Hungarian progress to be slow, given the terrain. He then belied even that limited confidence by complaining about the poor quality of the Austrian soldier. Although Tappen's diary cryptically noted that good progress was being made in the

Carpathians and although some Russian forces were diverted there from East Prussia, the reality was otherwise.[34] The true situation was summed up by Stolzmann, in a message he asked Cramon to bring to Conrad's attention. "After the experiences of the last 14 days," Stolzmann wrote, "it seems that the offensive power of the Third Army is broken." The fact that Stolzmann asked Cramon to inform Conrad of this certainly could be taken as an indication of how loose Conrad's hold on the front was. There was much criticism of the attack at OHL, including the kaiser lecturing Stürgkh on strategy, with a typically Wilhelmine misquotation of Bismarck.[35] Meanwhile Mackensen's attack, supported by 518 guns, was marked by limited gains and a failed attempt to employ poison gas.[36]

Undeterred by the failure of his first effort in the Carpathians, Conrad resolved to launch another offensive through the mountains to relieve Przemysl. Inserting the Austro–Hungarian Second Army between the Austro–Hungarian Third Army and Linsingen's Süd Army, Conrad ordered all three armies to attack. As the main road to the fortress lay in the Second Army's sector, the Second Army would constitute the main effort, assisted by the right flank of the Third Army. The attack, which began on February 27, again made little progress and was definitively brought to an end by a Russian counterattack against the Second Army on March 11. One attack did take place in the Gorlice sector, but the five-division attack by the Austro–Hungarian Fourth Army on March 7 was on too small a scale to threaten the Russian grip on Przemysl.[37]

Austro–Hungarian and German attempts to bring relief to Przemysl from more distant sectors on the eastern front were also unsuccessful. Although Pflanzer-Baltin's Austro–Hungarian Seventh Army was able to capture Czernowitz, this was too far away from Carpathian passes to matter. Likewise Ober Ost's offensive against the Russian 10th Army in the Masurian Lakes region, although successful tactically, did not bring about any strategic results. The Russians, with seemingly endless reserves of manpower, were able to create a strong position west of Grodno and south of the Bober River to stop the advance of the German Eighth and Tenth Armies. To stymie Conrad's offensive, Russian headquarters (Stavka) reinforced General Alexei Brusilov's 8th Army, which was able to press the Austro–Hungarians back from Dukla Pass.[38]

Meanwhile, the Russian 11th Army maintained the siege of the fortress. Inside Przemysl, Hermann Kusmanek von Burgneustädten, the garrison commander, had about 120,000 men at his disposal to hold the fortress. He had informed AOK that sufficient supplies were available to enable the garrison to hold out until sometime in March. The food situation, at least for the enlisted men, deteriorated rapidly. By the end of 1914, according to Przemysl resident Helena Jablonska, whenever Russian soldiers saw Austro–Hungarian troops, they would start neighing like horses to remind the garrison of what they were subsisting on now. Jablonska, a nurse, noted that while soldiers were dying from a combination of exposure to the cold and the aftereffects of drinking dirty water, the officers were well off. Certainly they were fed well enough to be able to expend energy on sex with the town's prostitutes, often paying for their services with food. Jablonska noted that a number of the officers were riddled with all manner of venereal disease.[39]

After the failure of Conrad's two relief attempts, Kusmanek launched an attempt to break out but failed to get through the siege lines of the Russian 11th Army. Likewise another Austro–Hungarian relief operation foundered, this time much more quickly than the first two offensives. By the latter half of March 1915, it was clear to everyone that the fall of the fortress was imminent.[40] On March 22, 1915. Kusmanek ordered the remaining ammunition to be blown up. He also had some 700,000 Kronen in paper burned. The Austro–Hungarians also destroyed some of the guns in the fortress. The Russians entered the next day and promptly began looting and mistreating city's remaining Jewish population.[41]

The period January–March 1915 was one of unparalleled disaster for Austro–Hungarian arms. Conrad's Carpathian offensives had cost the Austro–Hungarian Army about 600,000 men, many from noncombat causes. During the second Carpathian offensive, the Austro–Hungarian Second Army lost about 40,000 men, only 6,000 of whom were casualties in combat. The loss of Przemysl added a further 120,000 men to the roll of losses, in this case permanently. Vast quantities of equipment had been lost, including 900 guns in Przemysl. The Carpathian battles also effectively used up Conrad's last reserves of trained manpower.[42]

In retrospect, Conrad's best chance to relieve Przemysl was probably his first, since it was also his strongest attack. The location for it, however, left much to be desired. While Dukla Pass was the shortest route to Przemysl and comparatively broad, the terrain was difficult even in good weather and eminently defensible.[43] In addition, even if the attackers succeeded in getting through the pass, extending the advance all the way to the fortress would be problematic. A pencil-thin advance would be subject to Russian attempts to pinch it off via counterattack. This was a capability the Russians had demonstrated convincingly in thwarting Hindenburg's offensive into Poland in the fall of 1914. An offensive in the Gorlice–Tarnow sector would probably have been better from the standpoint of terrain to be crossed to get to Przemysl. Conrad did launch one of the later relief attacks in that sector, but as in the case of so many of his Conrad's endeavors, he tried to do far too much with far too little.

It is also interesting to consider briefly what Conrad would have done had his effort succeeded. Given the waning strength of the Austro–Hungarian Army, holding Przemysl indefinitely would have been impossible, at least without a good deal of German assistance. The best alternative for Conrad, assuming success, would have been to evacuate the garrison and withdraw to a more defensible position. Although that would have saved valuable manpower, the loss of Przemysl would still have been a serious blow to Austria–Hungary in terms of political prestige and conversely a considerable boost to Russia. In the actual event, Conrad had gotten the worst of all possible results; his army had been bled white and the fortress lost with both garrison and equipment.

By the end of March 1915 the Central Powers were in a situation that could be regarded as perilously close to defeat. Although the Anglo-French attempt to force the Dardanelles by means of sea power failed, it highlighted the need for Germany to open a secure overland line of communications to Turkey. The loss of Galicia also deprived the Germany Navy of its sole source of oil.[44] Far more worrisome was the situation facing Austria–Hungary. By late March both Cramon and OHL were concerned over the situation of both the Austro–Hungarian Second and Third Armies. Cramon described the atmosphere at AOK in Teschen as thick with worry and tension. Francis Joseph wept when he was informed of Przemysl's fall.[45]

Conrad's immediate response to the disasters experienced throughout March was to call on Germany for assistance. The first German assistance arrived in the form of the Beskiden Corps, commanded by General der Kavallerie Georg von der Marwitz. The Beskiden Corps was composed of 25th and 35th Reserve Divisions plus the 4th Infantry Division. The first two units were drawn, much to Ludendorff's irritation, from Ober Ost's Army Detachment Woyrsch and the German Ninth Army, respectively, while the 4th Infantry Division came from the Süd Army. Once assembled, Marwitz's force was sent to the Carpathians to shore up the Austro–Hungarian front at Dukla Pass.[46]

The arrival of the Beskiden Corps in early April proved timely, although not in the way Conrad had hoped. Marwitz's lead unit, the 25th Reserve Division, was assigned to support the Austro–Hungarian X Corps in an attack. The attack, begun on April 3, promptly fell apart under the impact of a determined Russian night counterattack. With his force now concentrated, Marwitz was able to launch an assault of his own on April 4, which recovered the original positions of the Austro–Hungarian X Corps. Marwitz, furious with what he regarded as gross misconduct on the part of the Austro–Hungarian X Corps commander, demanded the removal of the commander by AOK. The request was granted within 24 hours.[47]

Even worse, the Austro–Hungarian Army was beginning to show signs of considerable strain. The most notable example of this occurred on April 3, 1915, when the 28th Infantry Regiment, a Czech unit drawn mostly from Prague, in essence defected to the Russians at Zboro, near Dukla Pass. These ethnic strains could only be expected to worsen if Italy entered the war. Austria–Hungary had mobilized 85,000 Italian soldiers from the Tirol and the Trentino in 1914. High losses and a variety of other factors led soldiers from these areas to desert, with Switzerland and Italy as the two most common destinations.[48] Low morale extended upward as well. Cramon noted that the atmosphere at AOK was rife with dejection and despondency.[49]

The Russians, for their part, were seeking a knockout blow against Austria–Hungary. With Przemysl in his hands and the situation on the Northwest Front stabilized by mid-March, Grand Duke Nicholas of Russia decided to shift his main effort to the Southwest Front. The 8th Army was reinforced by the XXVIII Corps while the 3rd Army received the XXIX Corps, both of which were detached from the 11th Army. Once reinforced, Brusilov's 8th Army would make the main effort to break through Dukla Pass completely and reach the Hungarian plain, while the 3rd Army would support Brusilov's attack.[50]

Ivanov's offensive failed for the same reasons that Conrad's previous efforts had. Ivanov's force was too small to accomplish its mission. The infantry had to struggle through deep snow in the mountains, fighting the Austro–Hungarians all the way, while the thawing valley roads were now bottomless canals of mud. By April 10, the 8th Army's decimated and exhausted troops reached the western side of the Carpathians, while the 3rd Army's troops had reached the mountaintops on the 8th Army's right flank.[51]

As the fortunes of Austro–Hungarian arms continued to sink, Conrad amplified his calls for German assistance. This reached an apogee on April 6, when Conrad asked Falkenhayn for a total of 12 German divisions. Since Conrad now assumed "Italy's perfidy" as a given, as well as potential Romanian intervention against the Central Powers, he wanted 10 German divisions to relieve Austro–Hungarian divisions, which would then be committed against either Italy or Romania. Another two German divisions would be needed to shore up the Austro–Hungarian position in the Carpathians.[52]

Falkenhayn ultimately decided to send Conrad help, but not in the way Conrad expected. From the available documentation, it seems that Falkenhayn began thinking about employing OHL's strategic reserve on the eastern front during the third week of March 1915. His key sounding board for the decision was August von Cramon. On March 25, 1915, Falkenhayn wrote to Cramon that according to the former's calculations, some 34 Austro–Hungarian and German divisions on the Carpathian front were opposed by 24 Russian divisions. After asking Cramon whether this was correct, Falkenhayn also asked Cramon his opinion of how much of a difference the Beskiden Corps would make and if it could create an advantageous situation.[53]

Cramon answered Falkenhayn the same day. Although confirming the correctness of Falkenhayn's calculations, Cramon cautioned that the Russians were superior in combat strength, given the depleted state of the Austro–Hungarian divisions. Cramon added that the insertion of the divisions that would eventually become the Beskiden Corps would produce some local successes, but only in a defensive role.[54]

The next day Cramon followed up with a lengthy appreciation of the situation. After noting that not much could be expected from either Pflanzer-Baltin's force or the Süd Army in terms of offensive action, Cramon discussed the critical sector of the Austro–Hungarian front. Cramon stated that the large-scale Russian counterattack had forced the Austro–Hungarian Second and Third Armies back on the defensive and that, while the front had been stabilized, a renewed Russian attack might result in a severe defeat for an increasingly unreliable Third Army. None of the neighboring armies were in a position to help; Army Detachment Woyrsch and the Austro–Hungarian First and Fourth Armies were too weak to launch attacks or even give up substantial forces to the threatened sector. Cramon thus suggested that forces be drawn from other fronts and concentrated to attack the Russians. The three best places to concentrate such a force were either behind the right flank of the Austro–Hungarian Second Army, behind the Süd Army, or behind the right flank of the Austro–Hungarian Fourth Army.[55]

Falkenhayn's next step was to consult with Colonel Wilhelm Groener, head of the railway section of the German general staff.[56] From March 28–31, 1915, Falkenhayn met with Groener on a series of issues. On March 28, Falkenhayn asked Groener to examine the possibilities of moving reserves to the eastern front for an offensive in one of three places, namely north of the Nieman River, on both sides of the Pilica River, or against Serbia. The following day Falkenhayn had narrowed the field, asking for studies on mounting an operation from Silesia into Hungary in the case of an Austro–Hungarian collapse. Groener's task was narrowed even further on March 31, when Falkenhayn raised the idea of concentrating five or six corps (about 12 divisions) in upper Silesia and the adjacent Austro–Hungarian territory. This was ultimately refined that same day into the idea of concentrating a force on the line Neu Sandec–Tarnow.[57]

While Falkenhayn was considering all this, he made no mention of his thinking to Conrad, who had come to Berlin for a meeting on April 4, 1915. When asked by Falkenhayn whether the Carpathians could be held, all Conrad could do was to reassure Falkenhayn that everything possible was being done. Both Conrad and Falkenhayn agreed that a separate peace with Russia was unlikely, especially with an Italian intervention on the side of the Entente as a likely eventuality. When it came to discussing the prospect of the creation of new German formations and where they would be used, Falkenhayn remained elusive. Conrad came away from the meeting believing that Germany was going to raise a considerable number of new formations but that no definitive decision had been reached as to where they would be employed.[58]

Having investigated the strategic matters of shifting troops to the east, Falkenhayn now went to the operational level. He wrote to Cramon on April 4, 1915. While acknowledging that any decisions depended on the overall situation, Falkenhayn intimated to Cramon that "I have considered the matter of a powerful attack from the Gorlice region in the direction of Sanok personally for a long time." For the scale of the attack, Falkenhayn thought that four divisions, as proposed earlier by Conrad, would be insufficient, but that a force of four corps would be the right size. After acknowledging the difficulties posed by limited rail capacity in the Tarnow area and above Neu Sandec, Falkenhayn asked Cramon for his opinion of the operation. Falkenhayn also asked Cramon to provide information on the railroads and the ability of the local roads to support German vehicles. Absolute secrecy was requested of Cramon in carrying this out.[59]

Cramon responded two days later. After noting the poor state of the Austro–Hungarian Army and its command, Cramon provided Falkenhayn with the information requested. Given the dispositions of Russian forces, Gorlice–Tarnow offered the best prospects for the offensive outlined by Falkenhayn. Defended by about 56,000 Russian troops, the proposed force of four German corps, supported by some of the 60,000 Austro–Hungarian regular troops and 10,000 Landwehr in the area should be able to achieve the requisite superiority. The main rail line from Cracow to Tarnow could handle up to 26 trains, each of consisting of 50 cars, while the minor line from Oderberg to Neu Sandec could take up to ten 50-car trains. Although the terrain was hilly, the main roads could sustain German vehicular traffic, especially in dry weather, which was expected to arrive in the second half of April. Finally, Cramon suggested that the attack needed to be conducted by a well-staffed army headquarters under a German general officer.[60]

At this point, however, Falkenhayn had still not definitively made up his mind. Tappen and Wild remained obdurate that, given the primacy of the western front, such an operation should be undertaken only if absolutely necessary.[61] Two pieces of information that may have helped Falkenhayn arrive at his decision came to his attention. The first was a message from Cramon sent late on April 8, 1915. Cramon reported to Falkenhayn that the German military attaché in Sofia reported that according to his sources, Russia would not undertake any further operations in East Prussia. Instead, the major Russian effort would be made in the Carpathians. The Russian offensive would be accompanied by attacks launched by Romania and Serbia. When Falkenhayn asked Cramon's opinion of this, Cramon responded on April 12, 1915, that the attaché's information had hitherto always proved reliable. Cramon added that Conrad expected the arrival of at least two more Russian divisions in the Carpathians. In addition Conrad also indicated the desirability of an offensive, but it could not be undertaken without German assistance.[62]

The second was another appreciation, sent on April 10 by Cramon to OHL on the state of the Austro–Hungarian Army. Cramon described the condition of the Austro–Hungarian Second and Third Armies in dire terms. The troops of both armies, owing to months of combat, were "weary and demoralized." The Second Army alone, during March 1915, had lost almost two-thirds of its strength. Any further retreat by the Austro–Hungarian Second Army in the Uzsoker Pass area would compromise the left flank of the Süd Army. Having briefed the Gorlice plan to the Kaiser on April 10, Falkenhayn then had another night of lengthy discussions with Tappen on the April 12, as well as additional conversations with Groener, before making his decision.[63]

On April 13, 1915, Falkenhayn sent a message to Conrad. After a brief introduction indicating his opposition to simply sending German units to support the Austro–Hungarian front in the Carpathians, Falkenhayn told Conrad that an army of at least eight German divisions was being created and that it would be backed very strongly with artillery. This force would be deployed to the Gorlice area for an attack in the direction of Sanok. The offensive would be supported by the Austro–Hungarian Fourth Army. To ensure unity of effort, both armies should be under a unified command, and in this case the command would naturally be under a German general. The night before, Tappen had urged Falkenhayn to go to Vienna to clarify the Italian situation with Conrad and to negotiate with Austro–Hungarian Foreign Minister Stephan Graf von Burián von Rajecz, although the issue to be negotiated was not stated. Instead, Conrad would come to Berlin on the April 14 to discuss the proposed operation.[64]

As planned, Conrad came to Berlin on April 14 for a 6 P.M. meeting to discuss the operation. Present at the meeting were also Tappen and Groener, who would be involved in planning the deployment of the force by rail. Tappen noted in his diary that the meeting went smoothly as to the tactical details of the operation. The only issue that proved contentious was the command arrangements for the assault. In the end, however, Conrad agreed that the Austro–Hungarian Fourth Army, commanded by Archduke Joseph Ferdinand, would be subordinate to the German commander of the operation.[65] The choice of commander of the offensive is discussed in the next chapter. Thus by mid-April 1915, the die had been cast.

Perhaps the most contentious aspect of the decision to launch the Gorlice offensive has been the matter of who should receive the most credit for the idea. Support for the idea that the concept originated from Conrad comes from those who sought to bolster Conrad's reputation as one of the great strategic minds of the war. These writers included many of Conrad's protégés from the Austro–Hungarian Army, such as August Urbanski von Ostrymiecz, more naturally Conrad's wife Gina, and finally Conrad himself.[66]

Cramon suggests in his book that AOK and OHL, independent of each other, arrived at the same conclusion regarding both the situation in the east and the choice of Gorlice for the attack area. Many thoughtful participants in and critics of the war have agreed with Cramon's assessment.[67] In fact, the decision to launch an attack in the east should not have been surprising. Although Falkenhayn was much more of a westerner strategically, he could not devote resources there until two more immediate strategic goals had been achieved. The first of these was the elimination of the Russian threat to Austria–Hungary. This would then allow for a major offensive against Serbia to open a line of communications to Turkey.

Likewise the choice of the Gorlice–Tarnow sector for the attack should also have come as no surprise. Both Conrad and Falkenhayn could read a map. As Cramon noted in his analysis, of all the places on the eastern front, the Gorlice–Tarnow sector was the only place where an offensive could have operational consequences in regard to Austria–Hungary. An offensive from East Prussia was too far away from the Carpathians to influence events there, as was shown in the second battle of the Masurian Lakes. The same applied to the southern end of the Austro–Hungarian front. Conrad had spent far too much time and far too many lives trying to hammer his way through the Carpathians.

A breakthrough in the Gorlice–Tarnow sector, however, would have the advantage of turning the Russian flank in the northern edge of the Carpathian range. Although the terrain in the area was hilly, it was far less formidable than that in the Carpathian passes themselves, and the roads were able to support heavy German vehicles. Finally, an offensive in the Gorlice sector with the forces allotted to it by Falkenhayn was far more realistic than Conrad's typically grandiose idea of a double envelopment. This was to be accomplished by attacks from East Prussia by Ober Ost aimed at the Russian rail centers east of Warsaw, while Pflanzer-Baltin and the Süd Army would attack the left flank of the Russian Carpathian front from the south. Falkenhayn correctly rejected this in favor of the much more reasonable Gorlice attack, which also had objectives that were much more attainable.[68]

The strategic decision had been made and the area for its execution chosen. The conduct of the offensive would now rest on the skill of the German Army and those commanders assigned to execute the attack. It is to an examination of those instruments that we now turn.

Chapter 3

Forces, Plans, and Preparations

Our troops are brave but young, in the attack they are not as good as the old troops. In defense they are completely reliable.

—Erich Ludendorff, April 1, 1915[1]

I also came rapidly to trust the most important people in the newly created army command.

—August von Mackensen, late April 1915[2]

The attack of the 11th Army must press forward rapidly for it to accomplish its mission.

—German 11th Army Order, April 27, 1915[3]

The success or failure of the Gorlice offensive rested on the German and Austro–Hungarian Armies. The strengths and liabilities of both of these military establishments are now considered.

Like all of the armies of the major belligerents in 1914, the German Army had suffered serious casualties in the war's initial campaigns. When the war started in 1914, the total strength of the German Army was 3,823,000 officers and men, of which some 2,398,000 were in the field.[4] Losses suffered in the west during the 1914 summer campaign led to the committing of poorly trained volunteers in November at Ypres, remembered so vividly after the war as the sacrifice of the best of Germany's youth at Langemarck.[5] Between September and December 1914, the German Army suffered a total of 800,000 casualties on all fronts. The loss of so many junior officers and noncommissioned officers affected the army's tactical proficiency, as Ludendorff's letter to Moltke, quoted above, indicates.[6]

Nonetheless, the German Army of 1915 was a formidable weapon. The survivors of the 1914 campaigns on both fronts were battle-hardened. Many still retained the spirit of 1914, such as Ernst Günter Schallert. Writing to his parents to inform them of the death of his brother Helmut in a German field hospital near Douai on January 10, 1915, Schallert's sense of patriotism and duty remained undimmed. Despite the personal tragedy of his brother's death, Schallert told his parents "we must all do our duty to the Fatherland. And we offer our sacrifice willingly and gladly." Arthur, Count von der Groeben, a young officer in the Fusilier Battalion of the Prussian 1st Guard Grenadier (Kaiser Alexander) Regiment, wrote to his father on April 25, 1915, from Galicia about his excitement at the prospect of his being able to lead troops. "God grant," Groeben wrote, "that I may do it to the benefit of the Fatherland."[7]

Training and the incorporation of experience gained on the battlefield would improve the army's tactical performance over time. The biggest problem facing Germany was the number of units available to carry out the strategic decisions reached by Falkenhayn and Conrad and the men needed to staff them. By the second half of February 1915, the German Army in the west fielded 92 divisions, opposed by 97 Allied divisions. In the east, over 30 German infantry division and 9 German cavalry divisions, along with a like number of Austro–Hungarian formations, confronted 97 Russian infantry divisions and just over 33 Russian cavalry divisions. In terms of available military manpower, at the start of the war the Entente powers outnumbered Germany and Austria–Hungary by almost twice the number of men.[8] Casualties suffered in the 1914 campaigns, even allowing for the major victory at Tannenberg, did not improve this ratio.

Nonetheless, a strategic reserve had to be created. Falkenhayn had intimated to Conrad in their meeting at Oppeln on December 19, 1914, that such a reserve would be created, although its size was yet to be determined. On February 22, 1915, Falkenhayn met with Colonel (later Generalmajor) Ernst von Wrisberg, chief of the army section of the War Ministry. The two men discussed Wrisberg's proposal for a reorganization of the army that would produce the desired new formations. Falkenhayn accepted Wrisberg's proposal and was able to obtain the Kaiser's approval (something of a formality) on the same day.[9]

When the German Army went to war in 1914, its standard infantry division was organized on the square pattern. That is, the division had four subordinate infantry regiments organized into two brigades. The reorganization carried out under Wrisberg's plan called for a number of these divisions to give up one of their infantry regiments. The spare regiments would then be organized into new divisions. The artillery for the new formations would also be drawn from existing divisions, at least in part, as artillery batteries were reduced from six guns to four. One of the brigade headquarters would also disappear. The divisions losing units would be compensated by receiving 2,400 trained replacements, and all of the machine gun platoons in these divisions would get an extra machine gun. One major advantage to the plan was that all of the new divisions would have troops that had combat experience. The initial expectation was that this reorganization would produce as many as 24 new divisions by the end of March 1915.[10]

Once Wrisberg's proposed reorganization was put into place by Falkenhayn's order on February 25, 1915, problems arose. Initially designed to apply to only a portion of the German Army in the west, the plan had to be extended on March 3, 1915 to the whole of the army in the west. In addition, the peculiarities of the imperial German military system mandated that several states possessing a degree of autonomy would execute this plan through their own military establishments. The available military manpower did not allow for the formation of 24 new divisions while also providing 2,400 trained replacements to the divisions that were losing a regiment. The production of arms and equipment was insufficient to allow for the full equipping of the new divisions while maintaining existing units at the same time. The result was that by the end of March 1915, only 14 new divisions would be available. The order creating the Bavarian 11th Infantry Division, for example, was not issued until March 21, 1915.[11] Thus, by using eight divisions for the attack, Falkenhayn was committing over half of OHL's strategic reserve. Although major German forces were going to be involved, a considerable degree of Austro–Hungarian participation in the offensive would also be required.

By April 1915, the Austro–Hungarian Army was in as poor a state as could be imagined. Easily the weakest of all the military establishments among the major powers at the start of the war, the army had suffered severely between August 1914 and April 1915. It had sustained well over a million casualties, almost half of the Austro–Hungarian Army's total strength at the start of the war. This included several hundred thousand prisoners. Matters were made worse by the fact that Austria–Hungary had the smallest pool of military manpower available to any of the major belligerents.[12]

The strain of war against both Russia and Serbia exposed the weaknesses inherent in the multiethnic army and society of the dual monarchy. This was certainly illustrated in the surrender of the Czech 28th Infantry Regiment, as noted in the previous chapter. Ethnic tensions were heightened when Archduke Friedrich, the nominal Hungarian Army's commander in chief, asked Francis Joseph to officially disband the unit, which was done on April 17, 1915. This act, although understandable, was also counterproductive, as it served to exacerbate hostile feelings between the native Austrians and Czechs, especially in Vienna, which had a sizable Czech minority.[13]

For all of its problems, however, the Austro–Hungarian Army would prove surprisingly durable. It was able to hang on in the Carpathians, although this was done with the help of German units, including army-sized formations with both German and Austro–Hungarian units such as those commanded by Linsingen and Woyrsch. Hans von Seeckt, after long experience on the eastern front and with Austro–Hungarian troops, would eventually write an appraisal of the Austro–Hungarian Army that, while harshly critical of the army's leadership, was sympathetic to its common soldiers.[14] In April 1915, however, the amount of help the Austro–Hungarian Army could render in the offensive was uncertain.

Since battles are fought by opposing sides, a few words on the Russian Army are required as well. That army's record in the first eight months of combat was not one of unrelieved disaster. To be sure, it suffered a major defeat at Tannenberg. Nevertheless, the battles along the frontier with Austria–Hungary had resulted in the seizure of Austro–Hungarian Galicia, including all of dual monarchy's oil producing areas, the capital city of Lemberg, and the fortress of Przemysl. The Russians had also shown sufficient flexibility to conduct operational-level movements to thwart Hindenburg's attempt to take Warsaw. Although the second Masurian Lakes campaign in February 1915 had resulted in a defeat for the Russian 10th Army, it was still able to retreat back to the prewar Russo-German border, and Ober Ost's success came only by dint of hard fighting.[15]

Nonetheless, the first eight months of war had been very hard on the Russian Army. Although the loss of 83,100 men to sickness represented a major improvement over previous periods in Russian military history, combat was another matter. Losses incurred in battle ran close to a million in 1914 alone. Matters were not helped by a tremendous shortage of medical personnel at the regimental level. Losses in officers had been particularly heavy, and those lost could not be replaced quickly. The Russian Army claimed that in 1914 it could field some 3,500,000 reservists, which proved to be a considerable overstatement. Of these reservists, only about 200,000 could be considered trained replacements, a number that proved hopelessly inadequate. Although the Russian Army instituted a training program to generate the requisite number of replacements, comprising officers and specialists such as machine gunners, time would be required for such a program to become fully effective.[16]

In the realm of logistics, Russian industry proved unable to meet the needs of the army in terms of munitions and arms. In addition, the Russian rail system, although operating at increased capacity, proved unable to distribute the material that had been produced. It might be added here that since the Russians were operating inside Austro–Hungarian territory, they had the problem of overcoming the barrier presented by the narrower European rail gauge.[17]

Operationally, the course of events through March 1915 left the target of the impending Central Powers' offensive, General R. D. Radko-Dmitriev's Russian 3rd Army, in a vulnerable position. The demands of slowing the German advance after second Masurian Lakes campaign had consumed the reserves of the Russian Northwest Front. Likewise, on the southern end of the front, Conrad's Carpathian offensives and matching Russian counterattacks seeking to reach the Hungarian plain left the Russian Southwest Front with much of its combat power in or immediately behind the Carpathians.[18]

Russia's initial strategic plan for 1915 was formulated when Grand Duke Nicholas conferred with his senior staff and commanders at Siedlce on January 17, 1915. Three basic courses of action were considered. The first was an advance from the Konsk-Opoczna area to Petrikau. A second alternative was an offensive along the left bank of the Vistula. This attack was aimed at enveloping the left wing of the Germans and Austro–Hungarians south of the river. The third course of action discussed was a renewed invasion of East Prussia. The first alternative was the consensus choice. The attack would be carried out by a new force, the 12th Army, whose buildup was noticed by the Germans.[19] The events of March 1915, however, led the grand duke to shift his effort to the southwest front, with the results described in the previous chapter. The focus of effort would still be the 8th Army, which was now due to be reinforced with the III Caucasian Corps.[20]

The Russian positions in the Gorlice–Tarnow area, however, remained formidable. Radko-Dmitriev's troops had been in possession of the area for five months and had used the time to build up a powerful defensive system. Maximizing the advantages of the terrain, the Russians were able to develop three trench lines, with the second and third lines overlooking the forward line. All three lines were dotted with numerous machine gun nests and positions from which flanking fire could be delivered against an attacking force.[21]

With the strategic decisions having been made and plans drawn up in broad outline, they had to be put in motion. The first steps involved the assembly of the attack force and the equally important matter of deciding who was to command the German Eleventh Army. When they met in Berlin on April 14, 1915, Falkenhayn and Conrad had disagreed over the issue of command. Ultimately, since the preponderance of troops in the Eleventh Army would be German, Falkenhayn prevailed in his demand that the operation be entrusted to a German general. In addition, the German commander of the Eleventh Army would also have the Austro–Hungarian Fourth Army subordinated to him.[22] The question now was which German general?

According to Cramon and Fleck, there were four candidates up for the command of the German Eleventh Army. The first and least likely was Falkenhayn himself. Since Falkenhayn was the head of OHL, his appointment would simplify the issue of communications with AOK in Teschen. The idea of Falkenhayn as army commander, however, was impractical. First, Falkenhayn had more than enough on his plate with just running OHL. Even with a chief of staff as able as Seeckt, commanding a field army in an active campaign was a time-consuming task. Falkenhayn simply could not direct an operational-level campaign in the east given that OHL fully expected an Allied offensive in France during the spring. Personality would also be a factor. In the opinion of Cramon and Fleck, Falkenhayn was too "restless" to work with the Austro–Hungarians in such a direct manner. Given the nature of his duties, however, as well as the lack of any contemporaneous evidence, it does seem unlikely that Falkenhayn ever seriously considered himself as a possibility to command the German Eleventh Army.[23]

The second candidate for the job of commanding the offensive was Hindenburg. His position as the head of Ober Ost gave the idea of Hindenburg leading the attack a certain logic. Hindenburg would have the ability to coordinate attacks of the other German armies on the eastern front, especially the German Eighth, Ninth, and Tenth Armies. Several problems, however, militated against Hindenburg's selection as commander for the attack. The first of these was Hindenburg's own personality, described by Cramon and Fleck as much too "authoritarian" for the Austro–Hungarians. In addition, Hindenburg would have the rest of Ober Ost's staff in tow as well. The 1914 campaigns had shown a number of instances of strained relations between Hindenburg's staff and their Austro–Hungarian counterparts.[24]

The major reason why neither Falkenhayn nor Hindenburg would have been acceptable to lead the German Eleventh Army had to do with a broader issue, namely that of unified command. As the 1914 campaign in the east developed, Ober Ost was created as a command and control mechanism for the German forces on the eastern front. The complexity of the situation, however, certainly suggested the idea of an overall unified command element to control the forces of both allies over the entire eastern front. In late November 1914, a proposal for a unified command structure was proposed by the Austrians. Originated apparently by Artur Baron von Bolfras, the chief of Francis Joseph's military chancery, the proposal called for the creation of a unified command that would be headed by Austrian Archduke Friedrich. Ludendorff would fill the role of chief of staff. Although Francis Josef favored the idea, Conrad's opposition proved too strong to overcome. Conrad proved equally opposed to any scheme for a unified command under a German officer.[25]

The third candidate for command of the German Eleventh Army, according to Cramon and Fleck, was Ludendorff. Although his position as chief of staff at Ober Ost conferred the requisite stature for such a command, Ludendorff too seemed a highly unlikely choice. His antipathy toward Falkenhayn was guaranteed to make relations with OHL strained at best. Ludendorff's "hard edged" personality made the prospect of working with the Austro–Hungarians problematic as well. This was well manifested already in September 1914, as outlined in chapter 1. Given the lack of any mention of this prospect in Ludendorff's letters to Moltke, the idea of entrusting the German Eleventh Army to Ludendorff was never seriously considered by OHL.[26]

The last candidate on the list of Cramon and Fleck was Mackensen. Promoted Generaloberst after the successful conclusion of the Lodz campaign in December 1914, Mackensen's rank certainly qualified him for the position of German Eleventh Army commander. His conduct as a corps commander at Tannenberg and then as a de facto army commander during the Warsaw and Lodz campaigns late in 1914 certainly marked Mackensen as one of Germany's best field commanders, although he did have his critics.[27] In addition, Mackensen, unlike Hindenburg or Ludendorff, enjoyed a very close relationship with Wilhelm II. Finally, Mackensen would be a good fit when paired with the army's already posted chief of staff, a matter to be commented on later. On April 18, 1915, Mackensen traveled on a special train to OHL headquarters at Charleville, where he received his appointment and orders from Falkenhayn.[28]

At this point, a slightly more extended examination of the German Eleventh Army's command team is in order. Born on December 6, 1849, August von Mackensen was a member of a well-off nonnoble Saxon family. He entered the army on October 1, 1869, as a one-year volunteer with the 2nd Life Hussars and saw combat in the Franco-Prussian War. After a short stint as a student at the University of Halle, Mackensen reentered the army in 1873, obtaining a regular commission as a lieutenant. In 1880, then a captain, Mackensen was assigned to the general staff, even though he was not a graduate of the Kriegsakademie. While with the general staff, he served in the section that dealt with Russia, the Balkans, and Austria–Hungary. Service on the general staff was followed by a tour with the Life Hussars and then postings as an adjutant to Schlieffen and later the kaiser. Fortunate assignments and natural ability brought Mackensen advancements and honors. Association with the Life Hussars and service at the Hohenzollern court gained the attention of the kaiser, who raised Mackensen to the nobility on January 22, 1899. Promoted General der Kavallerie on January 27, 1908, he was given command of the XVII Corps. All things remaining the same, Mackensen's tenure as commander of the XVII Corps was going to be the capstone to what had been a fine military career.[29]

Things, however, did not remain the same after July 1914. Mackensen commanded the XVII Corps through the opening campaigns of 1914, playing an important role at Tannenberg. Named commander of the German Ninth Army on November 1, 1914, his conduct of the Lodz campaign in November and December 1914 made him one of the most popular figures in Germany, surpassed only by Hindenburg.[30]

More important than popularity was the experience gained by Mackensen in commanding field forces engaged in active combat operations. Mackensen's staff at the XVII Corps remembered their boss as the quintessential hard-driving cavalry officer. An avid and skilled horseman, Mackensen was capable of spending hours in the saddle on a nearly daily basis, either out on military exercises or hunting. As a corps commander, Mackensen tried to be as far forward as possible and engaged in this practice at both Gumbinnen and Tannenberg.[31] That approach to corps-level command would have been familiar to corps commanders 40 or 50 years earlier, such as James Longstreet or Constantine von Voigts-Rhetz.

The circumstances of high level operational command in World War I, however, changed drastically once the implications of technological developments over the period 1890–1914 became at least partially clear.[32] Mackensen obviously understood this change and captured it in a letter of November 14, 1914, from his headquarters at Hohensalza during the Lodz campaign. It is worth quoting here at length:

> It seems quite strange to me, that I sit here at my desk and map table, while my troops fight between the Warthe and the Vistula. Such, however, is the conduct of modern warfare. The distances of the march routes and the battlefield, the extent of the latter and the whole technical apparatus of the modern army brings it out so. Hohensalza is very good in this respect. It is valuable for the conducting of business when a headquarters remains in the same place for a longer time and becomes a traffic center. Units report by telephone and wireless radio and receive orders by the same means. One is far from particular staffs and still speaks constantly with them and is constantly in contact with the battle front. The business area of my headquarters here is in a Gymnasium. All of my sections make demands on my time. I work in the room with the directors.[33]

Although Mackensen understood the parameters by which high-level operational command was conducted, as the passage above indicates, he did not let himself become totally desk-bound. He would head to decisive points to personally observe the progress of operations.

Finally, Mackensen had one more quality that recommended him very much for the position, namely tact. Service as Wilhelm II's adjutant in Berlin taught Mackensen the importance of observing the niceties of protocol. This would prove to be an important element of coalition warfare. Mackensen's personality also made him an ideal fit for the relationship that German military practice demanded between a commander and his chief of staff.

From the days of the Prussian military reformers of the Napoleonic Wars through the end of the Second Reich, the relationship between a commander and his chief of staff was central to the conduct of military operations. Although the commander ultimately bore responsibility for success or failure, his chief of staff enjoyed equal authority when it came to casting plans and making decisions, as long as the decisions made corresponded to the commander's intent.[34]

This system demanded that the selection of both commanders and chiefs of staff be given careful consideration. The officers chosen for these positions had to possess complementary personalities. Often they knew each other personally. Such military matchmaking, engineered by the military cabinet and the great general staff, had served the Imperial German Army's Prussian forebear well during the Wars of German Unification. This was best exemplified by the relationship between Crown Prince Friedrich Wilhelm (later Kaiser Friedrich III) and his chief of staff, Generalleutnant (later Generalfeldmarschall) Carl Constantine Graf von Blumenthal.[35]

The tradition of carefully pairing commanders and chiefs of staff was faithfully followed during World War I. Certainly the most famous such duumvirate was Hindenburg and Ludendorff, but it was not the only one. Another fruitful

German military marriage was that of Crown Prince Rupprecht of Bavaria and the brilliant Hermann von Kuhl, his chief of staff. For the Gorlice operation, a similarly compatible couple had to be created. Even before Mackensen was appointed to the command of the German Eleventh Army, his chief of staff had already been chosen.

Born on April 22, 1866, Hans von Seeckt was the son of an army officer, and his family was part of the Pomeranian nobility. He entered the army as an officer cadet in the Kaiser Alexander Guards Regiment in 1885. After obtaining his commission in 1887, Seeckt was admitted to the Kriegsakademie in 1893. Between his graduation from the Kriegsakademie in 1896 and the outbreak of war in 1914, Seeckt served in a variety of command and staff assignments. He spent the war's opening campaigns in the west as chief of staff of the III Corps. On October 30, 1914, Seeckt helped engineer an attack on the French at Vailly, the success of which depended heavily on careful artillery preparation. Seeckt was able to repeat this accomplishment in January 1915 at Soissons, an event that cemented his reputation as a brilliant staff officer whose organizational abilities were matched by steely nerves. Seeckt, who also enjoyed a good relationship with Falkenhayn, was selected on March 9, 1915, as the chief of staff for the then forming headquarters of the German Eleventh Army.[36]

The practice of assigning first a chief of staff and then a commander to a headquarters has served to create the impression that in the German system, it was the chief of staff, such as Ludendorff or Seeckt, who was the brains behind the operations, while commanders such as Hindenburg or Mackensen were mere front men. From John Wheeler-Bennett's description of Hindenburg, for example, one gets the feeling that Hindenburg was an empty vessel, totally dominated by Ludendorff. The only purpose Hindenburg served, in this depiction of the relationship, was to calm down his chief of staff, especially during times that were particularly difficult or stressful.[37] In effect, Hindenburg was nothing more than an ambulatory tranquilizer.

Mackensen likewise has been portrayed more as Seeckt's assistant than as his superior.[38] The old hussar's appearance at times conveyed an impression that he belonged to an earlier age. A tall, thin man with deep-set eyes and a handlebar mustache, Mackensen, although he had successively commanded an infantry division and then a corps, often wore the uniform of the Life Hussars, topped by the large fur busby with its distinctive death's head insignia. This singular exception to the regulations governing how German generals could dress gave Mackensen a rather fearsome countenance, reminding contemporaneous German authors of Gebhard von Blücher, hero of the Napoleonic Wars.[39] Mackensen's rather anachronistic appearance presented a stark contrast to Seeckt's, whose sphinx-like expression, along with his blue eyes and monocle, exuded an icy coolness.

To be sure, there was some truth to the notion that Hindenburg's rock-like imperturbability served to steady Ludendorff's jangled nerves at several critical times during the war. To paint generals such as Hindenburg and Mackensen simply as front men, however, is to do a disservice to both. Both men had had long careers in the army, and both had served in numerous staff positions that required extensive use of their brains. Although Mackensen had not attended the Kriegsakademie, that was true of most officers who reached the rank of general officer before 1914.[40] Seeckt, while mentioning the inevitable comparison to Blücher, noted in his memoirs that Mackensen possessed an impressive range of both theoretical and practical knowledge. Even Ludendorff, not known for throwing around compliments with abandon, described Mackensen as both "a distinguished man and a brilliant soldier." A colonel is, as a rule, not given a lobotomy when he is promoted to general.[41]

Unlike Hindenburg and Ludendorff, who were polar opposites in terms of personality, Mackensen and Seeckt were very similar in personality. In the stress of combat operations, Mackensen proved every bit as phlegmatic as his chief of staff. In addition, the two men had known each other for a while. They apparently first met in 1901 when Seeckt was on the staff of the XVII Corps and Mackensen was the commander of the Life Hussar Brigade while the two units were on maneuvers near Danzig.[42]

Having received his orders on April 18, 1915, Mackensen headed for Neu Sandec, the location of the German Eleventh Army's headquarters, where he arrived during the evening of April 25. Later on, Mackensen wrote that at first he could only really trust himself, as "everything else—terrain, troops, officers, staff and not least allies—was new." He quickly came to trust his staff, however, especially Seeckt and Major Fedor von Bock, the staff's operations officer. Seeckt was equally pleased with his new boss. He wrote to his wife that the army's headquarters had a most positive atmosphere, and that he and Mackensen got along very well. Seeckt was particularly happy that Mackensen had very few "vanities" that had to be placated.[43] As a general, Mackensen could be regarded, to use modern parlance, as "low maintenance."

When Mackensen met with Falkenhayn on April 18, 1915, Mackensen received the plan in broad outline. Further map study convinced Mackensen that a successful attack could be launched only in the area between the Vistula and the Carpathians.[44] When the German Eleventh Army commander arrived on April 25, Mackensen's staff was busy doing the detailed planning necessary for the conduct of the offensive, a matter to be commented on shortly. Given that the staff was gainfully employed putting the plan together, Mackensen had other matters to deal with, namely the Austro–Hungarians.

On April 26, 1915, Mackensen, accompanied by Seeckt and Bock, drove to Teschen to see Conrad and Archduke Friedrich, the nominal Austro–Hungarian commander in chief. Although he was then 66 years old, Mackensen presented an appearance to the Austro–Hungarians that Cramon described as "youthful" and "fresh" as well as elegant. Mackensen depicted the Archduke as "soldierly" and "frank." The old hussar insightfully regarded Conrad as a clever man but one

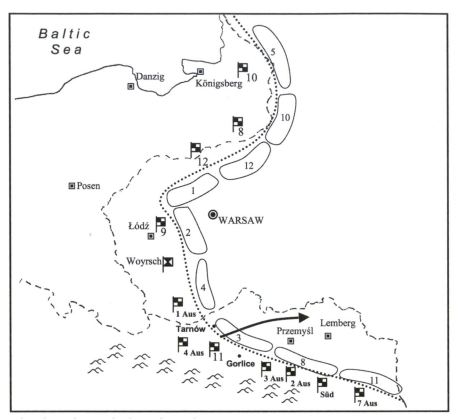

The Eleventh Army's Planned Attack, May 1915.

who was borne down by his weighty responsibilities and "the poor turn of events."[45]

The most important issue that needed to be clarified was command relationships. Mackensen made it clear that while AOK might issue directives to Mackensen, no orders would be given without Falkenhayn's agreement. This reflected the agreement reached by Falkenhayn and Conrad in their April 14 meeting in Berlin. In addition, Mackensen would be able to issue orders to elements of the Austro–Hungarian Fourth Army through that army's headquarters. The Austro–Hungarians, however, did receive assurances from Mackensen that he would not allow Austro–Hungarian prestige to be damaged. Cramon also asked OHL's operations section that situation reports from Mackensen's headquarters also go to him, a request to which OHL agreed.[46]

Once arrangements with AOK had been settled, Mackensen and his small entourage drove over to Brzesko to visit the headquarters of the Austro–Hungarian Fourth Army and Archduke Joseph Ferdinand, its commander. While the respective chiefs of staff discussed the situation, Mackensen took the measure of his Austro–Hungarian colleague. The Austrian archduke struck Mackensen as a good man and a capable soldier on whose support Mackensen could rely. Mackensen also believed that making the archduke a close acquaintance gave the trip added value.[47] It is difficult to imagine any of the other candidates for the post of German Eleventh Army commander exercising the kind of personal touch, so critical in coalition warfare, as shown here by Mackensen.

While Mackensen's staff completed the detailed plans for the attack, the German Eleventh Army completed its assembly. Although Wrisberg's plan had resulted in the creation of 14 new divisions, only two of these, the Bavarian 11th Division and the 119th Infantry Division, were actually employed in the attack. The state of training of new recruits in the depots was regarded as wholly insufficient, exacerbated by shortages of needed items such as live ammunition.[48] Thus, the new divisions were used to relieve experienced divisions from the western front that would be used in the offensive.

The German Eleventh Army was composed largely of picked troops. These units had fought under difficult circumstances in the west and had experienced commanders.[49] The elite of the German Army was represented in Mackensen's force by the Prussian Guard Corps. Composed of the Prussian 1st and 2nd Guard

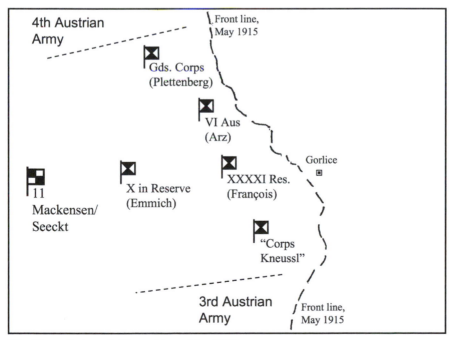

The Eleventh Army's Dispositions, May 1915.

Divisions, the Guard fielded 24 battalions, 6 squadrons, and 108 guns, totaling about 25,000 officers and men. The Guard's component divisions were the only units to retain the old square pattern organization. The oversized corps was commanded by General der Infanterie Karl Freiherr von Plettenberg, who had led the Guard through its initial campaigns in 1914. His division commanders were Prince Friedrich of Prussia and Generalleutnant Arnold von Winckler.[50]

The next German corps in Mackensen's force was the XXXXI Reserve Corps. This corps, composed of the 81st and 82nd Reserve Divisions, put 18 battalions, 4 squadrons, and 108 guns in the field—about 20,000 officers and men. The corps was commanded by General der Infanterie Hermann von François, one of the more controversial German figures of World War I. Born on January 31, 1856, François obtained his first commission as a second lieutenant in the First Guard Regiment in 1875. After graduating from the Kriegsakademie in 1887, he spent most of his career in the Prussian Guard Corps. Promoted to General der Infanterie just after the outbreak of the war, François led the I Corps during the Tannenberg campaign. He proved to be a difficult subordinate to manage for both Prittwitz and then Hindenburg. He was successful enough, however, that, as senior corps commander in the German Eighth Army, he took over command of the army after the creation of Ober Ost. Promotion to army command did little to ease the strained relationship between François and Ober Ost. He was relieved and sent west to command the XXXXI Reserve Corps in France. The Gorlice operation would mark his return to the eastern front. Whether he could work successfully with Mackensen and Seeckt, however, was an open question.[51] His division commanders were Generalmajor Leo von Stocken (81st Reserve Division) and Generalmajor Sigfried Fabarius (82nd Reserve Division).[52]

The most direct manifestation of OHL's newly created strategic reserve was provided in the form of "Corps Kneussl." Commanded by Generalmajor Paul Ritter von Kneussl, it was composed of the Bavarian 11th and 119th Infantry Divisions, both of which were created under Wrisberg's plan. The units that would compose the Bavarian 11th Infantry Division were assembled in early April. The Bavarian 3rd Infantry Regiment, for example, was withdrawn from its frontline position on the night of 1–2 April and sent by night march to Douai. Most of the other troops arrived by train, and the assembly of the division was completed by April 6, 1915, although the creation of the division was announced officially by Kneussl in a stirring order of the day published on April 5, 1915.[53]

The two divisions possessed 18 battalions and 6 squadrons, altogether a combat strength of about 20,000 men. The Bavarian 11th Infantry Division alone had a combat strength of 9,060 officers and men. Although the corps had a generous allotment of 40 machine guns, it was a bit light on artillery, fielding only 56 guns.[54]

Born on June 27, 1862, Kneussl obtained his first commission as an officer in the Bavarian Army in 1884. By 1910 he was a colonel. Promoted Generalmajor

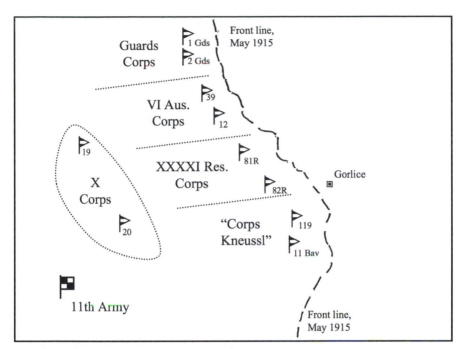

The Eleventh Army's Dispositions in Detail, May 1915.

on March 27, 1913, Kneussl did a brief stint as commander of the Bavarian 8th Infantry Brigade before taking positions first in the Bavarian War Ministry and later Bavarian Army Headquarters. When the Bavarian 11th Infantry Division was created, a commander had to be named. Kneussl was proposed as commander of the division by the Bavarian War Ministry, probably by Generaloberst Otto Freiherr Kress von Kressenstein, the war minister, to King Ludwig III of Bavaria. Ludwig III named Kneussl as commander in early April 1915. Kneussl's chief of staff was Captain Wilhelm Ritter von Leeb.[55] Aside from commanding the corps, Kneussl also remained commander the Bavarian 11th Infantry Division. The 119th Infantry Division was commanded by Generalmajor Karl von Behr.[56]

The third German corps-sized unit under Mackensen's command was the German X Corps, commanded by General der Infanterie Otto von Emmich. Like François's XXXXI Reserve Corps, the German X Corps possessed 18 battalions, 6 squadrons, 53 machine guns, and 108 artillery pieces—about 20,000 officers and men. Emmich himself was an old hand. Born on August 4, 1848, he obtained his first commission as a lieutenant on February 8, 1868. By 1887, Emmich was both a colonel and commander of the 114th Infantry Regiment. On September 25, 1909, Emmich was promoted to General der Infanterie and appointed commander of the German X Corps. One of the few German generals who entered World War I with combat experience, Emmich led the German X Corps through the 1914 campaigns.[57] Emmich's two subordinate infantry divisions, the 19th and 20th, were commanded by Generalleutnant Max Hofmann and Generalleutnant Horst Ritter und Edler von Oetinger, respectively.[58]

The Austro–Hungarian contingent of Mackensen's force was the Austro–Hungarian VI Corps, commanded by Feldmarschalleutnant Artur Arz von Straussenberg. Although composed of two divisions, Feldmarschalleutnant Paul Kestranek's Austrian 12th Infantry Division and Feldmarschalleutnant Emmerich Hadfy von Livno's Hungarian 39th Honved Division, the corps could field about 33,000 officers and men in 28 battalions or 4 squadrons, with 64 machine guns and 106 artillery pieces.[59]

Arz was considered a rising star in the Austro–Hungarian Army. Born on June 11, 1857, he entered the army in 1878. Nine years later he graduated from the Austrian Kriegsakademie and then did a tour on the general staff. By 1908, Arz had been promoted to Generalmajor and appointed commander of the Austro–Hungarian 61st Infantry Brigade in Budapest. This was followed by a stint as commander of the Austro–Hungarian 31st Infantry Division. In 1914, Arz led the Austro–Hungarian 15th Infantry Division. Later in 1914, he was promoted to Feldmarschalleutnant and given command of the Austro–Hungarian VI Corps, which he commanded with success at Limanowa–Lapanow.[60] The corps represented the best effort that Austria–Hungary could muster. It was transferred from control of the Austro–Hungarian Fourth Army to that of the German Eleventh Army on April 22, 1915.[61]

The true power of Mackensen's army, however, lay in the additional artillery attached to his component corps. Each corps with the exception of the German X Corps, whose guns were still in transit, had large amounts of attached heavy artillery, either German or Austro–Hungarian. This included batteries of 100-mm guns and 150-mm howitzers. More important was the inclusion of a large number of heavy mortars, including German 210-mm and the more advanced Austro–Hungarian 305-mm pieces. Used in 1914 to subdue fortresses, the most notable of which was Liege, this would mark their first employment against field fortifications.[62]

Before a force can be employed, it has to be trained and deployed. In the case of the German Eleventh Army, this involved moving the Guard, XXXXI Reserve X Corps, and Kneussl's Corps from the western front to the east. Prior to their transfer, all these divisions were concentrated behind the western front and given training to attack and break through prepared positions. The Bavarian 11th Infantry Division, for example, was trained extensively in cooperation between the infantry and artillery. The infantry were given marching exercises to prepare them for mobile warfare. Units were also trained in resupplying individual batteries or guns with ammunition during an attack. Cavalry units practiced the art of reconnaissance against fortified positions. Exercises were progressive in terms of the size of units involved. In the space of five days, the division went from having regimental-size exercises to conducting a division-size exercise from April 13–15. That would be the last training the division engaged in before its transfer to the east.[63]

Orders for the eastward movement went out to the units and to the German railroad authorities on April 15, 1915, and deployment began two days later. The Guard Corps left from Strassburg in Alsace, while the XXXXI Reserve Corps departed from Busigny. The 119th Infantry Division left from Mörchingen, while the Bavarian 11th Infantry Division boarded its trains at Valenciennes. Once the trains began rolling, the X Corps would be sent as a second echelon. The movement was carried out in the greatest possible secrecy, so the men who boarded the trains were in the dark as to their destination. The trains also took a circuitous route through Germany. Only when the trains carrying the Guard Corps turned south after reaching Posen did the men realize what their final destination would be. To cover the movements from the prying Anglo-French eyes, a limited attack by the German Fourth Army in the area of Ypres was conducted in late April.[64]

As the trains approached the Austro–Hungarian border, orders, presumably from AOK, went out to the Austro–Hungarian railroad authorities. Matters regarding the arrival of the German troops by rail had been discussed at a conference in Berlin involving Groener and his Austro–Hungarian counterpart on April 16, 1915. This was a very complicated issue, as the movement of the Guard Corps, XXXXI Reserve Corps, the 119th Infantry Division, and the Bavarian 11th Infantry Division of the German Eleventh Army required no less than 500 trains. Each German unit was allotted a specific railroad and destination for off loading. These sites were located behind the front of the Austro–Hungarian Fourth Army. The Guard Corps, for example, detrained at Brzesko, located on the double-tracked line between Cracow and Tarnow. On average, the trip for German units sent from the western front took four to five days. The Bavarian 11th Infantry Division, for example, left France on April 20. Several stops along the way were made to allow troops to be fed. The division's units arrived at Grybow in stages on April 23–24. The trip was not an easy one. The cars were cramped and, given that the trains were running nonstop, rest for both men and horses was hard to come by.[65]

Once the units reached their respective destinations by rail, they had to be off loaded. Once that was accomplished, the divisions had to move to their assembly areas. This was hard as well; the Germans regarded the Austro–Hungarian rail facilities as poor. Once off the trains, men, horses, and vehicles had to travel over poor roads, which were often very stony or consisted of deep sand, so that the troops were sometimes covered with a thick coat of dust.[66]

The German deployment was facilitated by the Austro–Hungarian Army, which made parks of Austrian vehicles—which were lighter than the German equipment—available to Mackensen's units. Each cart, drawn by two horses, could haul as much as 880 pounds of food and forage. Turned in German vehicles would be collected in a designated park run by the German Eleventh Army. To ease the difficulties of moving guns and heavier equipment, the Germans made use of corduroyed roads. Although Russian aerial reconnaissance was scanty, the needs of operations security required that German troops move only at particular times in the day.[67]

The first elements to be deployed were the heavy artillery, as these required the most time to position as well as having a stockpile of ammunition created. Infantry units then moved to their assembly areas, relieving Austro–Hungarian troops. The idea was to have the German troops reach their attack positions between April 26 and 28. This was also a matter of operational security, since in 1915 German troops still used the leather *Pickelhaube* helmet with its distinctive spike. The presence of German troops was to be kept as quiet as possible until the last moment before the attack.[68]

Although the French did notice the removal of German units from the western front and informed the Russian high command, the presence of Mackensen's force was not discovered by the Russians until April 25. The Germans also sought to maintain their operational security in a couple of ways. The first was that advance parties of German officers wore Austrian uniforms while reconnoitering their respective sectors. Where full uniforms were not available, officers just used Austrian or Hungarian caps.[69]

The second method of maintaining operational security involved the civilian population. The presence of a large civilian population, the Germans thought, represented a threat in the form of Russian espionage. To mitigate this, the Germans evacuated the civilian population (Austro–Hungarian subjects) from the area as rapidly as possible. In his sector at least, François made it policy that any civilian caught tampering with German telephone lines would be executed. Although harsh, this policy served to disrupt precisely the kind of intelligence operation the Russians were attempting to mount in this area.[70]

The German deployment was not without its problems. The biggest difficulty came from Russian snipers. In the Guard Corps sector, for example, the 1st Guard Infantry Regiment lost Lieutenant Graf von Finckenstein on April 30. Finckenstein imprudently allowed himself to be seen and was killed instantly by a shot to the head. The 1st Guard Grenadier (Kaiser Alexander) Regiment lost several officers to Russian sniping on April 29 and 30, including one battalion and one company commander, serious casualties for a unit on the eve of an important offensive.[71]

One matter that deserves discussion here is the size of Mackensen's force. As actually constituted, Mackensen had almost 130,000 officers and men under his command, 180,000 if one includes those elements of the Austro–Hungarian Fourth Army over which Mackensen could exercise operational control. The German Eleventh Army alone was supported by over 400 guns, including 146 heavy guns and mortars. If the artillery of the Austro–Hungarian Fourth Army is included, the number of guns supporting the attack rises to just over 1,000 guns of all types, ranging from mortars and light 77-mm field guns to heavy 150-mm howitzers and 210- and 305-mm heavy mortars, the most modern artillery Germany was capable of fielding.[72]

The guns of the assault force would consume a massive quantity of shells. An important part of the preparations for the offensive was the stockpiling of artillery ammunition. By the end of April this had been accomplished. Each field battery had about 1,200 shells at its disposal. Thus, for example, the 24 organic field batteries of the Guard Corps' two divisions amassed some 28,800 shells, about 266 shells per gun. The heavy howitzer and gun batteries had 600 rounds each, while the heaviest artillery batteries (210-mm and up) had about 500 rounds each. In all, well over 300,000 shells had been stockpiled for the attack.[73]

A secondary question here is whether Mackensen's force could have been even bigger than it was. This issue really revolves around the employment of the German X Reserve Corps. On April 22, 1915, Conrad sent a telegram asking Falkenhayn for an additional German corps to be used as a force for exploitation of the breakthrough. After the war, critics of Falkenhayn, such as Hermann von Kuhl, faulted Falkenhayn for not making the German Eleventh Army large enough to exploit any major success.[74]

To be sure, Falkenhayn did discuss the prospect of sending the German X Reserve Corps to the east, first with Tappen on April 30 and with Groener on May 1, 1915.[75] Falkenhayn, however, rejected the idea of sending the German X Reserve Corps to the east. The chief of the general staff regarded a major Franco-British offensive in the west as a certainty, the Allied landing at Gallipoli notwithstanding. The German X Reserve Corps had to be held back for such an eventuality.[76]

Falkenhayn's thinking in this regard was quite logical. Given the situation in France, some sort of major offensive by the western allies in the spring of 1915 had to be expected. Given that OHL was risking over half of its new strategic reserve for the coming Gorlice offensive, Falkenhayn had to retain an operational reserve for the western front. Subsequent events proved Falkenhayn correct. In fact, as early as March 1915, Joffre indicated to the French government his intention of launching a major offensive in Artois with British cooperation. The British were of like mind, although ironing out command problems on the western front still remained a vexatious issue for the Franco-British coalition.[77]

After a reconnaissance, Mackensen decided to shorten the attack front to about 25 miles, allowing his army to concentrate as much of its fighting power as possible. As the Germans deployed, Mackensen's forces were arrayed as follows from north to south. The German Eleventh Army's left flank was held by the powerful Prussian Guard Corps. The Guard's left flank maintained contact with the Austro–Hungarian Fourth Army at Tursko, while its right flank was located at Staszowka. To the right of the Guard Corps was the Austro–Hungarian VI Corps, whose line extended southeast along a chain of hills directly in front of Arz's objective, the Pustki massif. Just southwest of the Pustki massif, the Austro–Hungarian VI Corps' right flank touched the left flank of the German XXXXI Reserve Corps, whose line went through the hills directly opposite Gorlice, François's initial objective. Just southwest of Gorlice, the German XXXXI Reserve Corps' right flank met with the left flank of Corps Kneussl, whose line ran to just north of Malastow, where the sector of the Austro–Hungarian Third Army began. Since the German X Corps was still in the process of arriving, the German 19th Infantry Division would complete its assembly at Podole behind the Guard, while the 20th Infantry Division would concentrate around Grybow, behind the German XXXXI Reserve Corps. The Hungarian 11th Cavalry Division, although assembling in the Austro–Hungarian Fourth Army's sector, was also part of the German Eleventh Army's reserve.[78]

The plan that the allied field armies would execute was, in theory, relatively simple. The plan developed by Seeckt and the army's staff called for the German Eleventh and Austro–Hungarian Fourth Armies to effect a penetration of the Russian positions between Gorlice and Tarnow by attacking northeast. Corps Kneussl would be the *Schwerpunkt* (main weight) of the attack. According to the basic instructions for the attack, published on April 29, 1915, once the Russian position was broken, Mackensen's force would drive east toward Zmigrod.[79] Taking Zmigrod and blocking the roads to the south and southeast of it would outflank the Russian position in the Carpathians, especially at Dukla Pass. The Austro–Hungarian Fourth Army would advance its right flank north of Tursko toward the Biala River, covering the German Eleventh Army's left flank. Other elements of the Austro–Hungarian Fourth Army would hold the line extending north to the Vistula River. The Austro–Hungarian Third Army was asked (via AOK) to make a limited attack to cover the German Eleventh Army's right flank.[80]

The true complexity of the plan lay in the employment of the artillery. Here Seeckt and the staff played a broad supervisory role. The key part here was played by Generalmajor Alfred Ziethen, Mackensen's artillery commander.[81] Consequently, a special order for the conduct of the artillery was issued by the army's headquarters on the evening of April 29, 1915. Harassing artillery fire would be conducted at intervals during the night before the attack. During the periods when artillery fire ceased, infantry patrols and engineers would go forward, conducting last-minute reconnaissance of Russian positions and clearing paths through the Russian wire. Harassing fire would continue into the morning. The whole of the artillery would then fire for effect for about four hours. The moment the barrage was lifted, the infantry would go forward according to the standard infantry tactics of the day.[82]

In the best tradition of the elder Moltke, much was left to Mackensen's subordinate commanders. Each corps developed its own target list for the artillery. Commanders were aided in this by a combination of aerial photography and ground reconnaissance, prisoner interrogations, and excellent terrain maps supplied by the Austro–Hungarian Army. Consequently, each corps had its own "artillery commander," who exercised control over the guns in his sector.[83] Likewise, unit boundaries beyond the area of penetration were to be determined by the units involved. Army headquarters would intervene only when absolutely required.[84]

Another important part of the plan, and a most interesting one, was that the fire plan developed by the German Eleventh Army called for the creation of a mobile artillery ammunition reserve. Artillery commanders in each sector also designated individual guns or batteries to be held in reserve. These guns would be placed at the disposal of the respective corps commanders. This would enable them to give advancing infantry the kind of firepower needed to deal immediately with any Russian pockets of resistance.[85]

As the plans for the attack matured, Mackensen and Seeckt determined the date for the attack. On April 27, 1915, Seeckt, when questioned by Falkenhayn as to how soon the attack would start, indicated that he hoped the artillery preparation would start on the evening of May 1, while the attack would jump off the next day. Likewise on April 27, Mackensen expressed the hope that the attack could begin on May 2, after the conclusion of the artillery bombardment. "Longer," the old hussar wrote, "I cannot wait." The Russians had become aware of the German presence on April 25, and the Germans had confirmed this through prisoner interrogation.[86]

The target of Mackensen's force was Radko-Dmitriev's Russian 3rd Army. More specifically, the sector designated for the Gorlice attack was defended by the Russian X Corps, whose 9th and 31st Infantry Divisions, plus corps troops, totaled about 34,000 officers and men. These troops were strung out on a thin line and, in Brusilov's opinion, mistakenly posted in the most forward trenches. Both artillery and ammunition were lacking, although apparently the Russians had enough machine guns to make taking the position a potentially difficult proposition.[87]

Plans and preparations on the part of the Central Powers are worthy of comment. Credit for the first part of the deployment must go to Falkenhayn and the OHL staff, especially Groener. In the space of about a week, the Germans were able to shift large forces from the west to the east, deploy them in an area noted for relatively poor communications, and do so without a major hitch. This bespeaks the high level of staff work for which the German Army has always been renowned.

Another interesting aspect of the Eleventh Army's plan was its limited objectives. The furthest geographic point mentioned in the Eleventh Army's order was Zmigrod, less than 10 miles from the Eleventh Army's front line. The idea that Mackensen's force was aiming at the San River and retaking Przemysl seems to be a classis case of crediting the victors with foresight after the event.[88]

The deployment of the German Eleventh Army also represented one of the few high points in terms of cooperation between the Germans and their

Austro–Hungarian allies. The Austro–Hungarian railroad authorities were crucial to the successful deployment of Mackensen's force. A good part of the heavy artillery involved in the attack was provided by the Austro–Hungarian Army. The carts and light vehicles provided to the Germans by the Austro–Hungarian Army proved a pleasant surprise for the Germans. The vehicles were sturdy and performed excellently on the poor roads and rough terrain of Galicia. German commanders studied their respective sectors with the aid of accurate and detailed maps from the Austro–Hungarian Army. Finally, the at times thorny relations between the Germans and Austro–Hungarians were smoothed over by Mackensen, as felicitous a choice for the command of the attack force as could have been made.[89]

The plan put together by the German Eleventh Army's staff reflected the state of tactical thinking in the German Army in early 1915. Artillery, heavy artillery in particular, represented the key to undertaking a successful attack against field fortifications. This was a concept with which both Mackensen and Seeckt were familiar, and both had experience in employing such tactics.[90] The creation of a mobile reserve of both guns and ammunition, however, represented an interesting innovation; one that was designed to allow a force not only to break into a position but actually to break through it.

Although the discovery of the German Eleventh Army's presence by the Russians on April 25 deprived Mackensen of tactical surprise, the Germans had nonetheless achieved operational surprise. Although the reaction of General Ivanov's Southwest Front has been criticized for being lethargic, it is difficult to imagine any real alternatives for him other than to order a precipitate retreat east for Radko-Dmitriev's Russian 3rd Army. Norman Stone's suggested alternative, a new offensive by the Russian 9th Army on the Dniestr River, would probably have occurred too far away to exert any influence over events occurring at the opposite end of the Carpathians.[91]

By the end of April, all was in readiness for the attack. The weather had cooperated fully, being generally sunny and dry. Would the infantry and more importantly, artillery, allocated to the attack be sufficient to obtain a breakthrough of the Russian position at Gorlice? Mackensen, Seeckt, and their Austro–Hungarian allies were about to find out.

Chapter 4

Punching the Hole: May 2–5, 1915

Six o'clock! The 120-mm gun on Hill 696 fires the signal shot and all batteries at the ready, from the field guns to the heavy mortars, fire a salvo at the Russian positions.

—Hermann von François[1]

On May 2 we stormed the Russian position and took six kilometers of ground.
—Prussian Guards Officer, May 1915[2]

Up to now all goes forward. The tactical situation will clarify tomorrow, when the enemy commits his reserves.
—August von Mackensen, May 2, 1915[3]

On April 30, 1915, a large number of fires were spotted behind the Russian lines, presumably by aerial reconnaissance. The Russians were apparently setting the oil tanks ablaze. At OHL, Tappen fretted that this was the beginning of a Russian retreat that would frustrate the well-laid plans of the Central Powers. Slightly more ominous was the fact that no new information had come in on Russian troop movements behind the Russian 3rd Army's front.[4]

The first moves were actually made on April 29 and 30, respectively. Both the Bavarian 11th Division and the Austro–Hungarian VI Corps had to do some fighting in order to secure the jump-off positions for the infantry. The goal was to secure such positions that were no more than 200 yards from the forward Russian trenches. This was in keeping with standard German practice of the time. Although the Bavarians were able to gain a closer assault position easily,

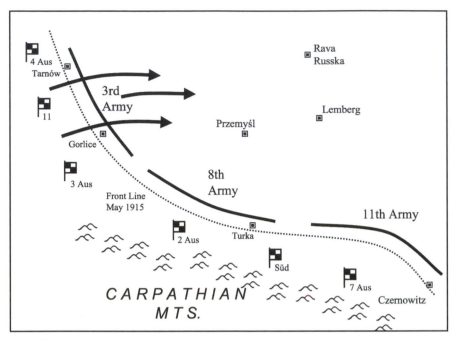

The Offensive Starts, May 1915.

the Austro–Hungarians had to engage in some hard combat on the 29th and 30th, including having to repulse a local Russian counterattack.[5]

As planned, the artillery bombardment began on May 1. Any final adjustments for artillery fire were made between 1 P.M. and dark, after the corps artillery commanders had received the final version of their target lists and then distributed them to the battery commanders. Light harassing fire from the field artillery would begin at 9 P.M., with batteries firing two or three rounds at five-minute intervals. Fire would halt for one hour at 10 P.M., resume again at 11 P.M. in the same manner, with a two-hour break from 1 to 3 A.M. During the periods of harassing fire, aside from high explosives and shrapnel, signal flares would be fired, to bring Russian soldiers out of their shelters and expose them to subsequent firing phases. The German fire plan was also designed to conserve ammunition as well as wear on artillery tubes. During the two lulls, infantry patrols went forward to conduct last-minute reconnaissance while engineers removed obstacles.[6]

The weather on May 2 was sunny and warm. With the harassing fire part of the artillery plan completed, the artillery now moved to firing for effect. François describes the memorable scene:

> Six o'clock! The 120-mm gun on Hill 696 fires the signal shot and all batteries at the ready, from field guns to the heavy mortars, fire a salvo at the Russian posi-

tions. It is followed by thunder and booming, slamming and banging, as 700 guns open fire and hurl hissing iron and steel through the air. The shells explode in the ground, throwing heaps of earth, wood splinters and obstacles yards high into the air.[7]

Like the initial phase of the artillery preparation, this part of the barrage was also graduated. At 6 A.M. all of the field batteries began firing. At 9 A.M. the heaviest howitzers joined the barrage, and the artillery fire reached its height at about 9:30. Counterfire from the Russian batteries was almost nonexistent. In the Guard's sector, the artillerymen gained the impression that the infantry would meet with little resistance.[8] At 10 A.M. the German artillery fire shifted from the Russian front line toward known or suspected enemy rear positions as the German and Austro–Hungarian infantry left their own trenches to storm the Russian defenses. To follow the progress of the German Eleventh Army's attack, we proceed from right to left.

The rightmost of Mackensen's corps was Corps Kneussl. This formation, with the 119th Infantry Division and the Bavarian 11th Division, represented Mackensen's main effort. The Bavarian 11th Division got off to a good start. With the Bavarian 3rd Infantry Regiment on the left and the Bavarian 22nd Infantry Regiment on the right, the 3rd was able, with one exception, to take the first Russian trench in a few minutes. The 22nd Regiment and one battalion of the 3rd Regiment had some problems. Many of the obstacles in front of the Russian trenches remained intact, and the rolling barrage moved too quickly for the infantry to keep up. The Russian defenses recovered quickly and began to lay down heavy small arms and machine-gun fire on the Bavarians.[9]

Aided by excellent observation posts, the Germans were able to shift their artillery back to the still untaken Russian trenches. The new bombardment was very short, designed to deal with specific parts of the Russian line and allow the infantry to renew the assault. The artillery had an effect, as the infantry was able to storm up the steep slopes of the Bavarian 11th Division's major objective, Hill 507. After heavy fighting, the hill was secured by the Bavarians by 11 A.M. The attack then moved further east, against a strongly built Russian position on Hill 469 and the Mecina Valley, south of the Zamcyzsko Plateau. Serious fighting took place once more, but by 2 P.M. a Russian counterattack had been broken by the power of German artillery. Bavarian losses were heavy. The 3rd Regiment lost more than a quarter of its strength, with 20 officers and 700 men killed and wounded.[10]

The left side of Kneussl's front was held by Behr's 119th Infantry Division. At 10 A.M. the division's two leading regiments, the 46th and 58th, went forward. The 46th Regiment, the division's right, drove the Russians out of the village of Sekowa and pressed on to keep abreast of the Bavarian 11th Division's left flank. Meanwhile, the 58th Regiment had to fight its way through the southern suburbs of Gorlice, south of the Ropa River. This involved considerable house-to-house fighting and heavy losses, although hundreds of prisoners were taken. The 119th Division then turned slightly north. The gap that now opened between the 119th and Bavarian 11th Divisions was filled by the Bavarian 11th Division's composite cavalry regiment. The advance of Behr's 58th Regiment served to protect the right flank of the adjacent XXXXI Reserve Corps. By nightfall on May 2, Kneussl's corps had driven the Russian 9th Infantry Division back to the northeast about one and a quarter miles.[11]

Adjacent to Corps Kneussl was François's XXXXI Reserve Corps. François's command post was located on Hill 747. This dominating eminence afforded François a rare luxury for a commander in World War I, a panoramic view of his entire sector. François placed the 82nd Reserve Division on the right and the 81st Reserve Division on the left. Fabarius's 82nd Reserve Division had a particularly difficult task, as the city of Gorlice lay in its sector. Given that the 82nd Reserve Division's front was shorter than that of the 81st Reserve Division, François held back three battalions (two from the 270th Regiment and one from the 272nd Regiment) as the corps reserve.[12]

While the bombardment was in progress, Fabarius was worried about the strength of the Russian position. At 9:30 A.M. he called Behr to ask for help from the 119th Infantry Division. When Behr declined, Fabarius called François to ask that the corps reserve be returned to his control. François denied the request but allowed Fabarius to confine his attack to the Jewish cemetery and Hill 357 and take Gorlice from the north.[13] With that change, the infantry went over the top at 10 A.M.

To aid command and control and prevent fratricide from short artillery rounds, François's skirmish lines carried flags that showed an unmistakable red-and-white side toward the German lines. Careful reconnaissance and artillery preparation paid off as the 82nd Reserve Division's 271st Regiment, after a short stiff fight, secured the Jewish cemetery and Hill 357. The adjacent Russian front line trench was taken by the 2nd Battalion of the 270th Regiment, while the 272nd Regiment fixed the Russian defenders in the town. By 11 A.M. all of the hills north of the town and the Jewish cemetery were in German hands.[14]

Having secured his initial objectives, Fabarius now extended his attack in the afternoon to take Gorlice itself. After a short artillery preparation, the 1st and 2nd Battalions of the 272nd Regiment would attack into the town, taking care not to move south over the Ropa River into the sector of the neighboring 119th Infantry Division. The 271st Regiment and the 2nd Battalion of the 270th Regiment would aim at extending their gains to the village of Glinik, a village centered on a chain of hills northeast of Gorlice. Some German field guns were also displaced forward to Hill 357.

Over the course of the afternoon, before darkness halted operations, the 82nd Reserve Division's attack made the desired progress. Gorlice was taken by a combination of artillery fire and some house-to-house fighting by the

272nd Regiment. The 272nd was also able to establish contact with the 119th Infantry Division. The 82nd Reserve Division's other elements were able advance just past Glinik without encountering serious resistance. The Russians did attempt to mount a brigade-size counterattack from Biecz. Discovered by aerial reconnaissance, the Russian attack was broken up by Fabarius' artillery, now on Hill 357.[15]

François's 81st Reserve Division went forward as well. Stocken made his major efforts on both of his sector's flanks, with the 267th Regiment on the right and the 269th Regiment on the left. The 3rd Battalion of the 268th Regiment would maintain contact with both regiments in the center. The remainder of the 268th was held out as the Division reserve. Stocken's major objective was the Kamieniec Forest.

The 269th Regiment in particular had a hard time. The first two waves of the attack encountered machine-gun fire, particularly from a corner of the forest to the left of the regiment. The two waves of men eventually were able to reach the cover of a railroad embankment in front of the first Russian trench. The intensity of Russian fire, however, made any further progress impossible unless the two Russian machine guns in the corner of the forest could be knocked out.

Observing the situation, the commander of the 269th, Lieutenant Colonel Vorberg, directed his adjutant, Lieutenant Pagels, to telephone Division headquarters and request renewed artillery support. For 15 minutes, the division's artillery bombarded the forest corner. When the attack resumed, however, the Germans found Russian resistance as tough as ever. The commander of the 2nd Company, Captain Reichhelm, was killed. By noon, the 81st Reserve Division's attack had still not moved forward from the railroad embankment.[16]

Fortunately for Stocken, events on both flanks aided his attacks. The 82nd Reserve Division's success removed any major threat to Stocken's right flank. Meanwhile the advance of the Austro–Hungarian VI Corps had compromised the Russian position in the Kamieniec Forest. While this was occurring, another round of artillery preparation was conducted, and Vorberg decided to commit his last battalion to the next infantry assault. Major Lindemann, the artillery zone commander, also ordered the 1st Battery of the 67th Field Artillery to go forward to deliver artillery fire against the Russian positions at point-blank range. This time the assault succeeded. The Russian trench near the railroad embankment was seized, and the 269th continued to push into the forest. By the time the 81st Reserve Division's attack halted, the Germans had taken the forest, pursuing the Russians to the villages of Zagorzany and Moszezenica, which they took in the evening.[17]

By nightfall on May 2, the XXXXI Reserve Corps had driven the Russians back anywhere from just under two miles to about two and a half miles along the line. The 81st Reserve Division took an estimated 4,000 prisoners. The 269th Regiment captured a large Russian encampment in the Kamieniec Forest, taking large amounts of equipment, including six machine guns. Success, however, had been expensive. The 81st Reserve Division alone suffered 8 officers and 159 men killed, plus another 17 officers and 554 men wounded.[18]

The Austro–Hungarian VI Corps actually began its part of the offensive on the day before the full attack began. During May 1, both of Arz's divisions, the Austrian 12th Infantry Division on the right and the Hungarian 39th Honved Division on the left, had to eject Russian defenders from the villages and foothills before the Pustki massif. This was done initially in a relatively short firefight, although Austro–Hungarian artillery was needed to breakup a Russian counterattack. Fortunately for the Austro–Hungarians, casualties were light, with 40 killed and 192 wounded.[19]

Having secured their assault positions, the attack proceeded in the same manner as in the other corps sectors of the German Eleventh Army. The artillery bombardment reached its height between 9 and 10 A.M. The focus of Austro–Hungarian artillery activity, including Austrian 305-mm howitzers, was the Pustki massif. The Austrian 12th Infantry Division was able to overrun the Russian trench at the foot of the mountain and then gradually move up the south slope. By 11:30 A.M. elements of the Austrian 56th Infantry Regiment reached the summit.

After repulsing a Russian counterattack, the Austrians continued their attack in two directions. Elements of the Austrian 20th and 100th Infantry Regiments moved against the flank of the Russian defenses in the Kamieniec Forest, aiding the efforts of the German 81st Reserve Division. The rest of the Kestranek's infantry moved down the east slope of the Pustki toward the next geographic objective, Hill 320. By 6:45 P.M. the Austrians had taken Hill 320 and reached the Moszczenica–Gorlice road.[20]

The Hungarian 39th Honved Division had a much harder time. The mission for the division was to first seize a line of hills, from which they would then attack the Wiatrowki Hill, the dominant military feature in the sector and the major objective for the attack. Hadfy's initial attack suffered, however, for a couple of reasons. First, Arz had made the Austrian 12th Infantry Division the focus of his effort, so it got the lion's share of the heavy artillery. Hadfy compounded this problem by dispersing the artillery available to him. Thus very little damage was done to the Russian defenses. Consequently the initial attack made little headway, reaching a point about seventy paces from the main Russian position.[21]

The Hungarians, however, were able to eventually reach their objective. The artillery was recommitted in a more concentrated fashion against parts of the Russian position, most notably Wiatrowki Hill. The Hungarians were further aided by the Prussian Guard successfully storming Staszkowka. In the course of the afternoon of 2 May, the Hungarian 39th Honved Division was able carry the Russian position, ultimately reaching a chain of hills north of Moszczenica. Arz's troops had driven the Russians back a bit over four miles, taking an estimated 1,700 prisoners and 4 machine guns. Losses, however, had been considerable.[22]

Mackensen's largest German unit, the Prussian Guard Corps, had perhaps the hardest fight among all of the German Eleventh Army's subordinate units. Plettenberg placed the 2nd Guard Division on the right and the 1st Guard Division on the left. The immediate objective was a series of positions centered around Hill 437 (southwest of Staszkowka), Hill 382 (east of Siezkowice), and Hill 358 (northeast of Siezkowice). The more distant objectives were Turza and Rzepiennik, the former about two and a half miles from the German line, while the latter was a little over a mile from the Guard's start line.[23]

The artillery preparation in the 2nd Guard Division's sector was focused on Hills 437 and 405, with the greater emphasis being placed on the latter hill. The two hills and the village of Staszkowka were in the sector assigned to the 3rd Guard Brigade, commanded by Generalmajor von Petersdorff. The 3rd Guard Infantry Regiment (Queen Elizabeth) would tackle Hill 405 and the northern half of Staszkowka, while Hill 437 and the southern half of Staszkowka would be taken by the 1st Guard Grenadier Regiment (Kaiser Alexander).[24]

The Queen Elizabeth Regiment was able to take Hill 405 without much trouble. Hill 437 and Staszkowka proved to be another matter. Both the hill and the village were well fortified. The Kaiser Alexander Regiment's Fusilier Battalion was able to take the most forward Russian trench after a short but stiff fight, the attempt to move from there came under intense Russian machine-gun fire. The troops here remained pinned down for about two hours.[25]

The rapid taking of Hill 405, however, allowed the Germans to shift their artillery fire to Hill 437 and Staszkowka. The fusiliers were also aided by several batteries of the 2nd Guard Field Artillery Regiment, which moved up right behind the taken Russian trench to provide direct support. With this assistance, the renewal of the attack in the afternoon made much better progress. Hill 437 was taken, while elements of both the Elizabeth and Alexander Regiments fought their way through the destroyed village of Staszkowka, repulsing a Russian counterattack as well. Once these positions were taken, the Brigade advanced east, finally stopping east of Turza.[26]

Meanwhile the 4th Guard Brigade, composed of the 2nd Guard Grenadier Regiment (Kaiser Franz) and the 4th Grenadier Guard Regiment (Queen Augusta), had a tough fight for Hill 382. Although the artillery preparation allowed the Queen Augusta Regiment to grab the Russian trench at the base of Hill 382, getting up the steep slopes to the top proved time consuming and costly. Finally, with aid from the Franz Regiment, the Augusta grenadiers were able to seize Hill 382. The Brigade then resumed its advance, finally reaching a line of hills north of Turza. While the infantry were advancing east during the afternoon and evening, the 2nd Guard Division displaced its artillery forward to Hills 382 and 405.[27]

The leftmost of Mackensen's divisions, the 1st Guard Infantry Division, had a somewhat easier time of it. When the 1st Guard Infantry Regiment went over the top at 10 A.M., the only resistance encountered was from two Russian machine guns. Thus the 1st Guard Infantry Brigade was able to secure Hill 358 a mere 15 minutes after the start of the attack.[28] The 1st Guard Division followed this with a rapid advance against Hill 376. The 1st Guard Division advanced so rapidly that it lost contact with the Austro–Hungarian IX Corps on its left.[29]

By the time the Guard Corps halted for the night, they had driven the Russians back between three and three-and-a-half miles. Plettenberg's success, however, came at a price. Although the 1st Guard Division's losses were relatively light, the 2nd Guard Division had been badly shot up. The Kaiser Alexander Regiment, for example, lost 280 officers and men killed. The Queen Elizabeth Regiment lost 206 killed, 396 wounded, and 10 missing. Among the officers killed was Lieutenant Wilhelm von François, the nephew of the XXXXI Reserve Corps commander.[30]

On both of the German Eleventh Army's flanks, elements of the Austro–Hungarian Third and Fourth Armies were involved in the attack. The Austro–Hungarian IX and XIV Corps were part of Archduke Joseph Ferdinand's Austro–Hungarian Fourth Army. Feldmarschalleutnant Rudolf Kralicek's IX Corps was able to win a number of local successes, thus covering the Prussian Guard Corps' left flank. To Kralicek's left, Feldmarschalleutnant Paul Roth's XIV Corps was able to take its objectives, most notably Hill 481 and Sugar Loaf Hill, although only at a frightful cost. At the opposite end of the attack front, the Austro–Hungarian X Corps, part of Feldmarschalleutnant Svetozar Boroević von Bojna's Austro–Hungarian Third Army, was able to drive the Russian 9th Infantry Division from the hills east of Malastow. The Austrians did this under Boroević's watchful eye. At about noon Boroević was joined at his observation post by several dignitaries, including Archduke Friedrich and Conrad. The hundreds of Russian prisoners taken were escorted to the rear by a single cavalryman. The prisoners taken would then be turned over to an Austro–Hungarian Landsturm, a company composed of over aged reservists that was detailed to the corps for this duty. This arrangement extended to every corps in the German Eleventh Army.[31]

The X Corps also moved up during the course of the day. The 20th Infantry Division marched to Ropa, while the 19th Infantry Division reached Olszowa.[32] Emmich's lead elements in the 20th Infantry Division were now in the rear of Kneussl's sector, a proper place for them, given that Mackensen's main effort was being made on the right.

Mackensen and Seeckt spent the day at their headquarters in Neu Sandec, sifting through the reports as they came in. There was some excitement as a Russian aircraft flew over the headquarters, but German antiaircraft fire was able to drive the intruder away before he could drop any bombs.[33]

As the troops halted late on the night of May 2, the Germans began to move their support elements and supply trains forward. Units received a resupply of ammunition. The artillery moved forward, and German field kitchens came up to provide hot food for the men. This was particularly welcome, not only because the men were hungry. While the weather during the day was warm, spring nights in the northern end of the Carpathians could be cold.[34] Resupplied and fed, the Germans would be able to resume the advance on the May 3.

Reaction to the events of May 2 on the German side can generally be described as cautious optimism. At OHL, the immediate hope was that the success achieved might still deter Italy from entering the war. Falkenhayn decided to reinforce Mackensen with another infantry division, the 56th, from the western front. While Mackensen and Seeckt were pleased with the outcome of the day's events, they regarded the situation as still not clear enough to make definitive judgments.[35] The Russians' reserves had yet to be heard from, and the Germans had lost track of two divisions that had last been seen moving toward the German Eleventh Army's sector. In Mackensen's opinion, the situation would become clearer once it was certain where Radko-Dmitriev had committed his reserves. Mackensen expected Russian reserves to appear in the Biecz–Jaslo area.[36]

Given what he knew about the events of May 2, Mackensen decided on the night of that day to continue the attack along the line on May 3. Orders went out at 7 P.M. on the night of May 2, and it took some time for the orders to reach the corps. In the case of the XXXXI Reserve Corps, the Army Order for May 3 arrived at 1 A.M., after François had already issued orders for his corps an hour earlier. As before, the main effort would be made on the right. For this purpose Corps Kneussl would be subordinated to Emmich's X Corps headquarters. Aside from the Bavarian 11th Division and the 119th Infantry Division, Emmich would also have the 20th Infantry Division as well.[37] The Guard Corps would be reinforced by the 19th Infantry Division's artillery, and the remainder of the 19th Infantry Division was designated as the army reserve. Orders were given to the Austro–Hungarian Fourth Army to continue its attack as well. The goal was for the troops to advance a little over six miles (ten kilometers). This would put the German Eleventh Army in a position to advance to and cross the Wisloka River on May 4.[38]

Now responsible for Mackensen's right flank, Emmich decided to make the 119th Infantry Division his main effort. Kneussl's Bavarians, on the Eleventh Army's extreme right flank, were initially going to assault the chain of hills north and south of Mecina Wk. Reconnaissance by the Division's cavalry, however, revealed that the Russians had retreated further east to Wapienne and Rozdziele and the nearby hills. This was the southern part of the Russian 3rd Army's second position. Unlike the first position, the Russians had more artillery available to them in the second position. Thus, when the Bavarian 3rd Infantry Regiment reached the northeast edge of the Zamczysko Forest, they came under artillery fire from the villages of Kryg and Rozdziele.[39]

Under the new circumstances, preparation for the attack took time, so that Kneussl's infantry could not start until late in the morning. Impeded by wooded and hilly terrain, Russian defenses and a cloud of thick smoke from burning oil tanks, the Bavarians made slow progress. By the afternoon of May 3, the

Bavarians had reached a chain of hills, the most notable of which was Hill 488 west of Rozdziele. Over the course of the afternoon, the hills west of Rozdziele were taken, but the advance on Wapienne made little progress. Contact between the Bavarian 13th and 22nd Infantry Regiments was lost, and had not been reestablished by 7 P.M. To assault the Wapienne position successfully, sufficient artillery support required, and only a portion of the light artillery had been able to move up over the poor roads. Thus the exhausted Bavarians dug in to await the expected Russian counterattack.[40]

While the Bavarians were dealing with Russian defenses and difficult terrain, the 119th Infantry Division had a relatively easy time. By 1 P.M. Kryg and Kobylanka had been taken, as well as the southern part of Libusza. The end of the day saw the 119th Infantry Division holding a lengthy salient that extended eastward to a point just north of Bednarka, threatening the rear of the Russian positions facing Kneussl's Bavarians. The 20th Infantry Division moved from Gorlice to Sokol, while 79th Infantry Regiment was sent forward to Kryg as Corps reserve.[41]

On May 4 the main effort in Emmich's sector shifted back to the Bavarians. Kneussl's first objective was a chain of hills east of Rozdziele. Once the initial objective was seized, Kneussl's men would advance up to the Wisloka River. Crossing the Wisloka would be left to Emmich's freshest division, Oetinger's still uncommitted 20th Infantry Division. If all went well, Oetinger's division would be able to cross the Wisloka at Zmigrod. The 119th Infantry Division would cover the corps' left flank.[42]

For Corps Emmich, May 4 was a busy day. In Emmich's rear area, troops worked feverishly to keep the roads clear. Traffic jams on the roads during the previous night had earned Emmich a blistering postscript in army special orders.[43]

During the night of May 3–4, the Russians had evacuated the hills in front of the Bavarians, and morning aerial reconnaissance noted that Russian columns were moving from Krempna toward Zmigrod, apparently reinforcing their defenses with forces from the Carpathian front. Kneussl's men thus moved into the hills, and the Bavarian 3rd Regiment reached the Gorlice–Dukla road after taking Rozdziele. Bednarka was also taken, but two miles to the east the Bavarians encountered a new position between Wola Cieklinska and Cieklin. The Bavarians could not storm the position on the run, and thus had to wait until the artillery came up in the afternoon. Good cooperation between the infantry and artillery allowed Kneussl's men to evict the Russians from the position, and advance another mile or two east. At 8 P.M. Kneussl established his headquarters in Bednarka.[44]

The 119th Infantry Division covered Kneussl's left during the day. Late in the afternoon, however, a strong Russian counterattack broke through the Behr's line. The position was restored, however, and the Russian forces retreated to the northeast. The Russians facing Kneussl's Bavarians retreated towards the Wisloka River.[45]

On May 5 Mackensen's first operational objective was achieved. Emmich inserted the 20th Infantry Division into line, and it was able to enter Zmigrod and cross the Wisloka River at an intact bridge that the retreating Russians, in their haste, had failed to demolish. Oetinger's men then headed for the next river, the Jasiolka. By the time the division stopped for the night on May 5, they had reached Wietrzno, opposite the Jasiolka.[46]

The 119th Infantry Division and the Bavarian 11th Infantry Division covered the flanks of the 20th Infantry Division. Kneussl's Bavarians moved on Krempna. Although the town itself was not taken, the Bavarians were able to cover the roads that led from the Carpathians to the north, thus preventing the Russians from directly threatening the 20th Infantry Division's right flank. The 119th Infantry Division secured the 20th Infantry Division's left flank while also seeking to establish contact with the right hand division of Francois' XXXXI Reserve Corps. Stung by the Eleventh Army's dressing down, Emmich issued detailed orders for the rear areas of all three divisions, making certain that the roads were kept reserved for high-priority material. Both divisions encountered Russian counterattacks, especially in the 119th Infantry Division's sector. Once stopped, the Russians quickly retreated to the east and northeast.[47]

By the time the Eleventh Army's order for May 3 arrived, François had already issued his orders for the XXXXI Reserve Corps. The tardy army order did not severely affect François' corps other than to necessitate a slight shift of its right boundary to the south. François's main objective was Wilczak Mountain, the dominating eminence in his sector north of the Ropa River and the key to the second Russian defensive position. Aerial reconnaissance had indicated a considerable degree of confusion on the Russian side. Francois thus decided to make the 82nd Reserve Division his main effort, committing the whole division, while only two of the 81st Reserve Division's regiments, the 267th and 268th, would be involved in the attack, while the 269th would be kept as the corps reserve.[48]

François's attack made slow progress initially. The Russians had excellent observation from Wilczak Mountain, plus enough artillery to make the Germans uncomfortable. In addition, rain in the morning made it difficult for François to get the heavy guns forward to new firing positions. Thus the battle had to be borne by the German field batteries in the morning. While Russian heavy artillery hit the area where the 269th was placed in reserve, the attacking forces needed all morning to reach the foot of the mountain.

At last, German heavy artillery was able to reach its new firing positions in the afternoon. Once again, the heavy artillery proved to be the German trump card. The 100-mm guns supporting Stocken's 81st Reserve Division shelled Biecz and the roads leading from there to Wilczak Mountain while the heavy field howitzers and mortars tore up the Russian positions. Fabarius's 82nd Reserve Division was able to make it up the slopes and after some close combat, stormed the summit of Wilczak Mountain, taking it by 7 P.M. German artillery also shot to pieces an attempted Russian counterattack from the Ropa Valley against Fabarius's right flank.[49]

With Wilczak Mountain secured, François, in keeping with the Eleventh Army's concept, wanted his corps to overrun the third Russian defensive line, a position located in a chain of hills and the villages of Harklowa and Glebowka, over a mile west of the Wisloka River. Possession of these hills would effectively eliminate the possibility of the Russians maintaining a defensive line west of the river as well as cover the left flank of Emmich's X Corps.[50]

The advance of the XXXXI Reserve Corps on May 4 began at 6 A.M. in warm, sunny weather. Early reconnaissance by a company of the 272nd Regiment revealed no organized Russian resistance north of Libusza (along the corps' southern boundary), and brought in 500 prisoners. The 82nd Reserve Division was able to cross the Ropa River, which ran to the northeast across François's sector. Fabarius's objective was the oil well south of Hill 350. After taking Wojtowa, resistance was encountered at Hill 348, south of the oil well. Meeting fire initially at 4:30 P.M., the division quickly deployed its accompanying field artillery. After a short bombardment, an attack by the Division took Hill 438 by 7 P.M. The 82nd pressed on, its lead elements reaching Pagorek by 9 P.M. The 81st Reserve Division made much slower progress. The 269th Regiment in particular had a hard fight for Harklowa, an action that started on the afternoon of May 4 and lasted into the morning of May 5 before the village was secured at the cost of 38 killed, 117 wounded, and 17 missing.[51]

The corps' advance continued on May 5. Once the 269th Regiment completed its seizure of Harklowa, it pressed on to Osobnica as the right flank of the 81st Reserve Division. As it neared Osobnica, the 1st Battalion of the 269th, advancing unsupported, encountered a stout Russian defense. Taken under fire, the battalion retreated under the pressure of a Russian counterattack. With the 269th stymied, the task of taking Osobnica, situated in the middle of the corps' sector, fell to the 82nd Reserve Division's leftmost regiments, the 270th and 272nd. The only support on which the two regiments could count was the division's field artillery, as the heavy artillery was on the Jaslo Road, the only road that could sustain that kind of traffic. Ultimately, after a couple of assaults culminating in bayonet fighting, Osobnica was taken during the evening of May 5. The 270th Regiment suffered considerably, losing 8 killed, 298 wounded and 65 missing.[52]

The fighting at Osobnica marked the effective limit of the XXXXI Reserve Corps' advance on May 5, although patrols followed the retreating Russians up to the Wisloka River. While the Corps did not reach the river, the XXXXI Reserve Corps' advance was sufficient to cover the left flank of the X Corps, allaying Emmich's concerns from that quarter.

The Austro–Hungarian VI Corps continued its slow slog through the Russian defenses after the first day. On May 3 the Austro–Hungarians were able to advance against another Russian position located in a chain of hills east of Rozembark, taking several thousand prisoners. Meanwhile Arz learned from a combination of aerial reconnaissance and spies of a third Russian defensive in the area around Biecz.[53] Thus, on May 4, the Austro–Hungarians fought their way through the next Russian position. Taking Biecz allowed Arz to get part of the Austrian 12th Infantry Division to get across the Ropa River, and the subsequent advance east was astride the river, reaching a somewhat jagged line between Kunowa as the right boundary and just outside of Swieczany on the left. The attack continued astride the Ropa River with Jaslo, located at the confluence of the Ropa and Wisloka Rivers, as the objective. The Hungarian 39th Honved Division experienced tough fighting on the left and made slow progress. The Austrian 12th Infantry Division was able to successfully storm Hill 349 northeast of Harklowa. Although Jaslo was not reached, Kestranek's Austrians had been able to establish solid contact with the XXXXI Reserve Corps on the right at Harklowa.[54]

Like the XXXXI Reserve Corps and the Austro–Hungarian VI Corps, Plettenberg's Guardsmen spent the period of May 3–5 gnawing their way through successive Russian positions. The 2nd Guard Infantry Division's situation on May 3 was similar to that of the XXXXI Reserve Corps in that the division was faced with taking a fortified mountain position much like Wilczak Mountain. The Kaiser Alexander and Queen Elisabeth Regiments started at 6 A.M. and by 11 A.M. had reached Rzepiennik and Suchy, an assault position under cover from which an attack could be launched on Hill 425, the key position for the possession of Lipie Mountain. After a reconnaissance, a short artillery preparation commenced, and the infantry attacked at 5:30 P.M., with the Alexander Regiment as the main effort. The fight for Lipie Mountain was brief, successful, and costly. The 1st Battalion of the Alexander Regiment alone lost 25 killed and 111 wounded. By 9 P.M. the mountain was effectively in German hands.[55]

The 1st Guard Infantry Division had a slightly easier time at least initially, but by midafternoon Prince Friedrich's infantry encountered stiff Russian resistance in the hills east of the Olszyny stream and the village of Olszyny. It was not until 9 P.M. that the 1st Guard Brigade was able to gain the upper hand. The 1st Guard Brigade reached the hills east of Olszyny while the 2nd Guard Brigade covered the corps' left flank.[56]

On May 4 the Guard advanced astride the Olszyny–Olpiny road towards the Wisloka River. Although flanking fire from the nearby Hill 385, the Queen Elisabeth Regiment took Hill 385 and the Augusta Regiment took Olpiny around 4:30 P.M. The 2nd Guard Division and most of the 1st Guard Division pressed forward towards Szerzyny. The 1st Guard Infantry Regiment was employed covering the division's left. Mackensen also reinforced the Guard with the 19th Infantry Division, marching in trace behind Plettenberg's left flank. That effectively broke Russian resistance in the Guard 's sector west of the Wisloka River. Thus on May 5 the Guard was able to close up to the river.[57]

After their exertions on May 2, the Austro–Hungarian Fourth Army remained quiet for the next few days, only extending its right flank to cover the left of the German Eleventh Army. The Austro–Hungarian IX and XIV Corps advanced slowly on May 4 against the reinforced Russian 42nd Infantry Division and the Russian 70th Infantry Division, often having to fend off counterattacks.[58] The slow progress by Austro–Hungarian Fourth Army thus necessitated the measures taken by Plettenberg to cover his lengthening left flank against possible Russian counterattacks. At the opposite end of Mackensen's front, the Austro–Hungarian Third Army was able to move up to Krempna, covering the Eleventh Army's right flank.[59]

The Russian response to Mackensen's attack was ineffective for several reasons, but surprise was not one of them. The Russians had become aware of the German presence by April 25.[60] Thus a heavy German attack could be expected. Once the offensive began, the Russian response was poorly coordinated combination of retreat and attack. The Russian 63rd Infantry Division, for example, the local reserve for the Russian X Corps sector, was effectively consumed in the fighting for Gorlice. Radko-Dmitriev planned to counterattack on a broader front, using the III Caucasian Corps recently assigned to the Southwest Front by Stavka. The Northwest front was also ordered by Stavka to send the II Siberian Corps (13th Siberian and 62nd Infantry Divisions) to the 3rd Army. Once the III Caucasian Corps marched to Zmigrod via Jaslo, Radko-Dmitriev wanted to blunt the German Eleventh Army's main effort south of the Ropa River, using the III Caucasian Corps and those elements of the X Corps who were still combat effective.[61]

Radko-Dmitriev's plan proved stillborn. Both the III Caucasian Corps and the II Siberian Corps ended up being caught up in fighting with elements of the Prussian Guard, the opposite end of where Radko-Dmitriev needed them the most. Local command, particularly at left end of Radko-Dmitriev's line, broke down completely. François noted that on May 3, aerial reconnaissance reported all manner of Russian columns moving past each other in opposite directions, both east and west. He considered that a sign of confusion on the part of the Russians as well as an inability to reestablish a defensive position, an assessment that proved correct.[62]

The attack launched by Mackensen on May 2 is worthy of several comments. First, the Germans were still using the conventional infantry tactics of 1914. Although the German War Ministry had officially decreed in January 1915 that the use of thick skirmish lines for daytime advances was eliminated, the Eleventh Army used precisely these kinds of formations. They did, however, in accordance with the War Ministry's views, conduct operations into the night hours.[63]

Given the employment of conventional infantry tactics, the scale and manner in which artillery was employed was critical to the success of the offensive.

The plan for the artillery preparation drawn up by Ziethen and Seeckt was careful and meticulous. Uncontested German control of the air allowed for fairly complete reconnaissance of the area. That plus excellent maps provided by the Austro–Hungarians proved a major benefit as well.[64]

The artillery plan was designed to create fire superiority at specific points in the attacking sector while husbanding ammunition at the same time. The use of heavy guns proved a trump card that the Russians could not match. The heavy howitzers provided the kind of high angled fire that was essential to knocking out known Russian artillery positions. Also, the Russian trenches were not well enough constructed to withstand heavy artillery fire. The decision to send forward individual guns or sections of batteries with the attacking infantry also paid dividends on several occasions. The Germans were also aided in this by the weakness of the Russian artillery response. Where German artillery support was lacking, Russian machine guns alone gave the attacking German or Austro–Hungarian forces trouble. German artillery was also crucial in stopping repeated Russian counterattacks.[65]

Another interesting aspect of Mackensen's attack was the use of the telephone and telegraph. Although still in many ways an emerging technology, telephone was a crucial component of German command and control over the operation. Since the advances made by the Eleventh Army from May 2 to 5 averaged about two to three miles per day, the Germans were able to move their telephone and telegraph lines forward as well. The corps orders that are still extant stress the importance of the component divisions establishing telephone or telegraph contact with the corps headquarters as soon as possible. The importance of telephone and telegraph technology to the Germans was also manifested by the draconian punishments threatened against anyone damaging the lines.[66]

By May 5, 1915, it had become clear that the Eleventh Army had smashed the Russian X Corps. Relentless pummeling by the Eleventh Army had reduced the Russian X Corps to a mere 4,000 to 5,000 infantry from its original strength of 34,000. Likewise, elements of the Russian IX Corps and the III Caucasian Corps had been badly mauled. According to German sources, almost half of the X Corps' men had surrendered.[67] Such success, however, did not come without cost. Parts of the Eleventh Army had taken considerable losses. The XXXXI Reserve Corps, for example, suffered over 2,000 casualties on May 2 alone, a loss of about 10% of its strength. Over the period of May 1–7, 1915, the Austro–Hungarian VI Corps incurred about 10,300 casualties—close to one third of its strength—on April 29. The Guard likewise lost a little over 10% of its strength, with most of the casualties being concentrated in the 2nd Guard Division. A reasonable estimate as to the total losses of the German Eleventh Army over the period of May 2–5 might be about 20,000 killed and wounded.[68]

From the start of the attack, Mackensen had kept OHL informed of its progress. While Mackensen and Seeckt remained cautiously optimistic, the mood at

OHL quickly turned euphoric. The Kaiser, for example, gave Tappan a bottle of champagne on May 3 and then issued a congratulatory message to the Eleventh Army, which was transmitted by Mackensen to his soldiers the next day. At AOK in Teschen, Cramon also noted the great sense of relief among the Austrians. It was not until noon on May 5, however, that Mackensen regarded the situation as secure enough to send a message to OHL confirming the achievement of the breakthrough. The old hussar praised the behavior of his German troops but also noted that "the Austrians responded gallantly."[69]

The well-planned and executed attack by the German Eleventh Army had torn a gaping hole in the Russian 3rd Army's front. The subsidiary attacks by the Austro–Hungarian Third and Fourth Armies served to widen the shoulders of the breakthrough. The issue now turned on the question of how far and how fast the Germans could exploit the opening they had created and how quickly the Russians could formulate a defense. This would apply particularly to the matter of the fortress of Przemysl.

Erich von Falkenhayn, director
of Germany's strategy in 1915.
(Courtesy of National Archives)

Conrad von Hötzendorf, chief of the
Austro–Hungarian general staff. His
plans often exceeded the capabilities
of his army. Here he is possibly
contemplating his two favorite
subjects, war and Gina. (Courtesy of
National Archives)

Archduke Friedrich. Although his title was commander of the Austro–Hungarian Army, he exercised very little influence over strategy. (Courtesy of National Archives)

Svetozar Boroević von Bojna. As commander of the Austro–Hungarian Third Army, he was responsible for the security of Mackensen's right flank. After the capture of Przemysl, Boroević went to the Italian front, where he commanded the Austro–Hungarian forces with distinction. (Courtesy of National Archives)

Eduard Baron von Böhm-Ermolli. He was the commander of the Austro–Hungarian Second Army, which took Lemberg on June 22, 1915. (Courtesy of National Archives)

Otto von Emmich. The leadership of veteran corps commanders like Emmich was a critical element of Mackensen's success. (Courtesy of National Archives)

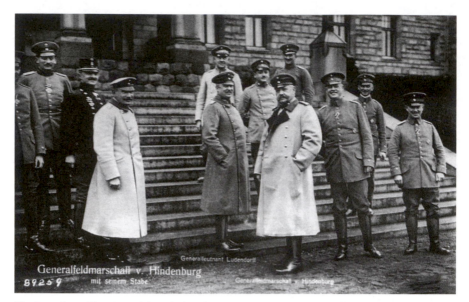

The boys from Ober Ost. Although this photo was taken during the Tannenberg campaign, most of the German Eighth Army staff moved up with Hindenburg, including Ludendorff (in the center of the picture) and Max Hoffmann (right, by Hindenburg's left arm). (Courtesy of National Archives)

Grand Duke Nicholas and Nicholas II. In August 1915. The tsar later replaced his uncle as the head of Stavka. (Courtesy of National Archives)

R.D. Radko-Dmitriev. A native Bulgarian, he commanded the Russian 3rd Army that was so severely mauled at Gorlice-Tarnow. (Courtesy of National Archives)

Elements of the German Eleventh Army in their deployment march in April 1915. Railroads, with raised roadbeds, were often the best routes on which to march, especially during wet weather. (Courtesy of National Archives)

A German field telephone detachment. Field telephone proved a vital asset to German commanders on the eastern front. (Courtesy of National Archives)

A short German pontoon bridge over the San River. (Courtesy of National Archives)

August von Mackensen on campaign. Arguably Germany's best field commander, he was a thoroughly modern soldier, his predilection for rather anachronistic looking cavalry uniforms notwithstanding. Here he is wearing a more conventional uniform. (Courtesy of National Archives)

A German infantry regiment takes a break in a Polish town during the campaign. (Courtesy of National Archives)

The final stage of the great offensive. Foot-sore infantry press on into the edge of the Pripet Marshes east of Brest Litovsk. (Courtesy of National Archives)

Chapter 5
The Capture of Przemysl: May 6–June 6, 1915

Any restraint in the continuation of the attack would undo all the success enjoyed so far.
> —Franz Conrad von Hötzendorf, May 9, 1915[1]

Our line is very extended, we cannot shuttle troops around it with the required speed, and the very weakness of our armies makes them less mobile; we are losing all capacity to fight.
> —Russian Staff Officer, May 10, 1915[2]

For the impending attack on Przemysl, it is expected that the attack will be under the command of the Austro–Hungarian Third Army.
> —Franz Conrad von Hötzendorf, May 23, 1915[3]

Przemysl is ours!
> —August von Mackensen, June 4, 1915[4]

World War I armies that had successfully affected a breach of an enemy defensive system were often in position of a dog that chases a passing car. The dog may catch up with the car, but then what? Mackensen's force, having chewed its way through successive Russian defense positions from May 2–5, 1915, was now in precisely that kind of situation. The focus of the orders issued before the attack was tactical. The German Eleventh Army's order, published on April 29, 1915, called for breaking through the Russian position between Gorlice and Rzepiennik and then advancing in the direction of Zmigrod and Kolaczyce. Beyond that, the rest of the order concerned itself with tactical details. The same went double for the German Eleventh Army's "Basic Instructions for the Attack."[5]

By May 9, 1915, one week after start of the attack, all of the objectives specified in the German Eleventh Army's order of April 27 were met. Zmigrod had been taken, and the Wisloka River had been crossed on a broad front. Mackensen had waited until May 6 before officially confirming to OHL the extent of the victory. Sensing success, the same day AOK in Teschen ordered the Austro–Hungarian Second Army of General der Kavallerie Eduard Baron von Böhm-Ermolli to join the advance. The basic instructions for the German Eleventh Army, however, remained essentially the same.[6] The next two days were taken up with the minutiae concomitant with a visit by the Kaiser to both the German Eleventh and Austro–Hungarian Fourth Armies. On May 9, however, Mackensen apparently got the ball rolling, by writing to OHL. After stating that the troops of the German Eleventh Army had accomplished their mission in defeating the Russian 3rd Army, Mackensen asked for some guidance in terms of the next set of objectives. Falkenhayn then communicated this to Conrad.[7]

Conrad, ever excitable when things were going well, responded immediately. His proposal had several elements. The first was that the attack needed to be pressed to throw the retreating Russians further back behind the San River. The second was a more familiar refrain: that additional German reinforcements be sent, in this case to the Austro–Hungarian Fourth Army, to join the division that Conrad was transferring to it from the Austro–Hungarian Third Army. This would allow the Fourth Army to assume the offensive along the full extent of its line. Finally, Conrad wanted to reinforce Pflanzer-Baltin's Austro–Hungarian Seventh Army, then facing an attack by superior Russian forces.[8]

Falkenhayn responded the following morning. He immediately scotched any idea of moving additional German troops from the western front to Galicia. Falkenhayn noted that the long-awaited Anglo-French offensive had begun the day before southwest of Lille. This attack had effectively tied down all available German reserves on the western front.[9] Falkenhayn did ask Ober Ost to release two divisions for transfer to Mackensen. While Falkenhayn agreed that the offensive in western Galicia should be pressed, the Austro–Hungarians, he thought, had more troops available to reinforce the attacking armies than the Germans did. Finally, Falkenhayn noted that since the decisive result could be sought in Galicia, the two divisions Conrad wanted to send to Bukovina and the Austro–Hungarian Seventh Army could be better employed with Mackensen's forces.[10]

Conrad's immediate response was to raise the issue of the attitude of the neutral states, especially Romania. Although noting that events in western Galicia had made a major impression on Romania, something that was confirmed for Falkenhayn two days later by the German military attaché in Bucharest, a major defeat in Bukovina could undo that, enticing Romania to enter the war against Austria–Hungary.[11] Although Conrad and Falkenhayn agreed on the need for exploitation of the breakthrough in Galicia, no specific objective had been set for Mackensen's force. Thus the outcome of the exchanges between Conrad and Falkenhayn was inconclusive, resulting in the need for another personal meeting.

In the midst of these weighty strategic discussions, more mundane issues had to be resolved. One of these was the name that should be given to the battle. Although the Kaiser had ordered church bells rung across Germany in celebration of the successful attack, the battle did not have a proper name. Falkenhayn told Cramon to consult the Austro–Hungarians on this, while Falkenhayn himself thought that the title "May Battle in Galicia" would be appropriate. Mackensen favored the title "Battle of Gorlice or Jaslo." Conrad, responding to the German request, suggested the title "Battle of Gorlice–Tarnow." The Kaiser and Falkenhayn agreed, so that from there on, the battle of May 1915 would be referred to as the battle of Gorlice–Tarnow in official communications.[12]

Another routine matter concerned the disposal of captured material. During the first several days of the offensive, units could make use of captured enemy weapons, ammunition, and equipment as they deemed proper. With an advance under way, Falkenhayn now wanted captured Russian weapons and ammunition sent back to Germany. Conrad replied, with some justice, that if Austria–Hungary was going to be responsible for the care of prisoners taken, booty captured should go to Austria–Hungary as well. It would seem that Conrad got his way on this issue.[13] The final routine matter dealt with awards. Given the success achieved thus far, awards were due to be given out. Eager to reward his old adjutant, Wilhelm quickly bestowed the Grand Cross of the Royal Order of the House of Hohenzollern, with Swords, on Mackensen. Conrad supported the idea of Falkenhayn's receiving an award from Francis Joseph, but he also wanted some recognition given to the army commanders and to high-ranking Austro–Hungarian officers involved in the attack.[14]

With nothing definitive coming from either Teschen or Pless in terms of a long-term objective, Mackensen proceeded according to his original orders. Over the course of May 7–8, the German Eleventh Army made a series of short advances. The main effort was to continue to block any roads leading from the Carpathians by which the Russian troops in Dukla Pass could escape to the northeast. All the corps of the Eleventh Army were able to cross the Wisloka River, either over bridges that the Russians had failed to destroy or on pontoon bridges constructed by the advancing divisions.[15]

On the German Eleventh Army's flanks, the Austro–Hungarian Third and Fourth Armies began to extend their offensive efforts. The Austro–Hungarian Third Army enjoyed its best success, driving the Russians out of Dukla Pass. In the process, the Austrians were able to surround and destroy the Russian 48th Infantry Division over several days. General Lavr Kornilov, the division commander, was captured on May 7.[16]

The flurry of memoranda traded by Conrad and Falkenhayn over May 9–10 finally produced a degree of consensus regarding the German Eleventh Army and its Austro–Hungarian neighbors. This was effectively ratified in a conference at Pless on May 12, 1915. The German Eleventh Army would advance to the San River on a broad front and establish bridgeheads. The Austro–Hungarian Third Army would be entrusted with the capture of Przemysl. Further south, the Austro–Hungarian Second Army and the German Süd Army would advance up to the Dniestr River.[17]

With relative harmony prevailing between OHL and AOK, Mackensen and Seeckt could launch the next phase of the offensive. Aerial reconnaissance and intercepted Russian wireless radio messages provided some idea as to the extent of the Russian retreat. The Russians were continuing to retreat to the north and east. Intercepted messages also indicated a degree of uncertainty on the part of the Russians in regard to the matter of holding Przemysl. Nonetheless, all available information indicated that Przemysl and Jaroslau were strongly garrisoned.[18]

On May 12, the German Eleventh Army published two orders for the continuation of the offensive. The first, issued at 11 A.M., set forth the broad objectives for the attack. The goal for the German Eleventh Army was now to reach the San River on a broad front to the north and east of Przemysl. The river was to be crossed and bridgeheads created. Given the San's considerable width, the two critical crossing points on the river to be captured were Jaroslau and Radymno. Their capture would serve to isolate Przemysl partially in an operational sense, as the rail line that ran north from Przemysl ran through those places, both located west of the San. The Austro–Hungarian Fourth Army would continue to cover the Eleventh Army's left, between the Wislok and Vistula Rivers. The Austro–Hungarian Third Army would advance on Przemysl from the west and south, and if possible, take the fortress by coup de main.[19]

The second order, issued at 7:45 P.M. on May 12, outlined a reorganization of the Eleventh Army. The Bavarian 11th Infantry Division was now to be subordinated to François's XXXXI Reserve Corps. Emmich's X Corps would now include the 19th Infantry Division and the newly arrived 56th Infantry Division, commanded by Generalmajor Schach von Wittenau.[20] The X Corps would also be shifted from the Eleventh Army's right flank to its left, in effect becoming the leftmost corps on the army's front. The 20th Infantry Division would be posted at Tyczyn, behind the X Corps.[21]

The reorganization of the army was based on operational considerations. Since Jaroslau was now Mackensen's major target, the main effort of the Eleventh Army had to be shifted from the right flank to the left. The principal elements of the army tasked with capturing Jaroslau were the Guard Corps and the Austro–Hungarian VI Corps. The artillery ammunition situation reflected the Eleventh Army's new operational priorities. By mid-May 1915, the Eleventh Army was down to a little over 11,000 shells of all types. Well over half of these were held by the Guard and the X Corps. The most critical shortage was in the largest calibers, especially the 210-mm heavy howitzers. The extent of the German and

Austro–Hungarian advance exacerbated the problem of supply. By mid-May the Eleventh Army had advanced over 90 miles from its railheads. Motor vehicles were lacking, and horses suffered from a shortage of fodder. The paucity of good roads was another problem, one that could be mitigated only partially by stringent traffic-control procedures. Reaching the San would mark the effective limit of the Eleventh Army's operational range until the railroads could be advanced east.[22]

On May 13 the German Eleventh Army made another short advance. The Bavarians were able to go forward along the north bank of the San and reach Helusz. The XXXXI Reserve Corps conducted reconnaissance to the east, covering the area north of Przemysl. The Austro–Hungarian VI Corps moved up to the Mleczka stream, which would allow Arz's troops to approach Jaroslau from the southwest. Meanwhile the Guard, after building a bridge over the Mleczka, took the rail junction of Przeworsk. The 19th Infantry Division covered the Guard's left.[23]

The short advances from May 11–13, involving minimal combat, brought some welcome respite to Mackensen's troops, especially given the exertions of the previous nine days. The weather during daylight was generally warm and pleasant during the first half of May. The nights, however, were often much colder. In addition, the pursuit marches during the first week of the offensive often lasted well into the night. The short marches from May 11–13 demanded minimal exertion on the part of both men and horses while also affording the opportunity for rest and food.[24]

Aside from the supply situation, the biggest problem facing Mackensen and Seeckt was trying to divine the intentions of the Russian Southwest Front. Although aerial reconnaissance clearly showed the Russians to be retreating, there was nothing definitive to indicate where they were going to make a stand. A radio intercept on May 12 indicated that the Russian high command had had a change of heart regarding the question of Przemysl. Given that the Russians had taken the precisely opposite tack just a few days earlier, one could not take the latest intercept as definitive. Thus, the assumption that Mackensen and Seeckt made on May 13 was that the Russians would try to avoid any kind of a decisive battle on the San.[25]

On May 14, Mackensen and Seeckt decided to reorganize the German Eleventh Army. The Bavarian 11th Infantry Division and the 119th Infantry Division were combined as the reconstituted Corps Kneussl. The recreated corps would be reinforced by a half battery of 100-mm guns from the XXXXI Reserve Corps.[26] This reorganization was based on a combination of experience with an assumption. Events of May 14 showed the earlier impression that the Russians were not going to make a stand on the San River to be false. The Prussian Guard encountered "lively" resistance on the part of the Russians, who had taken up a well-entrenched position west of Jaroslau. Thus, the active participation of the XXXXI Reserve Corps in the thrust to the San would be required. With the balance of the German Eleventh Army moving east, a corps-sized unit would be required to guard the army's right flank against any possible sorties from the

Przemysl garrison to the north.[27] In addition, if the Austro–Hungarian Third Army proved unable to take Przemysl, the Eleventh Army would have units ready to undertake offensive operations against the fortress.

Consequently, the Eleventh Army's subordinate corps spent May 14 doing a combination of reconnaissance, advance, and assault. The XXXXI Reserve Corps began moving toward Radymno, with the 81st and 82nd Reserve Divisions reaching their day's respective objectives of Zamiechow and Chlopie by the evening. The Austro–Hungarian VI Corps and the Guard, after a morning reconnaissance, launched an attack in the evening. The focal points of Plettenberg's and Arz's efforts was Hill 264 and Jaroslau castle, the collective key to the Russian defenses west and south of Jaroslau. Starting at 7 P.M., elements of the Guard were able to reach the forward Russian position.[28] Tackling the Russian main line would be on the next day's agenda.

The German Eleventh Army's eastward offensive continued on May 15 in a somewhat staggered fashion. The 119th Infantry Division took over the security of the Eleventh Army's right flank, allowing elements of the Bavarian 11th Infantry Division to cover the right flank of the XXXXI Reserve Corps. François's corps spent the day making a thorough reconnaissance of the Russian positions. Those efforts were hampered a bit by the weather, which remained rainy through the morning. A sunnier afternoon, however, allowed François to get his aircraft aloft to examine the Russian positions and photograph them. All photos and reports were sent to the subordinate commanders, supplementing their own ground-based reconnaissance efforts.[29]

The major action on May 15 involved the Austro–Hungarian VI Corps and the Guard. After a short artillery bombardment, the Austro–Hungarians and the 2nd Guard Division renewed the assault on Hill 264 and the castle. The 1st Guard Division would attack Jaroslau itself. The attack started in the morning, and immediately ran into tough Russian resistance. The Hungarian 39th Infantry Division was able to take Hill 264 in the morning, only to be evicted by a Russian counterattack. The German Alexander and Elisabeth Regiments likewise made little headway in the morning.

The timely arrival of artillery ammunition allowed for a renewed bombardment, followed by a renewed assault. These efforts ultimately brought a degree of success. The 2nd Guard Division was able to reach the railroad embankment and the castle, while the Hungarians were able to gain a foothold on Hill 264 by 7 P.M. Although the left flank of the 1st Guard Division was able to force the Russians over the San, Jaroslau itself remained in Russian hands.[30] Even this limited success was dearly bought. The 1st Guard Foot Regiment lost 52 killed and 140 wounded, while the Elisabeth Regiment lost 33 killed and 101 wounded. The 2nd Guard Artillery Regiment also suffered casualties from Russian small-arms fire, proof of its efforts supporting the infantry.[31]

The X Corps enjoyed somewhat more success, spending most of the day driving the Russians back, ultimately forcing them back across the San. Although the

20th Infantry Division reached the San crossing point at Nielepkowice, crossing the river on the jump was another matter. In Emmich's sector, the San was about 70 yards wide. A deliberate crossing would have to be made.[32]

Although aerial reconnaissance had confirmed that, as of the evening of May 15, there were still significant Russian forces west of the San, Mackensen and Seeckt were confident that several crossings could be achieved on the 16th. Emmich's X Corps was to cross the San and then advance on Sienawa. This would serve the dual purpose of guarding the Eleventh Army's left flank while also facilitating the advance of the Austro–Hungarian Fourth Army. The Guard and the Austro–Hungarian VI Corps would take Jaroslau and cross in the area. Once across the river, the Guard would head for Makowisko with Arz's Austro–Hungarians to the right, with the Szklo River as the corps boundary. The XXXXI Reserve Corps would take Radymno, cross the San, and advance on Michalowka. Kneussl's Bavarians would continue their security mission; the 56th Infantry Division was assigned as the army reserve. The bridgehead the Eleventh Army expected to create would be relatively shallow. Given the supply situation, however, the Eleventh Army would have to undertake a series of limited operations.[33]

As expected, the limited operation produced limited results. Although hampered by the low-lying terrain of the San valley, the 20th Infantry Division was able to get its 92nd Infantry Regiment across the San west of Miazownica. The regiment was able to advance far enough to allow the 5th Company of the 10th Pioneer Regiment to begin building their pontoon bridges. By the evening of May 16, Emmich's X Corps had a shallow but firm lodgment on the east bank.[34]

The major action was at Jaroslau. During the night, the Russians evacuated the area west and south of Jaroslau. The town itself, however, was still defended by elements of three different divisions. The 2nd Guard Division and the Austrian 12th Infantry Division occupied Jaroslau and advanced up to the west bank of the river. Members of Jaroslau's Jewish population warned the Alexander Regiment, Winckler's lead element, that the bridge over the San had been mined by the Russians. That information was confirmed moments later by a shattering blast that destroyed the bridge.[35]

Plettenberg had given instructions that the division send only patrols to the opposite bank. Winckler, however, decided to pursue a more aggressive course of action. The Elisabeth Regiment located a crossing site. Artillery was slightly repositioned, machine guns were put in supporting positions and pontoons brought up. The artillery opened fire at 4:30 P.M., and machine guns suppressed Russian snipers. At 5:30 P.M. the Elisabeth Regiment's Fusilier Battalion reached the east bank in pontoon boats (150 yards distant), followed by the 1st Battalion. After beating off a Russian counterattack, the 2nd Battalion crossed, and was able to make contact with elements of the Alexander Regiment that had crossed the river about 300 yards north of the destroyed bridge. Although the 1st Guard Division, with its artillery displacement held up by bad roads, remained on the west bank of the San, Plettenberg had his bridgehead.[36]

Over the next several days, the Eleventh Army worked to expand its bridgeheads over the San. Already across the river, the X Corps and the Guard fought off Russian counterattacks, connected their bridgeheads, and gained some depth and protection, especially against the Russian artillery. The Austrian VI Corps was able to cross the San as well. The XXXXI Reserve Corps moved slightly toward Radymno and then went over to the defensive, while Kneussl's Bavarians and the 119th Infantry Division continued the security mission for the army's right flank.[37]

Once the German and Austro–Hungarian forces had gotten across the San, a longer operational pause became necessary. The Eleventh Army had reached the edge of its operational range. The ammunition situation, poor at the start of the limited operations of May 16–18, was now critical. Ammunition shortages forced François to cancel attacks scheduled for May 19. Although German and Austro–Hungarian efforts had advanced the railroads, the forward units of the Eleventh Army were still over 62 miles from the nearest railhead. Matters were made worse by poor roads, although the weather remained generally favorable.[38] Ultimately, the supply problem could be solved only by moving the railheads closer to the front line and rebuilding the army's artillery ammunition stocks. The Germans were fortunate that the Russians were in worse shape. Although still capable of defense, they were incapable of counterattacking successfully. François noted that in some local counterattacks on May 18 and 19, Russian soldiers were armed only with grenades or even clubs.[39]

As the offensive ground to a halt just after mid-May, Conrad and Falkenhayn assessed the general strategic situation and the operational situation in Galicia. Strategically, the matter of Italy's entry into the war on the side of the Entente was now regarded as a certainty.[40] How to respond to an Italian entry was becoming an increasingly vexatious point of contention between Falkenhayn and Conrad, a matter that is discussed in the next chapter. Operationally, Conrad agreed that the San–Dniestr line was still the objective. Falkenhayn also fended off attempts by Conrad to alter the command arrangements. The attack on Przemysl would continue. As before, this decision was reached after exchanges of memoranda and another conference, this time at Teschen on May 18.[41]

The operational pause on the San was useful for another reason: namely, the fact that the direction of the Eleventh Army's offensive would have to be changed yet again. The original concept for the operation agreed to by Conrad and Falkenhayn at their meeting in Pless on May 12, 1915, was that the capture of Przemysl would be left to the Austro–Hungarian Third Army.[42] As May progressed, however, it became ever more evident that Boroević's forces had made relatively little progress on the western and southern approaches to Przemysl. Russian defenses in these sectors remained resolute, and the Austro–Hungarians were experiencing difficulties trying to bring supplies through the poor mountain roads, especially in regards to heavy artillery ammunition.[43]

With the Austro–Hungarian Third and Second Armies stymied, Falkenhayn turned to his trump card. Falkenhayn and the Eleventh Army headquarters exchanged a flurry of messages on May 18, 1915. Falkenhayn raised the question of the Eleventh Army shifting the direction of its attack to the southeast, thus advancing against Przemysl from the north. Mackensen and Seeckt agreed but noted that this would require a pause to build up stocks of artillery ammunition. This would be followed by an offensive to capture Radymno and widen the bridgeheads east of the San. Only after sufficient maneuvering space to the east had been won could the direction of the attack be shifted to the southeast.[44]

Once the revised plan for the operations of mid-May had been agreed to on May 18, most of the following six days were spent preparing for the attack. Ammunition stocks were built up. Commanders such as François had the corps air detachments fly numerous reconnaissance missions to develop the depth and strength of the Russian defenses at Radymno. Units such as the Alexander Regiment took advantage of the lull to rest, refit, and repair broken equipment. The one thing they did not receive was replacements. This was serious, as three weeks of hard fighting and marching had taken their toll. The Elisabeth Regiment, for example, was down to about half of the strength it had on May 2.[45]

German reconnaissance efforts paid off in that by May 23 a fairly detailed picture of Russian dispositions opposite the Eleventh Army had been formed. The most important sector of the upcoming attack, Radymno, was held by the Russian XXI Corps; 33rd and 44th Infantry Divisions, plus the 16th Cavalry Division. All told, the Russians had 18 infantry and 3 cavalry divisions arrayed against the Eleventh Army, controlled by the III Caucasian, XII, XXI, XXIV, and V Caucasian Corps. The Germans were well aware that the Russians were trying to bolster the 3rd Army with seven divisions from other parts of the front. These units, such as the 13th Siberian Rifle Division, had been engaged in hard fighting and had suffered correspondingly heavy losses. The only uncertainty concerned the respective size of the sectors of the Russian 3rd and 8th Armies. In fact, Ivanov was seeking to regain the initiative and wanted to launch a counterattack as soon as possible. Radko-Dmitriev, however, wanted to pull the 3rd Army as far back as possible in order to reorganize and rebuild his shattered force. Considering Radko-Dmitiev somewhat demoralized, Ivanov replaced him as 3rd Army commander with General Leonid Lesh and extended Brusilov's front to include the XXI and XII Corps.[46]

Mackensen issued an initial attack order on May 20 and then a final order on May 23. The plan did not call for the Eleventh Army to seize Przemysl but rather to sever the fortress's eastward communications. The capture of Przemysl would be left to the Austro–Hungarian Third and Second Armies, advancing from the west and south, respectively, in accordance with Conrad's desires. The Austro–Hungarian Fourth Army would keep the Russians busy on its front with an attack on Sandomierz.[47]

The German artillery preparation followed a by now familiar if not predictable pattern. Artillery fire would begin during the afternoon of May 23 and continue intermittently throughout the night to harass the Russians. Unlike prior attacks, this time registration fire would be used. Intervals in artillery fire would allow engineers to destroy obstacles and infantry to reach their assault positions. Fire for effect would begin at 6 A.M. on May 24 and last for two hours. The bombardment would reach its height starting at 7:15 A.M., and the artillery would expend one third of its ammunition during the last 45 minutes of fire for effect. The barrage would be lifted at 8 A.M., when the infantry would go over the top.[48]

Once again favored with warm spring weather, the Eleventh Army's attack went off on schedule. The X Corps, covering the Eleventh Army's left, was able to make a short advance. The 56th Infantry Division, Mackensen's left flank unit, made it to the western edge of Cetula. The 20th Infantry Division, after taking Olchowa, was able to reach Chodanie by 10 P.M., an advance of almost two and a half miles. From May 25–27, Emmich's Corps advanced a few more miles toward the Lubaczowka stream against tough Russian resistance.[49]

The Guard and the Austro–Hungarian VI Corps also had several days of hard fighting. The Guard was able to advance on both sides of the Szklo for about 12 miles while the Austro–Hungarian VI Corps was able to take Wietlin and Wysocko, in its 10-mile advance up to the Wisznia River. The Austro–Hungarian VI Corps took over 7,000 prisoners, 12 guns, and 7 machine guns, and the Guard took several thousand more. Casualties in the Guard were relatively light, with the biggest loss being the Elisabeth Regiment's 172 killed and wounded. The Austro–Hungarian VI Corps suffered a bit more severely, especially in prying the Russians out of Wietlin. By May 25, Arz had only about half of the men he had started the campaign with on May 2.[50]

The burden of the offensive was borne by the XXXXI Reserve Corps. The artillery barrage initiated a "lively duel" with the Russian artillery, including heavy guns from Przemysl. As the German barrage intensified, François noted that the Russian artillery fire weakened considerably. At 8 A.M. the infantry advanced against negligible opposition. By 8:45, the 81st Reserve Division took Ostrow, its initial objective. Elements of the 269th Infantry Regiment were able to get the drop on a Russian artillery battery as it was limbering up to retreat. The neighboring 82nd Reserve Division also made significant gains, reaching the Russian artillery positions in its sector. By the evening of May 24, it was clear that François's attack had collapsed the position of the Russian XXI and XII Corps at Radymno. Booty included 9,000 prisoners, 52 guns, and 42 machine guns. François had to use part of his corps reserve for prisoner escort. Casualties were light, only 13 officers and 633 men killed and wounded. The Bavarians and 119th Infantry Division covered François's right flank.[51]

Over the following three days, François continued his drive to the southeast. By the evening of May 27, Sosnica had been taken by the 81st Reserve Division and the 82nd was within easy striking distance of Naklo.[52] Seizure of that critical position would put German artillery within range of the Przemysl–Medyka railroad and the Przemysl–Mosciska Road, the fortress's last two open lines of communication.

Events on both flanks of the Eleventh Army, however, complicated the situation. On May 27, the Russians launched a strong attack against the 56th Infantry Division. Although the Division was able to hold its own, Mackensen had to bolster it with a regiment from the 19th Infantry Division. Further north, a Russian attack by the III Caucasian Corps collapsed the Austro–Hungarian Fourth Army's bridgehead at Sieniawa, forcing the Austrian 10th Infantry Division back across the San. The incident was marked by accusations of bad behavior by another Czech regiment. The Fourth Army was able to stabilize the situation, although help was required from Emmich. At the other end of the Fourth Army's

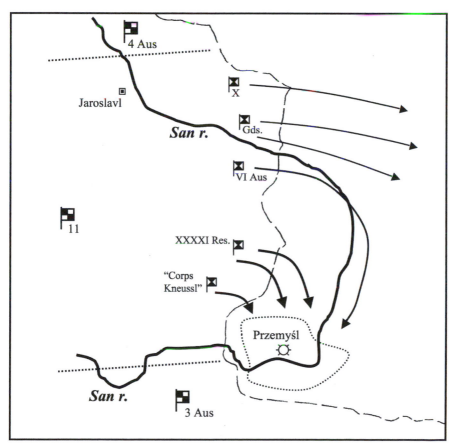

The Siege of Przemysl, May–June 1915.

front, the planned attack on Sandomierz never came off as the key unit, the German 47th Reserve Division, lacked the artillery needed.[53]

Mackensen's other problem was to his south. The Austro–Hungarian Third and Second Armies continued to make minimal progress. The lack of activity was sufficient to bring Conrad's belated attempted personal intervention, trying to get more action from the two armies.[54] Nonetheless, by May 29 it was clear that Przemysl's eastward communications could be threatened only from the north. With Mackensen's forces stretched to the limit and the Russians in Galicia apparently being reinforced, Falkenhayn tried to pry four divisions out of Ober Ost, but to no avail.[55] To Falkenhayn's mind, however, success had to be reinforced. Thus Tappen went to Eleventh Army headquarters in Jaroslau on May 30 to inform Mackensen and Seeckt the next day that help in the form of several more divisions would be on the way. Tappen was also briefed on the status of ongoing operations against Przemysl.[56]

To cover the potentially dangerous situation on the Eleventh Army's left flank, Mackensen and Seeckt pulled the 119th Infantry Division out of the line, leaving only the 46th Infantry Regiment with the Bavarians. The rest of Behr's division headed north to Jaroslau as army reserve. The majority of the Hungarian 11th Cavalry Division was also sent to Jaroslau. The X, Austro–Hungarian VI, and the Guard Corps were all ordered to go over to the defensive. In addition, aerial reconnaissance reported that the Russians were making all preparations to abandon Przemysl. These impressions were confirmed for François by a Jewish peddler he had sent to Przemysl a few days before.[57]

Given the new situation, Mackensen and Seeckt decided to shift the focus of the attack on Przemysl, much to François's irritation, to Kneussl's Bavarians. They would fight their way through the northern side of the fortifications, supported by the heaviest artillery at Mackensen's disposal. François would employ his heavy artillery to interdict Przemysl's road and rail communications, especially at Medyka. The irascible XXXXI Reserve Corps commander would have preferred to seize Medyka and Mosciska, a little over nine miles further east. François could not do that, however, without the 119th Infantry Division. The infantry of the XXXXI Reserve Corps would have to be content with holding their positions, especially at Naklo, against Russian counterattacks, while the artillery would carry the brunt of the battle.[58]

Przemysl was an old market city, dating back to the seventh century. The inner city extended out from both banks of the San as it ran in an east–west course before the river turned sharply to the north. The inner city had an old wall that was militarily useless, but Przemysl was surrounded by a ring of modern fortifications that extended several miles from the city itself. These fortifications, a series of permanent works of earth and concrete connected to each other with trenches, had been slightly damaged during the first Russian siege. These damages had been repaired by the Russians in the spring of 1915 using labor from the city's civilian population, by this time about 50,000 people. While these fortifications might be insurmountable to infantry, Seeckt, with his experience on the western front, expected that the German and Austro–Hungarian heavy artillery would be more than a match for Przemysl's forts.[59]

The Russian garrison, commanded by General Sergei Delvig, consisted of bits and pieces of the 14th, 15th, 34th, 35th, 60th, and 65th Infantry Divisions. Delvig's task was not helped by considerable confusion between Stavka and the southwest front over whether to abandon Przemysl or hold onto it. Ultimately, Delvig was ordered to hold it with his cobbled-together force, supported by a small amount of heavy artillery.[60]

The plan, developed by the Eleventh Army and executed by Kneussl, required a day of preparation. Artillery would be positioned on May 29, while the infantry obtained good observation posts for the heavy guns and reached jump-off positions. The bombardment would begin on May 30, with the infantry assault to follow the day after. Kneussl's chosen target was the area between Forts X and XI, which also covered Forts Xa and XIa. All of these forts were easily seen from a Bavarian observation post at Batyce, about a mile distant. The Bavarians were also reinforced by elements of the 119th Infantry Division, the Hungarian 11th Cavalry Division, and two battalions of the Guard.[61]

The German bombardment began at 11 A.M. on May 30. Kneussl's heavy guns engaged the forts while François's artillery, positioned at Naklo, started hitting Medyka. The XXXXI Reserve Corps' guns quickly had Medyka in flames, halting railroad traffic. The remaining Russian artillery, however, was able to hit back. A shell strike on the ammunition pile of François's 100-mm gun battery produced ghastly results; the battery was almost wiped out. Further west, the fire of Kneussl's heavy guns was not considered effective enough to let the infantry go forward. The scheduled infantry attack for May 31 was postponed to June 1, to give the artillery one more day to work. In the meantime, the Austrian 45th Infantry Regiment of the 24th Infantry Division, part of the Austro–Hungarian X Corps, was able to gain a lodgment on the western side of Przemysl's ring of fortifications at Pralkowce near Fort VII, a development of which Conrad immediately informed Falkenhayn.[62]

The bombardment continued through May 31. Austro–Hungarian success at Pralkowce proved of short duration. The Russians were able drive the Austrians out of Pralkowce. On the German side, a lucky hit from a heavy howitzer destroyed a key Russian trench on the west flank of Fort XI, and several other forts were severely battered. The German barrage's accuracy was improved by the excellent network of observation posts to the north. On June 1, the German infantry went in. The Bavarians took Forts X and XI, while the Augusta Regiment's Fusilier Battalion took Fort XII.[63]

By the evening of June 1, Przemysl's defenses had been penetrated. During the early morning hours of June 2, the Russians launched a heavy counterattack against the Bavarian 3rd Infantry Regiment at Fort XI, only to be defeated by rifle and machine-gun fire. With the last Russian counterattack's failure, the Russian defense quickly fell apart. The Russian troops that could escape east moved that way. Remaining supplies were burned and at 11 P.M. on June 2 the last bridge over the San was blown up. Kneussl's planned drive into the city on June 3 proved unnecessary. By the afternoon of June 3, the fortress was in Mackensen's hands.[64]

Although the offensive had produced immense numbers of prisoners and booty, the haul from Przemysl was disappointingly small. According to the Eleventh Army, no more than 8,000 prisoners were taken on June 3, the majority by the Bavarians. Also taken were 38 guns and 38 machine guns. A number of Austro–Hungarian guns that the Russians had captured in March were also taken.[65] For the Germans' part, while losses in the four-day siege were not as bad as they could have been, victory did not come cheaply. Total casualties for the XXXXI Reserve Corps, for example, for the period May 25–31, 1915, were about 1,400 killed, wounded, and missing. Meanwhile the Bavarians, who enjoyed better heavy artillery support, considered their casualties light: 13 officers and 424 men killed and wounded.[66]

After several months of Russian occupation marked by periodic spasms of anti-Semitic criminality, Przemysl's civilian population welcomed their deliverance at the hands of the Germans and Austro–Hungarians. Helena Jablonska noted the tumultuous reception given the Austro–Hungarian troops. Even François, whose suspicion of the Galician population was extraordinary even by the standards of the day, noted how well the civilians received the German soldiers.[67]

News of Przemysl's fall also triggered celebrations in other places. Mackensen announced the capture of the fortress in a message to Vienna, in which he laid Przemysl "at the feet" of Francis Joseph. The wording of the message, which implied that the Germans had cleaned up an Austro–Hungarian mess, ruffled feelings in Vienna. The message was a surprisingly tactless move on Mackensen's part, given his normal aplomb in dealing with allies.[68] Both Francis Joseph and Wilhelm II were more than happy, slights aside, to dole out awards to the various commanders who figured prominently in the operation. Chief among the recipients were Mackensen, Seeckt, François, and Kneussl.[69]

Diplomatically, the successes of May 1915 and the capture of Przemysl had mixed results. The original diplomatic goal of the attack was to dissuade Italy and Romania from entering the war on the side of the Entente. By mid-May, it had become plainly evident to both OHL and AOK that Italy was going to declare war on Austria–Hungary.[70] Italy did so on May 23 but refrained from issuing a declaration against Germany. A much greater impression was made on Romania. Russia had promised territorial compensation at Austria–Hungary's expense, but the collapse of the Russian position in the Carpathians made such a prospect unlikely.[71]

The phase of the campaign beginning with the aftermath of the breakthrough at Gorlice, which concluded with the capture of Przemysl, is worthy of comment in several respects. First, the goal for the offensive, the San–Dniestr line and the capture of Przemysl, developed only gradually over the first week after the initial attack of Mackensen's force had scored a clear breakthrough. That was the clear limit of the offensive as envisioned by Conrad and Falkenhayn. It is worth noting that in their correspondence of May 1915, one name that never appears is Lemberg. This pattern of strategic decision making is commented on later.

By the standards of 1915, the conduct of the campaign from the second week of May to the capture of Przemysl showed the German Army at its most nimble. Over the course of May, the Eleventh Army had to shift its *Schwerpunkt* (main effort) several times. The initial attack was weighted on the right, with the Bavarians. It was then shifted to the left, as Emmich's X Corps had to move across the army's sector to the left flank. Later, for the critical assault on Jaroslau, the Guard was the critical element in the attack. For the culminating attack on Przemysl, the *Schwerpunkt* was shifted again, back to the Bavarians and the XXXXI Reserve Corps. This showed a consistent level of staff work by the Eleventh Army and the subordinate corps commands that was simply superb.

Another key element in Mackensen's success was aerial reconnaissance. Operationally, aerial reconnaissance generally kept German commanders well informed of Russian large-scale troop movements. Tactically, given the limited amount of German artillery ammunition available, the ability of German reconnaissance aircraft to roam unchallenged over Russian positions was crucial, especially in mid-May.[72] The ability of aircraft to spot for German artillery, especially the heavy guns, allowed the Germans to maximize the effectiveness of this trump card. Repeatedly, German attacks turned on the ability of the heavy artillery to destroy Russian field fortifications and disrupt attempted Russian counterattacks. Although the first siege of Przemysl was a matter of the Russian 11th Army starving out the Austro–Hungarian garrison over several months, the four-day German siege was quickly resolved by the heavy artillery. Forts Xa and XIa, for example, were literally smashed by the big guns. François toured the damage and marveled at the devastation.[73]

For the Russians, the month of May 1915 was disastrous. Total losses for the southwest front in May were 412,000. By May 17, 1915, according to Falkenhayn's calculations, at least 170,000 prisoners had been taken.[74] While the decision to hold the line of the San at Jaroslau and Radymno was a reasonable one, once both places were lost, the loss of Przemysl should have been seen as unavoidable. Although the decision was eventually made to evacuate Przemysl, this occurred only after a considerable amount of dithering and indecision. Ivanov acted too slowly to reinforce the 3rd Army, and generally it took too long for reinforcements to arrive.[75]

With Przemysl now back under Austro–Hungarian control and the German Eleventh and Austro–Hungarian Fourth Armies having traversed the San, a new front was opening up with Italy. Therefore the offensive that had begun on May 2 could now go in one of several directions. The month of June 1915 would bring a new set of choices, decisions, and actions. The "Mackensen Phalanx" would march again, but in which direction?

Chapter 6
Liberating Lemberg: June 6–24, 1915

> Eastern Galicia should become part of Russia. Western Galicia, when its conquest has been completed, should form part of the kingdom of Poland, within the empire.
>
> —Count Vladimir Bobrinski, October 15, 1914[1]

> Lemberg has fallen.
>
> —August von Mackensen, June 22, 1915[2]

The breaking of the Russian position on the San in late May and the ensuing capture of Przemysl presented Falkenhayn and Conrad with a whole new set of strategic choices in the late spring of 1915. Falkenhayn's position had been strengthened by events on both the eastern and western fronts. French offensive operations in May 1915, the most notable of which was the attack on Vimy Ridge in Artois by General Victor d'Urbal's French 10th Army, had collapsed in a welter of bloodshed, with the French suffering over 140,000 casualties by the end of May.[3] Germany's Turkish ally had been able to hold its own, stymieing the British advance at Gallipoli. Finally, Falkenhayn's decision to employ Mackensen's Eleventh Army had disposed of the Russian threat to Hungary, confirming the wisdom of Falkenhayn's decision to commit forces to the Gorlice attack. Although Italy had entered the war against Austria–Hungary, it was abundantly clear by early June that Romania was not going to take the plunge.[4]

These circumstances served to strengthen Falkenhayn's hold as head of OHL. After having fended off pressure by Ober Ost aimed at the kaiser, the successes of the spring of 1915 put Falkenhayn in the driver's seat. Although Wilhelm II's influence on operational matters was minimal at most, at this point in the war he could exercise considerable influence on the matter of who got to make strategic decisions. By late May 1915 Wilhelm was clearly in Falkenhayn's corner, much to the frustration of Ober Ost.[5]

Conrad's position was not in serious jeopardy. The successes in Galicia in May 1915 resulted in Conrad being showered with honors, all of which meant nothing to him. Perhaps the two most notable successes for Conrad were his promotion to Generaloberst and the fact that Gina's impending divorce from Hans von Reininghaus would allow Conrad to marry her, pending the emperor's permission.[6]

The result of the Gorlice–Tarnow breakthrough and the capture of Przemysl on June 3 had forced the collapse of the Russian position in the Carpathians and alleviated the threat to Hungary. The Russian response, the offensive against the seam between the Austro–Hungarian First Army and Army Detachment Woyrsch on the north side of the Vistula scored some local successes. Meanwhile, the offensive against Pflanzer-Baltin's Austro–Hungarian Seventh Army resulted in the capture of Czernowitz. Neither success, however, was near enough to influence events in Galicia, although Falkenhayn did have to provide some spine to Conrad, who was a bit panicked by Pflanzer-Baltin's situation in the south.[7]

As Mackensen's offensive rolled forward over the course of May, Conrad and Falkenhayn pondered what they should do once the San–Dniestr line had been reached. The most contentious problem was Italy. This issue seemed to bring out the worst in both Falkenhayn and Conrad. To avoid war with Italy, Falkenhayn suggested that Austria–Hungary buy off Italy with territorial concessions, including the Trentino. Conrad, with his finely honed sense of sarcasm, responded by suggesting that Germany cede Alsace–Lorraine to France. A further proposal by Germany to offer Austria–Hungary territorial compensation also came to naught from both Austrian and German resistance.[8] For Falkenhayn, the entry of Italy would be a problem, but in the context of the strategic situation in 1915, it would remain a secondary issue compared with the matter of opening a direct route to Turkey, let alone dealing with the main enemy, Britain.

For Conrad, the entry of Italy changed everything. Conrad was a man of serial obsessions. In 1914, Conrad's obsession with Serbia helped precipitate the war. His personal obsession, eventually satisfied, was Gina von Reininghaus. During the early winter of 1915, his fixation with Przemysl led to a series of ill-considered and costly offensives. During the spring of 1915, Conrad's new obsession was Italy. His letters, especially to Bolfras, reeked with hatred for Italy. One noted scholar suggests that Conrad felt about Italy much as certain figures in Germany felt about Britain. Conrad went so far as to suggest that arsenal workers in places like Pola be given weapons. He even called for guerrilla warfare to be conducted by irregular forces led by young, spirited officers, supported by loyal elements of the population, who would be armed.[9] In case of an Italian entry, Conrad wanted a concentration of at least 20 divisions, including the German Eleventh Army, for offensive operations against Italy, while a defensive posture would be assumed once the San–Dniestr line was reached.[10]

Falkenhayn, of course, would have none of that, given his strategic priorities. In the actual event, Italy itself solved the problem. On May 24, the government of Antonio Salandra declared war on Austria–Hungary but not on Germany and would not do so for a year, much to the irritation of France and Britain. Since Falkenhayn had no interest in fighting Italy, he made sure that the only kind of war Conrad could pursue against Italy would be defensive. By mid-June 1915, Falkenhayn made it clear to Conrad that once operations in Galicia were concluded, operations against Serbia would take precedence over those against Italy.[11]

Meanwhile, the matter of how to proceed in Galicia remained to be decided. Even before Przemysl was captured, it was apparent that Mackensen had won a victory of monumental proportions. The casualties inflicted on the Russian 3rd, 8th, and 11th Armies greatly exceeded those of Tannenberg. Material losses were also immense. In addition, Russian transportation difficulties were making the cobbling together of a coherent defensive position difficult. Sometime in late May, Falkenhayn decided to reinforce the Eleventh Army and continue operations east of the San.[12]

When it came to the concept of follow-on operations, the Germans were able to present Conrad with a fait accompli. When Tappen visited the Eleventh Army on May 31, aside from hearing about coming operations against Przemysl, he also sounded out Mackensen and Seeckt for their ideas on subsequent operations once the promised reinforcements had arrived. Mackensen and Seeckt regarded an advance on Lemberg as the natural next step to be taken in Galicia. Thus when Conrad telegraphed Falkenhayn on June 2 that, now that the situation at Przemysl had clarified itself and its fall was at hand—and that they should meet in Pless to discuss future operations—Falkenhayn was ready with an immediate response.[13]

Once the reinforcements had arrived and the supply situation improved, Mackensen's forces would be reorganized. Since the advance from the Gorlice sector and the Carpathians to Przemysl had shortened the front, the Austro–Hungarian Third Army would be broken up, with two of its corps, the Austro–Hungarian X and XVII Corps, shifted to the Austro–Hungarian Fourth Army. Böhm-Ermolli's Austro–Hungarian Second Army would now be on the German Eleventh Army's right flank. As before, the main effort would be made by the Eleventh Army. Its target would not be Lemberg itself but rather the critical communications center of Rava Russka. Possession of Rava Russka would, in effect, cut the most direct lines of communications between the Russian northwest and southwest fronts. This advance would also facilitate forward progress of Böhm-Ermolli's Second Army, in whose sector Lemberg would be located. The Austro–Hungarian Fourth Army would continue its normal mission of covering Mackensen's left flank.[14] Conrad had little choice but to agree with this proposal. More galling to Conrad was the fact that both commanders of the

Austro–Hungarian Fourth and Second Armies, Archduke Ferdinand and Böhm-Erolli, respectively, would be under Mackensen's orders, not those of AOK.[15]

In late May, with the Austro–Hungarian Third Army disbanded, Boroević was sent south to take over the newly forming Austro–Hungarian Fifth Army on the Isonzo front against the Italians. It would be one of the wisest choices of commanders Conrad would make. Boroević's successor, Feldzeugmeister Paul Puhallo von Brlog, would take over the Austro–Hungarian First Army from General der Kavallerie Viktor Graf Dankl von Krasnik, who would command the defense of the Tirol.[16]

While the next objective was being set and command arrangements refined, the Eleventh Army used the first two weeks of June to reinforce, refit, and resupply itself. Although the Eleventh Army had won magnificent victories in May and early June 1915, success was not cheap. During May the Eleventh Army suffered close to 28,000 casualties, including over 5,500 killed, over 20% of the Eleventh Army's original strength. Although a number of the wounded would return to duty, thanks to the efforts of the German medical services, these losses were still serious. Some of the Prussian Guard regiments had sunk to half of the strength they possessed on May 1. Arz's Austro–Hungarian VI Corps was also below half strength, and equipment was in poor shape. A month of hard campaigning had reduced uniforms to tatters, with civilian trousers often pressed into service as replacements.[17]

When Tappen visited the Eleventh Army on May 30, 1915, he brought the good news to Mackensen and Seeckt, communicated the next day, that several divisions would be sent to the Eleventh Army. The shape of these reinforcements was further clarified by Falkenhayn two days later. Instead of just three divisions, the Eleventh Army would receive over four. Falkenhayn had managed to pry two divisions, the 22nd and 107th, from Ober Ost. Most of the XXII Reserve Corps, consisting of the 43rd and 44th Reserve Divisions, would be sent from France, commanded by General der Kavallerie Eugen von Falkenhayn, Falkenhayn's older brother. Finally, Generalleutnant Hermann Freiherr von Stein's Bavarian 8th Reserve Division would also be sent from France. Aside from these units, two engineer companies and some additional batteries of 100-mm guns would also go to the Eleventh Army.[18]

The lull in operations also allowed the Eleventh Army to improve its manpower situation through the incorporation of replacements. Some regiments, such as the 269th Reserve Infantry Regiment, had received replacements as early as May 28, when 900 men arrived.[19] More replacements arrived after Przemysl's capture. A number of the Prussian Guard regiments also received replacements. Although the number of replacements was insufficient to cover the gaps in the ranks created by combat and disease, a degree of strength was restored to the regiments.[20]

The arrival of reinforcements and replacements rebuilt the Eleventh Army's strength to a considerable degree. Although definitive numbers are not available, it would be reasonable to assume—given the fact that almost five divisions were added to the army's order of battle, plus the replacements that arrived to fill the gaps at least partially—that by second week of June 1915 the Eleventh Army had about as many men as it did on May 2, 1915. Equally important was the fact that Mackensen's attacking forces were supported by 700 guns, including numerous heavy guns.[21]

The Eleventh Army's ability to get reinforcements and replacements was enhanced by the improvement of the railroad situation. By June 2 the railroad had reached Jaroslau and soon after would reach Przemysl.[22] The condition of the roads remained poor, although the favorable weather helped offset this to a degree.[23] Nonetheless, the advancing of the railroad by the Austro–Hungarian railroad authorities was critical in allowing for the continuation of offensive operations in Galicia.

The improvement in the Eleventh Army's supply situation was reflected in the size of its stocks of artillery ammunition. By mid-May, as seen previously, the Eleventh Army was down to a relative handful of artillery shells. By June 10, 1915, although the stocks had not been restored to the level attained before May 2, the situation had improved considerably. By May 15, 1915, for example, the entire Prussian Guard Corps had only 2,500 gun shells, 1,300 light field howitzer rounds, and 1,000 heavy field howitzer rounds. By June 10, 1915, the 2nd Guard Field Artillery Regiment alone had 600 rounds for each of its three batteries of guns and 900 rounds for its three light field howitzer batteries.[24]

The supply situation improved in other ways as well. Additional rations were brought up, including such treasures as sugar, beer, and wine. Morale in the 2nd Guard Artillery Regiment increased considerably when the Potsdam Guard Artillery League sent the regiment 7,000 cigars and 2,000 cigarettes.[25]

While the Eleventh Army was preparing to resume offensive operations, a matter arose that was as amusing as it was delicate. Before the start of the offensive on May 2, AOK and OHL agreed that for the first three days, any material captured would be used by the capturing unit in any way the unit saw fit. After the breakthrough was achieved, Conrad and Falkenhayn agreed that since the offensive was being conducted on Austro–Hungarian territory, any Russian material captured would be turned over to the Austro–Hungarian authorities.[26] The first unit of the Eleventh Army to enter Przemysl, however, was the Bavarian 11th Infantry Division. Kneussl's men captured a number of Austro–Hungarian guns that had been taken by the Russians in March. The Bavarians were now sending these items as trophies back to the Bavarian War Ministry in Munich.[27] AOK complained that these guns were Austro–Hungarian property and should be returned, as per the prior agreement. Falkenhayn did pass the order—that captured material should be turned over to the Austro–Hungarians—on to the Eleventh Army. Unfortunately we do not have Mackensen's response to Falkenhayn's message.[28]

Another delicate matter arose when a local attack at Josefowka, which was supposed to be carried out by the Austro–Hungarian XVII Corps and the XXXXI

Reserve Corps, miscarried. The attack was aimed at a position the Russians had created at Josefowka, a small village and dairy located near a chain of hills just north of the Przemysl–Lemberg rail line. Launched on June 7, the attack made some progress in some areas but no progress against the critical sector of the Russian defenses, the Josefowka dairy, located in the zone of the Austro–Hungarian XVII Corps. The Eleventh Army ordered the corps relieved by Kneussl's Bavarians, and the order was apparently couched in language that was sharply critical of the Austro–Hungarians. François attributed the problem to the unsettled command arrangements at the time, as the Austro–Hungarian Third Army headquarters was in the process of disbanding. The issue was smoothed over by shifting the Austro–Hungarian XVII Corps to the Austro–Hungarian Fourth Army, as had been planned anyway. In addition, after feelings had simmered down, Archduke Friedrich wrote Mackensen a lengthy letter vouching for the competence of the corps and its commander, General der Infanterie Karl Kritek.[29] Josefowka remained in Russian hands for the time being.

With Lemberg now set as the next objective, preparations for the offensive went forward. The new forces arriving were incorporated into the Eleventh Army while its existing forces were reorganized. The army's left flank would now be entrusted to the 56th and 119th Infantry Divisions and placed under the command of Behr, the 119th Infantry Division commander, designated as Corps Behr. To Behr's right was Emmich's X Corps. Falkenhayn's XXII Reserve Corps was inserted into the front on Emmich's left. To the left of the XXII Reserve Corps was the Guard, then the Austro–Hungarian VI Corps, and the rightmost corps was François's XXXXI Reserve Corps. Mackensen now had the luxury of retaining four infantry divisions, the 22nd, 107th, and Bavarian 8th Reserve and 11th Infantry Divisions, plus the Hungarian 11th Cavalry Division, in reserve. Meanwhile, the Austro–Hungarian X and XVII Corps were inserted into the Austro–Hungarian Fourth Army's right flank. The date for the next offensive was set as June 13, 1915.[30]

As usual, extensive reconnaissance was conducted, mostly by air. Aerial reconnaissance was critical in several ways. First, it was needed to spot targets for the heavy artillery. Even though the artillery ammunition situation had improved considerably, heavy artillery shells especially were still items that were not to be wasted. Since every shot needed to count, the best way to ensure that was by observation of every shot fired. This was best done either by aircraft or tethered balloon. Commanders were urged to make sure that artillery preparation was aided by observation, even after the start of the attack.[31]

Aerial reconnaissance was also critical in providing ground commanders with some idea as to the depth of the Russian defenses. On June 6, 1915, for example, the Eleventh Army issued detailed orders for aerial reconnaissance the following morning. The air detachments for all corps would conduct close reconnaissance, meaning to a depth of 5 miles beyond the front line. The area for distant reconnaissance extended a further 25 to 30 miles beyond the close reconnaissance zone. Any new Russian positions were to be photographed. In addition, any aerial reconnaissance reports sent to army headquarters were to be sent with nine copies (ten total) to enable better dissemination to subordinate commanders. The Rava Russka area was to be covered extensively. Finally, should the offensive assume a mobile character, aerial reconnaissance could provide operational intelligence to commanders, given the paucity of Central Powers' cavalry and their futility in operating against the veritable clouds of Cossacks employed by the Russians in such situations.[32]

Preparation went on in other ways as well. Stein's Bavarian 8th Reserve Division, coming from France, was new to the theater. Since they would be working with the Austro–Hungarian Army, troops were provided with information on the types of soldiers in the army, their uniforms and rank insignia.[33] Work also continued on defenses for the San line, although this was more precautionary than anything.[34]

The new offensive by Mackensen's forces would be conducted in a manner similar to the campaign's previous attacks. The first attack would be a supporting effort on 12 June by the Fourth Army and left flank of the Eleventh Army at Sieniawa. The main attack would begin with artillery registration and harassing fire during the night of June 12–13, during which time the infantry would move up to their assault positions. Artillery fire for effect would be conducted from 4 to 5:30 A.M. Where necessary, fire against particular targets could be brought in from neighboring sectors, a practice that depended heavily on excellent communication among corps artillery commanders, supported by constant observation. At 5:30 A.M. the infantry assault would commence.[35]

The Eleventh Army's major effort would be made by the Austro–Hungarian VI Corps, the Prussian Guard, and the newly arrived XXII Reserve Corps. The three corps would attack and drive forward to the northeast. The X Corps and Corps Behr would cover the left flank of the Eleventh Army's offensive, while also maintaining contact with the Austro–Hungarian Fourth Army. The XXXXI Reserve Corps would advance on a broad front across the Wisznia, covering Arz's right flank. François's corps would also have to maintain contact with the Beskiden Corps, the leftmost corps of the Austro–Hungarian Second Army. In addition Marwitz, commander of the Beskiden Corps, would also have the Austro–Hungarian IV Corps, commanded by Feldmarschalleutnant Albert Schmidt von Georgenegg, at his disposal. Although the corps of the Eleventh Army were given objectives to reach for June 13, they were not set in stone. Units could go beyond them if they were able. The boundaries that had to be adhered to were the lateral boundaries between the corps.[36]

The new offensive would be launched against a Russian defensive line that had been hurriedly cobbled together after the fall of Przemysl. Ivanov's southwest front defense still rested on the 3rd and 8th Armies, both of which were in poor shape and short of artillery pieces and ammunition. Reinforcements were also sent down from the northwest front. The new position rested on holding the Lubaczowka and Wisznia Rivers, covering Lemberg.[37]

The preliminary attack on June 12 got the offensive off to a good start. Corps Behr's two divisions were able to cross the Lubaczowka and overrun the Russian positions south of the Kotowka Forest. The 22nd Infantry Division, committed from army reserve, was able to occupy Sieniawa by 5 P.M. These advances enabled the Austro–Hungarian Fourth Army to complete the building of two bridges across the San at Lezachow in the Austro–Hungarian XVII Corps sector.[38]

The main offensive began on June 13 under cloudy skies, with the artillery preparation and infantry assaults starting on time. The XXXXI Reserve Corps faced a difficult task; the area around the Wisznia River, which ran parallel to the corps' front, was flat and provided little if any cover. The attacking units were able to reach the river, several hundred yards past their jump-off positions, when they were met by intense machine gun fire. Two attempts to cross the river revealed that the Russians were well dug in and that the 90-minute artillery preparation was insufficient. The 268th Regiment was able to get a request back to Stocken for a 15-minute artillery barrage against the village of Zakorby, the key to the Russian position in the 81st Reserve Division's sector. The barrage allowed the infantry to get across the river and take Zakorby around 2 P.M. To the 268th Regiment's right, the 267th Regiment was also able to cross the river on the third try and eventually seize the heights to the north overlooking its position. Although casualties were described as "heavy," they were not severe enough to warrant bringing the 269th Regiment forward from the second line.[39]

Further south, Fabarius's 82nd Reserve Division was able to take Ostrow, west of the Wisznia, fairly quickly. Upon reaching the river, the 82nd Reserve Division had an experience similar to that of the 81st Reserve Division.[40] Several attempts were required to get over the Wisznia. Nonetheless, by the evening of June 13, the XXXXI Reserve Corps was able to cross the river all along its front. Some 1,400 prisoners were taken, while François's corps suffered almost 1,000 casualties.[41]

On François's left, the Austro–Hungarian VI Corps made uneven progress, with the Austrian 12th Infantry Division on the left making slightly more progress than the Hungarian 39th Infantry Division. Nonetheless, by 6 P.M. Arz's troops had reached the eastern edge of a large forested area, when they encountered a new Russian position.[42] They had advanced over a mile.

Mackensen's main effort was in the hands of Plettenberg's Guard Corps. Although aided by additional heavy artillery, the Prussian Guard's two divisions had differing experiences when the infantry went over the top. The 1st Guard Infantry Division, tasked with having to cross the Szklo River, ran into tough opposition, so much so that another round of heavy artillery fire had to be called in. Russian resistance began to weaken after 9 A.M. In the afternoon Prince Friedrich's guardsmen were able to cross the Szklo River.[43]

To the left, Winckler's 2nd Guard Division found the artillery preparation to be quite effective. The village of Tuchla was taken quickly, and the advance was then pressed into the woods to the northeast. Ironically, the German Kaiser Alexander Regiment was opposed by the Russian King Friedrich Wilhelm III Life Guard Regiment. By nightfall on June 13, the Guard's advance had reached a depth of several miles, to just west of Wielkie Oczy. Several thousand prisoners were taken, while casualties were relatively light.[44]

Falkenhayn's XXII Reserve Corps found the going tough but was able to advance on June 13. Most importantly, the largest gain was made by the 43rd Reserve Division on the XXII Corps' right flank. This enabled the Guard to maintain contact with its left flank. The left flank, the 107th Infantry Division, was able to take Czerniawka.[45]

Unlike the other corps in the Eleventh Army, Emmich's X Corps attacked in a staggered fashion, with the 20th Infantry Division leading off. Overcoming tough resistance while advancing over open and swampy ground, Oetinger's men, supported by the 107th Infantry Division's left flank, were able to cross the Lubaczowka River. Hofmann's 19th Infantry Division extended the width of the attack with its right flank, echeloning the line back to the left.[46]

After its exertions on 12 June Corps Behr, now placed under Stein (commander of the Bavarian 8th Reserve Division) and renamed Corps Stein, made only a few limited attacks to expand its penetration. Meanwhile, the Austro–Hungarian Fourth Army, with the XVII and IX Corps, expanded its San bridgehead up to just short of Piskorowice.[47] At the opposite end of the Eleventh Army's line, the Beskiden Corps was finally able to take the Josefowka dairy, although heavy fighting was required.[48]

Early on June 14, Mackensen noted that the Russians were retreating. Thus he gave new orders for a pursuit to commence. The objective was to prevent the Russians from establishing a new defensive position west of Lemberg. The main effort would continue to be with the XXII Reserve, Guard and Austro–Hungarian VI Corps. The army's component corps were given objectives that François complained were too far away to reach on June 14 or even 15, although the Army order of June 14 noted that they were not set in stone, only the lateral boundaries between the corps had been fixed. As before, the Austro–Hungarian Second and Fourth Armies would continue to cover the Eleventh Army's flanks.[49]

Mackensen's instincts about the Russians proved half right. The Russians had clearly retreated before the Second Army. Böhm-Ermolli's forces followed, impelled in part by sharply worded orders from Mackensen and Seeckt for the Second Army to start attacking "forcefully." Once under way, the Second Army's attack was able, especially on the left with the Beskiden Corps and the Austro–Hungarian IV Corps, to cross the Wisznia on a broad front and advance about six miles.[50]

The Eleventh Army, while experiencing more hard fighting, also enjoyed success. The XXXXI Reserve Corps started its day by canceling the scheduled morning attack, as the Russians had retreated. An advance, ordered even before the arrival of new orders from the army, was put in motion in the morning. After a cautious advance of several miles and contending with Cossack cavalry screens, François's reservists discovered two new Russian positions. One faced the 81st Reserve Division at Sarny and the other opposed the 82nd Reserve Division at Mielniki.[51]

Given that the infantry strength of the corps was now slightly less than half its normal establishment, François decided on a cautious approach. After a personal reconnaissance that almost ended in disaster, with François being shot at by his own soldiers, an attack was launched in the afternoon. Fighting was severe in places, with bayonets being crossed in some spots, but brief. The corps reached the chain of hills east of Sarny and just south of Krakowiec Lake, taking 3,000 prisoners.[52]

The Austro–Hungarian VI Corps also made progress on June 14. Although the Hungarian 39th Infantry Division was not able to keep pace with François' 81st Reserve Division on the right, the Hungarians were able to reach Krakowiec Lake, and the Austrian 12th Infantry Division, in a difficult frontal assault against the Russian 20th and 34th Infantry Divisions, was able to cross the Szklo River north of the lake.[53]

For the Prussian Guard, June 14 was another day of hard but successful combat. After a short artillery barrage (one hour) in an afternoon attack, the 1st and 2nd Guard Divisions were able to drive the Russians from their defenses in the Bucznik and Bereznik Hills and take Wielkie Oczy. After moving ahead two miles, another Russian position was encountered. With night coming on, Plettenberg called a halt and decided that the attack would be resumed the next day. Commanders were pleased to note that the replacements the corps had received performed very well.[54]

Falkenhayn's XXII Reserve Corps also made significant progress on June 14. The corps was able to advance a couple of miles to the east (43rd Reserve Division) and northeast (107th Infantry Division). The slightly divergent directions of advance of the two divisions widened the corps' front, so that the interval between the two of them was filled by the 44th Reserve Division. Most importantly, the XXII Reserve Corps was able to keep pace with the Guard on its right.[55]

Emmich's X Corps had to fight its way through a Russian position in a forested area. The 20th Infantry Division was able to break into and turn the left flank of the Russian position in Emmich's sector. This allowed the X Corps to both clear the forest and the Lubaczowka River. Emmich's advance while not fully keeping pace with the XXII Reserve Corps' movement; nonetheless the X Corps was able to establish solid contact with Falkenhayn's left as the German line echeloned back to the northwest.[56]

On June 14, Corps Stein made only limited attacks, resulting in limited gains. The corps did succeed in its principal mission, namely establishing solid contact with the flanks of the X Corps on the right with the 56th Infantry Division and the Austro–Hungarian XVII Corps on the left with the 22nd Infantry Division. The Austro–Hungarian Fourth Army made only limited gains on June 14, but enough to allow Archduke Joseph Ferdinand to get six divisions across the San.[57]

For Mackensen and Seeckt, June 15 confirmed their expectations of success. Although the Austro–Hungarian Second and Fourth Armies made limited gains and Corps Stein saw some fighting, it was clear that the Russian defenses along the Eleventh Army's front had collapsed. Although the Guard had to deal with some pockets of resistance, no large-scale attacks were needed.[58] Statements from prisoners and reports from agents indicated that the Russians were creating a new position around Grodek and Janow. The Russian force, based on Lesh's 3rd Army, was composed of twenty infantry and two cavalry divisions, organized into eight corps.[59]

General agreement on the course of operations prevailed between Pless, Teschen, and Jaroslau. Mackensen noted on June 15 that since the start of the offensive on June 13, some 35,000 prisoners and 69 machine guns plus an artillery piece had been taken.[60] Although all of the major German and Austro–Hungarian commanders were aware of the Grodek position, none thought it would be difficult to tackle. Both Falkenhayn and Conrad thought that a decisive battle could be fought against the Russians around Magierow.[61] Seeckt believed that the Eleventh Army's offensive disrupted Russian plans to arrest the progress of the offensive in Galicia. As to the prospect of fighting through the Grodek position, Seeckt was confident that it would not stop Mackensen's forces as long as the pursuit followed closely enough to deny the Russians time needed to build up a formidable defensive line. Everyone agreed that Lemberg should be taken and eastern Galicia cleared. Beyond that, Seeckt had a concept of follow-on operations, discussed further on. For now, Lemberg, and the destruction of the Russian forces defending it, remained the objective.[62]

The Russian command was as dispirited as its German and Austro–Hungarian opponents were confident. The Russians had transferred forces from both the northwest front and Odessa to the southwest front. Among the reinforcements sent was the XXIII Corps, a unit that had been destroyed at Tannenberg and was in the process of reforming. These forces were to be concentrated as an attack force to strike the northern flank of any advance on Lemberg, which would continue to be held by Brusilov's 8th Army. Mackensen's attack on June 13, however, did indeed disrupt these plans, as Seeckt had conjectured.[63] Instead, many of these reinforcements got sucked into the vortex of combat in a futile efforts to slow down the Eleventh Army. On June 17, Stavka outlined the extent of the seriousness of the situation. Shortages of both men and ammunition were catastrophic. In the south, Ivanov's available reserves had been used up. The best the Russians could do was to retreat to the Grodek–Janow line and hold the Germans there, a prospect Brusilov thought unlikely.[64]

On June 16 and 17, the "Mackensen Phalanx," as the Russian press called it, moved forward as rapidly as possible over dusty roads. To the south, Böhm-Ermolli's Second Army closed up and took Grodek itself. In the Eleventh Army's sector, François's XXXXI Reserve Corps forged ahead, reaching the Russian positions at the southern edge of the Sosnina Forest on June 17. François, reverting to his old aggressive self, wanted to attack on June 18, but he was ordered by Mackensen to delay for a day until the rest of the army could get up and carefully prepare an attack.[65] Meanwhile, the Austro–Hungarian VI, Guard, XXII Reserve, and X Corps plus Corps Stein moved up toward the new Russian line. Aside from the occasional action against Russian rearguards, no major fighting took place. The Austro–Hungarian Fourth Army was able to get all of its corps across the San and moved northeast. On June 18, Tarnogrod was taken and the Austro–Hungarians moved up to the Tanew River, once again covering the Eleventh Army's left flank.[66]

The Grodek position was a hastily prepared line incorporating the chain of lakes north and south of Grodek and, on the forested areas and rivers connected to lakes between Janow and the Sosnina Forest. The principal river valley in the position, the Wereszyca, was broad and marshy.[67] Artillery was in short supply, and by this time so were rifles and ammunition of all sorts. Soldiers with adequate training were equally scarce.[68]

For the attack on June 19, Mackensen and Seeckt planned to stick with the army's major attack group, the Austro–Hungarian VI, Guard, and XXII Reserve Corps. Despite the poor visibility on June 19, the Eleventh Army spent the day reconnoitering the position. Aerial reconnaissance spotted long columns leaving Lemberg, with concentrations to the northeast. Tactically, close reconnaissance was examining the Russian defenses, especially in the Guard's sector. This was particularly important because artillery commanders did not like the observation positions available to them. It was already standing policy in the Eleventh Army that the fall of every heavy artillery shot needed to be observed in order to maximize the effect. The army headquarters noted that the heavy howitzer shells had a remarkable effect on the Russians.[69]

The target for the attack was well chosen. The objective was to gain control of the railroad between Rava Russka and Lemberg. This would bypass the strongest part of the Grodek position, since the attack zone would be north of the lakes and rivers that constituted the heart of the Russian line. Were the road and better yet, Rava Russka itself seized, the Grodek position would be compromised and Lemberg rendered vulnerable. A successful attack would also split the Russian 3rd and 8th Armies.[70]

In the event, the attack on June 19 was about as effective as Mackensen and Seeckt expected but not as successful as they had hoped. After the customary two-hour bombardment, the infantry assault began at 7 A.M. Given the nature

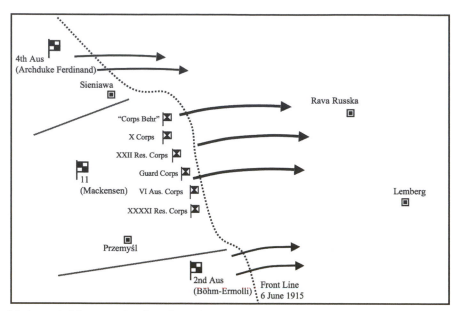

Mackensen's Advance on Lemberg, June 1915.

of the Russian defenses in his sector, François decided to use the 82nd Reserve Division to fix the enemy while the 81st Division would attack and roll up the Russian defenses from the north. As with prior attacks, the initial infantry assault discovered that the artillery preparation had been insufficient. Matters were made worse by the boggy ground over which the 267th, 268th, and 269th Regiments had to attack. The attackers, however, were able to call in another round of heavy artillery fire on revealed Russian strong points. A renewal of the infantry attacks in the evening brought success. The 267th Regiment was able to overrun two Russian positions and take an artillery battery. Similar success was enjoyed by the other regiments, and enemy counterattacks served only to pile up Russian losses. By the end of 19 June, the 81st Division had taken 2,000 prisoners and four guns and had moved its battle front forward past the Sosnina Forest and beyond the swampy ground in the 82nd Reserve Division's sector.[71]

The Austro–Hungarian VI Corps, like the XXXXI Reserve Corps, had to contend with some hilly terrain, and the northern part of the Sosnina Forest was in its sector. The initial attack was halted about 150 paces in front of the Russian trenches. A second round of artillery fire and some hard fighting allowed the Hungarian 39th and Austrian 12th Infantry Divisions to get through the forest and wrest the Horodysko massif from the Russian XXVIII Corps while keeping contact with both the XXXXI Reserve and Guard Corps.[72]

The Guard, with Behr's 119th Infantry Division attached, made the key penetration on June 19. After the initial attack had been stopped, the ability to direct fire from heavy howitzer batteries against specific Russian machine-gun nests made the difference. The key position in the 2nd Guard Division's sector, Hill 345, had been taken by the Alexander and Elisabeth Regiments, with the kaiser himself watching. Although the advance continued beyond Hill 345, Russian counterattacks served to slow the momentum of the attack. By the evening, the 2nd Guard Division was just short of the railroad. Aided by the 2nd Guard Division's success, the 1st Guard Division able to reach its objective. The division's most forward element, the 1st Guard Regiment of Foot, crossed the Rava Russka–Lemberg railroad in the afternoon and then assumed an arc-like line to defend its hold on the rail line. The 119th Division moved up to Magierow.[73]

Like the other corps of the Eleventh Army, Falkenhayn's XXII Reserve Corps required several attacks to crack the Russian position. The 43rd Reserve Division was able to take advantage of the 2nd Guard Division's success and capture Lawrykow. The 44th Reserve Division found the going slow as well, but the commitment of the 107th Infantry Division provided enough assistance to allow the 44th Reserve Division to draw up to the 43rd Reserve Division's left flank.[74]

Emmich's X Corps maintained a generally defensive posture but did make a short advance to take Dubrowka. Some regiments, like the 77th, engaged in some aggressive patrolling and the occasional trench raid, which did net some prisoners. Corps Stein was on the defensive, repulsing a couple of Russian attacks. Likewise the Austro–Hungarian Fourth Army remained on the defensive on its front. The Austro–Hungarian Second Army spent the day trying to attrite the Russian defenses in the Grodek position, making a limited penetration.[75]

The importance of the Eleventh Army's attack on June 19 was highlighted by the presence of Falkenhayn as well as the kaiser and his retinue. After meeting the imperial train in Jaroslau at 7:30 A.M., Mackensen and Seeckt accompanied them to Radymno and from there went forward to observe the Guard's attack. The kaiser then went to visit the Beskiden Corps and Marwitz. Although Marwitz was certain of Lemberg's imminent fall, he was also not sanguine about the prospects for a decisive victory. In the evening after dinner, Seeckt and Falkenhayn discussed the ideas for operations after Lemberg's capture. Satisfied as to the course of operations, Falkenhayn and the kaiser returned to Pless.[76] The following day Falkenhayn and Conrad met at Pless, agreeing to the continuance of operations in Galicia up to the capture of Lemberg and to the subsequent operation, which are discussed in the next chapter.[77]

Although Rava Russka, the Eleventh Army's target, had not been reached on June 19, both Mackensen and Seeckt realized that the results of the attack presented a major opportunity. It was clear by the evening of June 19 that the Russian front facing Mackensen's forces was splitting. The seizure of Rava Russka would force Lesh's Russian 3rd Army to continue retreating in a northerly direction while the neighboring 8th Army would have to retreat east. In addition, aerial reconnaissance showed the Russians to be in movement. Thus Mackensen and Seeckt ordered a renewal of the advance to both widen and strengthen the

Eleventh Army's hold on the railroad between Rava Russka and Zolkiew, a distance of about 25 miles.[78]

The course of June 20 confirmed the impression that the Russians were in headlong retreat. The Austro–Hungarian Second Army was able to advance on a broad front, reaching the western side of Lemberg's ring of fortifications. The Eleventh Army also advanced, especially with the XXXXI Reserve and X Corps, to achieve the desired widening of the front. François, with the Bavarian 11th Infantry Division attached to his corps, aimed at Glinsko and was given Zolkiew as his objective. Hampered more by bad roads than anything, the XXXXI Reserve Corps moved up to a new Russian position just west of Glinsko, which François decided he would attack the next day.[79]

In the Guard's sector, the 1st Guard Division fought off a Russian attempt to dislodge the 1st Guard Regiment's hold on the railroad. Meanwhile, the 2nd Guard Division was able to cross the railroad and relieve the 1st Guard Division's left flank. By the evening of June 20, Plettenberg's hold on the railroad had been strengthened and over 1,600 prisoners taken.[80] The Guard's neighbors on each side were able to draw even with its flanks. Arz's Austro–Hungarian VI Corps was able to come up on the Guard's right, taking about 900 prisoners in the process. The XXII Reserve Corps also made a short advance, having to contend only with cavalry screens. To Falkenhayn's left, Emmich's X Corps moved up and was able to establish that the Russians had evacuated Rava Russka. Corps Stein and the Austro–Hungarian Fourth Army remained relatively stationary.[81]

Only limited offensive operations were undertaken on June 21. Under a light rain, the XXXXI Reserve Corps found the going slow against the Russian position at Glinsko. Thanks to some help from the Bavarians and the gallantry of Private Kukuk, a flag bearer from the 267th Regiment, the Russian position was taken. The Austro–Hungarian VI Corps also made a short advance. The Beskiden Corps was able to advance across the Lemberg–Rava Russka railroad toward Kulikow, possession of which would threaten Lemberg from the north.[82]

On the Russian side, the breaching of the Grodek line made holding Lemberg problematic. Brusilov found the mood on the Southwest Front despondent. Stavka, fearful of encirclement, thus decided to evacuate Lemberg and abandon Galicia. Brusilov's 8th Army retreated east, seeking safety behind the lower reaches of the Bug River. Lesh's 3rd Army retreated north from Rava Russka. At midnight of June 25, in fact, operational control of the 3rd Army passed from Ivanov's Southwest Front to General Mikhail V. Alexeyev's Northwest Front.[83]

On June 22, 1915, Mackensen and Seeckt won the prize of the campaign. The Austro–Hungarian XIX Corps was able to take two of Lemberg's western forts and then, with the IV Corps, press into the city and beyond. Böhm-Ermolli and his staff entered the city late in the afternoon. The rest of the Austro–Hungarian Second Army fanned out on a line east of Lemberg. The next day a parade was held as Archduke Friedrich arrived from Teschen.[84] Two of the Eleventh Army's corps, François's XXXXI Reserve Corps and Arz's Austro–

Hungarian VI Corps, moved on past Zolkiew and up to Turynka, respectively. In a final organizational touch, Corps Stein was disbanded on June 23. The campaign in Galicia was over.[85]

Between May 2 and June 22, 1915, the German Eleventh and Austro–Hungarian Third, Fourth, and Second Armies had advanced about 186 miles. The real estate, however, came with a price. During the campaign, the Eleventh Army suffered some 87,000 casualties, including 12,000 dead. Most of the latter were from combat; among them were the guardsmen Schallert and Groeben, both of whom were killed in May at Jaroslau. Others, such as Major Brauer, the commandant of François's headquarters, died of disease. Among the wounded were men and officers, such as Lieutenant von Stutterheim of the Alexander Regiment, who had been wounded several times in the course of the campaign.[86] These losses were not evenly spread over the units of the Eleventh Army. The XXXXI Reserve Corps and the Guard, for example, had taken heavy losses during the campaign, and their infantry units were often down to half or less of authorized strength. On the other hand, Kneussl's Bavarians, while they had fought quite often in May, saw very little action after Przemysl's capture.[87]

Russian losses in the campaign can be described only as immense. The forces facing Mackensen's armies lost perhaps as many as 250,000 men as prisoners alone, not counting dead and wounded, which also ran into the hundreds of thousands. Matters were not helped by the practice of constant counterattacks, which served only to pile up losses. In addition, 224 artillery pieces, hundreds more machine guns, and hundreds of thousands of rifles were lost, all items that were not easily replaced. Russian morale was also shattered. François noted that the prisoners taken in the Grodek line seemed quite content with the prospect of captivity. Certainly in the south, Russian offensive military power had been neutralized for some time to come.[88]

The capture of Lemberg had a number of consequences. Austro–Hungarian troops entered first Przemysl and then Lemberg to scenes of "indescribable joy" among the population, and bringing to an end the Russian occupation of Galicia. Although the Russians had practiced a "scorched earth" policy during their retreat across Galicia, the destruction inflicted on Austro–Hungarian oil facilities involved, for the most part, easily replaceable wooden derricks. Refineries were relatively undamaged, as were oil tanks containing 480,000 tons of oil, although another 350,000 tons were destroyed.[89]

In Austria–Hungary, after the failures of the winter of 1914–1915 and the entry of Italy into the war, Mackensen's victories in May and June provided a major morale boost for both Vienna and Teschen. When Archduke Friedrich, Conrad, and their entourage left Teschen for Lemberg on June 23, they were greeted with warm ovations from the local population, which had gathered along the road to the train station. For Conrad, the recapture of Lemberg was bittersweet, in that he was able to make a trip to Rava Russka and visit the grave of his son Herbert, who had been killed there the previous September.[90]

Spirits were high in Pless as well. The outcome of the campaign clearly strengthened Falkenhayn's position. The capture of Przemysl and then Lemberg, along with the associated losses inflicted on the Russians, had vindicated Falkenhayn's judgment, first in creating the Eleventh Army and then reinforcing it in June.[91] Mackensen and Seeckt were certainly the men of the hour. At dinner on June 22, 1915, amid the flowing champagne, the kaiser announced that Mackensen was being promoted to Generalfeldmarschall and Seeckt to Generalmajor. Seeckt somewhat cynically noted in a letter to his wife that these were precisely the same honors that were bestowed on Hindenburg and Ludendorff after Tannenberg, suggesting that Falkenhayn was possibly setting up the Mackensen–Seeckt team as a counterweight to Ober Ost. At Ober Ost, aside from the usual complaining by the usual suspects, even Ludendorff was writing of the Austro–Hungarian Army as being "invigorated" by the course of operations in Galicia.[92]

Strategically, the campaign was only partly successful. As noted previously, Italy was not dissuaded from entering the war, while the removal of the Russian presence from the Carpathians and Galicia had a clear deterrent effect on Romania. Finally, Turkey may also have benefited from the campaign. The Russians had been assembling a large force, about 25 divisions, in the Odessa region. With the Turkish forces fully engaged in Gallipoli, Palestine, Mesopotamia, and the Caucasus, a Russian descent on the Black Sea coast near Constantinople could have caused serious problems. Much of this force, however, was sucked into the vortex created by Mackensen's offensive.[93]

In his memoirs, Hindenburg likened Mackensen's offensive to an avalanche, a landslide that starts small but grows to a size that destroys anything in its path.[94] Although a colorful description, it was not quite true. The avalanche stopped twice after the capture of Przemysl. The first time was before the attack on June 13 to break the position on the Wisznia. Four days later, Mackensen's armies halted before the Grodek position, taking a day to prepare before resuming the offensive. In both cases the sectors for each attack were carefully chosen, so that Mackensen's trump card, his heavy artillery, would be effective in relatively narrow areas. This certainly reflected the lessons gained from prior experiences against the Russians. The improved artillery ammunition situation led to the lengthening of the time allotted for artillery preparation. The initial bombardment on May 2 lasted for four hours. The scarcity of ammunition by mid-May was illustrated by limiting the artillery preparation for the attack on May 15 to a mere 90 minutes. The situation had improved by late May and then into June, so that the time for artillery preparation was lengthened to two hours.[95]

Tactically, Mackensen and Seeckt insisted that the respective corps restrict their actions to their sectors. Several times during the campaign, corps commanders sought to launch operations that would involve either units passing over corps boundaries or cooperating in joint attacks. Each time, Mackensen and Seeckt scotched the idea. This was also reflective of the improvement in communications equipment available to the Germany Army in both quantity and mobility since the start of the war in 1914.[96]

Once the defensive positions had been broken, all corps were given relatively distant objectives. Although François complained that the objectives were too far away, the army orders outlining them also noted that these were objectives to be achieved if possible. The underlying idea was to deny the Russians time to construct new defensive positions with any depth. This policy paid particular dividends in regard to the Grodek position. Given only a day to build, in the event the Grodek line proved rather brittle, breaking in only one day, with the Guard driving a deep wedge into the Russian positions.[97]

For the Russians, the campaign in Galicia should have demonstrated the futility of their infantry tactics. Their penchant for immediate counterattack, often heedless of circumstances and in thick waves, proved an excellent way for the Germans to maximize the effectiveness of their precious artillery ammunition and machine guns. The cavalry was able to screen the retreats well, although the scarcity and ineffectiveness of German cavalry was mitigated by aerial reconnaissance.[98]

Operationally, Mackensen and Seeckt had achieved their objective, namely splitting the Russian forces in Galicia. By the end of June 1915, Ivanov's southwest front had been reduced to the Russian 8th, 9th, and 11th Armies. With the 3rd Army retreating in shambles to the north, new opportunities and choices presented themselves to Falkenhayn, Conrad, Mackensen, and Seeckt. The campaign was now going to take a turn in a different direction, but which?

Chapter 7

Decisions and Preparations: June 25–July 13, 1915

The goal of operation would be to have the Second and Eleventh Armies advance between the Bug and Vistula against the line Brest Litovsk–Warsaw, while the Fourth Army advances on both sides of the Vistula. Thus a decision would be brought about against the Russian west and northwest fronts.
—Hans von Seeckt, June 15, 1915[1]

A brilliant idea! But? . . . .
—Erich von Falkenhayn, June 16, 1915[2]

Generalfeldmarschall von Mackensen attacks between the Vistula and the Bug with the Fourth, Eleventh, and Bug Armies.
—AOK–OHL Directive, July 11, 1915[3]

The recovery of most of Galicia, culminating in the recapture of Lemberg, following the retaking of Przemysl, had solved a major problem. Falkenhayn put it very simply when he said that "the threat to Hungary had been completely removed."[4] The lull in operations after Lemberg's fall provided a convenient occasion for the Central Powers to reconsider their strategic options. The situation demanded no less.

In the west, a British attack at Ypres on June 15, coming after the end of the last major German attack there in late May, initiated another round of bloody fighting. Some, such as German Chancellor Theobald von Bethmann-Hollweg, thought that matters on the western front had reached a crisis point. Falkenhayn, phlegmatic as ever, did not think this was the case, and events proved him right. Nonetheless one almost had to expect that there would be renewed

Anglo-French offensives, given the now known scale of German commitment to the eastern front, and Russian calls for help as disaster unfolded. Although the situation in the west had quieted down, Falkenhayn still regarded the number of reserve formations available on the western front as low enough that OHL ordered Mackensen to send four divisions there.[5]

On the new Italian front, the Austro–Hungarians profited from Italian lassitude. Although Italy had started its mobilization on May 22, just one day prior to the Salandra government's declaration of war on Austria–Hungary, General Luigi Cadorna, the Italian commander, wasted a month, much to Conrad's relief. The Italian armies tentatively advanced across the border in late May, but it was not until June 21 that Cadorna issued orders for an offensive aimed at Gorizia and Trieste. The Italian Second and Third Armies then attacked the main Austro–Hungarian defensive line in the Carnic Alps east of the Isonzo River.[6]

Given the precious gift of a month by Cadorna, Boroević made the most of it, cobbling together a defensive line with a force of eight divisions. The combination Boroević's inspiring leadership, sheer toughness on the part of the outnumbered Austro–Hungarian Fifth Army, plus inexperience and poor tactics on the part of the Italians brought Cadorna's first offensive on the Isonzo to a bloody halt by July 7, 1915.[7]

Boroević's dauntless defense of the Isonzo front averted what could have been a dangerous situation, but the Italian front had now become a strategic concern for Falkenhayn and a strategic obsession for Conrad. Although the successful creation of the Isonzo front kept Conrad from having to resort to guerrilla warfare, a defensive posture against "perfidious Italy" did not suit him. Throughout May and June, Conrad called for an offensive against Italy with an insistence that was increasingly irksome to Falkenhayn, especially as Conrad's proposed strike force of at least 20 divisions would include several German units.[8]

From Falkenhayn's perspective, sending more than the barest minimum of German troops to the Italian border would be a useless diversion, wasting units that were badly needed elsewhere. Matters were made a bit more complicated by the fact that Italy had not declared war on Germany, only on Austria–Hungary. In his memoirs, Falkenhayn claimed that it "would have been very ill-advised to break off voluntarily the communications with the outside world, which were maintained through the medium of Italy."[9] That Falkenhayn was being less than truthful was shown by the fact that Germany did sever both political and economic ties with Italy, in effect breaking of communications voluntarily. The hope was that such measure by themselves would be sufficient to force Italy to rapidly abandon its resort to arms.[10]

Unlike Ludendorff, who was positive that Italy could not sustain its war effort after a defeat, Falkenhayn had to assume that Italy's conflict with Austria–Hungary would last for some time. In addition, given his strategic priorities, that would require the commitment of forces elsewhere, Falkenhayn sought to minimize the scale of the commitment to the Italian front, for both Germany and Austria–Hungary. In regard to the latter, the only thing he could and did do was to urge Conrad to adopt a defensive posture, aided by the excellent terrain available to the Austro–Hungarians. Italy's failure to declare war on Germany gave Falkenhayn the excuse to make a minimal response to Conrad's calls for help. Whereas Conrad had asked for several German divisions, Falkenhayn sent only one, and under no circumstances was it to enter Italian territory.[11]

With the Italian front now set on the back burner, Falkenhayn considered the next concern on his strategic priority list, namely Serbia. The matter of Serbia was inevitably connected with that of Turkey. By late June 1915 the Turkish forces in Gallipoli had stopped the British attempt to force the Dardanelles and take Constantinople. Although British progress up the Tigris River toward Baghdad was a potential problem, the Turks were holding their ground, both in Palestine against the British and in the Caucasus against the Russians.

Nevertheless, Turkey was still isolated, with no direct overland route between Berlin and Constantinople. This was highlighted by messages from the leading German military advisor at Gallipoli, Generalleutnant Otto Liman von Sanders, speaking to the critical ammunition situation of the Turkish forces there.[12] The only direct route by rail to Turkey lay through Serbia. An offensive against Serbia would be easier to conduct with Bulgarian participation. Bulgaria and Serbia had been allies in the First Balkan War, but then, in the Second Balkan War, they turned on each other. Bulgaria, like every other country in the Balkans, entertained notions of a "greater" stature, meaning territorial expansion. The territory that Bulgaria claimed as its own was Macedonia, at that time more a "geographical notion" (to use the phrase of the Austrian Prime Minister Clemens von Metternich) than a country, which was divided between Serbia and Greece.

Like those of other countries that had stayed out of the war in 1914, Bulgaria's government had competing factions, both susceptible to the blandishments that each side was willing to dangle before it. Historically, Bulgaria's government had always manifested a strong streak of Russophilia, owing to Russia's part in the creation of an independent Bulgaria after the Russo-Turkish War of 1877–1878. This was most clearly manifested in person of Radko-Dmitriev's leaving Bulgaria for the Russian Army.

Both sides courted Bulgaria with promises of the same territory. Ultimately, however, only the Central Powers were in a position to make the promises stick. Mackensen's victories, effectively removing the Russian presence from Galicia, were a severe setback for the pro-Russian faction in the government. The upswing in the fortunes of the Central Powers, fears of Serbian expansionism, plus the sheer desire for revenge would ultimately swing King Ferdinand's government to the side of Germany and Austria–Hungary.[13]

Even before Italy's entry, Falkenhayn was quite certain that Serbia could be dealt with before the Italians could pose a really serious problem, even if they did intervene. The danger of a Serbian offensive was regarded as minimal by Falkenhayn, given Serbia's need to keep substantial forces on its borders with both Romania and especially Bulgaria, plus the high water level of the defended rivers the Serbs would have to cross.[14] In the actual event, with Italy contained and Romania quieted by events in Galicia, and realizing that Serbia could not be successfully invaded without German and Bulgarian forces, Falkenhayn had the leverage he needed to get his way. Serbia would be next, after the conclusion of operations against Russia.[15]

With the answers to broader, long-term questions taking shape, the major issue that had to be resolved was what to do in regard to the situation in Russia. The offensive operations conducted in May and June had also provided a range of choices for Germany and Austria–Hungary. By late June 1915, the Russians were clearly on the run. The question now was whether Russia could be driven to a state where the government of Nicholas II would be willing to conclude a separate peace.

The notion of pursuing operations against a Russia isolated from its allies to force it from the war appealed to both Conrad and Falkenhayn for obvious reasons. For Conrad, a major undertaking against Italy remained at the top of his agenda. The forces for that, however, had to be freed up from somewhere, and the best place would be the eastern front if Russia could be put out of the war. Aside from dealing with Italy, forces freed up from the Russian front could also be employed in furtherance of Austria–Hungary's aims in the Balkans.[16]

Given his other strategic concerns, especially in the west, Falkenhayn was also interested in driving Russia from the war. At the very least, a shortening of the line on the eastern front, especially in Galicia, could free up forces for employment against Serbia and France. That at least was his thinking in mid-May, when it looked as though the San and Przemysl would mark the limit of Mackensen's advance.[17]

The Mackensen "avalanche" (as Hindenburg put it) and the recapture of Lemberg, however, altered Falkenhayn's thinking. Others in OHL, such as Groener, thought that the withdrawal of the XXXXI Reserve Corps (81st and 82nd Reserve Divisions), the Bavarian 8th Reserve Division, and the 56th Infantry Division on June 20 was premature, given the state of affairs in Galicia. Likewise, Wild thought it foolish to let go when they had the Russians "by the throat."[18] Thus the mood at Pless was to strike while the iron was hot.

The offensive had dramatically changed the shape of the front line in the east. In May 1915, the front started up on the Baltic coast and then generally followed the Russo-German border except for a shallow penetration into Lithuania. The line then curved west, again running along the prewar border, until just south of Tannenberg, when the line turned south into Russian Poland, running anywhere from 20 to 100 miles east of the prewar border. Upon entering Austro–Hungarian territory, the line curved gently to the southeast until it reached neutral Romania's border near Czernowitz.

By the end of June 1915, the southern part of the line had changed considerably. The advance of Mackensen's armies had wiped out the line that had curved so gradually to the southeast. The line east of Lodz now ran more to the east until it reached the Bug River, where it turned sharply south. A large Russian salient, encompassing the remaining part of Poland still under Tsarist control, bulged away to the west.

The campaign in Galicia had also drastically altered the Russian order of battle. In May 1915, Ivanov's southwest front in Galicia had under its control the Russian 3rd, 8th, 9th, and 11th Armies, plus a large force assembling at Odessa. Alexeyev's northwest front covered the rest of the front, with the Russian 1st, 2nd, 4th, 5th, 10th, and 12th Armies. By the end of June 1915, the southwest front had been severely mauled. The force at Odessa had dissipated as its divisions were sucked into the Galician maelstrom. The armies under Ivanov's command were reduced to the 8th, 9th, and 11th. Lesh's battered 3rd Army, forced to retreat northeast from Lemberg, was incorporated into Alexeyev's Northwest Front.[19]

The idea for having Mackensen's forces turn north apparently originated with Seeckt. On June 13, 1915, Falkenhayn wrote to Conrad of the urgent need to reinforce the Süd Army to facilitate the Eleventh Army's drive to the east, and Conrad still thought that a decisive action could be fought west of Lemberg.[20] Seeckt, however, was thinking in much bigger terms. On June 15, 1915, the German Eleventh Army chief of staff wrote a lengthy estimate of the situation. After dealing with prospects for the impending operations west of Lemberg and the capture of the city, Seeckt then dealt with the next phase of operations.

Seeckt regarded the prospect of encircling Russian forces in the immediate vicinity of Lemberg as unlikely, as the Russians would be able to evade them. Once Lemberg and its immediate environs had been secured, Seeckt regarded the current mission of the Eleventh Army as accomplished. Any further advances east to recover the remaining sliver of eastern Galicia still in Russian hands could be undertaken by the Austro–Hungarian Seventh Army and the Süd Army.

With the eastern advance of the Eleventh Army concluded, Seeckt now proposed that the Eleventh Army as well as the Austro–Hungarian Second and Fourth Armies would turn north. The prospective advance would use the land bridge bordered by the Bug River to the east and the Vistula River to the west. The armies would advance on Lublin and Cholm. The ultimate objective of the offensive would be Brest–Litovsk, one of the major centers of the Russian rail network in Poland. "Thus," concluded Seeckt, "a decision would be brought about against the Russian West and Northwest Front."[21]

Falkenhayn's marginalia, quoted at the beginning of this chapter, indicate at least a modicum of skepticism. Seeckt, however, got another chance to press his case when the Kaiser, Falkenhayn, and the whole OHL entourage came for a visit to the Eleventh Army on June 19. Seeckt and Falkenhayn met that night, and Seeckt once again pitched his concept. A continuation of the advance in Galicia in an easterly direction would yield no decisive result. A move north against the Russian armies in Poland had a much greater chance of producing the desired decision. Mackensen was also supportive of Seeckt's thinking.[22]

Immediately upon his return to Pless, Falkenhayn met with Conrad to discuss Seeckt's concept. Conrad agreed, although more details were required. Seeckt provided these when he briefed both Falkenhayn and Conrad at Eleventh Army headquarters in Jaroslau on June 24.[23] By late June, it was fairly clear that both Falkenhayn and Conrad were in agreement. The two general staff chiefs met again at Pless on June 28 to finalize their understanding for Mackensen's next offensive and to set details for the subsidiary operations that would accompany the offensive against Brest–Litovsk.[24] While Conrad was daily becoming ever more painfully aware that it was the Germans who were calling the shots, the idea of turning north had a considerable appeal. Since Falkenhayn was implacably opposed to any major move against Italy in the near term, making the attempt to wrap up the Russian front was, for Conrad, the next best thing. In addition, the evolving plan for the offensive north was very much reminiscent of the long-discussed prewar concept of the joint German and Austro–Hungarian offensive to cut off Russian Poland.[25]

Once the Austro–Hungarians were on board for the turn north, Falkenhayn had two other ducks to line up, namely the kaiser and Ober Ost. The first was relatively easy. Wilhelm II's adjutant, the 74-year-old Generaloberst Hans von Plessen, noted on June 28, 1915, that the kaiser agreed with the idea of continuing the offensive in Galicia in a northerly direction.[26]

Ober Ost and its willingness to participate in the offensive and how it would do so was another question. When Seeckt put forward his idea on June 15, 1915, he was silent as to what the forces under Hindenburg's control would do to support Mackensen's offensive. One could easily infer, however, that Ober Ost was to launch some sort of action to fix those Russian forces in Poland that were to the west and north of Mackensen's oncoming offensive.[27]

Ober Ost did indeed have ideas for the conduct of operations, and they differed rather substantially from Falkenhayn's. Ober Ost was thinking in terms of an operation that would lead to a penetration deep into the Russian rear. This would be accomplished by an offensive by the German Tenth Army, supported by the recently formed Nieman Army, to take Kovno and then press on to Vilna, thus severing a major Russian line of communications to Poland. The capture of Vilna would also put the Germans within striking distance of Minsk. That, combined with the seizure of the Brest–Litovsk rail hub, would in theory cut off all the Russian armies of the Northwest Front fighting in Poland. To put some meat on the bones of this concept, Ober Ost shifted the 41st Infantry, 76th Reserve, and 4th Cavalry Divisions from the German Eighth Army to the Nieman Army.[28]

Falkenhayn preferred a much less audacious solution. While Mackensen attacked from the south with the Austro–Hungarian Fourth and the German Eleventh Armies, two subsidiary attacks would be launched. One would be launched by Army Group Gallwitz, commanded by General der Artillerie Max von Gallwitz, against the Russian 1st and 12th Armies holding the lower reaches of the Narew River, generally northeast of Warsaw.[29] A second subsidiary attack would be launched by Army Detachment Woyrsch, and the Austro–Hungarian First Army would cross the Vistula River between Warsaw and Ivangorod. Meanwhile the German Ninth Army, commanded by Generalfeldmarschall Prince Leopold of Bavaria, would advance directly on Warsaw from the west.[30] This set of attacks would support Mackensen more directly and were more feasible logistically.

To hash out these issues, a meeting was convened at Posen on July 2, 1915. The principal attendees were Falkenhayn, Conrad, Hindenburg, Ludendorff, and the kaiser. Neither Mackensen nor Seeckt was present, but Falkenhayn had conferred with them the day before. Hindenburg and Ludendorff laid out their concept of operations. The operation against Kovno and Vilna offered, in their opinion, the greatest possible result; taking Kovno would not require an inordinate amount of time. An offensive on the Narew, owing to the swampy terrain and tough Russian defenses, would yield too little result for too much effort. In addition, the offensive would be pressing the Russians in a general direction from west to east, the kind of pursuit, as Hindenburg argued, that is more tiring to the pursuer than those being pursued.[31]

In response, Falkenhayn noted the disappointing results when Ober Ost attempted another large-scale encirclement in February 1915, culminating in the tactically successful but operationally inconclusive second battle of the Masurian Lakes. The Russians were sufficiently acquainted with attempted envelopment operations against them to evade this one, aided by the Russian railroad network. Although it was daring, the proposed Kovno operation was logistically difficult to support. The proposed offensive by OHL would serve to erode the Russian armies to the point where there might be a chance for a separate peace.[32]

Since Falkenhayn had already gotten the kaiser's support, and given that Falkenhayn was in high standing with him, it was a forgone conclusion that the kaiser would side with Falkenhayn. In addition, the kaiser was probably more than happy to give Hindenburg some payback after his resignation threat over the matter of Ludendorff's prospective posting to the Süd Army. The Posen conference represented Falkenhayn's most significant victory over his enemies at Ober Ost. The reaction at Ober Ost was predictably angry. Hoffmann noted that Ludendorff in particular returned from Posen to Ober Ost headquarters at Lötzen in a very "savage" mood.[33]

In actuality, Falkenhayn's ideas were more attuned to the realities of the situation than those of Ober Ost. Although Hoffmann and Ludendorff both noted that Kovno fell quickly in August, by the that time the Russians were in retreat along that entire sector of the front. The logistics of the situation were also problematic from the standpoint of sustaining the offensive. A mere wedge made by elements of the Tenth and Nieman Armies, François noted, would require far more troops to secure the sides of the salient against Russian attempts to cut it off.[34] Sustaining the German effort meant advancing a single rail line against a barrier created by the differences between the German and Russian rail gauges. Although Hoffmann argued that, while the Russians normally demolished everything in the course of their retreat, this practice did not slow down the German advance. German officers who were familiar with railroad matters, however, were far more cognizant of the difficulty in advancing railroads, a time-consuming and manpower-intensive activity. In the case of Kovno, even Ludendorff noted that the attack was facilitated by the fact that the railroad had been advanced sufficiently to improve the supply situation, particularly the delivery of heavy artillery ammunition. Finally, François noted that even if Kovno were taken quickly, making the 162-mile leap via Vilna to Minsk would have taken much too long to close the trap on the Russian armies. The Russians had shown sufficient operational dexterity to be able to evade such an attempted envelopment.[35]

In his book, François suggests a third alternative: an offensive by the German Eighth Army aimed at Bialystok and Grodno. Once those were taken, the advance would press on a further 70 miles or so to Brest–Litovsk, to meet Mackensen's oncoming forces from the south. The terrain, François argued, was more favorable than that of the more northern route proposed by Ludendorff.[36] The biggest drawback to François's idea was the lack of railroads to support the advance. The only rail line that ran northwest from Bialystok had only a single track, the gauge of which would have to be altered as well. In addition, the terrain on both sides of Bialystok was swampy.

Falkenhayn's concept was based more on the recent successes scored by Mackensen. Thorough preparation and careful execution had not produced the spectacular encirclement but rather major advances and very large numbers of prisoners, let alone dead and wounded Russians. The more conservative approach would also be more manageable logistically. Control of Warsaw would give access to several rail lines, although the gauge barrier, having to convert the broad-gauge Russian tracks to the narrower European gauge, would continue to present problems. Finally, the offensive proposed by Falkenhayn would have the advantage of flattening out the Russian front, thus freeing up troops for use elsewhere.[37]

Now that the broad outlines of the next phase of German operations had been decided upon, preparations could go forward. In the case of the forces north of Lemberg, preparation involved overcoming several major challenges. The first of these was logistical. Mackensen's forces still depended on the railroad for supply. On June 26, the railroads for his armies crossed the San, the railheads respectively reaching Mosciska (east of Przemysl) and Lubaczow (east of Jaroslau). The main railroad line to Lemberg, which was double-tracked, would not be reopened by the Austro–Hungarians until late July. The Germans and Austro–Hungarians were relatively fortunate, from a logistical standpoint, that Mackensen's operations in May and June were conducted almost entirely on Austro–Hungarian territory, so that the troops tasked with repairing the railroads did not have to contend with a gauge barrier. Even when repaired, however, the railroads still had a limited capacity. The lines that ran north from Lemberg were all single-track. These circumstances served to make the assembling of sufficient troops, equipment, and ammunition a slow and laborious process.[38]

The next challenge involved having to undertake several supporting operations to cover Mackensen's flanks. These were the attacks that Conrad and Falkenhayn had agreed upon at their meeting of June 28 in Pless.[39] Southeast of Lemberg, Linsingen's German Süd Army fought its way forward across the Dniestr River on June 30 and then stopped briefly to assess its gains and losses before moving on its next objective, the Gnila Lipa River. To Linsingen's left, Böhm-Ermolli's Austro–Hungarian Second Army tried to keep abreast of the Süd Army but fell a bit short.[40] The two armies inched forward, however, and by July 12 the Süd Army had reached the Zlota Lipa and the Austro–Hungarian Second Army attained the Zlota Lipa and the lower Bug River.[41] The line created by the Austro–Hungarian Second Army and the German Süd Army served to cover both Pflanzer-Baltin's Austro–Hungarian Seventh Army's left flank and Mackensen's right and rear.

Meanwhile, Pulhallo's Austro–Hungarian First Army, engaged in local combat around Tarlow, occupied a small sector between Army Detachment Woyrsch and the Austro–Hungarian Fourth Army at the end of June. In early July, the First Army was withdrawn and sideslipped forward via Lemberg across the rear areas of the Austro–Hungarian Fourth and German Eleventh Armies to take position on the left flank of the Austro–Hungarian Second Army. The area vacated by the First Army was taken over by Woyrsch.[42]

The purpose of these operations was to facilitate the redeployment of Mackensen's Eleventh Army. After the fall of Lemberg and Rava Russka, the German Eleventh Army was oriented to the northeast. The next phase of the offensive required the Eleventh Army to reorient itself to the north. This would be accomplished by a series of attacks and marches in a roughly northwesterly direction until the army's right flank rested on the Bug River and its front faced north. These tasks did not require much combat over the last full week of June. The marches, however, were strenuous. The troops also had to contend with a different environment. In the northern edge of the Carpathians, the terrain was hilly and the roads were mere forest trails but the weather was excellent. Now the summer was at its hottest; the terrain was relatively flat, but with swampy forests in some areas. The roads were very sandy, becoming bottomless ruts of mud after a heavy rain.[43]

On June 28 and 29, the Eleventh Army's troops crossed the border into Russian Poland with loud cheers. Aside from some weak rearguards, Russian resistance was nonexistent. Even the normally ubiquitous Cossacks were absent.

To Mackensen's left, the Austro–Hungarian Fourth Army crossed the Tanew River and advanced into the area east of Vistula River, extend toward the Wieprz, where its right flank met the X Corps, Mackensen's left flank unit.[44] Somewhat problematic was the lengthening right flank of the Eleventh Army along the Bug River. This caused OHL and Mackensen to recall the XXXXI Reserve Corps, which was heading toward Jaroslau for transport to the west. Instead, only François would go back to the west, with an appointment as commander of the VII Corps.[45]

Russian activity now confirmed worries about the Eleventh Army's right flank. On July 1, the Eleventh Army encountered a new Russian position on both sides of the Wieprz River. In fact, the Russians had indeed retreated during the last week of June to a much shorter and straighter line on the southern side of the Russian salient in Poland. The Augusta Regiment had a hard fight at Sitno, taking the village at a cost of 18 dead and 57 wounded. The next day the Russians launched a major counterattack on Mackensen's ever-lengthening right flank on the Bug River. Although the attack was beaten off by elements of the Guard, both the Eleventh Army and OHL reached the conclusion that the Russians had concentrated major forces against Mackensen. This was confirmed when at least four new enemy units—the Russian Imperial Guard, XXXI, II Siberian, and VI Siberian Corps—were identified, along with the headquarters of General Vladimir Gorbatovski's Russian 13th Army. In addition, measures had to be taken to cover the Eleventh Army's right flank.[46]

OHL decided to reorganize the forces in Mackensen's area. Since the stretch of the Bug River north of Pulhallo's Austro–Hungarian First Army was the most critical sector in regard to Mackensen's right flank, a new army-level organization was to be created that would be subject to Mackensen's orders. Given the recent practice of designating armies in geographic terms, such as the Nieman Army, the new force was named the Bug Army. Based on recommendations from Mackensen and Seeckt, the Bug Army was composed of the Beskiden Corps, transferred from the Austro–Hungarian Second Army as well as the Austro–Hungarian XXIV Corps headquarters, headed by General der Infanterie Friedrich von Gerok. Although an Austro–Hungarian headquarters, the corps would have two German divisions—the 107th Infantry and the Bavarian 11th Infantry—under its command. The Bug Army's order of battle was rounded out by the XXXXI Reserve Corps, now commanded by Winckler, who was moved over from the 2nd Guard Division to replace the departed François. Winckler's old command was now taken over by Generalleutnant Walter Freiherr von Lüttwitz.[47] Command of the Bug Army was entrusted to Linsingen, transferred from his position as commander of the Süd Army. To replace Linsingen, Falkenhayn picked General der Infanterie Felix Graf von Bothmer, the Süd Army's senior corps commander.[48]

In addition to the creation of the Bug Army and repositioning of the Austro–Hungarian First Army, Falkenhayn also wanted operational unity of command for the southern end of the coming offensive. Thus far, during the opening phase of the offensive, Mackensen had exercised control over the Eleventh Army and elements of the Austro–Hungarian Third and Fourth Armies. During the advance on Lemberg, Mackensen gave orders to the Austro–Hungarian Second and Fourth Armies. Falkenhayn now wanted Mackensen to have operational control over the German Eleventh and Bug Armies as well as the Austro–Hungarian First and Fourth Armies.[49]

Conrad agreed with Falkenhayn's proposed order of battle for the Bug Army. For reasons that remain unclear, however, he opposed the choice of Linsingen to command the army. Conrad also said he would prefer that neither the Austro–Hungarian VI Corps nor the Hungarian 11th Cavalry Division be assigned to the Bug Army. Finally, Conrad pushed another pet idea: that should the offensive in the south be resumed, the Austro–Hungarian Seventh and German Süd Armies would be subordinated to Pflanzer-Baltin.[50]

Falkenhayn's response might be described succinctly as curt sarcasm. He started off by telling Conrad in essence that the matter of who is selected to command a German army was none of his business. Falkenhayn wrote that he had not sought Conrad's agreement to Linsingen's new appointment but merely informed him of it as part of the operational decision to weaken the Süd Army in order to reinforce Mackensen. In regard to Linsingen, Falkenhayn pointed out that Linsingen had compiled a fine record and that he had received the warmest congratulations and thanks from both AOK and OHL for his victories on the Dniestr and the Gnila Lipa.

Although Falkenhayn thought it unlikely that either Arz's Austro–Hungarian VI Corps or the Hungarian 11th Cavalry Division would be subsumed into the Bug Army, they would be if the situation demanded it. Falkenhayn then said he was "grateful" to be informed of Conrad's opposition to subordinating the Austro–Hungarian First Army to Mackensen, because Falkenhayn had regarded the correctness of such a command relationship as "self evident." Finally, after a few words extolling Bothmer's capabilities, Falkenhayn told Conrad that he considered the idea of subordinating the Süd Army to Pflanzer-Baltin to be "unnecessary."[51] In the end, once again Falkenhayn got his way; Linsingen and Bothmer assumed the positions for which they had been selected. For his part, Conrad enlisted both Archduke Friedrich and even the Austro–Hungarian Foreign Ministry in keeping the Austro–Hungarian VI Corps and 11th Cavalry Division directly under Mackensen, and apparently he got his way on that issue.[52]

On the heels of this testy exchange came another embarrassment for Conrad. During the night of July 6–7, the Russian XXV Corps, part of General Alexei Evert's Russian 4th Army, attacked the Austro–Hungarian X Corps, part of the Austro–Hungarian Fourth Army, at Krasnik. The left flank of the X Corps was driven back by the Russian 3rd Grenadier Division. Evert then sent his VI Siberian Corps into action. By the afternoon of July 7, the Austro–Hungarian

VIII, X, and XIV Corps had been driven back over a mile. Although Archduke Joseph Ferdinand was able to bring the stampede to a halt after a day, he did so by using all of his available reserves.[53]

This latest Austro–Hungarian setback proved more embarrassing than serious. The Krasnik affair prompted the usual complaints from the OHL staff about the value of Austria–Hungary as an ally. Although Conrad assured Falkenhayn that the situation was not threatening, both leaders agreed that the Austro–Hungarian Fourth Army needed reinforcement. Ultimately, the Austro–Hungarian II Corps, originally scheduled to reinforce the Austro–Hungarian First Army, was sent instead to Archduke Joseph Ferdinand. The German 103rd Infantry Division on the Serbian border would go to the First Army.[54] The forthcoming offensive by Army Group Mackensen would begin on time.

Preparations went forward in other ways as well. Campaigning over May and June had taken a considerable toll on the various corps. The troops had outrun their supplies, especially in the move on Lemberg and Rava Russka. By late June, soldiers were living on coffee and not much else.[55] The lull in operations allowed the troops to get some much-needed rest and for their supplies to catch up. Some units also received replacements. On July 4, 1915, for example, the Kaiser Alexander Regiment received about 60 to 80 replacements per company as well as a large number of officers to refill depleted ranks.[56] Nonetheless, manpower would be a concern for the commanders.

The fact that Mackensen's units were going into a major campaign below strength undoubtedly heightened the concern about noncombat casualties, although there was a cultural component to this as well. During the campaign in Galicia, there was considerable concern on the part of the Eleventh Army regarding disease. Casualties were kept to a minimum, although the average incidence of disease in the east was higher than in the west. The appearance of eight cholera cases in the 268th Regiment's 1st Battalion (part of the XXXXI Reserve Corps' 81st Reserve Division) caused the regiment's panicky medical officer to declare the unit unfit for operations. That earned the hapless physician a chewing out from an enraged François.[57] Units tried not to quarter soldiers in the local houses that the Russians had not destroyed because of the risk of diseases such as cholera, typhus, and spotted fever. The Eleventh Army also issued orders on June 26 that the sick were to be moved away from the front as quickly as possible, first to Radymno and Lubaczow and then to Jaroslau, from which they could be moved back to Germany.[58]

Fear of disease was not something peculiar to the forces operating under Mackensen but rather was a phenomenon infecting the entire German Army, or at least that part of it which operated in the east. German leaders such as the kaiser, Foreign Minister Gottlieb von Jagow, and Moltke, to name but a few, all accepted the notion of a "Slavic peril" threatening to overwhelm German civilization.[59] More broadly, Germans of every class accepted the notion of the "east," which also included the eastern reaches of Austria–Hungary, as a place that was dirty, culturally backward, and rife with disease. Such perceptions among the German leadership were only heightened when they had a personal impact. Bernhard Plessen, for example, the son of the Kaiser's adjutant, contracted typhus in eastern Galicia. Although only a mild case, incidents such as Plessen's and the death of the commandant of the XXXXI Reserve Corps headquarters served to reinforce already deeply held perceptions.[60]

Unlike Mackensen's previous attacks, this one would be part of a much larger effort. Mackensen was now in command of four armies, two German and two Austro–Hungarian. All other German armies operating to the north of Mackensen's forces came under the aegis of Ober Ost. Since they were all supposed to participate, a considerable degree of coordination was required. Those details had to be hashed out between OHL and Ober Ost.

Representing Falkenhayn, Tappen (promoted to Generalmajor on June 26) traveled to Ober Ost headquarters at Lötzen on July 10. Tappen's presence in Lötzen was not appreciated at Ober Ost. Hindenburg, Ludendorff, and Hoffmann thought that Tappen had been sent to make sure that Ober Ost was carrying out its part of the plan. For his part, Tappen noted the unfriendly attitude at Ober Ost. Although Hindenburg was "decent," Ludendorff in particular struck Tappen as uncooperative and irritable. Meanwhile, Hoffmann congratulated himself for exercising admirable self-control in regard to Tappen's unwanted and (in Hoffmann's view) unwarranted intrusion. The date for Ober Ost's offensive was set for July 13.[61]

Tappen returned to Pless just in time to observe another argument between Falkenhayn and Conrad. The matter to be decided was the Austro–Hungarian First Army's attack on Władimir Wołynsk. Conrad thought that three Austro–Hungarian divisions would be sufficient, a force Tappen thought utterly inadequate. Eventually a much larger force was assigned to the task, although not as large as Tappen desired. The initial draft of the joint OHL–AOK directive called for the Austro–Hungarian First Army, supported by Linsingen's Bug Army, to attack on July 14 toward Władimir Wołynsk and Hrubieczow. Mackensen's other two armies would begin their attacks on the next day. The final directive left the timing to Mackensen, who set the start of the operation back one day. The attack on Hrubieczow and Władimir Wołynsk would begin on July 15, and the rest of the army group would start the next day.[62]

The decision to undertake the offensive against Russian Poland was regarded by François as not only "logical but imperative."[63] Given the size of the salient that constituted the Russian position in Poland, it was a tempting target in the minds of people such as Seeckt. In addition, flattening out the salient, even if it did not result in any kind of grand encirclement envisioned by Ludendorff and Conrad, would shorten the line to an extent, thus freeing up troops for use elsewhere. In addition, if it did not provide the basis from which a separate peace with Russia could be negotiated, the offensive power of the Russian Army could be crippled for at least a year.[64] In addition, the basic decision to continue the offensive against the Russians produced a rare degree of unanimity among OHL and Ober Ost and even Conrad, although that was only his best alternative to his real desire, an attack on Italy.

The crucial matter that had to be decided was the shape the offensive would take. In looking at the competing ideas of Ober Ost and OHL, it does seem that Ober Ost's proposal for the Kovno operation, with follow-on thrusts against Vilna and Minsk, was too ambitious. In many ways, it reflected the dismissal of logistical realities that was so illustrative of the German way of war. The more cautious concept advocated by Falkenhayn, relying on the methodical bludgeoning employed so effectively by Mackensen, was better suited to the tactical, operational, and logistical realities of 1915. As Norman Stone so shrewdly observed, Conrad and Ludendorff, still chasing the chimera of grand envelopments and battles of annihilation, were the ones who were out of date. It was Falkenhayn and Mackensen, the old hussar, who were much better attuned to the realities of modern warfare.[65]

The Posen conference of July 2, 1915, at which Falkenhayn's proposal for the offensive into Poland was approved, was a masterpiece of bureaucratic infighting on Falkenhayn's part. Lining up the support of Conrad and the kaiser in late June 1915 in effect reduced the Posen meeting to a mere formality. Although Ober Ost was able to have a say, the outcome of the meeting was never in doubt.[66]

By mid-July 1915, Mackensen's forces had been reorganized and expanded. The German Eleventh Army had completed the difficult task of changing the orientation of its front to the north, and the great offensive could now begin.

Chapter 8

The Conquest of Poland:
July 13–August 31, 1915

My deployment for the new operation has been executed undisturbed and on schedule.

—August von Mackensen, July 13, 1915[1]

It is unfair to ask any troops to stand this nerve-wracking unless they have a regular rabbit-warren of trenches.

—British Observer, late July 1915[2]

In their flight the Russians set fire to the villages, and especially the bridges.

—Peter Frenzel, Summer 1915[3]

What began on the day of Gross Görschen ended on the day of the Katzbach.

—August von Mackensen, August 26, 1915[4]

Every war has two sides, and World War I was no exception. Just as the Germans and Austro–Hungarians were considering various courses of action in tackling the salient that was Russian Poland, the Russians had to contemplate their own course of action as well in regard to the salient.

The first basic decision that Stavka had to make concerned whether to even hang on to the salient. Theoretically, evacuating the salient was a simple matter, given that all of the rail lines in the salient, both single- and double-tracked, were operating. That was where simplicity ended.

Although the salient was an inviting target, it was also a good jumping-off point. If the Russians were ever to regain the initiative, it would best be done from a point where an attack on the enemy could produce the greatest gains.

The salient was the best possible place in that regard. A successful attack on Mackensen's forces in the south could restore Russian control of at least a part of Austro–Hungarian Galicia, which they had had wrested from them in 1914. The salient was also the best place from which to threaten or invade East Prussia, a desire always close to the hearts of some in Stavka, such as Danilov.[5] Such actions would give Russia a bit more leverage in terms of Stavka's calls for action by its Anglo-French allies. Evacuation of the salient could send a very negative message to the French and British, further straining a relationship already frayed by accusations of each ally wanting to fight the war to the other's last soldier.[6]

Aside from the strategic consequences of evacuating the salient, there were practical issues as well. During the 1880s and into the 1890s, the Russian Army had invested much effort and resources in the construction of fortresses at critical points in Russian Poland. Novogeorgievsk (present day Modlin) guarded the confluence of the Vistula and Narew, while Ivangorod covered the Vistula. Brest–Litovsk controlled the middle Bug; Kovno and Grodno covered the rail lines that crossed the Nieman River into Lithuania. During his tenure as war minister, General Vladimir A. Sukhomlinov sought to maintain only the most important fortresses on the Vistula while scrapping the rest, using the resources saved to enhance the capabilities of the field army. This effort, however, ran afoul of the more conservative elements in the army, who clustered around the person of Grand Duke Nicholas. Ultimately, all of the fortresses were kept, even though some, such as Kovno, had become museum pieces by 1914. The field forces went short of artillery, a trade-off that had serious consequences in 1914.[7]

To be sure, some of the fortresses served a useful purpose in 1914. Ivangorod in particular played an important part in the Russians' thwarting of Hindenburg's offensive against Warsaw in the autumn of 1914.[8] The circumstances of 1915, however, were very different. Russian experiences at Przemysl clearly showed that fixed fortifications were no match for the destructive power of German and Austro–Hungarian heavy artillery. The problem was that the sheer amount of material in these fortresses greatly exceeded the hauling capacity of the Russian railroads. Novogeorgievsk alone had 1,680 guns, many of them modern, and over a million shells. Evacuating this mass of material required at least 1,000 trains, and the evacuation of Warsaw would have demanded another 2,000 trains, an amount of rolling stock well beyond Russian capabilities.[9] Thus, the size of the investment already made in Poland served to make the Russians exert every effort to hold it.

Finally, the Russian position in Poland, while vulnerable, also had considerable strengths, especially in regard to the coming German offensive. The Russian defensive line confronting the German Eleventh and Austro–Hungarian Fourth Armies ran through rather hilly terrain. The further north one proceeded south of the Lublin–Cholm rail line, the area became marshy, and routes by which guns and other heavy equipment could be moved from south to north were very limited. On the northern side of the salient, the Narew and Bobr Rivers were considerable military obstacles.[10] If it was properly manned and adequately supported with well-handled artillery, the Germans and Austro–Hungarians would find taking the salient a very tough proposition at the very least.

By early July the Russians had cobbled together a defensive force against Army Group Mackensen. Opposite the Austro–Hungarian Fourth Army was part of Evert's Russian 4th Army, with the XXV, XV, and VI Siberian Corps plus two and a half cavalry divisions. Buoyed by their recent success at Krasnik, Evert's men held the front from the left bank of the Vistula to the area south of Lublin. On Evert's left, Lesh's Russian 3rd Army, with the IX, X, III Caucasian, XIV, XXIV, II Siberian, and Russian Guard Corps plus a cavalry division, held the front to just west of Grabowiec, a few miles south of Cholm. There the line was picked up by Gorbatovski's Russian 13th Army, with the II Caucasian, XXIII, XXIX, XXXI, and V Caucasian Corps plus five cavalry divisions. This force held a line astride the Bug River up to Zdary. The major problem for the Russians was weapons and equipment or rather the lack of them. Small arms were in short supply, and in the rear regimental commanders drilled unarmed troops.[11]

While Falkenhayn was fighting the successful bureaucratic battles in early July, preparations for the attack went forward. The biggest problem remained the rate of advance of the railroad, which Falkenhayn regarded as wholly insufficient.[12] Groener personally traveled to Galicia on July 12 to see how things were getting on and if they could be speeded up, but apparently there was not much else that could be done. Nonetheless, preparations went forward. Replacements continued to arrive, although the number of officers and men could not come close to filling the gaps. Even after receiving replacements, by July 13, 1915, the Elisabeth Regiment, for example, could muster only 1,300 officers and men, just under half of the regiment's normal strength. Ammunition was stockpiled and reconnaissance was conducted on both the air and the ground.[13]

Although Falkenhayn was unhappy with the pace of preparations, the course of affairs was quite satisfactory to Mackensen. On July 13, Mackensen wrote that the deployment of his force was complete. He now commanded four armies containing 41 infantry and 5 cavalry divisions, a very capable force. The Army Group had also received additional heavy artillery. He summed up his mental state in one simple sentence: "I have complete confidence."[14] The fourth army under Mackensen's command was the Austro–Hungarian First Army, which was officially subordinated to Army Group Mackensen after a meeting between Conrad and Falkenhayn at Pless on July 11.[15]

Confidence notwithstanding, Army Group Mackensen had several major operational and tactical problems to overcome. The start of the Gorlice offensive was aided by the fact that although the Germans had lost tactical surprise by

April 26, the Russians' inability to counter the German and Austro–Hungarian concentration before May 2 meant that operational surprise had been maintained. In the circumstances of July, neither operational nor tactical surprise was possible.

Another major operational problem was logistical. The Austro–Hungarian railroads that ran north from Lemberg were all single-tracked, and all stopped at the Russian border. There were no railroads on the Russian side of the border, and it was just over 60 miles from the border to the Lublin–Cholm rail line. There was a line that ran from Rozwadow, just inside the Austro–Hungarian border, to Lublin, but it had been thoroughly destroyed by the Russians.[16] The objective for the Eleventh Army, the Lublin–Cholm rail line, was at the very edge of its operational range. Sustaining the offensive over the area north of the border, even though the Germans and Austro–Hungarians had already made some headway, would be problematic, especially in regard to the matter of ammunition for the heavy artillery.

Two other operational matters presented problems, both of which concerned the right flank. The first, as previously mentioned, was the size of the force needed to attack Władimir Wołynsk. Falkenhayn and Conrad differed considerably one the size of the force needed for the mission, Conrad preferring no more than three divisions, which Falkenhayn regarded as hopelessly inadequate. Ultimately the matter was resolved in Falkenhayn's favor, although the size of the force allocated for the job represented a compromise.[17]

The other problem concerned the Bug Army. The AOK–OHL directive of July 11, 1915, called for the Bug Army to advance astride the river. Linsingen had grave misgivings about this. The terrain east of the Bug, laced with lakes and streams, was not particularly favorable for offensive operations.[18] Nonetheless, the offensive would go forward. The capture of Władimir Wołynsk was critical to the success of Mackensen's offensive proceeding north. Possession of Władimir Wołynsk would deprive the Russians of their nearest railhead. Any potential Russian counterattack aimed at Mackensen's right flank would then have to be supplied from Kovel, almost 40 miles northeast. The importance of Władimir Wołynsk was indicated by the fact that Mackensen's offensive would begin on July 15 with attacks by the Austro–Hungarian First and Bug Armies. Connection between the Bug Army's right flank and the Austro–Hungarian First Army's would be maintained by an ad hoc cavalry corps, Group Heydebreck. Composed of the German 5th and Austro–Hungarian 4th and 11th Cavalry Divisions, it was commanded by German Generalleutnant Ernst von Heydebreck. With the right flank secured, the main attack with the German Eleventh Army would begin on July 16.[19]

Meanwhile Ober Ost's offensive began on time. Gallwitz's Army Group, actually the XI, XVII and XIII Corps, seven divisions plus three in reserve, occupied a front of about 24 miles. Gallwitz had accumulated some 500 guns and 400,000 rounds of artillery ammunition for the offensive, more than what

Mackensen's Eleventh Army had before Gorlice.[20] On July 13, Gallwitz's force, with Hindenburg and several Ober Ost staff officers in attendance, attacked along its front. The assault apparently caught General A. I. Litvinov's Russian 1st Army off guard. The first two days of the attack made excellent progress, capturing the first two Russian defense positions to a depth of up to nine miles, while taking 7,100 prisoners, 13 guns, and 30 machine guns. Litvinov's insistence that every inch of ground be held contributed to the effectiveness of the German bombardment.[21]

The forces on each side of Gallwitz's sector made more limited progress. The German Eighth Army, commanded by General der Infanterie Otto von Below, attacked with its right flank, keeping abreast with Gallwitz's left.[22] The 75th Reserve Division, Below's rightmost unit, successfully stormed a Russian positions in the hills south of Lipniki, covering Gallwitz's left and taking 1,800 prisoners.[23] Prince Leopold's German Ninth Army also attacked on July 13, with the

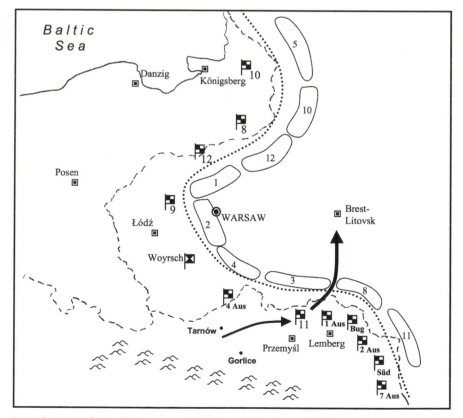

Army Group Mackensen's Advance on Brest Litovsk, July–August 1915.

army's left wing advancing with Gallwitz's right in a converging attack aimed at Novogeorgievsk. Leopold's center units moved toward Warsaw. Army Detachment Woyrsch also attacked on July 13, seeking to take Radom and push on toward the Vistula and Ivangorod. By the late July, as the offensive slowed on Ober Ost's front, the Narew and Vistula Rivers had been reached and German forces were closing in on Novogeorgievsk, Warsaw, and Ivangorod. Gallwitz's success at Przasnz had split the seam between the Russian 1st and 12th Armies.[24]

The onset of Mackensen's attack did not get off to a sterling start. Pulhallo's Austro–Hungarian First Army and Linsingen's Bug Army first had to cross the Bug River, whose steep banks posed a considerable obstacle and thus limited the number of places where bridgeheads could be established. The Russians had well-constructed positions, which they defended stoutly. Russian air defenses were formidable enough to cost Germans several aircraft and air crews. Even Russian reconnaissance aircraft put in a rare appearance. Their discovery of some of German artillery positions allowed the Russians to employ effective counterbattery fire against part of the XXXXI Reserve Corps' artillery.[25]

Linsingen soon reported that he had to contend with 19 divisions. Unless he received additional heavy artillery and infantry, he might have to confine his operations to those of a defensive nature on the western side of the Bug. The Austro–Hungarian First also made little progress on July 15 at Sokal, the designated crossing point on the Bug for the army. During the night of July 15–16, elements of Kirchbach's Austro–Hungarian I Corps were able to wade across the river north of the town and establish a small bridgehead.[26]

Mackensen's response to Linsingen's calls for help was to turn him down. The main effort of the Army Group was on the left, and Mackensen was willing to accept some risk to the right side of his line in order to achieve success in the more important sector. Ultimately, events showed Mackensen's judgment to be correct. Aided by progress on the more critical left side of the line, the situation on the Bug was partially resolved after a week of hard fighting. The Austro–Hungarian First Army was able to create its bridgehead on the east side of the Bug at Sokal on July 18 and widen it the following day.[27] Likewise, on July 19, the Bug Army was able to establish the bridgeheads it needed that would allow it to prepare for its next objective, the town and rail junction of Cholm.[28]

Mackensen's main effort was more toward his left, based on the left flank of the German Eleventh Army and the adjoining right flank of the Austro–Hungarian Fourth Army. The key sector was located where the Guard and the XXII Reserve Corps were operating. Although the German line ran astride the Wieprz River, the course of the river required the Germans to mount a crossing.

The Guard began its attack on July 16 at 11 A.M., after three hours of artillery preparation. The Eleventh Army quickly discovered that the left side of its line, the Guard, XXII Reserve Corps and the X Corps, the army's left flank corps, faced an "immensely strong" Russian defensive system extending some 18 miles along the Eleventh Army's front. At the same time, Arz's Austro–Hungarian VI Corps had a difficult time crossing the Wolica, a swampy tributary of the Wieprz to the east.[29]

Undeterred, the Eleventh Army renewed the attack on July 17. The Augusta Regiment of the 2nd Guard Division was able to take Krasnostaw, along with 1,270 prisoners and two machine guns, with the relatively light casualties of 10 killed and 77 wounded. The Elisabeth Regiment was then able to cross the Wieprz at Krasnostaw and establish a bridgehead while fighting off the usual Russian counterattack. The Russian positions west of Krasnostaw were successfully tackled by the 1st Guard Division, although casualties were considerably heavier than those suffered at Krasnostaw.[30] The right of the Guard's line was extended by the commitment of the 105th Infantry Division from the Army reserve, which aided a renewed attack by Arz. One of the interesting aspects of the fighting in the Guard's sector was that its opponent was the Russian Guard.[31] The XXII Reserve Corps, supported by elements of the Guard, spent several days fighting is way through the Russian positions. Likewise the X Corps also spent the first three days of the attack clawing its way through Russian positions in villages such as Pilaszkowice and Izdebno.[32]

The Austro–Hungarian Fourth Army, with over 100,000 men and 593 guns, was tasked with taking the hills west of Lublin and then gaining control of the road to Lublin. Like the other attacks by Army Group Mackensen, the Austro–Hungarian Fourth Army made limited progress. The most notable advances were made on each of the Fourth Army's flanks, where the Austro–Hungarians were operating with German units adjacent to them. The perceived lack of progress by the Austro–Hungarians brought forth the usual complaints from OHL, which dispatched Tappen to Teschen in an attempt to prod the Austro–Hungarians to show a bit more urgency.[33]

By July 19, 1915, Mackensen's Army Group had driven back the Russian 3rd, 4th, and 13th Armies almost 7½ miles in some places on a 20-mile-long front. Some 15,000 prisoners had been taken, plus 22 machine guns. German and Austro–Hungarian losses, while less than those of the Russians, were "not insignificant." The Austro–Hungarian VI Corps suffered almost 7,000 casualties, while the Guard's losses were sufficient to reduce the entire corps to about 12,000 men. The Russians had enough artillery to make life uncomfortable for the German artillery and took a heavy toll on some of the ammunition columns.[34]

The unfolding of the German offensive over the course of July 13–18 was certainly cause for satisfaction at OHL. Even the normally cautious Falkenhayn thought that the offensive could yield decisive results, while the kaiser once again raided the stock of pink champagne at Pless for celebratory toasts at dinner. Even the rarely impressed Hoffmann confided to his diary about how "we are in the thick of the greatest battle that history has ever known."[35]

Just as it seemed that the Germans would complete at least the first stages of an envelopment of the Russian forces in Poland, the momentum of the offensive slowed to a crawl. The Germans discovered that the Russian defenses on the Narew were stoutly manned and well supported by artillery. The marshy terrain of the Narew and Bobr Rivers also served to slow Ober Ost's advance.[36]

On Mackensen's side of the salient, the terrain was similarly restrictive. The few causeways running north were easily blocked by the Russians. Local attacks launched by the Guard on July 20 miscarried. In addition, a major rainstorm swept over Army Group Mackensen's sector on the night of July 18–19. Having to bivouac on ground that was already swampy, German soldiers now woke up in veritable pools of standing water. Movement became very difficult, and Mackensen's forces were hit by another storm on July 20.[37] Finally the troops, especially those who had been in combat since May, were worn out. The soldiers needed a break, or at least a much slower tempo of operations, until they could recover some strength. Then the offensive north could be resumed.[38]

On the Russian side, fears of possible encirclement abounded at both the Northwest Front and Stavka. The approach of Gallwitz's Army Group and Below's German Eighth Army on the Narew caused considerable concern for Alexiev's hold on Warsaw. Grand Duke Nicholas authorized Alexiev to evacuate Warsaw if he thought it necessary. Already thinking along these lines, Alexiev quickly decided to evacuate the western face of the salient, including Warsaw, issuing the orders on July 22.[39]

The withdrawal was carried out in reasonably good order, and the Russians, with the example of 1812 in mind, practiced a scorched-earth policy much as they had in Galicia. This certainly served to slow the German pursuit, Hoffmann's sneering contempt of Russian behavior notwithstanding. German soldiers noted the ubiquity of chimneys, all that was left of innumerable farmhouses burned by the Russians.[40]

The biggest controversy associated with Alexiev's withdrawal was his decision to leave a large garrison and huge amounts of material in Novogeorgievsk. Although this decision was operationally sound, since the fortress controlled a critical rail and road crossing of the Vistula and the Narew, the size of the force left behind was another matter. The 92,000-strong garrison, even if composed of overaged reservists, as Grand Duke Nicholas's defenders have claimed, plus the 1,600 or so guns and ammunition, was a major investment in what was guaranteed to be a losing bet.[41] Given the general course of the campaign, it was highly unlikely that Novogeorgievsk could be regained. Even the most complimentary of Grand Duke Nicholas's opponents regarded this decision as a major error.[42]

While Stavka and the Northwest Front were making unpalatable decisions, another round of wrangling over command relationships and operations was happening on the German and Austro–Hungarian side. With thrusts from the north and south stalled, Falkenhayn decided to press forward where he was making progress, namely in the center. Since this would involve coordinating the movements of Gallwitz, Prince Leopold, and Woyrsch, Falkenhayn proposed that the three forces be subsumed into a new army group commanded by Prince Leopold. The army group would be under OHL's direction, not that of Ober Ost. Somewhat surprisingly, neither Hindenburg nor Ludendorff voiced major objections, although Hindenburg expressed some irritation when the organization was finally stood up on August 6, 1915. Conrad initially opposed the idea but eventually came around once his concerns about the left flank of the Austro–Hungarian Fourth Army were sufficiently dispelled. The arrangement went into effect officially in early August.[43]

Meanwhile the German forces on the western face of the salient pressed toward the Vistula River. Part of Gallwitz's force, which was redesignated on August 7 as the German Twelfth Army, would peel off to lay siege to Novogeorgievsk. Leopold's Ninth Army continued on toward Warsaw. The bone of contention between Falkenhayn and Conrad was the movement of Army Detachment Woyrsch. Falkenhayn quickly picked up from reports that the Russians were indeed retreating. He thought that a direct advance by Woyrsch on Ivangorod and crossing the Vistula south of the fortress at Novo Alexandria served no purpose. Instead, Falkenhayn desired that Woyrsch move to cross the Vistula between Warsaw and Ivangorod. Once across the river, an attack to the northeast by Woyrsch would aid both Prince Leopold's Ninth Army advancing from Warsaw and Gallwitz's Twelfth Army, still battling on the Narew. Forces in the east would be reinforced by two additional divisions from the west, as OHL's judgment was that there would be no major Franco-British offensive until September, an estimate that proved correct.[44]

Conrad did not share Falkenhayn's estimate of the situation. An attack by Woyrsch in the direction proposed by Falkenhayn would endanger the left flank of the Austro–Hungarian Fourth Army. While not opposed to a crossing between Warsaw and Ivangorod, Conrad wanted Woyrsch to detail one corps to work with the Austro–Hungarian VIII Corps, which would also be subject to Woyrsch's orders, and have this force secure the confluence of the Pilica and Vistula Rivers and take Ivangorod.[45]

Ultimately Falkenhayn was willing to accommodate Conrad to a degree. The Austro–Hungarian XII Corps, part of Army Detachment Woyrsch, moved on Ivangorod, while elements of Austro–Hungarian Fourth Army crossed the Vistula south of Ivangorod on July 29. Meanwhile Woyrsch's Landwehr Corps crossed the Vistula north of Ivangorod on the same day. In both cases careful bridging operations were required, as the Vistula was too wide and deep to be forded. At Woyrsch's crossing site, pontoon bridges over half a mile in length were erected Although the Russians were already retreating, Woyrsch's river crossing operation surprised them. Hoffmann, who seldom praised anyone or anything, later described it as a "pretty piece of work."[46]

Falkenhayn had two more battles to fight before July was over. The first was with Ober Ost. With the offensive on the Narew stalled, Ober Ost sought to revive the Kovno operation. Hindenburg and Ludendorff even went so far as to ask Conrad to send two 305-mm heavy artillery batteries from the Austro–Hungarian forces operating near Ivangorod. Once again Falkenhayn rejected the proposal, questioning the assumptions on which it was based. While thanking Conrad for his willingness to send Hindenburg the artillery, Falkenhayn asked Conrad to keep the artillery near Ivangorod until after the fortress was taken and the Vistula crossings were secured.[47]

Another conflict arose with Conrad when the matter of Italy reared its head. In late July, Cadorna launched the second battle of the Isonzo; by July 25, the situation on the Carso plateau and at Gorizia looked critical for the Austro–Hungarians.[48] Falkenhayn learned, probably from Cramon, that Conrad had ordered that the Austro–Hungarian XIV Corps be transferred from Archduke Joseph Ferdinand's Austro–Hungarian Fourth Army to Boroević's forces on the Italian front. On July 27, 1915, an irritated Falkenhayn quickly reminded Conrad that there should be no weakening of the Austro–Hungarian forces in Poland without OHL's consent. Conrad quickly backed off, proposing an alternative course of action for reinforcing Boroević. A friendly if somewhat condescending telegram from Falkenhayn the following day ended the matter. The crisis on the Italian front subsided, and the Austro–Hungarian XIV Corps remained in Poland.[49]

While operations proceeded apace against the western face of the Polish salient and Ober Ost prepared for a another effort on the Narew, Mackensen's army group spent the last week of July getting ready to resume its offensive to seize the Lublin–Cholm rail line. The Army Group was reinforced with Generalleutnant Robert Kosch's X Reserve Corps, the Guard Cavalry Division, and Generalmajor Ludwig von Estorff's 103rd Infantry Division.[50]

Mackensen and Seeckt decided to make the main effort on the left, west of the Wieprz River. The X, X Reserve, and XXII Reserve Corps, with the 119th Infantry and Guard Cavalry Divisions in reserve, were organized into an attack force under Emmich's command. The Guard and the Austro–Hungarian VI Corps would continue to operate east of the Wieprz. The Bug Army and the Austro–Hungarian First Army would continue their mission to advance north and cover the Eleventh Army's right flank. The Austro–Hungarian Fourth Army would continue its mission to cover the Eleventh Army's left flank. In the meantime Mackensen's forces slowly accumulated the needed supplies and ammunition, a task the Russian artillery occasionally made difficult. Nonetheless, Army Group Mackensen was ready to resume the offensive, with the attack set for July 29. The objectives remained the same as before.[51]

As was now customary in Mackensen's assaults, the attack opened with a massive artillery bombardment. This had a considerable impact on the Russian troops holding the trenches against Emmich's attack force. The II Siberian Corps, part of Lesh's 3rd Army, was severely cut up. The British observer with the II Siberian Corps considered the Russian trenches hopelessly inadequate to withstand the pounding administered by Mackensen's heavy artillery.[52] With

Russian artillery opposite Emmich either absent or silenced, the German offensive quickly overran the Russian positions. By the night of July 29, forward patrols of the 20th Infantry Division's 77th Infantry Regiment observed the Russians in headlong retreat on the Piaski–Biskupice road. Having had a good day, the 77th had an even better night, meeting with some canteen wagons that were well supplied with bottles of wine and cognac. Emmich's force had driven the Russians back over a mile, taking 4,000 prisoners, three guns, and several machine guns.[53]

East of the Wieprz, affairs did not go nearly as well. Emmich directed Falkenhayn's XXII Reserve Corps to cross to the east bank of the Wieprz to help turn the Russians out of their positions, but the effort met with limited success. The Guard renewed acquaintance with its Russian counterpart, spending the day launching frontal attacks that made only limited gains. Arz's Austro–Hungarians likewise made little progress.[54] Further east, the Bug Army continued its slow advance toward Cholm, while the Austro–Hungarian First Army inched its way toward Władimir Wołynsk. The Austro–Hungarian Fourth Army, as usual, made uneven progress.[55]

As per Mackensen's orders, the attack continued on July 30. The goal was to widen the breach created the day before by Emmich's attack force. The outcome was even better than that of the previous day, as the Russians had begun a retreat from before the Austro–Hungarian Fourth Army and Emmich's force. Opposed at best by negligible rearguards, the Austro–Hungarian Fourth Army reached its objectives for the day. Emmich also faced light resistance, while east of the Wieprz the Guard and Austro–Hungarian VI Corps—and further east the Bug and Austro–Hungarian First Armies—continued to struggle forward through stoutly defended positions.[56]

Under the impact of Mackensen's assault, Woyrsch's crossing of the Vistula and the renewal of the offensive on the Narew by Gallwitz and Below, Stavka now regarded the complete evacuation of Poland as a "strategic necessity."[57] The defenses in Poland now collapsed as the Russian armies began to retreat all along the line, leaving the ubiquitous screens of Cossacks to cover the withdrawal. Although Conrad was still unsure of the fact of a Russian retreat, Falkenhayn quickly drew the correct conclusions from the available reports. The Russians were retreating from Woyrsch and Mackensen, offering resistance worthy of the name only against Gallwitz.[58] Long-sought objectives now fell to the Germans and Austro–Hungarians like ripened apples from a tree. Elements of the Austro–Hungarian Fourth Army entered Lublin on July 31, while Linsingen's Bug Army moved into Cholm on August 1. Several days later, Kövess's Austro–Hungarian XII Corps marched into Ivangorod, the Austro–Hungarian First Army took Władimir Wołynsk, and Warsaw was occupied on August 5, 1915.[59]

The manner of the entry into Warsaw was a matter of minor controversy between Germany and Austria-Hungary. Stephan Graf Burián von Rajecz, the

Austro–Hungarian foreign minister, wanted at least one division of Austro–Hungarian cavalry present for the entry into Warsaw. The unit, either the Austro–Hungarian 2nd, 7th, or 9th Cavalry Division, then operating on the northern flank of Woyrsch's Army Detachment, could be drawn north in time to participate in the triumphal march into the Polish capital. This would make a major political statement and demonstrate the closeness of the alliance between Germany and Austria–Hungary.[60]

Since Burián had communicated his desires to Falkenhayn via Conrad, Falkenhayn responded to Conrad. Ever terse in his writing , Falkenhayn quickly scotched the idea of having Austro–Hungarian troops involved in taking Warsaw. Such a presence, noted Falkenhayn, would indeed make the march into Warsaw precisely the kind of political event Falkenhayn wanted to avoid. Still desirous of reaching a separate peace with Russia, Falkenhayn worried that such a triumphant display would only serve to harden Russian attitudes. In this Falkenhayn was supported by Conrad, who also thought that a softer approach to Russia might be more fruitful. Once again Falkenhayn got his way; Gallwitz's advance into Warsaw was very low key. Even church bells in Germany remained silent at Falkenhayn's behest.[61]

With Warsaw in German hands, the military question that now confronted Falkenhayn was how far the advance should go. With the salient rapidly flattening into a straight line, Falkenhayn wanted to bring the campaign to a close so that as many as 10 German corps could be sent back to the west. Falkenhayn regarded a series of rivers as reasonably good places to halt. In the south, this would include the Dniestr and the Zlota Lipa, while in the center the long, broad Bug River served as a good stopping point. To the north, the Nieman could serve the same purpose.[62]

Falkenhayn's early August concept had a couple of consequences. The first was that Ober Ost would now be able to mount its long-desired operations against Kovno and Grodno. In the area where Army Group Mackensen was operating, the obvious objective was Brest–Litovsk, one of the major crossing points on the Bug and the focal point of the rail net in eastern Poland. Mackensen and Seeckt began to consider their next objective as well, and their thinking also drew them to Brest Litovsk. After a bit of typical wrangling, Conrad and Falkenhayn agreed that Mackensen's army group should turn northeast. Tappen also considered Brest–Litovsk the Eleventh Army's next target.[63] The matter was settled definitively when Falkenhayn and Tappen traveled to Mackensen's headquarters in Lublin on August 11. The next objective would indeed be Brest–Litovsk.[64]

Turning Mackensen's army group back to the northeast held some interesting operational challenges for the commanders executing the movement. With the Eleventh Army turning east, its left flank would now be covered by Woyrsch, advancing east from the Vistula. The Austro–Hungarian Fourth Army was effectively pinched out of the front and had to be sent somewhere else. As early as August 5, Conrad had decided to remove the Austro–Hungarian X Corps from the Fourth Army and shift it to the Austro–Hungarian First Army, a move tacitly endorsed by Falkenhayn.[65]

The decision to turn Army Group Mackensen to the northeast also had an impact on the Bug Army. Redirecting the Eleventh Army northeast meant that the Bug Army would have to turn northeast as well, to cover the Eleventh Army's right flank. The new path of advance for the Bug Army would take it directly through part of the Pripet marshes. Mackensen, however, was unconcerned about this, as the summer of 1915 had been rather dry, thus making the marshes somewhat more trafficable than it normally would be. The Austro–Hungarian First Army, now returned to AOK control, would consolidate its hold on Władimir Wołynsk. Only Cavalry Corps Heydebreck would be allowed to advance on the rail junction of Kovel.[66]

While Mackensen, Falkenhayn, and Conrad made decisions on the next and what was regarded by OHL as the concluding phase of the campaign, the Eleventh and Bug Armies made ready for the attack. The operational pause after the seizure of the Lublin–Cholm rail line afforded the regiments the opportunity for rest and religious services. Farms that escaped burning by the Russians provided fodder for the horses. The 269th Reserve Regiment finally received replacements, who arrived at the regimental bivouac area after a six-week journey.[67]

Army Group Mackensen's final attack of the campaign began on August 11, 1915, even as the final objectives were being set. The first task for the Eleventh Army was to eject the Russians from a position north of the Lublin–Cholm rail line. The Eleventh Army saw heavy fighting over August 11–12 in the Guard's sector, and the commitment of the army's reserves was required before the Russians were driven out of their positions at Ostrow.[68] Very early on August 13, the Russians evacuated their positions before the Eleventh Army. As Mackensen's forces moved forward, the Eleventh Army's left flank made contact with Woyrsch's right in the area south of Miendzyrzec.[69]

Once the Russian position at Ostrow was broken, the campaign for Mackensen's troops took on the pattern of a classic delaying action by the Russians. Mackensen's troops would pursue for two or three days, only to encounter a new Russian position. After a short fight, the Russian rearguards would break contact, moving back to the next position. German aerial reconnaissance reported troops and equipment moving east from Brest–Litovsk.[70]

The Eleventh Army had to struggle forward over poor roads, which were very sandy at the best of times. The poor roads had a particular impact on the heavy artillery's ability to keep pace with the infantry. Units that had to contend with Russian rearguard positions often ended up having to assault positions with only the support of light artillery. Deprived of their trump card, German infantry wound up fighting costly slogging matches with equally battered Russian infantry. In one rearguard action, for example, the Alexander Regiment lost 82 killed and 200 wounded. The Russian Guard regiment opposing it suffered 200 killed. The Alexander Regiment took a couple of machine guns as well. By this time (the third week of August), the Alexander Regiment was reduced to a strength of 450 officers and men. The strength of the regiment was now so low that the 2nd and Fusilier Battalions had to be consolidated into a single unit.[71]

While the Eleventh Army fought its way toward Brest–Litovsk, Linsingen's Bug Army was ordered by Mackensen to cross the Bug River and create a bridgehead that would serve as a basis for further offensive operations. This was accomplished at Wlodawa. Once the bridgehead was widened on August 17, the Bug Army would be able to protect the Eleventh Army's right flank.[72]

On August 23, the XXII Reserve Corps crossed the Bug north of Brest–Litovsk, the last fortress in Russian Poland, with the Guard following the next day. With the Bug Army also on the east bank of the river, Mackensen and Seeckt wanted the two forces to cut the rail lines east of the fortress and perhaps any Russian forces still in the fortress.[73] After the experiences of the spring and summer, the Russians had no doubt about the viability of Brest–Litovsk; it was abandoned and its forts and bridges destroyed. On August 26, elements of the Beskiden Corps entered the ruins of forts demolished by the Russians. Arz's Austro–Hungarian VI Corps troops also passed through razed forts and entered the city, earning plaudits for themselves and the German *Pour le Mérite* for their commander from Wilhelm II.[74]

Further south, Heydebreck's ad hoc cavalry corps briefly reached Kovel, an event that unnerved the Russian high command beyond its importance. The Austro–Hungarian First Army, now back under AOK's control, was directed by Conrad to advance on Luck, which would bring the front up to the Styr River. This task was accomplished at the end of August. Puhallo was eventually supported on his left by the Austro–Hungarian Fourth Army, once it was withdrawn from Army Group Mackensen. This was done after Woyrsch's forces had made contact with the Eleventh Army, effectively pinching the Austro–Hungarians out of the battlefront in Poland. On August 22, Puhallo's army was once again subordinated to Mackensen, but with no real impact on the campaign.[75]

While the final stages of Mackensen's offensive were being played out between the Wieprz and the Bug, two other notable events were taking place. The siege of Novogeorgievsk can be dealt with briefly here. The blockading force consisted of Generalleutnant Karl Suren's XVII Reserve Corps and an ad hoc corps commanded by Generalleutnant Gustaf von Dickhuth-Harrach. The siege train was commanded by General der Infanterie Hans von Beseler, most notable for his conduct of the successful siege of Antwerp in 1914.[76]

The Russian garrison, commanded by General Nikolai Bobyr, consisted of a rather dispirited group of units. Some of them, such as the 63rd Infantry Division, had been severely mauled in Mackensen's May offensive in Galicia. Of the garrison's 92,000 soldiers, only 55,000 were capable of bearing weapons.

The fortifications of Novogeorgievsk were old, designed more to defend against artillery of the late 19th century than the heavy artillery of 1915. Heavy artillery was an asset Beseler had in abundance; 113 guns organized in 26 batteries, 21 of which were 150-mm or larger.[77]

Once the investment of the fortress was completed, Beseler set the start of the attack for August 13. Over the next five days, Beseler used a combination of artillery and infantry assaults against the outer forts. The heart of one fort was destroyed by a large-caliber German shell. On August 19, Bobyr surrendered, after destroying all bridges over the Vistula. The Germans took 90,000 prisoners, including 30 generals. About 1,600 guns were also taken, along with huge amounts of ammunition and all kinds of equipment.[78] The Vistula north of Warsaw was now open.

The other major event was the fall of Kovno. Ober Ost took two divisions from the Narew front and shifted them to Generaloberst Hermann von Eichhorn's German Tenth Army.[79] Launched on August 10, Eichhorn's attack made progress as the Russian defense, under the command of an elderly officer named Grigoriev, quickly fell apart. The fortress itself, more of a military fossil than a useful installation, proved worse than useless. By August 18, 1915, after some cursory demolitions, the Russians were fleeing the fortress. Grigoriev was among the fugitives. Tracked down by Russian authorities, Grigoriev was tried and sentenced to 15 years imprisonment. The Germans came away with another large haul of booty, some 20,000 prisoners and 1,300 artillery pieces, including 350 heavy guns, 100 machine guns, and 810,000 rounds of artillery ammunition.[80]

The true impact of the fall of Kovno was felt more in the Russian command structure. After the loss of Kovno, Nicholas II decided to dismiss his uncle and take personal command of Stavka. While the military merit of the decision has been hotly debated by both participants and historians, its political dimension was universally agreed upon. From then on the tsar would have to bear personal responsibility for any defeats.[81]

By the beginning of September 1915, it was clear that the offensive started by Mackensen at the start of May was winding down. The Austro–Hungarians continued the offensive in the south, the *Herbstsau,* which yielded little result for the effort put into it and the casualties incurred. At the other end of the front, Ober Ost continued its offensive into Lithuania, an operation derided by Seeckt as little more than a private war conducted by Ludendorff at the behest of the Pan German interest groups.[82] These, however, were but mere, if in the Austro–Hungarian case, costly sideshows. Some of the units that had been brought east in April to form the German Eleventh Army were now withdrawn from the front. The Guard was sent back to Nasielsk, where the corps paraded past the kaiser on September 15, 1915. Three days later, the Guard boarded trains bound for France. The X Corps was also withdrawn and sent west, and others would follow. On September 8, 1915, the Army Group Mackensen was disbanded. After a short time on leave, Mackensen and Seeckt would be sent south to lead the invasion of Serbia.[83]

Strategically, the most immediate result of the series of offensive operations that began in May 1915 in Galicia and concluded in early September on the Bug was the security afforded to Austria–Hungary. The Russian threat to Hungary, which had loomed so large in the spring after the loss of Przemysl, was now but a distant memory. The offensive power of the Russian Army had been so greatly diminished that the prospect of a renewed Russian offensive had been eliminated for at least the near future and possibly longer.[84]

The elimination of the Polish salient also met Falkenhayn's strategic need for a flatter front line, thus freeing up forces for use in other theaters, especially on the western front, where another allied offensive was expected.[85] Sufficient forces were also now available to execute another strategically necessary operation: the invasion of Serbia and the opening of an overland route to embattled Turkey. All that needed to be done was to complete a military convention with Bulgaria. And by the time the offensive in Poland was over, Bulgaria was indeed a member of the Central Powers.[86]

The one strategic goal that remained unmet was knocking Russia out of the war. To be sure, there was considerable disagreement among the Germans as to what kind of approach should be made toward Russia. The disagreements between Falkenhayn and the annexationist-minded alliance of Ober Ost and Chancellor Theobald von Bethmann Hollweg has remained a subject of much debate among historians and need not be rehashed here.[87] Likewise, the various discussions between Germany and Austria–Hungary on the future of Poland and how that related to the prospect of a separate peace with Russia also lie beyond the scope of this study.[88] The hopes of Falkenhayn and Conrad for a separate peace with Russia were decisively dashed when Nicholas II informed Danish intermediary Hans-Niels Andersen that Russia would continue to honor its commitments to France and Britain. Hoffmann's sense that Russia would prove unwilling to negotiate proved correct. Mackensen also regarded a separate peace with Russia as unlikely, but the recently won successes earned Germany some strategic breathing space, which would allow for a "squaring of accounts" in the west.[89]

The conquest of Poland and Russia's Baltic provinces also presented the Germans and Austro–Hungarians, especially after the tsar had squashed any prospects of a separate peace, with the issue of developing occupation policy. Although an interesting topic that has been too long ignored, it is outside the scope of this study.[90] The only observation one might make on the occupation of Poland and how Germany and Austria–Hungary envisioned its future is that ultimately the two allies took positions on the issue that left them poles apart.

Operationally, the outcome of the summer 1915 offensive in Poland was disappointing. To be sure, a great deal of territory was won, and the flattening of the front line in the east had as many operational consequences as strategic ones. Nonetheless, the Russian armies in the Polish salient were generally able to escape. Outside of the large hauls of prisoners and booty from Novogeorgievsk and to a lesser extent Kovno, the results of the campaign were not what had been hoped for. This was particularly illustrated in terms of captures of artillery pieces. During its advance against Cholm during the end of July, for example, Linsingen's Bug Army captured over 21,000 prisoners and 31 machine guns, but only a single artillery piece was taken. In contrast, over the course of May, the Eleventh Army took over 152,000 men and 160 guns. The Bavarian 11th Infantry Division took 37 guns between March 28 and August 31, 1915, none of those captures having occurred during the division's stint with the Bug Army. Being much closer to their rail lines, the Russians had a much greater degree of operational mobility than the Germans, and they exercised it to their advantage.[91]

Of the competing concepts for how operations in Poland should be conducted, Falkenhayn's more cautious concept was much better attuned to the logistical realities of the situation than the more ambitious schemes of Ludendorff and Conrad. The unfolding of events over late July and August, however, did nothing to change anyone's opinion, as the rather icy meeting between Falkenhayn and Ober Ost at Novogeogievsk just after Bobyr's surrender demonstrated.[92]

The Eleventh Army in particular showed the cumulative effects of hard campaigning over an extended period of time. The Guard alone, according to Seeckt's calculations, had marched over 450 miles between the end of April and the start of September 1915. By the time the offensive north into Poland began in mid-July, the troops were simply worn out and required some degree of rest. Regiments were also in desperate need of replacements, and the ever-lengthening lines of communications extended the time needed for replacements to arrive.[93] By the time they crossed the Bug and took Brest Litovsk, Mackensen's troops were at the end of their tether. Given these circumstances, Mackensen's slow and methodical massing of ammunition and troops before each successive attack was the most logical way to proceed. Equally sensible was the decision to entrust the main effort east of the Wieprz to Emmich, ensuring unity of command in the Eleventh Army's key sector, while Mackensen and Seeckt oversaw the activities of four armies.

By September 1915 the great offensive in the east had run its course. The "avalanche" created by the "Mackensen phalanx" had ground to a halt, and the phalanx itself had been dismantled. The casualties incurred by the victorious Central Powers were considerable. Austro–Hungarian casualties for all of 1915 totaled 2,100,000, of which 181,000 were killed. Excluding the 67,000 killed in the first four months of 1915, plus the perhaps 20,000 killed on the Italian front and the casualties incurred in overrunning Serbia, Austro–Hungarian losses on the eastern front for 1915 almost certainly ran into the hundreds of thousands.

German losses for all fronts in 1915 were 612,000. Some 87,000, including 12,000 killed, were lost in the course of Mackensen's operations in Galicia. Total German losses on the eastern front easily ran into over 200,000 killed, wounded, and missing. Among the wounded was Mackensen's son Eberhard, then serving as a regimental adjutant in the Guard Cavalry Division. Russian casualties were far greater, numbering 1,410,000 killed and wounded plus 976,000 prisoners.[94] The task set for the German and Austro–Hungarian forces on the eastern front had been achieved. The next strategically necessary operation, the invasion of Serbia, could proceed.

Chapter 9

Assessments

The entire operation from Gorlice to Brest–Litovsk made a huge impact in the world.

—Hans von Seeckt[1]

Only an ordinary victory.

—Anonymous, 1934[2]

The close cooperation of the artillery with aircraft was always a prerequisite for success.

—Lieutenant Colonel Schirmer[3]

Command of the corps was made easy for me by the competence and drive of the two division commanders, Generals von Stocken and Fabarius.

—Hermann von François[4]

Assessing a complex event or set of events such as the series of offensives conceived by Falkenhayn and Conrad and executed by Mackensen and Seeckt is a complicated task. First, the impact of the campaign at the time must be considered. Did the attack alter the situation as it was supposed to? Then we must examine how the event was regarded after the war. Was the Gorlice–Tarnow offensive still considered significant, and why or why not was importance still attached to it?

Having dispensed with the issue of contemporaneous and historical significance, an assessment must be made to explain why events transpired as they did. In this case, why were the Germans and, to a lesser extent, the Austro–Hungarians successful? Conversely, why did Russians fare so poorly? Finally, can some broad conclusions regarding the offensive in Galicia and its sequel in Poland be reached, especially in regard to the other theaters of war, most notably the western front?

The contemporaneous impact of Gorlice–Tarnow and the ensuing conquest of Russian Poland was felt in several ways. Although the offensive did not deter Italy from joining the Entente, neutrals closer to the scene of the action did react to events, especially in Galicia. It is difficult to imagine Romania remaining neutral in 1915 with Austria–Hungary liable to extinction by a Russian eruption into the Hungarian plain. By June of 1915 it was clear that Romania was going to continue to await events.[5] Likewise it is equally difficult to envision Bulgaria aligning itself with the Central Powers with a continuing major Russian presence in Galicia. Once it was clear that the Russian threat to Austria–Hungary had been eliminated and it appeared that the Central Powers were in the ascendant, Bulgaria was willing to take the risk, sign the military convention, and go to war against Serbia alongside Germany, Austria–Hungary, and Turkey.[6]

Gorlice–Tarnow and the later conquest of Poland also affected the contending alliances in direct ways. The retaking of Galicia and the rampage across Poland did put considerable strain on the Entente. Although Nicholas II ensured that Russia would remain committed to the Entente, there was much bitterness in Russia at what was regarded as French lassitude. Urgent calls for help, as the Russians saw it, went unanswered as the summer slipped by. Meanwhile the next French offensive was beset with repeated postponements that put the next attack later and later into September. By then there were certainly people in Russia who thought that the Entente was willing to "fight the war to the last Russian soldier."[7] In addition, the success in Galicia complicated Joffre's domestic situation, as French politicians who were unhappy with Joffre could point to Mackensen's glittering success while Joffre's offensives in Artois and especially Champagne fizzled.[8]

Within Russia, the spring 1915 campaign in Galicia and summer campaign in Poland had profound consequences. The most notable of these, of course, was the relief of Grand Duke Nicholas by Nicholas II and the tsar's personal assumption of command. The secondary consequence, the leaving of the home front to the Tsarina Alexandra and the burgeoning influence of Grigory Rasputin, is a well-known story that requires no repetition here.[9]

Another consequence of the disasters of 1915 was the search in Russia for scapegoats. This process had already begun after Second Masurian Lakes, with the arrest, trial, and execution of Lieutenant Colonel Sergei N. Miasoedov in March 1915 on vague charges of espionage. The course of the spring and summer of 1915 only heightened the mania about spies, and the witch hunt extended into the upper echelons of the Russian government, aided by attempts to settle personal vendettas. This sordid business culminated in the arrest of former War Minister Sukhomlinov and renewed outbursts of anti-Semitism.[10]

The impact on the Central Powers was even more pronounced. The sagging morale of the Austro–Hungarians, manifested in the tense atmosphere at AOK at the fall of Przemysl and after, had given way to the tumultuous celebrations in Teschen and Lemberg when the Russians were driven out of the capital of Galicia.[11] Likewise across Germany and at OHL in Pless, there was considerable joy, given the otherwise static nature of the war in other theaters and at sea, the Lusitania affair notwithstanding. Falkenhayn and Mackensen, the two principal men of the hour, each received honorary doctorate degrees. Mackensen received a doctorate from the University of Halle, which he had attended before joining the Prussian Army. Falkenhayn was awarded a doctorate from Friedrich-Wilhelm University in Berlin on the recommendation of Hans Delbrück, the noted military historian and one-time scourge of the general staff.[12]

For Falkenhayn personally, the impact of the 1915 campaigns cannot be overstated. The success of Mackensen's initial attack and the seizure of Przemysl and then Lemberg confirmed the wisdom of Falkenhayn's decisions, first to commit the Eleventh Army to the attack in May and then to reinforce it in June.[13] The victory attained in Galicia gave Falkenhayn the highest standing he would have in regard to the kaiser, whose support still mattered at this point in the war. The leverage gained by Falkenhayn allowed him to execute the well-planned bureaucratic ambush of Ober Ost at Posen on July 2. It would be the most significant triumph Falkenhayn would gain over Hindenburg and Ludendorff during the war. It also cleared the way for Falkenhayn to execute the rest of his strategic designs relatively unhindered.[14]

The campaign also intensified certain changes already taking place in the German Army, brought about by the experience of war. Even though the casualties suffered in the campaign were excessively heavy in and of themselves, the cumulative effect cannot be overstated. The last member of the Alexander Regiment's prewar officer corps, for example, was killed on June 27, 1915. Likewise the Elisabeth Regiment experienced a 100% turnover in its officer corps between August 1914 and August 1915. The officers lost in these regiments were replaced increasingly by officers with reserve commissions and men who were not nobles. In the Elisabeth Regiment, for example, by August 8, 1915, seven of the unit's companies were commanded by nonnobles. Seven of the twelve company commanders also held reserve commissions. The Machine Gun Company had four nonnoble reserve lieutenants.[15] Such a regimental officer corps would have been inconceivable in a Guard regiment before the war. In effect, the war was forcing institutions like the Guard to undergo a social revolution.

The most notable impact of the campaign on the two principal Central Powers was in the relationship between them. If there was any question as to who was the dominant power in the alliance in the spring of 1915, there was no doubt about the answer by the end of the summer. The losses suffered in the Carpathian battles, Przemysl, Gorlice–Tarnow, the Polish campaign, and the *Herbstsau,* plus the strains of the Italian front, left the Austro–Hungarian Army in a severely weakened state. The course of the campaign made it increasingly evident that Austro–Hungarian units needed German support.[16]

The imbalance in the relationship became even more pronounced when it came to the issue of command. As the German presence in Galicia increased, first with the Beskiden Corps and then the Süd Army and finally the German Eleventh Army, so did German influence in matters of command. This was convincingly demonstrated early on when Marwitz successfully demanded the relief of the commander of the Austro–Hungarian X Corps by Conrad after the mismanaged action of April 3.[17]

Once the Eleventh Army was installed and the campaign under way, the disparity became ever more pronounced, starting with the arrangements by which directives were issued to Mackensen and the authority Mackensen had over elements of the two neighboring Austro–Hungarian armies. By July the authority of Falkenhayn was clearly expressed in his July 5, 1915, message to Conrad, telling him in effect that the matter of command of the Bug Army was none of Conrad's business, while dismissing the notion of subordinating even the now shrunken Süd Army to Pflanzer-Baltin.[18] All this was infuriating to Conrad, but given the rapidly eroding strength of the Austro–Hungarian Army, there was little he could do.[19]

Controversy over Gorlice–Tarnow after the war revolved around two issues. The first was who should get the credit for the victory, Falkenhayn or Conrad. The second was what kind of a victory had been won by Mackensen. The immediate postwar period saw Conrad get the credit as the brain behind the Gorlice–Tarnow offensive. Conrad still had a coterie of admirers, some of whom were associated with him from his days as chief of the Austro–Hungarian general staff, and of course Gina Conrad.[20] This group included officers who were involved in the production of the Austrian official history of the war. The image of Conrad as the master strategist remained strong into the interwar period, with Liddell Hart being one of the exceptions, describing Conrad as "the man who juggled with armies, and broke them."[21] More recent scholarship has taken a much more critical view of Conrad, noting his numerous errors and misjudgments.[22]

Just as the question of Conrad's contribution to the victory was tied up with the matter of his personality, the same was true of Germany and Falkenhayn. Even the most ardent of Falkenhayn's critics agreed that the decision to attack was correct. Most, however, were more than willing to give the credit to Conrad for the concept of the offensive. In addition, Falkenhayn is faulted for not sending a larger force, which, it was argued, was needed to achieve a decisive victory in the east.[23] Much of this was based on the side that people took when Falkenhayn was dueling with Hindenburg and Ludendorff.

A second question went to the issue of the kind of victory that Gorlice–Tarnow was. Postwar analysis in Germany concluded that the fight for Gorlice–Tarnow, however brilliantly it may have been conducted, was just an ordinary victory. This argument, however, seems to rest on one fact: namely, that no great encirclement was achieved. Although Mackensen's forces had inflicted hundreds of thousands of casualties, taken a haul of prisoners dwarfing that of Tannenberg, caused immense losses of equipment to the Russians, at no time were the Germans and Austro–Hungarians able to envelop and annihilate all or part of Radko-Dmitriev's Russian 3rd Army.[24]

This analysis of Gorlice–Tarnow, however, was reflective of the basic thrust of German military thinking in the postwar period, which made envelopment something of a fetish. This was enhanced by the prolific writings of Ludendorff and the looming presence of Hindenburg, who in his long tenure as president of the Reich represented a link with better times. The forging of the link was completed with the building and dedication of the massive Tannenberg monument in 1927.[25] Any reasonable examination of the spring and summer campaigns conducted by Mackensen and Seeckt should conclude that an extraordinary victory had been won, a success that turned the course of the war at the time in the direction of the Central Powers.

As is the case with every victory and defeat, the question of "why" beckons. Why were Mackensen's forces able to mount repeatedly successful attacks, and why were the Russians not able to mount an effective response? The first element that must be considered is command. The combination of Mackensen and Seeckt proved as formidable as any put together by the German Army during the war. Mackensen, always mindful of Prussian military history, once referred to Seeckt as his Gneisenau, the brilliant chief of staff to Blücher during the campaigns of 1813–1815.[26] Mackensen, however, was much more than a simple hard charger. He was an experienced, thoughtful professional who was able to adapt to the complexities of modern warfare and harness the potential of both mature and emerging technologies in the waging of war. For the effective waging of coalition warfare, both Seeckt and Cramon thought Mackensen was an ideal commander. Tappen, who later served as Mackensen's chief of staff for the Romanian campaign, regarded Mackensen as Germany's best field commander in the war.[27]

For his part, Seeckt proved an ideal alter ego for his boss. Both enjoyed imperturbable temperaments and were slightly different in outlook, in that Seeckt considered Mackensen naturally predisposed to melancholy.[28] The two, however, enjoyed an excellent relationship, both professionally and personally, as Seeckt intimated to his wife. When the military marriage of Mackensen and Seeckt was dissolved when Seeckt was assigned as chief of staff to the Austro–Hungarian Seventh Army in June 1916, Seeckt wrote that his parting from Mackensen was "moving for both of us."[29] It is also worth pointing out that

Mackensen's partnership with his new chief of staff, Tappen, was every bit as successful as the one with Seeckt.

Mackensen and Seeckt were fortunate also in their subordinate commanders. At first glance, most of the corps and division commanders who served in the Eleventh Army between May and September 1915 might seem to be a relatively undistinguished group. Aside from Marwitz, who later went on to army-level command, and Arz, who succeeded Conrad as chief of the Austro–Hungarian general staff, none of Mackensen's subordinate commanders achieved really high rank. Two, Emmich and Fabarius, did not even survive 1915, the former dying of natural causes and the latter of wounds received on the eastern front.[30]

Nonetheless, Mackensen's subordinate commanders were competent and experienced professionals who were good at their jobs. Winckler, for example showed himself to be a good battlefield tactician who was attuned to the intent of his superior. Winckler was also willing to take risks when it improved the execution of the plan, as illustrated in his pushing the 2nd Guard Division across the San, when Plettenberg initially pursued a more cautious course. Likewise François paid tribute to his division commanders, Stocken and Fabarius, for their exceptional combat leadership.[31]

The leadership shown at the corps and divisional levels was certainly in the best traditions of the German Army. More importantly, the subordinate commanders in the German Eleventh Army, although they were willing to take risks when the situation demanded it, always did so within the parameters of the plan. This allowed Mackensen and Seeckt to maintain not just command but also control of the operations. This is in stark contrast to the British Army on the Somme, for example, where the higher commanders, Sir Douglas Haig and Sir Henry Rawlinson, lost control of events after a month, resulting in uncoordinated attacks, pointless fighting, and unnecessary casualties.[32]

The success of Mackensen's attacks rested on three overlapping factors: aircraft, heavy artillery, and communications. The Germans did not have a very large number of aircraft available to them, but it was enough to give them aerial superiority and allow the Germans and Austro–Hungarians to conduct almost uninterrupted aerial reconnaissance. During periods when the contending forces were in static situations, aerial reconnaissance was critical to locating key Russian positions, which could then be attacked by the artillery. The ability to spot for heavy artillery was especially critical at times when ammunition was in short supply and the Germans needed to make every shot count.[33]

During the more fluid parts of the campaign, aerial reconnaissance provided Mackensen and his staff with plenty of information on the movements of Russian troops and rail traffic. In addition aircraft delivered to commanders photos of new positions being constructed. Aerial reconnaissance was able to compensate for the inability of German and Austro–Hungarian cavalry to provide operational reconnaissance, given its ineffectiveness in overcoming the swarms of ubiquitous Cossacks employed by the Russians to screen retreats.[34] The available documentation makes it clear that the Eleventh Army commander and staff placed great importance in the rapid dissemination of aerial reconnaissance to subordinate commanders. Aerial reconnaissance, combined with wireless intercepts and prisoner interrogations, served to give Mackensen and Seeckt a reasonably clear picture of the operational situation.[35]

Throughout the campaigns in Galicia and Poland, the trump card of the Central Powers was their heavy artillery, especially howitzers larger than 150-mm, which were capable of high-angle fire. The ability of German aerial reconnaissance to enhance the aim of the artillery was vital, since even when ammunition was plentiful, it was in short supply as compared with ammunition usage on other fronts. The longest bombardment by Mackensen's forces during the campaigns in Galicia and Poland was four hours. More commonly, the time allotted for artillery preparation was limited to about two hours.[36]

The ability of German and Austro–Hungarian artillery to improve their accuracy via ground or aerial observation was critical in several ways. First, with ammunition relatively scarce, the Germans and Austro–Hungarians simply did not have the shells to waste; every shot had to count. In addition, the ability to observe allowed the artillery to be used against precise targets. This paid major dividends at Przemysl, where Forts Xa and XIa were shattered by the heavy guns. Finally, the accuracy of German and Austro–Hungarian artillery inflicted heavy casualties on the Russians, while the survivors often believed they were confronted with a demoralizing blizzard of shells. As one Russian corps commander complained, "the Germans expend metal, we expend life."[37]

Light artillery was also employed in an imaginative way, taking advantage of the unique combat conditions in the east. The idea of sending field guns forward behind the attacking infantry for direct support against still active Russian machine gun nests and strong points paid dividends in the opening of the attack on May 2.[38] If done on the western front, such a practice would have been suicidal. In addition, the use of light guns in that manner was possible because of the anemic response of the Russian artillery. Even then, such tactics with field guns were not repeated thereafter. The artillery also proved very effective in breaking up Russian counterattacks.[39]

Central to the conduct of the campaign and effective use of artillery during it was communication. The Germans were able to make very effective use of the telephone. Whenever the Eleventh Army moved forward, the corps orders issued by François to his division commanders required them to establish telephone communications as soon as possible.[40] The Germans were aided by the almost total lack of opposition on the part of the Russian artillery. This alleviated the problem of Russian shrapnel cutting German telephone wires, a problem that bedeviled the British on the Somme a year later. The threat of a swift death sentence to any civilian found near telephone lines also served to give the Eleventh Army's command structure a secure means of communication, the lack of humanity notwithstanding. In addition, wireless radio was employed both more extensively and effectively than before. Finally, aircraft were employed during the war in the delivery of messages and reports as a matter of course.[41]

Mackensen's campaigns in Galicia and Poland were also interesting in the lessons they imparted to some German commanders and failed to impart to others. For an old cavalryman, Mackensen at least tacitly gave up on the idea of using large cavalry units in any kind of exploitative role. For the initial attack, artillery would be the key element in punching the hole, and for exploitation the Eleventh Army would use an infantry corps. After that, reserves that were placed near the main weight of the attack were usually infantry divisions.[42] The Hungarian 11th Cavalry Division, although part of the Eleventh Army's reserve, played a very minor part in the campaign. Likewise the actions of Heydebreck's ad hoc cavalry corps in regard to Kovel was but a mere sideshow to the major operations being undertaken elsewhere. This is in stark contrast with the British on the western front, where Haig repeatedly piled up masses of cavalry behind the front in the expectation of their sweeping forward into the German rear once the great breakthrough had been achieved.[43]

Another lesson that was learned by some and not by others concerned the purpose of breaking through enemy defenses. When he had become the de facto head of OHL, Ludendorff made the famous comment "I object to the word 'operation.' We shall punch a hole into their line. For the rest, we shall see. We also did it this way in Russia."[44] All this statement illustrates is that Dennis Showalter was quite right in saying that intellectually, Ludendorff never got beyond the level of colonel.[45]

In point of fact, every hole punched by Mackensen's forces during the campaign was made for a specific purpose. The initial attack on May 2 was designed to set the conditions for an advance to Zmigrod, thus compromising the right flank of the Russian forces in the Carpathians. The approach to and crossing of the San was based on the need for operational space in which to maneuver, so that Przemysl could be attacked from the north if the need arose. The assault on the Grodek position was intended to break through the Russian position in order to seize Rava Russka, thus isolating Lemberg from the north.[46]

Carefully chosen operational objectives were also matched by operational pauses, which were also well considered. Mackensen, Seeckt, and Falkenhayn all understood that the forces they commanded had an operational range limit. The pauses were reasonably short, however, so that the Russians were never given enough time to cobble together a defensive line that could stand up to even a short bombardment by the German and Austro–Hungarian heavy artillery. Thus the Russian positions across Galicia became steadily more brittle. This was particularly true of the Grodek position, which fell apart rather quickly.[47]

Just as military campaigns have a winning side, they also have a losing side. While this study has focused on the actions of the Germans and their Austro–Hungarian allies, some brief comments on the Russian conduct of the campaign are warranted here. From the standpoint of command, the Russians suffered in several ways. The first was that the Russian conduct of the campaign was affected by an inability on the part of Stavka or the respective front headquarters to make decisions in a timely manner. Early on in operations in Galicia, decisions by Stavka and the southwest front were made slowly. This was compounded by the lack of transportation needed to move troops operationally in a timely fashion. Consequently, Russian reinforcements arrived piecemeal, and only in time to get caught up in the maelstrom of combat and be decimated in their turn. In addition, the Southwest Front was never able to concentrate a force sufficient to enable any kind of countermeasure that was capable of halting Mackensen's offensive.[48]

During the summer campaign, the consequences resulting from the lack of timely decisions was manifested in the debacles at Novogeorgievsk and Kovno. The Russians lacked the transportation necessary for the simultaneous evacuation of both of those places plus Warsaw. The vast amount of material in those fortresses could have been removed in a staggered fashion had a decision been made in a timely fashion, because the rail lines in Russian Poland were operating. No such decision, however, was made. When events forced a decision on the matter, Stavka had to prioritize, and Warsaw was put at the top of the list. Thus huge amounts of valuable equipment, supplies, and ammunition were lost.[49]

Russian defenses suffered from several other defects. First, the Russian defense systems, aside from the initial position that was overrun by Mackensen's forces in early May, lacked depth. The pace of Mackensen's advance was enough to deny the Russians time to build extensive positions. The Grodek position, for example, was rather shallow and was fatally compromised after an advance of a couple of miles. The trenches themselves were also inadequate in terms of being able to withstand German and Austro–Hungarian heavy artillery. Finally, Russian infantry tactics served more to amass casualties than to impede the Germans, especially given the disparity in artillery.[50]

In terms of comparing the conduct of these campaigns with that of those on the western front, the most interesting aspect that requires discussion is surprise. Although the French did detect forces being withdrawn from the western front, none of the Entente powers were able to anticipate precisely where they would appear. A carefully conducted deployment was able to preserve operational surprise. Even though the Russians discovered the German presence on April 26, the information came to late for either Ivanov or Radko-Dmitriev to formulate an effective response. Thus, although Mackensen had lost the element of surprise tactically, it was irrelevant, since operational surprise had been maintained.[51]

The relationship between operational and tactical surprise on the eastern front was quite different from that on the western front. In the west it was tactical surprise, achieved either by technological means such as tanks or the introduction of new tactical methods, that mattered more. The more developed transportation systems in the west precluded the sustaining of operational surprise, as events in 1918 showed.[52] The best one could do in the west was to achieve a series of tactical surprises that could all be tied together in support of a strategic plan. The biggest difference in the west in 1918 was simply that Ferdinand Foch, the Allies' supreme commander, had a plan; Ludendorff did not.[53]

How then can we conclude this study of the offensive begun by Mackensen in May in Galicia and concluded in September 1915 in Poland? In just four months, Falkenhayn and Mackensen had taken a situation fraught with peril for the Central Powers and turned it to one of strategic advantage. The calculated risk of holding the western front with minimal reserves had succeeded, as both French and British offensives had failed. Although Italy had joined the Entente, a dauntless defense by the Austro–Hungarian Fifth Army had held the Italians at bay along the Isonzo. Turkey had inflicted a disaster on the British at Kut and was still holding on grimly at Gallipoli. The commitment of Germany's strategic reserve on the eastern front had neutralized the Russian threat to Austria–Hungary. With Russia put out of the war in an active sense temporarily, Serbia could now be put out permanently. The war was going Germany's way.

APPENDIX

German and Austro–Hungarian General Officer Ranks

German	Austro–Hungarian	American
Generalmajor	Generalmajor	Brigadier general
Generalleutnant	Feldmarschalleutnant	Major general
General der Infanterie[a]	Feldzeugmeister[b]	Lieutenant general
Generaloberst	Generaloberst	General
Generalfeldmarschall	Feldmarschall	General of the Army

---

[a]Other equivalents included General der Kavallerie and General der Artillerie.
[b]Other equivalents included General der Infanterie, Kavallerie, and Artillerie.

Notes

INTRODUCTION

1. Winston Churchill, *The Unknown War: The Eastern Front* (New York: Charles Scribner's Sons; 1931), p. 18.

2. Just a sampling of the literature includes Gerard DeGroot, *Douglas Haig, 1861–1928* (London: Unwin and Hyman; 1988), Denis Winter, *Haig's Command: A Reassessment* (New York: Viking; 1991), Robin Prior and Trevor Wilson, *Command on the Western Front* (Oxford: Blackwell; 1992), Andrew A. Wiest, *Haig: The Evolution of a Commander* (Washington, D.C.: Potomac Books; 2005), Anika Mombauer, *Helmuth von Moltke and the Origins of the First World War* (Cambridge: Cambridge University Press; 2001), Roger Parkinson, *Tormented Warrior: Ludendorff and the Supreme Command* (New York: Stein and Day, 1979), Robert T. Foley, *German Strategy and the Path to Verdun: Erich von Falkenhayn and the Development of Attrition, 1870–1916* (Cambridge: Cambridge University Press; 2005), Tim Travers, *The Killing Ground: The British Army, the Western Front and the Emergence of Modern Warfare, 1900–1918* (London: Routledge; 1987), Prior and Wilson, *Passchendaele: The Untold Story* (New Haven, Conn.: Yale University Press; 1996), Ian Passingham, *Pillars of Fire: The Battle of Messines Ridge June 1917* (Stroud: Sutton Publishing; 1998), Michael S. Neiberg, *Foch: Supreme Allied Commander in the Great War* (Washington, D.C.: Brassey's; 2003), Leonard V. Smith, Stéphane Audoin-Rouzeau and Annette Becker, *France and the Great War 1914–1918* (Cambridge: Cambridge University Press; 2003) and Robert A. Doughty, *Pyrrhic Victory: French Strategy and Operations in the Great War* (Cambridge, Mass.: Harvard University Press; 2005).

3. Norman Stone, *The Eastern Front 1914–1917* (New York: Charles Scribner's Sons; 1975).

4. Holger H. Herwig, *The First World War: Germany and Austria–Hungary 1914–1918* (London: Arnold; 1997) and Hew Strachan, *The First World War,* Vol. I: *To Arms* (New York: Oxford University Press; 2001).

5. Graydon A. Tunstall Jr., *Planning for War Against Russia and Serbia: Austro-Hungarian and German Military Strategies, 1871–1914* (Boulder, Colo.: East European Monographs; 1993) and Lawrence Sondhaus, *Franz Conrad von Hötzendorf: Architect of the Apocalypse* (Boston: Humanities Press; 2000).

6. Dennis E. Showalter, *Tannenberg: Clash of Empires, 1914* (reprinted edition) (Dulles, Va.: Brassey's; 2004) and Richard L. DiNardo, "Huns With Web-Feet: Operation Albion, 1917," *War in History,* Vol. 12, No. 4 (November 2005): pp. 396–417.

7. Although Prussia was allied with Italy in 1866, the Austro-Prussian War of 1866 was really a case of Austria fighting two different enemies, Italy and Prussia, in two different theaters at the same time. There was no real collaboration between Italy and Prussia in their respective struggles against Austria. Richard L. DiNardo, *Germany and the Axis Powers: From Coalition to Collapse* (Lawrence: University Press of Kansas; 2005), p. 6.

8. See especially James S. Corum, *The Roots of Blitzkrieg: Hans von Seeckt and German Military Reform* (Lawrence: University Press of Kansas; 1993).

9. It should be noted that all general officer ranks are given in the German or Austrian style. Thus Generaloberst is given here, not Colonel–General. For a table of German and Austrian ranks and their American equivalents see appendix in chapter 9. All names are also in the German form. Thus the German emperor is Wilhelm II, not William II.

10. Theo Schwarzmüller, *Zwischen Kaiser und Führer. Generalfeldmarschall August von Mackensen: Eine politische Biographie* (Paderborn: Ferdinand Schöningh; 1996).

11. See, for examples, Hans Meier-Welker, *Seeckt* (Frankfurt-am-Main: Bernard und Graefe Verlag für Wehrwesen; 1967), pp. 56–57, and Correlli Barnett, *The Swordbearers: Supreme Command in the First World War* (reprinted edition) (Bloomington: Indiana University Press; 1975), p. 271.

12. Seeckt to wife, 28 June 1915, Nachlass Seeckt, File N 247/57, Bundesarchiv–Militärarchiv, Freiburg-im-Breisgau, Germany (hereafter cited as BA-MA N 247/57).

CHAPTER ONE

1. Field Marshal Franz Baron Conrad von Hötzendorf, *Aus meiner Dienstzeit 1906–1918* (6th ed.) (Vienna: Rikola Verlag; 1921), Vol. 3, p. 145.

2. Walter Görlitz (ed.), *The Kaiser and His Court: The Diaries, Note Books and Letters of Admiral Georg Alexander von Müller, Chief of the Naval Cabinet 1914–1918* (New York: Harcourt, Brace and World; 1961), p. 40.

3. Holger H. Herwig, "Why Did It Happen?" *The Origins of World War I* (Holger H. Herwig and Richard F. Hamilton eds.) (Cambridge: Cambridge University Press; 2003), pp. 466–467.

4. Herwig, *The First World War,* p. 19. The most famous student of German war aims in World War I remains Fritz Fischer, whose controversial thesis held that Germany consciously went to war in 1914 for the aim of world power. In this regard, I consider Herwig's skepticism to be well founded.

5. Antulio J. Echevarria II, *After Clausewitz: German Military Thinkers before the Great War* (Lawrence: University Press of Kansas; 2000), p. 212, David R. Jones, "Imperial Russia's Forces at War," *Military Effectiveness* (Allan R. Millett and Williamson Murray, eds.), (Boston: Allen and Unwin; 1988), Vol. I, p. 289, and Bruce W. Menning,

"The Offensive Revisited: Russian Preparation for Future War, 1906–1914," *Reforming the Tsar's Army: Military Innovation in Imperial Russia from Peter the Great to the Revolution* (David Schimmelpennick van der Oye and Bruce W. Menning, eds.) (Cambridge: Cambridge University Press; 2004), p. 289.

6. The literature on the development of German war plans between 1875 and 1914 has consumed whole forests. Some of the more essential works include Arden Bucholz, *Moltke, Schlieffen and Prussian War Planning* (Oxford: Berg Publishers; 1993), Gerhard Ritter, *The Schlieffen Plan: Critique of a Myth* (New York: Praeger; 1958), and the interesting if rather overstated revisionist work by Terence Zuber, *Inventing the Schlieffen Plan: German War Planning, 1871–1914* (Oxford: Oxford University Press; 2002). For the 1914 campaign in the west from the German perspective, one always has to start with Germany, Reichsarchiv, *Der Weltkrieg 1914 bis 1918* (Berlin: E. S. Mittler und Sohn; 1925), Vol. 1. A vast number of works incorporate the 1914 campaign in the west as part of a broader study. Some of these are Herwig, *The First World War,* pp. 96–106, Mombauer, *Helmuth von Moltke and the Origins of the First World War,* pp. 227–282, Strachan, *The First World War,* Vol. I, pp. 163–242, Jehuda Wallach, *The Dogma of the Battle of Annihilation: The Theories of Clausewitz and Schlieffen and Their Impact on the German Conduct of Two World Wars* (Westport, Conn.: Greenwood Press; 1986), pp. 87–106, and Martin van Creveld, *Supplying War: Logistics from Wallenstein to Patton* (2nd ed.) (Cambridge: Cambridge University Press; 2005), pp. 109–141. For the French Army's opening operations, see Doughty, *Pyrrhic Victory,* pp. 46–85.

7. Casualty figures for both sides vary greatly. Herwig gives losses as being about 250,000 on each side for the 1914 campaign in the west. Herwig, *The First World War,* p. 105. Doughty puts French casualties much higher, with the army losing about 400,000 killed in the opening campaign culminating in the Marne, plus a further 268,000 killed between October 1914 and March 1915, thus bringing total casualties to well over a million. Doughty, *Pyrrhic Victory,* pp. 104–107.

8. Gordon A. Craig, *Germany 1866–1945* (New York: Oxford University Press; 1978), p. 114.

9. General Georg Wetzell, *Der Bündniskrieg: Eine militärpolitisch operative Studie des Weltkrieges* (Berlin: E. S. Mittler und Sohn; 1937), p. 4, Tunstall, *Planning For War Against Russia and Serbia,* p. 31, Gunther E. Rothenberg, "Moltke, Schlieffen and the Doctrine of Strategic Envelopment," *Makers of Modern Strategy,* (Peter Paret, ed.) (Princeton, N.J.: Princeton University Press; 1986), p. 308, and Eberhard Kessel, *Moltke* (Stuttgart: K. F. Koehler; 1957), pp. 703–727.

10. For a mere sampling of the scholarship on Schlieffen's westward shift, see Doughty, *Pyrrhic Victory,* p. 25, Tunstall, *Planning for War against Russia and Serbia,* p. 34, Robert M. Citino, *The German Way of War: From the Thirty Years' War to the Third Reich* (Lawrence: University Press of Kansas; 2005), pp. 196–208, Echevarria, *After Clausewitz,* pp. 193–197, and Bucholz, *Moltke, Schlieffen and Prussian War Planning,* pp. 127–213.

11. Herwig, *The First World War,* p. 50, Gunther E. Rothenberg, *The Army of Francis Joseph* (West Lafayette, Ind.: Purdue University Press; 1976), p. 175, Tunstall, *Planning for War against Russia and Serbia,* p. 46, Richard L. DiNardo and Daniel J. Hughes, "Germany and Coalition Warfare in the World Wars: A Comparison," *War in History* Vol. 8, No. 2 (April 2001): p. 168, and Lothar Höbelt, "Schlieffen, Potiorek und das Ende der gemeinsam deutsch–österreichisch–ungarischen Aufmarschpläne im Osten," *Militärgeschichtlichen Mitteilungen* No. 36 (1984): p. 17.

12. Tunstall, *Planning for War against Russia and Serbia*, p. 28, Wetzell, "Der Bündniskrieg," p. 840 and DiNardo and Hughes, "Germany and Coalition Warfare in the World Wars," p. 167.

13. Gerhard Ritter, *The Sword and the Scepter: The Problem of Militarism in Germany* (Coral Gables, Fla: University of Miami Press; 1970), Vol. 2, p. 239.

14. Walter Görlitz, *History of the German General Staff 1657–1945* (New York: Praeger; 1954), p. 139, and Rothenberg, *The Army of Francis Joseph*, p. 142.

15. Colonel General Helmuth von Moltke, *Erinnerungen-Briefe-Dokumente* (Eliza von Moltke, ed.) (Stuttgart: Der Kommende Tag, 1922), p. 252, Mombauer, *Helmuth von Moltke and the Origins of the First World War*, p. 113, Ritter, *The Sword and the Scepter,* Vol. 2, pp. 243–246, Conrad, *Aus meiner Dienstzeit 1906–1918,* Vol. 1, pp. 379–393, 403–404, 631–634, Gerhard Seyfert, *Die militärischen Beziehungen und Vereinbarungen zwischen dem deutschen und österreichischen Generalstab vor und bei Beginn des Weltkrieges* (Leipzig: J. Moltzen; 1934), pp. 53–61, Hew Strachan, "Die Ostfront. Geopolitik, Geographie und Operationen," *Die Vergessene Front. Der Osten 1914/15: Ereignis, Wirkung, Nachwirkung* (Gerhard P. Gross, ed.) (Paderborn: Ferdinand Schöningh; 2006), p. 16 and Tunstall, *Planning for War against Russia and Serbia*, p. 74.

16. Sondhaus, *Franz Conrad von Hötzendorf,* p. 125, and István Deák, *Beyond Nationalism: A Social and Political History of the Habsburg Officer Corps, 1848–1918* (New York: Oxford University Press; 1990), p. 145. A slightly different version of Redl's end is in Harold C. Deutsch, "Sidelights on the Redl Affair: Russian Intelligence on the Eve of the Great War," *Intelligence and National Security* Vol. 4, No. 4 (October 1989): pp. 827–828. The standard work on the Redl affair remains Georg Markus, *Der Fall Redl* (Vienna: Amalthea Verlag; 1984).

17. Sondhaus, *Franz Conrad von Hötzendorf,* p. 126 and Conrad, *Aus meiner Dienstzeit 1906–1918,* Vol. 3, p. 368.

18. Rothenberg, *The Army of Francis Joseph,* p. 152, Conrad, *Aus meiner Dienstzeit 1906–1918,* Vol. I, pp. 404–405 and Manfred Rauchensteiner, *Der Tod des Doppeladlers: Österreich-Ungarn und der Erste Weltkrieg* (Vienna: Verlag Styria; 1993), p. 54.

19. Karl von Kageneck Diary, August 4, 1914, BA-MA MSg 1/1914. Shortly after this, Waldersee was posted to the German Eighth Army as the chief of staff. Born May 10, 1871, Karl Graf von Kageneck was commissioned a lieutenant in 1891. After graduating from the *Kriegsakademie* in 1901, Kageneck was eventually promoted to captain in 1904. Assigned to Vienna in 1907, he eventually became German military attaché to the Dual Monarchy. While serving in that capacity, he was promoted to lieutenant colonel in 1914 and then colonel in 1916. After the war he retired with general officer's rank. He died in 1967. BA-MA MSg 109/10863.

20. Conrad, *Aus meiner Dienstzeit 1906–1918,* Vol. 4, p. 161, Moltke, *Erinnerungen-Briefe-Dokumente,* pp. 16–20, Kaganeck diary, August 7, 1914, BA-MA MSg 1/1914, and Count Josef Stürgkh, *Im Deutschen Grossen Hauptquartier* (Leipzig: Paul List Verlag; 1921), p. 23.

21. Kaganeck Diary, August 6, 1914, MSg 1/1914. "Parallel war" is a phrase that well describes the relationship between Germany and some of its Axis allies, most notably Finland and to a lesser extent Italy, in the Second World War. DiNardo, *Germany and the Axis Powers,* p. 195.

22. Major General Max Hoffmann, *War Diaries and Other Papers* (Eric Sutton trans.) (London: Martin Secker; 1929), Vol. II, p. 20, Showalter, *Tannenberg,* p. 158, and

Gerhard P. Gross, "Im Schatten des Westens. Die deutsche Kriegführung an der Ostfront bis Ende 1915," *Die vergessene Front,* p. 52.

23. Germany, Reichsarchiv, *Der Weltkrieg 1914–1918,* Vol. 2, p. 93, Stone, *The Eastern Front 1914–1917,* pp. 60–61, Hoffmann, *War Diaries and Other Papers,* Vol. I, pp. 38–39, Citino, *The German Way of War,* p. 227 and Showalter, *Tannenberg,* p. 187.

24. Görlitz, ed., *The Kaiser and His Court,* p. 23, John Wheeler-Bennett, *Wooden Titan: Hindenburg in Twenty Years of German History 1914–1934* (New York: William Morrow; 1936), p. 14, Hoffmann, *War Diaries and Other Papers,* Vol. II, p. 31, and Showalter, *Tannenberg,* pp. 198–199. Technically, Hindenburg's actual name was Paul von Beneckendorff und Hindenburg. For the purposes of this work, however, his name is noted simply as Hindenburg.

25. Born January 25, 1869, Max Hoffmann was commissioned as a lieutenant on September 19, 1888. After graduating from the *Kriegsakademie* in 1898, he was promoted to lieutenant colonel on January 27, 1914. After serving on the staff of OberOst, he was promoted to colonel on August 18, 1916, and became chief of staff for OberOst at the end of August 1916. Promoted to Generalmajor on October 29, 1917, he remained in the army through the early postwar period, being named commander of the 10th Infantry Brigade on January 10, 1919. He retired from the army on March 31, 1920, and died on July 8, 1927. Holger H. Herwig and Neil M. Heyman, *Biographical Dictionary of World War I* (Westport, Conn.: Greenwood Press; 1982), p. 188 and BA-MA MSg 109/10862.

26. In his corps order for August 25, 1914, Mackensen urged his troops on by saying that "the success of our operation depends upon the marching performance of the XVII Corps." Wolfgang Foerster, ed., *Mackensen: Briefe und Aufzeichnungen des Generalfeldmarschalls aus Krieg und Frieden* (Leipzig: Bibliographisches Institut; 1938), p. 48. This was not idle talk, as on August 25 the XVII Corps covered about 30 miles on foot, a most impressive performance when one considers the time of the year and the circumstances. Germany, Reichsarchiv, *Der Weltkrieg 1914 bis 1918,* Vol. 2, p. 169.

27. Stone, *The Eastern Front 1914–1917,* pp. 64–66, Germany, Reichsarchiv, *Der Weltkrieg 1914–1918,* Vol. 2, p. 175, Hoffmann, *War Diaries and Other Papers,* Vol. I, pp. 40–41, Foerster, ed., *Mackensen: Briefe und Aufzeichnungen,* p. 59, Franz Uhle-Wettler, *Erich Ludendorff in seiner Zeit: Soldat-Stratege-Revolutionär. Eine Neubewertung* (Augsburg: Kurt Vowinckel Verlag; 1996), pp. 142–143, and Showalter, *Tannenberg,* pp. 286–319.

28. Günther Kronenbitter, "Die Macht der Illusionen. Julikrise und Kriegsausbruch 1914 aus der Sicht des deutschen Militärattachés in Wien," *Militärgeschichtliche Mitteilungen* Vol. 57, No. 2 (1998): p. 541, Kaganeck diary, August 4, 1914, BA-MA MSg 1/1914, Conrad, *Aus meiner Dienstzeit 1906–1918,* Vol. 4, p. 161, and Rothenberg, *The Army of Francis Joseph,* pp. 178–179.

29. Kronenbitter, "Die Macht der Illusionen," p. 538, and Herwig, *The First World War,* p. 18.

30. Strachan, *The First World War,* Vol. I, p. 337, and Herwig, *The First World War,* p. 88.

31. Kaganeck Diary, September 14, 1914, BA-MA MSg 1/1914, Herwig, *The First World War,* pp. 88–89, and Strachan, *The First World War,* Vol. I, p. 346.

32. Stone, *The Eastern Front 1914–1917,* pp. 80–81, and Rothenberg, *The Army of Francis Joseph,* p. 179.

33. Herwig, *The First World War*, p. 90, Stone, *The Eastern Front 1914–1917*, pp. 80–81, and General der Infanterie Hermann von Kuhl, *Der Weltkrieg 1914–1918* (Berlin: Verlag Tradition Wilhelm Kolk; 1929), Vol. I, p. 22.

34. Strachan, *The First World War*, Vol. I, pp. 352–353, Stone, *The Eastern Front 1914–1917*, pp. 84–85, Herwig and Heyman, *Biographical Dictionary of World War I*, pp. 193–194, and Yuri Danilov, *Russland im Weltkriege 1914–1915* (Jena: Frommannsche Buchhandlung; 1925), pp. 223 and 227.

35. Strachan, *The First World War*, Vol. I, p. 356, Stone, *The Eastern Front 1914–1917*, pp. 90–91, Rothenberg, *The Army of Francis Joseph*, p. 180, Conrad, *Aus meiner Dienstzeit 1906–1918*, Vol. 4, p. 894, Yuri Danilov, *Russland im Weltkrieg 1914–1915*, p. 246 and Sondhaus, *Franz Conrad von Hötzendorf*, p. 156.

36. Herwig, *The First World War*, p. 94, Kuhl, *Der Weltkrieg 1914–1918*, Vol. I, p. 59, and Stürgkh, *Im Deutschen Grossen Hauptquartier*, p. 40.

37. General Erich von Falkenhayn, *The German General Staff and Its Decisions, 1914–1916* (New York: Dodd, Mead, 1920), p. 24, Foerster, ed., *Mackensen: Briefe und Aufzeichnungen*, p. 68 and Herwig, *The First World War*, p. 95.

38. Herwig, *The First World War*, pp. 106–107.

39. Tunstall, *Planning for War against Russia and Serbia*, pp. 255–256.

40. Germany, Reichsarchiv, *Der Weltkrieg 1914 bis 1918*, Vol. 5, pp. 412–413, Erich Ludendorff, *Meine Kriegserinnerungen 1914–1918* (Berlin: E. S. Mittler und Sohn; 1919), pp. 58–59, Kaganeck Diary, September 21, 1914, BA-MA MSg 1/1914, and Hoffmann, *War Diaries and Other Papers*, Vol. I, p. 43.

41. Germany, Reichsarchiv, *Der Weltkrieg 1914 bis 1918*, Vol. 5, p. 600, and Foerster, ed., *Mackensen: Briefe und Aufzeichnungen*, p. 68.

42. Germany, Reichsarchiv, *Der Weltkrieg 1914 bis 1918*, Vol. 5, p. 428, Strachan, *The First World War*, Vol. I, p. 363, and Foerster, ed., *Mackensen: Briefe und Aufzeichnungen*, p. 69.

43. Hoffmann, *War Diaries and Other Papers*, Vol. I, p. 45, Foerster, ed., *Mackensen: Briefe und Aufzeichnungen*, p. 70, Paul von Hindenburg, *Aus meinem Leben* (Leipzig: Verlag von S. Hirzel; 1920), p. 106 and Wolfgang Foerster, ed., *Wir Kämpfer im Weltkrieg: Feldzugbriefe und Kriegstagebücher von Frontkämpfer aus dem Material des Reichsarchivs* (Berlin: Neufeld und Henius Verlag; 1929), p. 123.

44. Foerster, ed., *Mackensen: Briefe und Aufzeichnungen*, pp. 71–72, Germany, Reichsarchiv, *Der Weltkrieg 1914 bis 1918*, Vol. 5, p. 438, Conrad *Aus meiner Dienstzeit 1906–1918*, Vol. 5, p. 21, and Ludendorff, *Meine Kriegserinnerungen*, p. 66.

45. Germany, Reichsarchiv, *Der Weltkrieg 1914 bis 1918*, Vol. 5, pp. 443–444, and Hindenburg, *Aus meinem Leben*, pp. 107–108.

46. Herwig, *The First World War*, p. 108, Danilov, *Russland im Weltkriege 1914–1915*, pp. 310–311, Svetlana Palmer and Sarah Wallis, eds., *Intimate Voices from the First World War* (New York: William Morrow; 2003), p. 70, and Conrad, *Aus meiner Dienstzeit 1906–1918*, Vol. 5, p. 92.

47. Germany, Reichsarchiv, *Der Weltkrieg 1914 bis 1918*, Vol. 5, p. 471, Foerster, ed., *Mackensen: Briefe und Aufzeichnungen*, pp. 80–84, Stone, *The Eastern Front 1914–1917*, p. 99, Hoffmann, *War Diaries and Other Papers*, Vol. I, pp. 46–47, Austria, Bundesministerium für Landesverteidigung, *Österreich–Ungarns Letzter Krieg 1914–1918* (Vienna: Verlag der Militärwissenschaftlichen Mitteilungen; 1930), Vol. 1, p. 431, Gross, "Im Schatten des Westens," *Die vergessene Front*, p. 57 and Hindenburg, *Aus meinen Leben*, p. 110.

48. Strachan, *The First World War*, Vol. I, p. 366. Conrad would later claim that these successes set the preconditions for the Gorlice–Tarnow offensive. Conrad to Arthur, Baron von Bolfras, 12 May 1915, Military Chancery File 78, Österreichischer Staatsarchiv-Kriegsarchiv, Vienna, Austria (hereafter cited as ÖSA-KA, MKSM 78), and Conrad, *Aus meiner Dienstzeit 1906–1918*, Vol. 5, p. 791.

49. Hindenburg, *Aus meinem Leben*, p. 112, Hoffmann, *War Diaries and Other Papers*, Vol. I, p. 49, Schwarzmüller, *Generalfeldmarschall August von Mackensen*, p. 99, Holger Afflerbach, *Falkenhayn: Politisches Denken und Handeln im Kaiserreich* (Munich: R. Oldenbourg; 1996), p. 197 and Conrad, *Aus meiner Dienstzeit 1906–1918*, Vol. 5, p. 340.

50. Adolph Wild von Hohenborn was born on July 8, 1860. He was commissioned a second lieutenant on February 14, 1880, and graduated from the *Kriegsakademie* in 1892. From 1901 to 1904, Wild served as aide to Prince Friedrich of Prussia. Promoted to colonel on March 24, 1909, he was eventually promoted to Generalmajor and appointed commander of the Third Guards Infantry Brigade on June 4, 1912, and commander of the 30th Infantry Division on August 31, 1914. Promoted Generalleutnant on January 20, 1915, he was named war minister the next day, as Falkenhayn's successor. Wild was appointed commander of the XVI Corps on October 29, 1916. He retired from the army with the rank of General der Infanterie on November 3, 1919, and died on October 25, 1925. Short Biographical Chronology, BA-MA MSg 109/10873.

51. Falkenhayn, *The German General Staff and Its Decisions, 1914–1916*, p. 33, Germany, Reichsarchiv, *Der Weltkrieg 1914 bis 1918*, Vol. 6, p. 37, Ludendorff, *Meine Kriegserinnerungen*, p. 75, Foley, *German Strategy and the Path to Verdun*, p. 117, Afflerbach, *Falkenhayn*, p. 230, and Lamar Cecil, *Wilhelm II* (Chapel Hill: The University of North Carolina Press; 1996), Vol. II, *Emperor and Exile, 1900–1941*, p. 219. Afflerbach suggests that Wilhelm still exercised some authority in the appointment of people to the top positions in the government. Holger Afflerbach, "Wilhelm II as Supreme Warlord in the First World War," *The Kaiser: New Research on Wilhelm II's Role in Imperial Germany* (Annika Mombauer and Wilhelm Deist, eds.) (Cambridge: Cambridge University Press; 2003), p. 208. For a more traditional interpretation, see Isabell V. Hull, *The Entourage of Kaiser Wilhelm II 1888–1918* (Cambridge: Cambridge University Press; 1982), p. 268.

52. Falkenhayn, *The German General Staff and Its Decisions, 1914–1916*, pp. 30–31, Germany, Reichsarchiv, *Der Weltkrieg 1914 bis 1918*, Vol. 6, p. 37, Gross, "Im Schatten des Westens," *Die Vergessene Front*, p. 56, Foley, *German Strategy and the Path to Verdun*, pp. 98–104, and Uhle-Wettler, *Erich Ludendorff in seiner Zeit*, p. 159.

53. Hermann von Kuhl, one of Germany's most perceptive critics of the war, who served in a variety of high-ranking staff positions during the war, considered the movement by rail of the German Ninth Army from Silesia to Posen a superb use of railways. Kuhl, *Der Weltkrieg 1914–1918*, Vol. I, p. 84.

54. Citino, *The German Way of War*, p. 233, and C.R.M.F. Cruttwell, *A History of the Great War 1914–1918* (Oxford: Oxford University Press, 1934), p. 87.

55. Foerster, ed., *Mackensen: Briefe und Aufzeichnungen*, pp. 105–109, and *Generalleutnant* Gerhard Tappen, War Diary, November 25, 1914, BA-MA W 10/50661. (Hereafter cited as Tappen diary.)

56. Herwig, *The First World War*, p. 109, Stone, *The Eastern Front 1914–1917*, pp. 104–107, Schwarzmüller, *Generalfeldmarschall August von Mackensen*, p. 99, Foerster, ed., *Mackensen: Briefe und Aufzeichnungen*, pp. 117–118, Hindenburg, *Aus*

meinem Leben, p. 115, Wheeler-Bennett, *Wooden Titan,* p. 46, and Otto Kolshorn, *Unser Mackensen: Ein Leben und Charakterbild* (Berlin: E. S. Mittler und Sohn, 1916), p. 112. Hoffmann was rather critical of Mackensen. Hoffmann, *War Diaries and Other Papers,* Vol. I, p. 51.

57. Showalter, *Tannenberg,* p. 328, Foerster, ed., *Mackensen: Briefe und Aufzeichnungen,* pp. 87–89, and Germany, Reichsarchiv, *Der Weltkrieg 1914 bis 1918,* Vol. 5, p. 444.

58. Ludendorff, *Meine Kriegserinnerungen,* p. 72.

59. Kaganeck Diary, September 21, 1914, BA-MA MSg 1/1914, Lundendorff, *Meine Kriegserinnerungen,* pp. 58–59, and Hoffmann, *War Diaries and Other Papers,* p. 43.

60. Gary W. Shanafelt, *The Secret Enemy: Austria–Hungary and the German Alliance, 1914–1918* (Boulder, Colo.: East European Monographs; 1985), p. 35, and Rauchensteiner, *Der Tod des Doppeladlers,* p. 56.

CHAPTER TWO

1. Conrad, *Aus meiner Dienstzeit 1906–1918,* Vol. 5, p. 755. The quote is from a report by Conrad to Austrian Prime Minister Count Leopold von Berchtold.

2. Erich Ludendorff to Helmuth von Moltke, January 2, 1915, *Nachlass* Ludendorff, BA-MA N 77/2.

3. Hoffmann, *War Diaries and Other Papers,* Vol. I, p. 53.

4. Afflerbach, *Falkenhayn,* p. 9. A short biographical chronology for Falkenhayn can also be found in BA-MA MSg 109/10859.

5. Afflerbach, *Falkenhayn,* pp. 107–108, and biographical chronology, BA-MA MSg 109/10859. See also Herwig and Heyman, *Biographical Dictionary of World War I,* pp. 145–146. It must be remembered that Imperial Germany was in point of fact a collection of states. Militarily, the three states that had separate armies were Prussia, Bavaria, and Württemberg. Prussia and Bavaria's military establishments were of such size that each maintained a separate war ministry and general staff, although the Prussian general staff encompassed all of Germany. Gordon Craig, *Germany 1866–1945* (New York: Oxford University Press, 1978), p. 41.

6. Afflerbach, *Falkenhayn,* p. 144, Cecil, *Wilhelm II,* Vol. II, pp. 189–194, and Erich Dorn Brose, *The Kaiser's Army: The Politics of Military Technology in Germany during the Machine Age, 1870–1918* (New York: Oxford University Press; 2001), p. 151.

7. Foley, *German Strategy and the Path to Verdun,* p. 91.

8. Seeckt "Diary Notes," January 24, 1915, *Nachlass* Seeckt, BA-MA N 247/22, Adolf Wild von Hohenborn, *Briefe und Tagebuchaufzeichnungen des preussischen Generals als Kriegsminister und Truppenführer im Ersten Weltkrieg* (Helmut Reichold, ed.) (Boppard-am-Rhein: Harald Boldt Verlag; 1986), p. 53, and Foley, *German Strategy and the Path to Verdun,* pp. 95 and 114. Falkenhayn's failure to gain the full confidence of the general staff was a major contributing factor to his downfall as head of OHL. Lieutenant Colonel Georg Wetzell, *Von Falkenhayn zu Hindenburg-Ludendorff: Der Wechsel in des deutschen Oberstes Heeresleitung im Herbst 1916 und der rümanische Feldzug* (Berlin: E. S. Mittler und Sohn; 1921), p. 1.

9. Ludendorff to Moltke, January 2, 1915, *Nachlass* Ludendorff, BA-MA N 77/2, Hoffmann, *War Diaries and Other Papers,* Vol. I, p. 60, and Cecil, *Wilhelm II,* Vol. II, p. 225. Ludendorff's antipathy toward Falkenhayn was also undoubtedly fueled by the for-

mer's great regard and even affection for Moltke, something that is clearly shown in Ludendorff's letters to him during 1915. See, for example, Ludendorff to Moltke, January 27, 1915, *Nachlass* Ludendorff, BA-MA N 77/2.

10. Foley, *German Strategy and the Path to Verdun*, p. 97.

11. Sondhaus, *Franz Conrad von Hötzendorf*, pp. 2–3.

12. August von Cramon, *Unser Österreich–Ungarischer Bundesgenosse im Weltkrieg. Erinnerungen aus meiner vierjährigen Tätigkeit as bevollmächtiger deutscher General beim k.u.k. Armeeoberkommando* (Berlin: E. S. Mittler und Sohn; 1920), p. 105. The details of Conrad's early career are covered in Sondhaus, *Franz Conrad von Hötzendorf*, pp. 19–80.

13. Conrad, *Aus meiner Dienstzeit 1906–1918*, Vol. 1, pp. 503–510, and Tunstall, *Planning for War against Russia and Serbia*, pp. 56–57.

14. Stürgkh, *Im deutschen Grossen Haupquartier*, p. 103, Afflerbach, *Falkenhayn*, p. 196, Conrad, *Aus meiner Dienstzeit 1906–1918*, Vol. 5, p. 340, and Sondhaus, *Franz Conrad von Hötzendorf*, p. 167. Tappen did not even mention Kundmann's name in his diary, noting only that the meeting was attended by "Conrad's adjutant." Tappen Diary, October 30, 1914, BA-MA W 10/50661.

15. Afflerbach, *Falkenhayn*, pp. 256–257, Sondhaus, *Franz Conrad von Hötzendorf*, p. 169, Conrad to Bolfras, April 6, 1915, ÖSA-KA MKSM 78, and Cramon, *Unser Österreich–Ungarischer Bundesgenosse im Weltkrieg*, p. 22. One can get a good sense of how much Falkenhayn traveled as the head of OHL from Tappen's diary. See, for example, Tappen Diary, January 11, 1915, BA-MA W 10/50661.

16. Compare, for example, Conrad to Falkenhayn, May 18, 1915, BA-MA W 10/50683, and Falkenhayn to Admiral Henning von Holtzendorf, March 30, 1916, BA-MA RM 28/53.

17. Cramon, *Unser Österreich–Ungarischer Bundesgenosse im Weltkrieg*, pp. 22–23.

18. Kaganeck Diary, April 12, 1915, BA-MA MSg 1/2514, Herwig, *The First World War*, p. 140, Sondhaus, *Franz Conrad von Hötzendorf*, p. 165, and Stone, *The Eastern Front 1914–1917*, p. 53. After Hans Reininghaus divorced Gina in the summer of 1915, she and Conrad were married in October 1915. She then moved to Teschen. While most satisfying emotionally to Conrad, this did serve to excite further derision among both the Germans and Conrad's enemies at the Habsburg court in Vienna. Gina Grafin Conrad von Hötzendorf, *Mein Leben mit Conrad von Hötzendorf; Sein geistiges Vernächtnis* (Leipzig: Grathlein, 1935), p. 132, Cramon, *Unser Österreich–Ungarischer Bundesgenosse im Weltkrieg*, pp. 65–66, Rauchensteiner, *Der Tod des Doppeladlers*, p. 354, and Sondhaus, *Franz Conrad von Hötzendorf*, p. 181.

19. Cramon, *Unser Österreich–Ungarischer Bundesgenosse im Weltkrieg*, p. 106. Cramon noted that this was a complete reversal of attitude on the part of AOK, which issued extremely detailed orders to the army commanders in the opening campaign of the war.

20. Hamilton and Herwig, *Decisions for War, 1914–1917*, p. 195, and Moltke, *Erinnerungen–Briefe–Dokumente*, p. 9.

21. Unsigned, "Die Führung Falkenhayn," 1934, p. 18, BA-MA W 10/50704, and Seeckt, "Diary Notes," January 18, 1915, *Nachlass* Seeckt, BA-MA N 247/22.

22. Foley, *German Strategy and the Path to Verdun*, p. 110, The poor personal regard in which Falkenhayn and Tirpitz held each other is laid out in Afflerbach, *Falkenhayn*, p. 201.

23. Ludendorff to Moltke, January 27, 1915 and Ludendorff to Moltke, March 12, 1915, *Nachlass* Ludendorff, BA-MA N 77/2, Hoffmann, *War Diaries and Other Papers,* Vol. I, p. 58, Seeckt, "Diary Notes," January 18, 1915, *Nachlass* Seeckt, BA-MA N 247/22, and OHL, Beurteilung der Feindlage im Osten durch die oberste Heeresleitung im Januar 1915, c. February 1915, BA-MA W 10/51373.

24. Rauchensteiner, *Der Tod des Doppeladlers,* p. 201, and Sondhaus, *Franz Conrad von Hötzendorf,* p. 167.

25. Ludendorff to Moltke, January 2, 1915, *Nachlass* Ludendorff, BA-MA N 77/2, and Tappen Diary, January 2,1915, BA-MA W 10/50661.

26. Ludendorff to Moltke, January 2, 1915, *Nachlass* Ludendorff, BA-MA N 77/2, Tappen Diary, January 7, 1915, BA-MA W 10/50661, Falkenhayn, *The German General Staff and Its Decisions, 1914–1916,* p. 58, and Cramon, *Unser Österreich–Ungarischer Bundesgenosse im Weltkrieg,* p. 6.

27. Born on February 10, 1850, Alexander von Linsingen was commissioned as a lieutenant on October 14, 1869. His major promotions and command positions were often simultaneous. On November 18, 1897 he was promoted to colonel and to command of the Fourth Grenadier Regiment; on June 16, 1901, Linsingen was promoted to Generalmajor and named commander of the 81st Infantry Brigade. Four years later, he was promoted to Generalleutnant and, on April 22, 1905, appointed commander of the 27th Infantry Division and subsequently advanced to General der Infanterie and made commanding general of the II Corps on September 1, 1909. Appointed commander of the Süd Army on January 1, 1915, he was later named commander of the Bug Army on July 6, 1915. Linsingen was promoted to Generaloberst on April 7, 1918; he retired on November 17, 1918, and died on June 5, 1935. Herwig and Heyman, *Biographical Dictionary of World War I,* p. 227, and short biographical chronology, BA-MA MSg 109/10865. Remus von Woyrsch was born on February 4, 1847 and commissioned as a second lieutenant on October 13, 1866. Promoted to colonel on May 15, 1894, Woyrsch was advanced to Generalmajor and appointed to command the Fourth Guards Infantry Brigade on November 18, 1897. After his promotion to *Generaloberst* on December 3, 1914, Woyrsch was named army detachment commander on December 14, 1914. After spending the entire war on the eastern front, Woyrsch was promoted to Generalfeldmarschall on December 21, 1917. He retired in 1918 and died on August 6, 1920. Herwig and Heyman, *Biographical Dictionary of World War I,* pp. 360–361, and short biographical chronology, BA-MA MSg 109/10874.

28. Ludendorff to Moltke, January 9, 1915, *Nachlass* Ludendorff, BA-MA N 77/2, excerpt from diary of Generaloberst von Plessen, January 15, 1915, BA-MA W 10/50656 (hereafter cited as Plessen diary), and Foley, *German Strategy and the Path to Verdun,* p. 121.

29. Cramon, *Unser Österreich–Ungarischer Bundesgenosse im Weltkriege,* pp. 1–3, and short biographical chronology, BA-MA MSg 109/10858.

30. Cramon, *Unser Österreich–Ungarischer Bundesgenosse im Weltkriege,* pp. 3–4.

31. Cramon, *Unser Österreich–Ungarischer Bundesgenosse im Weltkriege,* p. 104, Cramon to Falkenhayn, April 8, 1915, 11:26 P.M., and Cramon to OHL, June 18, 1915, BA-MA W 10/51388. Mackensen thought Cramon was a particularly fortunate choice for the position. Foerster, ed., *Mackensen: Briefe und Aufzeichnungen,* p. 137.

32. Stürgkh, *Im Deutschen grossen Hauptquartier,* p. 102.

33. Rauchensteiner, *Der Tod des Doppeladlers,* p. 203 and Foerster, ed., *Mackensen: Briefe und Aufzeichnungen,* p. 125. Karl Baron von Pflanzer-Baltin was born on June 1, 1855. After graduating from the Theresa Military Academy in 1875, Pflanzer-Baltin attended the War College in 1879–1880. Over the ensuing 31 years, Pflanzer-Baltin rose steadily through the army, filling a variety of command and staff positions, until ill health compelled his retirement in 1911. Recalled to service in 1914, Pflanzer-Baltin was given command of a cavalry corps and later the Austro–Hungarian Seventh Army. He led the Seventh Army until he was relieved of command in September of 1916. After a stint as inspector general of infantry, Pflanzer-Baltin was given command of Austro–Hungarian forces in Albania in July 1918, a position he held until the end of the war. He died on April 8, 1925. Herwig and Heyman, *Biographical Dictionary of World War I,* pp. 280–281.

34. Ludendorff to Moltke, January 27, 1915, *Nachlass* Ludendorff, BA-MA N 77/2, Tappen Diary, 27 January 1915, BA-MA W 10/50661, OHL, "Beurteilung der Feindlage in Osten im Februar 1915," c. March 1915, BA-MA W 10/51373, Höbelt, "Österreich–Ungarns Nordfront 1914/15," *Die vergessene Front,* p. 99, and Rauchensteiner, *Der Tod des Doppeladlers,* p. 203.

35. Chief of Staff of German Süd Army to Cramon, February 6, 1915, BA-MA W 10/51373, Cramon, *Unser Österreich–Ungarischer Bundesgenosse im Weltkrieg,* p. 106, and Stürgkh, *Im Deutschen Grossen Hauptquartier,* p. 114.

36. Foerster, ed., *Mackensen: Briefe und Aufzeichnungen,* p. 125, Archivist von Gontard, "Ninth Army From January 1 to February 5, 1915," c. 1927, p. 60, BA-MA W 10/51443 and Herwig, *The First World War,* p. 135.

37. Germany, Reichsarchiv, *Der Weltkrieg 1914 bis 1918,* Vol. 7, pp. 116–117, and Rothenberg, *The Army of Francis Joseph,* p. 184.

38. Tappen Diary, February 22, 1915, BA-MA W 10/50661, Ludendorff to Moltke, March 12, 1915, *Nachlass* Ludendorff, BA-MA N 77/2, Rauchensteiner, *Der Tod des Doppeladlers,* p. 205, and General A. A. Brusilov, *A Soldier's Note-Book 1914–1916* (reprinted edition) (Westport, Conn.: Greenwood Press; 1970), pp. 120–121.

39. OHL, "Beurteilung der Feindlage in Osten im Februar 1915," c. March 1915, BA-MA W 10/51373, Bernard Pares, *Day by Day With the Russian Army 1914–1915* (Boston: Houghton Mifflin; 1915), p. 160, and Palmer and Wallis, eds., *Intimate Voices from the First World War,* pp. 77 and 80.

40. Hoffmann, *War Diaries and Other Papers,* Vol. I, p. 53 and Rauchensteiner, *Der Tod des Doppeladlers,* p. 206.

41. Palmer and Wallis, eds., *Intimate Voices from the First World War,* pp. 83–85, Herwig, *The First World War,* pp. 137–139, Germany, Reichsarchiv, *Der Weltkrieg 1914 bis 1918,* Vol. 7, p. 123, and Foley, *German Strategy and the Path to Verdun,* p. 128. For a brief survey of relations between the Russian Army and the Jewish populations in both Russia and Austria–Hungary, see Eric Lohr, "The Russian Army and the Jews: Mass Deportations, Hostages, and Violence During World War I," *The Russian Review,* Vol. 60, No. 3 (July 2001):pp. 404–419.

42. Höbelt, "Österreich–Ungarns Nordfront 1914/15," *Die vergessene Front,* p. 100, Rauchensteiner, *Der Tod des Doppeladlers,* p. 205, Afflerbach, *Falkenhayn,* p. 275, Danilov, *Russland im Weltkriege 1914–1915,* p. 457 and Austria, Bundesministerium, *Österreich–Ungarns Letzter Krieg 1914–1918,* Vol. 2, p. 271. After the breakthrough had

been achieved at Gorlice, Conrad would claim that not only the Austro–Hungarian victory at Limanova-Lapanov in December 1914 but also the costly winter battles in the Carpathians had created the preconditions that allowed the Gorlice offensive to succeed. Conrad to Bolfras, May 12, 1915, ÖSA-KA MKSM 78.

43. Douglas Wilson Johnson, *Topography and Strategy in the War* (New York: Henry Holt; 1917), p. 79.

44. According to an agreement between the two countries, Austria–Hungary was to provide Germany with 10,000 tons of oil per month. Prior to 1914, the United States was Germany's principal supplier of oil. Alison Fleig Frank, *Oil Empire: Visions of Prosperity in Austrian Galicia* (Cambridge, Mass.: Harvard University Press; 2005), p. 184.

45. Cramon to Falkenhayn, March 24, 1915, 10 P.M., and Cramon to Falkenhayn, March 26, 1915, 10 A.M., BA-MA W 10/51388, Tappen diary, March 31, 1915, BA-MA W 10/50661, Germany, Reichsarchiv, *Der Weltkrieg 1914 bis 1918*, Vol. 7, p. 124, Herwig, *The First World War*, p. 139, and Cramon, *Unser Österreich–Ungarischer Bundesgenosse im Weltkrieg*, p. 10.

46. Extract from diary of Wilhelm Groener, *Nachlass* Groener, BA-MA N 46/41, Cramon to Falkenhayn, March 24, 1915, 10 P.M., BA-MA W 10/51388, Ludendorff to Moltke, April 1, 1915, *Nachlass* Ludendorff, BA-MA N 77/2, Germany, Reichsarchiv, *Der Weltkrieg 1914 bis 1918*, Vol. 7, p. 129, and Stone, *The Eastern Front 1914–1917*, p. 122.

47. Germany, Reichsarchiv, *Der Weltkrieg 1914 bis 1918*, Vol. 7, p. 131, and Cramon to Falkenhayn, April 6, 1915, BA-MA W 10/51388.

48. Lawrence Sondhaus, *In the Service of the Emperor: Italians in the Austrian Armed Forces 1814–1918* (Boulder, Colo.: East European Monographs; 1985), p. 105, and Oswald Überegger, "Auf der Flucht vor dem Krieg. Trentiner und Tirolen Deserteure im Ersten Weltkrieg," *Militärgeschichtliche Zeitschrift* Vol. 62, No. 2 (2007): p. 356.

49. Herwig, *The First World War*, p. 139, Tappen diary, April 3, 1915, BA-MA, W 10/50661, and Cramon to Falkenhayn, April 6, 1915, BA-MA W 10/51388.

50. Danilov, *Russland im Weltkriege 1914–1915*, p. 458, and Stone, *The Eastern Front 1914–1917*, p. 120.

51. Danilov, *Russland im Weltkriege 1914–1915*, pp. 462–463, and Herwig, *The First World War*, p. 139.

52. Tappen diary, April 6, 1915, BA-MA W 10/50661, Conrad to Falkenhayn, April 2, 1915, and Conrad to Falkenhayn, April 6, 1915, are reprinted in Hermann Wendt, *Der italienische Kriegsschauplatz in europäischen Konflikten: Seine Bedeutung für die Kriegführung an Frankreichs Nordostgrenze* (Berlin: Junker und Dunnhaupt Verlag; 1936), pp. 420 and 426, Conrad to Bolfras, April 10, 1915, ÖSA-KA MKSM 78, and Falkenhayn, *The German General Staff and Its Decisions, 1914–1916*, p. 84.

53. Falkenhayn to Cramon, March 25, 1915, BA-MA W 10/51388.

54. Cramon to Falkenhayn, March 25, 1915, BA-MA W 10/51388, and Cramon, *Unser Österreich-Ungarischer Bundesgenosse im Weltkrieg*, p. 8.

55. Cramon to Falkenhayn, March 26, 1915, 10 A.M., BA-MA W 10/51388, and Germany, Reichsarchiv, *Der Weltkrieg 1914 bis 1918*, Vol. 7, p. 349.

56. Born November 22, 1867, Groener was commissioned as a second lieutenant on September 9, 1886. He graduated from the Kriegsakademie in 1896 and was promoted to lieutenant colonel on September 13, 1912, and posted to the general staff the

same day. Appointed head of the railway section on August 1, 1914, Groener was promoted to colonel on September 5, 1914. After being promoted to Generalmajor on June 26, 1915, he was appointed head of the war office and promoted to Generalleutnant on November 1, 1916. On March 28, 1918, Groener was named chief of staff for Army Group Eichhorn. Later, on October 27, 1918, he succeeded Ludendorff as first quartermaster general. He retired from the army on September 30, 1919. Groener was appointed defense minister in 1932. He died on May 3, 1939. Herwig and Heyman, *Biographical Dictionary of World War I,* pp. 170–171, and short biographical chronology, BA-MA MSg 109/10861.

57. Groener diary extract, *Nachlass* Groener, BA-MA N 46/41, and Afflerbach, *Falkenhayn,* p. 287.

58. Sondhaus, *Franz Conrad von Hötzendorf,* p. 174, Afflerbach, *Falkenhayn,* p. 276, and Conrad to Arthur, Baron von Bolfras, April 6, 1915, ÖSA-KA File 78/14.

59. Falkenhayn to Cramon, April 4, 1915, BA-MA W 10/51388, and Cramon, *Unser Österreich–Ungarischer Bundesgenosse im Weltkrieg,* p. 11.

60. Cramon to Falkenhayn, April 6, 1915, BA-MA W 10/51388.

61. Tappen diary, April 7, 1915, BA-MA W 10/50661.

62. Cramon to Falkenhayn, April 8, 1915, 11:26 P.M., Falkenhayn to Conrad, April 12, 1915, 7:40 P.M., Cramon to Falkenhayn, April 12, 1915, 11:23 P.M., BA-MA W 10/51388, and Wendt, *Der italienische Kriegsschauplatz in europäischen Konflikten,* pp. 426–427.

63. Tappen diary, April 12–13, 1915, BA-MA W 10/50661, Afflerbach, *Falkenhayn,* p. 290, and Germany, Reicharchiv, *Der Weltkrieg 1914 bis 1918,* Vol. 7, pp. 356–358.

64. Falkenhayn to Conrad, April 13, 1915, Wendt, *Der italienische Kriegsschauplatz in europäischen Konflikten,* pp. 428–429, Falkenhayn, *The German General Staff and Its Decisions, 1914–1916,* pp. 92–93, Tappen diary, April 13, 1915, BA-MA W 10/50661, and Rauchensteiner, *Der Tod des Doppeladlers,* p. 211.

65. Tappen diary, April 14, 1915, BA-MA W 10/50661, Germany, Reichsarchiv, *Der Weltkrieg 1914 bis 1918,* Vol. 7, pp. 361–362, and Austria, Bundesministerium, *Österreich–Ungarns Letzter Krieg 1914–1918,* Vol. 2, p. 306.

66. August Urbanski von Ostrymiecz, *Conrad von Hötzendorf: Soldat und Mensch* (Vienna: Ulrich Mosers Verlag; 1938), p. 310, Gina Conrad, *Mein Leben mit Conrad von Hötzendorf,* pp. 132–133, and Conrad, *Aus meiner Dienstzeit 1906–1918,* Vol. 5, p. 791.

67. Cramon, *Unser Österreich–Ungarischer Bundesgenosse im Weltkrieg,* p. 12, Foerster, *Mackensen: Briefe und Aufzeichnungen,* p. 144, and Kuhl, *Der Weltkrieg 1914–1918,* Vol. I, p. 183. Writing after the war, Seeckt alluded to the old truism about victory having a thousand fathers while defeat is an orphan. Germany, Reichsarchiv, *Der Weltkrieg 1914 bis 1918,* Vol. 7, p. 439. For a more recent assessment that is also kind to Falkenhayn, see Afflerbach, *Falkenhayn,* pp. 287–290.

68. Cramon, *Unser Österreich–Ungarischer Bundesgenosse im Weltkrieg,* p. 12, Tappen diary, February 22, 1915, BA-MA W 10/50661, Ludendorff to Moltke, March 12, 1915, *Nachlass* Ludendorff, BA-MA N 77/2, Germany, Reichsarchiv, *Der Weltkrieg 1914 bis 1918,* Vol. 7, p. 357, and Urbanski, *Conrad von Hötzendorf,* p. 315. For a more positive view of Conrad's double envelopment plan, see unsigned, "Die Führung Falkenhayn," 1934, p. 20, BA-MA W 10/50704. More supportive of Falkenhayn is Kuhl, *Der Weltkrieg 1914–1918,* Vol. I, p. 183.

CHAPTER THREE

1. Ludendorff to Moltke, April 1, 1915, *Nachlass* Ludendorff, BA-MA N 77/2.

2. Foerster, ed., *Mackensen: Briefe und Aufzeichnungen,* p. 143.

3. General der Infanterie Hermann von François, *Gorlice 1915: Der Karpathendurch-bruch und die Befreiung von Galizien* (Leipzig: Verlag von K. F. Koehler; 1922), p. 34.

4. Holger Afflerbach, "Bis zum letzten Mann und letzten Groschen? Die Wehrpflicht im Deutschen Reich und ihre Auswirkungen auf das militärische Führungsdenken im Ersten Weltkrieg," *Die Wehrpflicht: Entstehung, Erscheinungsformen und politisch–militärische Wirkung* (Roland G.Foerster, ed.), (Munich: R. Oldenbourg Verlag; 1994), p. 90.

5. Among those who fought at first Ypres was an Austrian volunteer serving in the Bavarian Army, one Adolf Hitler. Naturally, the tragedy of Langemarck assumed an important place in Nazi mythology. Jay W. Baird, *To Die for Germany: Heroes in the Nazi Pantheon* (Bloomington: Indiana University Press; 1992), p. 10. For a very different look at the composition of the German forces at first Ypres, see Strachan, *The First World War,* Vol. I, p. 274.

6. Two examples illustrate the level of German officer losses in the opening campaigns of the war. The Prussian 1st Guards Grenadier (Kaiser Alexander) Regiment lost 30 officers killed between August 1914 and February 1, 1915. The Prussian 3rd Guards Grenadier (Queen Elisabeth) Regiment, lost 27 officers killed in 1914. If one includes even a small number of wounded, both regiments would have lost over half of their officers. Thilo von Bose, *Das Kaiser Alexander Garde-Grenadier-Regiment Nr. 1 im Weltkriege 1914–1918* (Zeulenroda, Germany: Bernhard Sporn; 1932), p. 592 and Hans-Oskar von Rosenberg-Lipinsky, *Das Königin Elisabeth Garde-Grenadier-Regiment Nr. 3 im Weltkriege 1914–1918* (Zeulenroda, Germany: Verlag Bernhard Sporn; 1935), p. 715.

7. Philipp Witkop (ed.), *German Students' War Letters* (Philadelphia: Pine St. Books, 2002), pp. 100 and 115 and Bose, *Das Kaiser Alexander Garde-Grenadier-Regiment Nr. 1 im Weltkriege 1914–1918,* p. 161.

8. Germany, Reichsarchiv, *Der Weltkrieg 1914 bis 1918,* Vol. 7, p. 302, unsigned, "Die Führung Falkenhayn," pp. 9 and 13, BA-MA W 10/50704, OHL, Beurteilung der Feindlage in Osten im Februar 1915, c. March 1915, BA-MA W 10/51373, and Afflerbach, "Bis zum letzten Mann und letzten Groschen?" *Die Wehrpflicht,* p. 90.

9. Rauchensteiner, *Der Tod des Doppeladlers,* p. 201, Germany, Reichsarchiv, *Der Weltkrieg 1914 bis 1918,* Vol. 7, p. 303, and Afflerbach, *Falkenhayn,* p. 286.

10. Ludendorff, *Meine Kriegserinnerungen,* p. 106, Foley, *German Strategy and the Path to Verdun,* pp. 132–133, Hoffmann, *War Diaries and Other Papers,* Vol. II, p. 99, Germany, Reichsarchiv, *Der Weltkrieg 1914 bis 1918,* Vol. 7, p. 303, Stürgkh, *Im Deutschen grossen Hauptquartier,* p. 127 and Afflerbach, *Falkenhayn,* p. 286.

11. Germany, Reichsarchiv, *Der Weltkrieg 1914 bis 1918,* Vol. 7, pp. 303–306, Gerhard Tappen, "Kriegserinnerungen," unpublished, no date, p. 91, BA-MA W 10/50661, and Bavarian War Ministry to Bavarian I, II, and III Corps, 21 March 1915, Bayerisches Hauptstaatsarchiv, Abteilung IV, Kriegsarchiv, Bavarian 11th Infantry Division, Bund 52, Akt 2 (hereafter cited as BH-KA File 11/52/2).

12. Rauchensteiner, *Der Tod des Dopeladlers,* pp. 167, 205–208, Sondhaus, *Franz Conrad von Hötzendorf,* p. 165, Höbelt, "Österreich-Ungarns Nordfront 1914/15," *Die vergessene Front,* p. 100 and Afflerbach, "Bis zum letzten Mann und letzten Groschen?" *Die Wehrpflicht,* p. 90.

13. Rothenberg, *The Army of Francis Joseph*, p. 185, and Maureen Healy, *Vienna and the Fall of the Habsburg Empire: Total War and Everyday Life in World War I* (New York: Cambridge University Press; 2004), p. 152.

14. Seeckt, Report on the KuK Army with Organizational Plans for the KuK Army, c. December 1917, *Nachlass* Seeckt, BA-MA N 247/32.

15. Stone, *The Eastern Front 1914–1917*, p. 119, Boris Khavkin, "Russland gegen Deutschland. Die Ostfront des ersten Weltkrieges in den Jahren 1914 bis 1915," *Die vergessene Front*, pp. 72–73 and 75, OHL, Beurteilung der Feindlage in Osten im Februar 1915, c. March 1915, BA-MA W 10/51373, Ludendorff to Moltke, 12 March 1915, *Nachlass* Ludendorff, BA-MA N 77/2, and Dennis Showalter, "Imperial Russia and Military History," *Reforming the Tsar's Army*, p. 327.

16. Bernard Pares, *Day by Day with the Russian Army 1914–15* (Boston: Houghton Mifflin, 1915), pp. 112–113, Jones, "Imperial Russia's Forces at War," *Military Effectiveness*, Vol. I, pp 312–313, Lieutenant General Nicholas N. Golovine, *The Russian Army in the World War* (New Haven, Conn.: Yale University Press; 1931), p. 46 and Danilov, *Russland im Weltkriege 1914–1915*, p. 365.

17. Stone, *The Eastern Front 1914–1917*, pp. 160–162, Golovine, *The Russian Army in the World War*, pp. 34–35 and Peter Gatrell, "Poor Russia: Mobilizing a Backward Economy for War, 1914–1917," *The Economics of World War I* (Stephen Broadberry and Mark Harrison, eds.) (New York: Cambridge University Press; 2005), pp. 260 and 268.

18. Jones, "Imperial Russia's Forces at War," *Military Effectiveness*, Vol. I, p. 305, and Brusilov, *A Soldier's Notebook 1914–1918*, pp. 125–126.

19. Danilov, *Russland im Weltkriege 1914–1915*, pp. 414–416 and OHL, Beurteilung der Feindlage in Osten im Februar 1915, c. March 1915, BA-MA W 10/51373

20. Danilov, *Russland im Weltkriege 1914–1915*, p. 464.

21. François, *Gorlice 1915*, p. 46 and Germany, Reichsarchiv, *Der Weltkrieg 1914 bis 1918*, Vol. 7, p. 370.

22. Cramon to Falkenhayn, April 6, 1915, BA-MA W 10/51388, Tappen diary, April 14, 1915 and Tappen, "Kriegserinnerungen," p. 96, BA-MA W 10/50661, Germany, Reichsarchiv, *Der Weltkrieg 1914 bis 1917*, Vol. 7, p. 362, and Austria, Bundesministerium, *Österreich–Ungarns Letzter Krieg 1914–1918*, Vol. 2, p. 306.

23. August von Cramon and Paul Fleck, *Deutschlands Schicksalsbund mit Österreich–Ungarn: Von Conrad von Hötzendorf zu Kaiser Carl* (Berlin: Verlag für Kulturpolitik, 1932), p. 102.

24. Ludendorff, *Meine Kriegserinnerungen*, pp. 58–59, Kaganeck diary, 21 September 1914, BA-MA MSg 1/1914, Hoffmann, *War Diaries and Other Papers*, Vol. I, p. 43, and Cramon and Fleck, *Deutschlands Schicksalsbund mit Österreich–Ungarn*, p. 102.

25. DiNardo and Hughes, "German and Coalition Warfare in the World Wars," p. 178, and Shanafelt, *The Secret Enemy*, p. 47.

26. Cramon and Fleck, *Deutschlands Schicksalsbund mit Österreich–Ungarn*, p. 102, Ludendorff, *Meine Kriegserinnerungen 1914–1918*, pp. 58–59, Kaganeck diary, 21 September 1914, BA-MA MSg 1/1914, Hoffmann, *War Diaries and Other Papers*, Vol. I, p. 43, Ludendorff to Moltke, April 1, 1915, and Ludendorff to Moltke, April 5, 1915, *Nachlass* Ludendorff, BA-MA N 77/2.

27. Hoffmann was critical of Mackensen's conduct of the campaign. Hoffmann, *War Diaries and Other Papers*, Vol. I, p. 51. Even after the Gorlice victory, Wilhelm II's adjutant, the aged Generaloberst Hans von Plessen (born 1841), regarded Mackensen

as "a splendid man, but a mediocre commander!" Plessen diary, June 2, 1915, BA-MA W 10/50656, and Cecil, *Wilhelm II*, Vol. II, p. 20.

28. Cramon and Fleck, *Deutschland's Schicksalsbund mit Österreich–Ungarn*, p. 102, Schwarzmüller, *Generalfeldmarschall August von Mackensen*, p. 103, and Tappen diary, April 18, 1915, BA-MA W 10/50661.

29. Herwig and Heyman, *Biographical Dictionary of World War I*, p. 235, Schwarzmüller, *Generalfeldmarschall August von Mackensen*, pp. 18–91, and Short Biographical Chronology, BA-MA MSg 109/10865.

30. Schwarzmüller, *Generalfeldmarschall August von Mackensen*, p. 99, Foerster, ed., *Mackensen: Briefe und Aufzeichnungen*, pp. 117–118, and Kolshorn, *Unser Mackensen*, p. 112.

31. Germany, Reichsarchiv, *Der Weltkrieg 1914 bis 1918*, Vol. 2, p. 90, and Foerster, ed., *Mackensen: Briefe und Aufzeichnungen*, pp. 29 and 67.

32. Wolfgang Foerster, "Das Bild des modernen Feldherrn," Deutsche Gesellschaft für Wehrpolitik und Wehrwissenschaften, *Heerführer des Weltkrieges* (Berlin: E. S. Mittler und Sohn, 1939), p. 2, and Echevarria, *After Clausewitz*, p. 65.

33. Foerster, ed., *Mackensen: Briefe und Aufzeichnungen*, pp. 93–94.

34. Citino, *The German Way of War*, p. 150, and Rothenberg, "Moltke, Schlieffen, and the Doctrine of Strategic Envelopment," *Makers of Modern Strategy*, p. 301.

35. Kaiser Friedrich III, *Das Kriegstagebuch von 1870/71* (Heinrich Otto Meissner, ed.) (Berlin: Verlag von K. S. Koehler; 1926), p. 6, and Field Marshal Carl Constantine Graf von Blumenthal, *Tagebücher des Generalfeldmarschalls Graf von Blumenthal aus den Jahren 1866 und 1870/71* (Albrecht Graf von Blumenthal, ed.) (Berlin: I. G. Gotta'sche Buchhandlung Nachfolger; 1902), pp. 9, 50, and 285–286.

36. Corum, *The Roots of Blitzkrieg*, pp. 25–26, Herwig and Heyman, *Biographical Dictionary of World War I*, p. 316, Major Bullrick, "Die Schlacht bei Vailly. Am Oktober 30, 1914, als Ausgangspunkt für der Erfolge bei Gorlice entscheidener neuer taktischer Grundsätze," Potsdam, February 27, 1920, *Nachlass* Seeckt, BA-MA N 247/22, Edgar von Schmidt-Pauli, *General von Seeckt: Lebensbild eines Deutschen Soldaten* (Berlin: Verlag Reinar Hobbing; 1937), p. 33, and Hans von Seeckt, *Aus meinem Leben 1866–1917* (Leipzig: von Hase & Koehler Verlag; 1938), p. 99.

37. Wheeler-Bennett, *Wooden Titan*, p. 17, B. H. Liddell Hart, *Through the Fog of War* (New York: Random House; 1938), p. 226, and Herwig, *The First World War*, p. 83. See also Uhle-Wettler, *Erich Ludendorff in seiner Zeit*, p. 177.

38. See, for example, Herwig and Heyman, *Biographical Dictionary of World War I*, p. 236, and B. H. Liddell Hart, *History of the First World War* (reprinted edition) (London: Cassell; 1970), p. 197.

39. Foerster, ed., *Mackensen: Briefe und Aufzeichnungen*, p. 28. Indeed, Mackensen later became known as the "new Marshal Forward," the moniker given Blücher a century before. See, for example, Karsten Brandt, *Mackensen: Leben, Wesen und Wirken des deutschen Feldherrn* (Leipzig: Gustav Schloessmanns Verlagbuchhandlung; 1916), p. 47.

40. Daniel J. Hughes, *The King's Finest: A Social and Bureaucratic Profile of Prussia's General Officers, 1871–1914* (Westport, Conn.: Praeger; 1987), p. 85.

41. Seeckt, *Aus meinem Leben 1866–1917*, p. 116, Ludendorff, *Meine Kriegserinnerungen*, p. 109, and Robert M. Citino, *Quest for Decisive Victory: From Stalemate to Blitzkrieg in Europe, 1899–1940* (Lawrence: University Press of Kansas; 2002), p. 157.

42. Seeckt, *Aus meinem Leben 1866–1917,* p. 38, and Foerster, ed., *Mackensen: Briefe und Aufzeichnungen,* p. 138.

43. Foerster, ed., *Mackensen: Briefe und Aufzeichnungen,* p. 143, Schwarzmüller, *Generalfeldmarschall August von Mackensen,* p. 105, Seeckt to wife, April 27, 1915, *Nachlass* Seeckt, BA-MA N 247/57, and Meier-Welcker, *Seeckt,* p. 52. Bock would be promoted Generalfeldmarschall by Adolf Hitler in World War II.

44. Foester, ed., *Mackensen: Briefe und Aufzeichnungen,* p. 144.

45. Cramon, *Unser Österreich–Ungarischer Bundesgenosse im Weltkriege,* p. 14, and Foerster, ed., *Mackensen: Briefe und Aufzeichnungen,* p. 137.

46. Schwarzmüller, *Generalfeldmarschall August von Mackensen,* p. 104, Germany, Reichsarchiv, *Der Weltkrieg 1914 bis 1918,* Vol. 7, p. 369, Afflerbach, *Falkenhayn,* p. 291, Cramon to OHL Operations Section, April 27, 1915, and OHL Operations Section to Cramon, April 27, 1915, BA-MA W 10/51388.

47. Born on May 24, 1872, Archduke Joseph Ferdinand graduated from the Austro–Hungarian War Academy in 1897. After his promotion to colonel in 1905, the Archduke held a series of command positions at successively higher levels until he was commander of the Austro–Hungarian XIV Corps in 1914. It was in that capacity that he fought in the opening campaign of the war. By late 1914 the Archduke had been promoted to command of the Austro–Hungarian Fourth Army. Although he commanded the army with success in the 1915 campaign, he suffered a major defeat at Russian hands in the Brusilov offensive of June 1916. He was relieved of command but appointed in 1917 by Emperor Karl to be the head of the Austro–Hungarian air forces. The Archduke died in Vienna on August 26, 1942. Herwig and Heyman, *Biographical Dictionary of World War I,* p. 200, personal diary of August von Mackensen, April 26, 1915, *Nachlass* Mackensen, BA-MA N 39/220, and Foerster, ed., *Mackensen: Briefe und Aufzeichnungen,* p. 146.

48. German War Ministry, Viewpoints on Training and Equipping of Infantry, 14 January 1915, and Corps Bothmer to Süd Army, April 26, 1915, BA-MA W 10/50755, Germany, Reichsarchiv, *Der Weltkrieg 1914 bis 1918,* Vol. 7, p. 305, and Heinrich Kraft, *Der Anteil der 11. Bayer. Inf. Div. an der Durchbruchsschlacht von Gorlice–Tarnow* (Munich: C. H. Beck'sche Verlagsbuchhandlung, 1934), p. 5.

49. Tappen, "Kriegserinnerungen," p. 97, BA-MA W 10/50661.

50. Information on the German Eleventh Army's order of battle is drawn from Oskar Tile von Kalm, *Schlachten des Weltkrieges,* Vol. 30, *Gorlice* (Berlin: Oldenburg, 1930), pp. 196–198. Plettenberg left the army under unclear circumstances on February 6, 1917. He died on February 10, 1937. Short Biographical Chronology, BA-MA MSg 109/10868. Born on July 7, 1883, Prince Friedrich of Prussia obtained his first commission as a lieutenant in 1904. After extensive service in the Prussian Guard, the prince was promoted colonel on August 1, 1914, and appointed division commander on January 27, 1915. He was promoted to Generalmajor on May 18, 1918. The prince died in Potsdam on December 8, 1942. Short Biographical Chronology, BA-MA MSg 109/10868. Arnold von Winckler was born on February 17, 1856, and commissioned as a second lieutenant on November 12, 1874. After graduating from the Kriegsakademie in 1886, Winckler held a series of command and administrative positions until his promotion to Generalleutnant and appointment as commander of the 2nd Guard Infantry Division in 1912. He later commanded the XXXXI Reserve Corps and was promoted to General der Infanterie on March 22, 1917. Winckler retired from the army on January 15, 1919 and died on July 27, 1945. Short Biographical Chronology, BA-MA MSg 109/10874.

51. Short Biographical Chronology, BA-MA MSg 109/10859 and Showalter, *Tannenberg*, p. 350.

52. Leo von Stocken was born on May 7, 1862, and obtained his first commission as a lieutenant on April 16, 1881. After graduating from the *Kriegsakademie* in 1891, Stocken rose gradually over time and was promoted to *Generalmajor* on January 27, 1913. Later that year he was appointed chief of staff of the IV Corps and served during the 1914 campaign in that capacity. Stocken was appointed to command the 81st Reserve Division on December 24, 1914. Although he was promoted to Generalleutnant on October 5, 1916, Stocken held no other commands of major importance. He died on December 22, 1926. Short Biographical Chronology, BA-MA MSg 109/10871. Born on August 22, 1853, Sigfried Fabarius obtained his commission as a lieutenant on October 17, 1876. After graduating from the Kriegsakademie in 1891, Fabarius had a successful if undistinguished career, reaching the rank of Generalmajor on October 1, 1912. He was appointed commander of the 82nd Reserve Division on December 24, 1914. Short Biographical Chronology, BA-MA MSg 109/10859.

53. Franz Freiherr von Stengel, *Das K.B. 3. Infanterie-Regiment Prinz Karl von Bayern 1914–1918* (Munich: Verlag Bayerisches Kriegsarchiv, 1924), p. 11, Bavarian 11th Infantry Division, Kriegstagebuch, April 5–6, 1915 (hereafter cited as KTB), BH-KA File 11/4/1 and Bavarian 11th Infantry Division, Division Order of the Day, April 5, 1915, BH-KA File 11/52/2.

54. The division's ration strength was considerably higher, 13,617 officers and men plus 4,549 horses. Bavarian 11th Infantry Division, KTB/April 11–12, 1915, BH-KA File 11/4/1, Germany, Reichsarchiv, *Der Weltkrieg 1914 bis 1918*, Vol. 7, p. 305, and Kraft, *Der Anteil der 11. Bayer. Inf. Div. an der Durchbruchsschlacht von Gorlice–Tarnow*, p. 5.

55. Kneussl later commanded the XXV Reserve Corps and the Bavarian I Reserve Corps. He retired from the army on August 11, 1919, and died in Munich on February 16, 1928. Short Biographical Chronology, BA-MA MSg 109/10863, Kraft, *Der Anteil der 11. Bayer. Inf. Div. an der Durchbruchsschlacht von Gorlice-Tarnow*, p. 5, and Kalm, *Gorlice*, p. 197.

56. Karl von Behr was born on December 9, 1857, and commissioned as a lieutenant on February 10, 1877. After graduating from the Kriegsakademie in 1890, Behr followed a standard career path, attaining the rank of Generalmajor on June 27, 1913. His appointment as commander of the 119th Infantry Division was apparently temporary, although his position was apparently made official on September 5, 1916. Although promoted to Generalleutnant on June 18, 1917, he held no other field commands in the war. Behr was appointed governor of Graudenz on December 23, 1918, and retired on May 24, 1919. He died in Detmold on March 25, 1926. Short Biographical Chronology BA-MA MSg 109/10856.

57. Short Biographical Chronology, BA-MA MSg 109/10859.

58. Max Hofmann (not to be confused with the Max Hoffmann who was one of Ober Ost's key staff officers) was born on March 9, 1854. He obtained his first commission as a lieutenant on October 12, 1875. Hofmann did not attend the Kriegsakademie but prospered anyway, being promoted to colonel on September 13, 1906. On March 22, 1913, he was promoted to Generalleutnant and appointed commander of the 19th Infantry Division. Hofmann was promoted to General der Infanterie on January 27, 1918; he died on November 28, 1918. Short Biographical Chronology, BA-MA MSg

109/10862. Horst Ritter und Edler von Oetinger was born on December 31, 1857, and obtained his first commission as a lieutenant on October 12, 1878. Graduating from the *Kriegsakademie* in 1890, Oetinger was promoted to colonel on May 18, 1908. After a short stint as commander of the 55th Infantry Brigade in the rank of Generalmajor, Oetinger was appointed to command the 20th Infantry Division on September 24, 1914. He was promoted to Generalleutnant on January 27, 1915. Later on he was appointed commander of the109th Infantry Division. Oetinger retired with the rank of General der Infanterie on October 20, 1919, and died in Baden Baden on September 27, 1928. Short Biographical Chronology, BA-MA MSg 109/10867.

    59. Kalm, *Gorlice*, p. 198. The Honved was theoretically the Hungarian equivalent of the German or Austrian Landwehr. Created as part of the reorganization of the government of the dual monarchy after 1867, the Hungarian government regarded the Honved as a national military force. Rothenberg, *The Army of Francis Joseph*, pp. 76–78.

    60. Herwig and Heyman, *Biographical Dictionary of World War I*, p. 71.

    61. Austro–Hungarian VI Corps, "Vorbereitung der Schlacht bei Gorlice–Tarnow," c. June 1915, BA-MA W 10/51393.

    62. General Alfred Ziethen, "Aus grosser Zeit vor Zwanzig Jahren. Die Durchbruchsschlacht von Gorlice," *Militär Wochenblatt*, Vol. 119, No. 41 (4 May 1935): p. 1628, Kalm, *Gorlice*, pp. 196–198, Herbert Jäger, *German Artillery of World War One* (Ramsbury, UK: Crowood Press, 2001), p. 34, Brose, *The Kaiser's Army*, p. 188, J. Scheibert, *Illustrirtes Deutsches Militär-Lexikon* (Berlin: Verlag von W. Pauli's Nachf.; 1897), p. 484, and Falkenhayn, *The German General Staff and Its Decisions, 1914–1916*, p. 90.

    63. Germany, Reichsarchiv, *Der Weltkrieg 1914 bis 1918*, Vol. 7, p. 367, Kraft, *Der Anteil der 11. Bayer. Inf. Div. an der Durchbruchsschlacht von Gorlice–Tarnow*, p. 8, Kalm, *Gorlice*, p. 24, Bavarian 11th Infantry Division, Experiences in Attack against Fortified Enemy Positions, April 10, 1915, BH-KA File 11/4/2 and Bavarian 11th Infantry Division KTB/April 13–15, 1915, BH-KA File 11/4/1.

    64. Groener diary extract, *Nachlass* Groener, BA-MA N 46/41, Germany, Reichsarchiv, *Der Weltkrieg 1914 bis 1918*, Vol. 7, pp. 367–368, Tappen diary, April 17, 1915, BA-MA W 10/50661, Tappen memoirs, p. 99, BA-MA W 10/50661, Kraft, *Der Anteil der 11. Bayer. Inf. Div. an der Durchbruchsschlacht von Gorlice–Tarnow*, p. 10, Kalm, *Gorlice*, p. 20, Witkop, ed., *German Students' War Letters*, p. 101, and Prince Friedrich of Prussia, *Das Erste Garderegiment zu Fuss im Weltkrieg 1914–1918* (Berlin: Junker und Dünnhaupt; 1934), p.87.

    65. Groener diary extract, *Nachlass* Groener, BA-MA N 46/41, Austria, Bundesministerium, *Österreich-Ungarns Letzter Krieg 1914–1918*, Vol. 2, p. 316, Germany, Reichsarchiv, *Der Weltkrieg 1914 bis 1918*, Vol. 7, p. 368, Witkop, ed., *German Students' War Letters*, p. 101, Bavarian 11th Infantry Division KTB/April 22–23, 1915, BH-KA File 11/4/1, and Paul von Keussl diary, April 24, 1915, *Nachlass* Paul von Kneussl, BH-KA NL 3, Rosenberg-Lipinsky, *Das Königin Elisabeth Garde-Grenadier-Regiment Nr. 3 im Weltkriege 1914–1918*, p. 136, and Kalm, *Gorlice*, p. 24.

    66. François, *Gorlice 1915*, p. 15, Kalm, *Gorlice*, p. 24, and Kraft, *Der Anteil der 11. Bayer. Inf. Div. an der Durchbruchsschlacht von Gorlice–Tarnow*, p. 13.

    67. Germany, Reichsarchiv, *Der Weltkrieg 1914 bis 1918*, Vol. 7, p. 373, German Eleventh Army, Special Orders Nr. 1, April 24, 1915, BH-KA File 11/43/4, German

Eleventh Army, "Die Durchbruchsschlacht in Westgalizien," c. May 1915, *Nachlass* Seeckt, BA-MA N 247/24, and General of Cavalry Ernest von Hoeppner, *Germany's War in the Air: The Development and Operations of German Military Aviation in the World War* (Nashville, Tenn.: Battery Press; 1994), p. 45.

68. Germany, Reichsarchiv, *Der Weltkrieg 1914 bis 1918*, Vol. 7, p. 374.

69. Doughty, *Pyrrhic Victory*, pp. 153–154, Germany, Reichsarchiv, *Der Weltkrieg 1914 bis 1918*, Vol. 7, p. 374, Kalm, *Gorlice*, p. 24, Rosenberg-Lipinsky, *Das Königin Elisabeth Garde-Grenadier-Regiment Nr. 3 im Weltkriege 1914–1918*, p. 138 and Fritz von Unger, *Das Königin Augusta Garde-Grenadier-Regiment Nr. 4 im Weltkriege 1914–1919* (Berlin: Gebr. Ohst Verlag; 1922), p. 90.

70. François, *Gorlice 1915*, pp. 43–44, Kalm, *Gorlice*, p. 27 and General A.A. Novikov, "Der russische Nachrichtendienst vor dem Gorlice-Durchbruch," *Militär Wochenblatt* Vol. 119, No. 42 (11 May 1935): p. 1671. The Russians held a similar attitude toward the area's population as well. Mark von Hagen, *War in a European Borderland: Occupations and Occupation Plans in Galicia and Ukraine, 1914–1918* (Seattle: University of Washington Press; 2007), p. 31.

71. Prince Friedrich of Prussia, *Das erste Garderegiment zu Fuss im Weltkrieg 1914–1918*, p. 89, and Bose, *Das Kaiser Alexander Garde-Grenadier-Regiment Nr. 1 im Weltkriege 1914–1918*, p. 162.

72. Ziethen, "Die Durchbruchsschlacht von Gorlice," p. 1628, Brose, *The Kaiser's Army*, p. 228, and Austria, Bundesministerium, *Österreich-Ungarns Letzter Krieg 1914–1918*, Vol. 2, p. 318.

73. Germany, Reichsarchiv, *Der Weltkrieg 1914 bis 1918*, Vol. 7, p. 372, Walter Luyken, *Das 2. Garde-Feldartillerie-Regiment im Weltkrieg* (Berlin: Verlag Tradition Wilhelm Kolk; 1929), p. 73, Kalm, *Gorlice*, p. 196, and Ziethen, "Die Durchbruchsschlacht von Gorlice," p. 1628.

74. Germany, Reichsarchiv, *Der Weltkrieg 1914 bis 1918*, Vol. 7, p. 363, Kuhl, *Der Weltkrieg 1914–1918*, Vol. I, p. 121, and unsigned, "Die Führung Falkenhayns," p. 20, BA-MA W 10/50704.

75. Tappen diary, April 30, 1915, BA-MA W 10/50661, and Groener diary extract, *Nachlass* Groener, BA-MA N 46/41.

76. Groener diary extract, *Nachlass* Groener, BA-MA N 46/41.

77. Doughty, *Pyrrhic Victory*, p. 155 and Elizabeth Greenhalgh, *Victory through Coalition: Britain and France during the First World War* (Cambridge: Cambridge University Press; 2005), pp. 40–41.

78. Germany, Reichsarchiv, *Der Weltkrieg 1914 bis 1918*, Vol. 7, p. 371, François, *Gorlice 1915*, pp. 31–32, Meier-Welcker, *Seeckt*, p. 52, and Austria, Bundesministerium, *Österreich–Ungarns Letzter Krieg 1914–1918*, Vol. 2, p. 317.

79. François, *Gorlice 1915*, pp. 31.

80. François, *Gorlice 1915*, p. 31, Germany, Reicharchiv, *Der Weltkrieg 1914 bis 1918*, Vol. 7, p. 373, and Seeckt, *Aus meinem Leben 1866–1917*, p. 118.

81. Born on August 7, 1858, Alfred Ziethen obtained a commission as a lieutenant on February 11, 1882, rising to the rank of colonel on January 27, 1911. Ziethen spent most of his career with the heavy artillery. This service included a tour as commander of the Heavy Artillery School. Promoted to Generalmajor on January 17, 1914, Ziethen was appointed to the command of the 5th Foot Artillery Brigade (a heavy artillery

unit) on August 25, 1914. After a tour as commander, Ziethen was assigned to Mackensen's staff in April 1915. Later on, Ziethen was appointed inspector general of artillery schools on October 16, 1917 and promoted to Generalleutnant on November 6, 1917. Ziethen retired from the army with the rank of General der Artillerie and died on February 14, 1944. Short Biographical Chronology, BA-MA MSg 109/10874.

82. Ziethen, "Die Durchbruchsschlacht von Gorlice," p. 1629, Foley, *German Strategy and the Path to Verdun*, pp. 136–137, and Bruce I. Gudmundsson, *Stormtroop Tactics: Innovation in the German Army, 1914–1918* (reprinted edition) (Westport, Conn.: Praeger; 1995), p. 110.

83. Kalm, *Gorlice*, p. 27, Hoeppner, *Germany's War in the Air*, p. 44, and Ziethen, "Die Durchbruchsschlacht von Gorlice," p. 1629.

84. François, *Gorlice 1915*, p. 33. One of the virtues of François's book is that it contains the full text of a number of orders that were published either at the army or corps level. Seeckt's memoirs also include the German Eleventh Army's order of April 30, 1915, but only in handwritten form. Compare François, *Gorlice 1915*, pp. 31–33, with Seeckt, *Aus meinen Leben 1866–1917*, pp. 120–121.

85. Germany, Reichsarchiv, *Der Weltkrieg 1914 bis 1918*, Vol. 7, p. 377, François, *Gorlice 1915*, p. 37, and Ziethen, "Die Durchbruchschlacht von Gorlice," p. 1630.

86. Seeckt, *Aus meinem Leben 1866–1917*, p. 119, Foerster, ed., *Mackensen: Briefe und Aufzeichnungen*, p. 146, Kalm, *Gorlice*, p. 24, Stone, *The Eastern Front 1914–1917*, p. 136, and Novikov, "Der russische Nachrichtendienst vor dem Gorlice-Durchbruch," p. 1671.

87. Stone, *The Eastern Front 1914–1917*, pp. 136–137, Kalm, *Gorlice*, pp. 27 and 199, and Brusilov, *A Soldier's Notebook, 1914–1918*, p. 130.

88. François, *Gorlice 1915*, p. 31. For a couple of good examples of attributing foresight after the event, see Meier-Welcker, *Seeckt*, p. 52, and Rosenberg-Lipinsky, *Das Königen Elisabeth Garde-Grenadier-Regiment Nr. 3 im Weltkriege 1914–1918*, p. 168.

89. Kalm, *Gorlice*, pp. 25–27, Austro–Hungarian VI Corps, "Vorbereitung der Schlacht bei Gorlice-Tarnow," BA-MA W 10/51393, Cramon, *Unser Österreich–Ungarischer Bundesgenosse im Weltkriege*, p. 14, Höbelt, "Österreich–Ungarns Nordfront 1914/15," *Die vergessene Front*, p. 102, Bavarian Eighth Reserve Infantry Division, "Billeting, Supply and Road Conditions in Galicia," April 10, 1916, BH-KA File 8R/1/3, and Sondhaus, *Franz Conrad von Hötzendorf*, p. 174. Sondhaus goes a bit over the top when he questions the idea of Gorlice–Tarnow as a "German" victory by cleverly including all of the Austro–Hungarian troops in the Austro–Hungarian Third and Fourth Armies. In reality, however, the plan made it abundantly clear that it was the Germans who would be doing the heavy lifting.

90. Major Bullrick, "Die Schlacht bei Vailly. Am October 30, 1914. als Ausgangspunkt der für der Erfolge bei Gorlice entscheidener neuer taktischen Grundsätze," *Nachlass* Seeckt, BA-MA N 247/22, Seeckt, *Aus meinem Leben 1866–1917*, pp. 87–88, Bavarian 11th Infantry Division, "Experiences in Attack against Fortified Enemy Positions," April 10, 1915, BH-KA File 11/4/2, Foerster, ed., *Mackensen: Briefe und Aufzeichnungen*, p. 125, and Archivist von Gontard, "Ninth Army From January 1 to February 5, 1915," BA-MA W 10/51443.

91. Novikov, "Der russische Nachrichtendienst vor dem Gorlice-Durchbruch," p. 1671, and Stone, *The Eastern Front 1914–1917*, p. 136.

CHAPTER FOUR

1. François, *Gorlice 1915*, p. 47.
2. Foerster, ed., *Wir Kämpfer im Weltkrieg*, p. 182.
3. Foerster, ed., *Mackensen: Briefe und Aufzeichnungen*, p. 148.
4. Tappen Diary, April 30, 1915, BA-MA W 10/50661 and Germany, Reichsarchiv, *Der Weltkrieg 1914 bis 1918*, Vol. 7, p. 378.
5. François, *Gorlice 1915*, p. 43, Kraft, *Der Anteil der 11. Bayer. Inf. Div. an der Durchbruchsschlacht von Gorlice-Tarnow*, p. 17, Austro–Hungarian VI Corps, Preparation for the Battle of Gorlice-Tarnow, BA-MA W 10/51393, Bavarian 11th Infantry Division, "Experiences in Attack Against Fortified Enemy Positions," April 10, 1915, BH-KA File 11/4/2 and Kalm, *Gorlice*, p. 41.
6. Ziethen, "Die Durchbruchsschlacht von Gorlice," p. 1630, François, *Gorlice 1915*, p. 39, Kalm, *Gorlice*, p. 43, and Gudmundsson, *Stormtroop Tactics*, p. 110.
7. François, *Gorlice 1915*, p. 47. The 120-mm gun was almost certainly from the half battery of Austro–Hungarian 120-mm guns assigned to the XXXXI Reserve Corps. Germany, Reichsarchiv, *Der Weltkrieg 1914 bis 1918*, Vol. 7, p. 468.
8. Germany, Reichsarchiv, *Der Weltkrieg 1914 bis 1918*, Vol. 7, p. 379, Kalm, *Gorlice*, p. 44, François, *Gorlice 1915*, p. 48, Kraft, *Der Anteil der 11. Bayer. Inf. Div. an der Durchbruchsschlacht von Gorlice-Tarnow*, p. 23, and Luyken, *Das 2. Garde-Feldartillerie-Regiment im Weltkriege*, p. 73.
9. Germany, Reichsarchiv, *Der Weltkrieg 1914 bis 1918*, Vol. 7, p. 379, Bavarian 21st Infantry Brigade to Bavarian 11th Infantry Division, 9:55 A.M., May 2, 1915, BH-KA File 11/4/2, and Kraft, *Der Anteil der 11. Bayer. Inf. Div. an der Durchbruchsschlacht von Gorlice-Tarnow*, p. 24.
10. Germany, Reichsarchiv, *Der Weltkrieg 1914 bis 1918*, Vol. 7, p. 379, Kalm, *Gorlice*, p. 55, Kraft, *Der Anteil der 11. Bayer. Inf. Div. an der Durchbruchsschlacht von Gorlice-Tarnow*, pp. 25–27, Ziethen, "Die Durchbruchsschlacht von Gorlice," p. 1630, Bavarian 11th Infantry Division KTB/2 May 1915, BH-KA File 11/4/1 and Stengel, *Das K.B. 3. Infanterie-Regiment Prinz Karl von Bayern 1914–1918*, p. 15.
11. Germany, Reichsarchiv, *Der Weltkrieg 1914 bis 1918*, Vol. 7, p. 380, Ziethen, "Die Durchbruchsschlacht von Gorlice," p. 1630, and Kalm, *Gorlice*, p. 64.
12. François, *Gorlice 1915*, p. 48, and Walther Engelberg, *Das Reserve-Infanterie-Regiment Nr. 270 im Weltkrieg 1914/1918* (Berlin: Verlag Bernard & Graefe, 1934), p. 34.
13. François, *Gorlice 1915*, p. 49.
14. Germany, Reichsarchiv, *Der Weltkrieg 1914 bis 1918*, Vol. 7, p. 381, François, *Gorlice 1915*, p. 51, and Engelberg, *Das Reserve-Infanterie-Regiment Nr. 270 im Weltkriege 1914/1918*, p. 36.
15. Kalm, *Gorlice*, pp. 84–85, Germany, Reichsarchiv, *Der Weltkrieg 1914 bis 1918*, Vol. 7, p. 382, François, *Gorlice 1915*, p. 53, Engelberg, *Das Reserve-Infanterie-Regiment Nr. 270 im Weltkriege 1914/1918*, pp. 36–38, and Ziethen, "Die Durchbruchsschlacht von Gorlice," p. 1631.
16. François, *Gorlice 1915*, p. 54, Max Eder, *Das Preussische Reserve-Infanterie-Regiment 269* (Zeulenroda, Germany: Bernhard Sporn Verlag; 1937), p. 34 and Germany, Reichsarchiv, *Der Weltkrieg 1914 bis 1918*, Vol. 7, p. 382.
17. François, *Gorlice 1915*, pp. 56–57, and Eder, *Das Preussische Reserve-Infanterie-Regiment 269*, p. 38.

18. Kalm, *Gorlice,* p. 82, Germany, Reichsarchiv, *Der Weltkrieg 1914 bis 1918,* Vol. 7, p. 382, and François, *Gorlice 1915,* pp. 56–57.

19. Austro–Hungarian VI Corps, "Schlacht bei Gorlice-Tarnow," BA-MA W 10/51393.

20. Kalm, *Gorlice,* pp. 91–92, François, *Gorlice 1915,* pp. 58–59, Ziethen, "Die Durchbruchsschlacht von Gorlice," p. 1631, and Austro–Hungarian VI Corps, "Schlacht bei Gorlice-Tarnow," BA-MA W 10/51393.

21. Kalm, *Gorlice,* p. 92 and Austro–Hungarian VI Corps, "Schlacht bei Gorlice-Tarnow," BA-MA W 10/51393.

22. François, *Gorlice 1915,* pp. 58–59, Kalm, *Gorlice,* pp. 93–94, Ziethen, "Die Durchbruchschlacht von Gorlice," p. 1631, Germany, Reichsarchiv, *Der Weltkrieg 1914 bis 1918,* Vol. 7, p. 384, and Austro–Hungarian VI Corps, "Schlacht bei Gorlice-Tarnow," BA-MA W 10/51393.

23. Germany, Reichsarchiv, *Der Weltkrieg 1914 bis 1918,* Vol. 7, p. 385.

24. Ironically, the Prussian 1st Guards Grenadier Regiment, formed in 1814, was designated the Kaiser Alexander Regiment in honor of Tsar Alexander I of Russia.

25. Bose, *Das Kaiser Alexander Garde-Grenadier-Regiment Nr. 1 im Weltkriege 1914–1918,* p. 164.

26. François, *Gorlice 1915,* p. 59, Ziethen, "Die Durchbruchsschlacht von Gorlice," p. 1632, Luyken, *Das 2. Garde-Feldartillerie-Regiment im Weltkriege,* p. 74, Rosenberg-Lipinsky, *Das Königin Elisabeth Garde-Grenadier-Regiment Nr. 3 im Weltkriege 1914–1918,* p. 150, and Bose, *Das Kaiser Alexander Garde-Grenadier-Regiment Nr. 1 im Weltkriege 1914–1918,* pp. 165–167.

27. Germany, Reischarchiv, *Der Weltkrieg 1914 bis 1918,* Vol. 7, p. 385, Unger, *Das Königin Augusta Garde-Grenadier-Regiment Nr. 4 im Weltkriege 1914–1919,* p. 94, and François, *Gorlice 1915,* p. 59.

28. Prince Friedrich of Prussia, *Das Erste Garderegiment zu Fuss im Weltkrieg 1914–1918,* pp. 91–92.

29. Germany, Reichsarchiv, *Der Weltkrieg 1914 bis 1918,* Vol. 7, p. 385.

30. Foerster, ed., *Wir Kämpfer im Weltkrieg,* pp. 182–183, Prince Friedrich of Prussia, *Das Erste Garderegiment zu Fuss im Weltkrieg 1914–18,* p. 93, Witkop, ed., *German Students' War Letters,* p. 117, Bose, *Das Kaiser Alexander Garde-Grenadier-Regiment Nr. 1 im Weltkriege 1914–1918,* 167, Rosenberg-Lipinsky, *Das Königin Elisabeth Garde-Grenadier-Regiment Nr. 3 im Weltkriege 1914–1918,* pp. 144 and 153, and François, *Gorlice 1915,* p. 63.

31. Austria, Bundesministerium, *Österreich-Ungarns Letzter Krieg 1914–1918,* Vol. 2, pp. 321–323, and German Eleventh Army, Special Orders Nr. 13, 2 May 1915, BH-KA File 11/43/4.

32. Germany, Reichsarchiv, *Der Weltkrieg 1914 bis 1918,* Vol. 7, p. 387.

33. Foerster, ed., *Mackensen: Briefe und Aufzeichnungen,* p. 148.

34. Kraft, *Der Anteil der 11. Bayer. Inf. Div. an der Durchbruchsschlacht von Gorlice-Tarnow,* p. 30, Luyken, *Das 2. Garde-Feldartillerie-Regiment im Weltkriege,* p. 74, Rosenberg-Lipinsky, *Das Königin Elisabeth Garde-Grenadier-Regiment Nr. 3 im Weltkriege 1914–1918,* p. 152, and Bose, *Das Kaiser Alexander Garde-Grenadier-Regiment Nr. 1 im Weltkriege 1914–1918,* p. 168.

35. Groener diary extract, *Nachlass* Groener, BA-MA N 46/41, and Stürgkh, *Im Deutschen Grossen Hauptquartier,* p. 131. Mackensen and Seeckt learned on the

morning of May 3 that 12,000 prisoners and 15 guns had been taken, plus many machine guns. Foerster, ed., *Mackensen: Briefe und Aufzeichnungen,* p. 148.

36. Tappen Diary, May 2, 1915, BA-MA W 10/50661, Görlitz, *The Kaiser and His Court,* p. 76, Seeckt, *Aus meinem Leben 1866–1917,* p. 123, and Foerster, ed., *Mackensen: Briefe und Aufzeichnungen,* p. 148.

37. Bavarian 11th Infantry Division KTB/3 May 1915, BH-KA File 11/4/1 and Kneussl Diary, May 3, 1915, *Nachlass* Kneussl, BH-KA NL 3. François regarded this as a vast improvement in the command arrangements, having a regular corps headquarters controlling matters on Mackensen's right flank, instead of an ad hoc organization such as Corps Kneussl. François, *Gorlice 1915,* p. 71.

38. Germany, *Der Weltkrieg 1914 bis 1918,* Vol. 7, p. 390, François, *Gorlice 1915,* p. 69, Kalm, *Gorlice,* p. 134, Foerster, ed., *Mackensen: Briefe und Aufzeichnungen,* p. 148, and Ziethen, "Aus grosser Zeit vor zwanzig Jahren. Die Durchbruchsschlacht von Gorlice," *Militär Wochenblatt* Vol. 119, Nr. 42 (11 May 1935): p. 1667. (To distinguish this article from the one with the exact same title in the May 4, 1915, issue of *Militär Wochenblatt,* hereafter this article is cited as "Die Durchbruchsschlacht von Gorlice II." The May 4, 1915, article is cited hereafter as "Die Durchbruchsschlacht von Gorlice I.")

39. Kraft, *Der Anteil der 11. Bayer. Inf. Div. and der Durchbruchsschlacht von Gorlice-Tarnow,* p. 31.

40. Germany, Reichsarchiv, *Der Weltkrieg 1914 bis 1918,* Vol. 7, pp. 392 and 394, François, *Gorlice 1915,* p. 72, Bavarian 11th Infantry Division KTB/3 May 1915, BH-KA File 11/4/1, Kraft, *Der Anteil der 11. Bayer. Inf. Div. an der Durchbruchsschlacht von Gorlice-Tarnow,* pp. 34–35, and Stengel, *Das K. B. Infanterie-Regiment Prinz Karl von Bayern 1914–1918,* p. 16.

41. Kalm, *Gorlice,* pp. 139–140, and François, *Gorlice 1915,* p. 72.

42. Germany, Reichsarchiv, *Der Weltkrieg 1914 bis 1918,* Vol. 7, p. 398.

43. German Eleventh Army, Special Orders Nr. 16, May 4, 1915, BH-KA File 11/43/4.

44. Germany, Reichsarchiv, *Der Weltkrieg 1914 bis 1918,* Vol. 7, p. 398, Bavarian 11th Infantry Division KTB/May 4, 1915, BH-KA File 11/4/1, Kneussl Diary, *Nachlass* Kneussl, BH-KA NL 3, and Stengel, *Das K.B. 3. Infanterie-Regiment Prinz Karl von Bayern 1914–1918,* p. 16.

45. Germany, Reichsarchiv, *Der Weltkrieg 1914 bis 1918,* Vol. 7, p. 399, and Ziethen, "Die Durchbruchsschlacht von Gorlice II," p. 1667.

46. Foerster, ed., *Mackensen: Briefe und Aufzeichnungen,* p. 151, and Germany, Reichsarchiv, *Der Weltkrieg 1914 bis 1918,* Vol. 7, p. 401.

47. Bavarian 11th Infantry Division KTB/May 5, 1915, BH-KA File 11/4/1, Kraft, *Der Anteil der 11. Bayer. Inf. Div. an der Durchbruchsschlacht von Gorlice-Tarnow,* p. 44, Corps Emmich, Special Orders For May 5, May 4, 1915, BH-KA File 11/44/10, Germany, Reichsarchiv, *Der Weltkrieg 1914 bis 1918,* Vol. 7, p. 401, and Stengel, *Das K.B. 3. Infanterie-Regiment Prinz Karl von Bayern 1914–1918,* p. 17.

48. François, *Gorlice 1915,* pp. 68–69, and Kalm, *Gorlice,* p. 135.

49. Germany, Reichsarchiv, *Der Weltkrieg 1914 bis 1918,* Vol. 7, p. 395, François, *Gorlice 1915,* pp. 70–71, and Kalm, *Gorlice,* p. 159.

50. François, *Gorlice 1915,* p. 75.

51. Germany, Reichsarchiv, *Der Weltkrieg 1914 bis 1918,* Vol. 7, p. 404, François, *Gorlice 1915,* pp. 76–77, and Eder, *Das preussische Reserve-Infanterie-Regiment 269,* pp. 48–49.

52. Germany, Reichsarchiv, *Der Weltkrieg 1914 bis 1918,* Vol. 7, p. 399, François, *Gorlice 1915,* pp. 80–81, and Engelberg, *Das Reserve-Infanterie-Regiment Nr. 270 im Weltkriege 1914/1918,* p. 39.

53. Austro–Hungarian VI Corps, "Schlacht bei Gorlice-Tarnow," BA-MA W 10/51393.

54. Germany, Reichsarchiv, *Der Weltkrieg 1914 bis 1918,* Vol. 7, p. 399, and Austro–Hungarian VI Corps, "Verfolgungskampfe nach der Schlacht bei Gorlice-Tarnow," BA-MA W 10/51393.

55. Germany, Reichsarchiv, *Der Weltkrieg 1914 bis 1918,* Vol. 7, p. 396, Bose, *Das Kaiser Alexander Garde-Grenadier-Regiment Nr. 1 im Weltkriege 1914–1918,* pp. 169–170, Rosenberg-Lipinsky, *Das Königin Elisabeth Garde-Grenadier-Regiment Nr. 3 im Weltkriege 1914–1918,* pp. 154–155, and Luyken, *Das 2. Garde-Feldartillerie-Regiment im Weltkriege,* p. 75.

56. Germany, Reichsarchiv, *Der Weltkrieg 1914 bis 1918,* Vol. 7, p. 396, Kalm, *Gorlice,* p. 146, and Prince Friedrich of Prussia, *Das Erste Garderegiment zu Fuss im Weltkrieg 1914–18,* p. 93.

57. Germany, Reichsarchiv, *Der Weltkrieg 1914 bis 1918,* Vol. 7, p. 404, François, *Gorlice 1915,* p. 79, Rosenberg-Lipinsky, *Das Königin Elisabeth Garde-Grenadier-Regiment Nr. 3 im Weltkriege 1914–1918,* p. 156, and Unger, *Das Königin Augusta Garde-Grenadier-Regiment Nr. 4 im Weltkriege 1914–1919,* p. 97.

58. Austria, Bundesministerium, *Österreich-Ungarns Letzter Krieg 1914–1918,* Vol. 2, p. 326.

59. Germany, Reichsarchiv, *Der Weltkrieg 1914 bis 1918,* Vol. 7, p. 404, and Austria, Bundesministerium, *Österreich-Ungarns Letzter Krieg 1914–1918,* Vol. 2, p. 329.

60. Novikov, "Der russische Nachtrichtendienst vor dem Gorlice–Durchbruch," p. 1671.

61. Germany, Reichsarchiv, *Der Weltkrieg 1914 bis 1918,* Vol. 7, p. 402, and Danilov, *Russland in Weltkriege 1914–1915,* p. 490.

62. Kraft, *Der Anteil der 11. Bayer. Inf. Div. an der Durchbruchsschlacht von Gorlice-Tarnow,* p. 47, Danilov, *Russland in Weltkriege 1914–1915,* p. 490, Bose, *Das Kaiser Alexander Garde-Grenadier-Regiment Nr. 1 im Weltkriege 1914-1918,* p 171, Rosenberg-Lipinsky, *Das Königin Elisabeth Garde-Grenadier-Regiment im Weltkriege 1914–1918,* p. 156, Jones, "Imperial Russia's Forces at War," *Military Effectiveness,* Vol. I, pp. 305–306, and François, *Gorlice 1915,* p. 69. For an eyewitness account of the Russian retreat, see Florence Farmborough, *With the Armies of the Tsar: A Nurse at the Russian Front 1914–18* (New York: Stein and Day, 1975), pp. 56–57.

63. German War Ministry, Viewpoints on Training and Equipping of Infantry, January 14, 1915, Rosenberg-Lipinsky, *Das Königin Elisabeth Garde-Grenadier-Regiment Nr. 3 im Weltkriege 1914–1918,* p. 154, and Engelberg, *Das Reserve-Infanterie-Regiment Nr. 270 im Weltkriege 1914/1918,* p. 35.

64. Hoeppner, *Germany's War in the Air,* p. 44, Austro–Hungarian VI Corps, "Vorbereitung der Schlacht bei Gorlice-Tarnow," June 1915, W 10/51393, and Kalm, *Gorlice,* p. 27.

65. Ziethen, "Die Durchbruchsschlacht von Gorlice I," p. 1628, Austro–Hungarian VI Corps, "Schlacht bei Gorlice-Tarnow," June 1915, BA-MA W 10/51393, François, *Gorlice 1915,* p. 55, and Bose, *Das Kaiser Alexander Garde-Grenadier-Regiment Nr. 1 im Weltkriege 1914–1918,* p. 166.

66. François, *Gorlice 1915*, pp. 44 and 51, and Corps Emmich, Special Orders for May 5, May 4, 1915, BH-KA File 11/44/10. Later on, the laying in of telephone and telegraph networks assumed a symbolic importance as a sign of Germany spreading its culture to the "uncivilized east." Vejas Gabriel Liulevicius, *War Land on the Eastern Front: Culture, National Identity and German Occupation in World War I* (Cambridge: Cambridge University Press; 2000), p. 160.
67. Austria, Bundesministerium, *Österreich-Ungarns Letzter Krieg 1914–1918*, Vol. 2, p. 328, and Stone, *The Eastern Front 1914–1917*, p. 137.
68. Kalm, *Gorlice*, pp. 201–202, and Austro–Hungarian VI Corps, "Verfolgungs-kampfe nach der Schlacht bei Gorlice Tarnow," BA-MA W 10/51393.
69. Tappen diary, May 3,1915, BA-MA W 10/50661, German Eleventh Army Order, May 4, 1915, *Nachlass* Seeckt, BA-MA N 247/24, Cramon, *Unser Österreich-Ungarische Bundesgenosse im Weltkriege*, p. 15, and Foerster, ed., *Mackensen: Briefe und Aufzeichnungen*, p. 152.

CHAPTER FIVE

1. Conrad to Falkenhayn, May 9, 1915, AOK Operations Bureau, Conrad–Falkenhayn correspondence, Russia, ÖSA-KA File 512 (hereafter cited as ÖSA-KA R512).
2. Quoted in Stone, *The Eastern Front 1914–1917*, p. 139.
3. Conrad to Falkenhayn, May 23, 1915, AOK Operations Bureau, Conrad–Falkenhayn correspondence, Russia, ÖSA-KA R512.
4. Foerster, ed., *Mackensen: Briefe und Aufzeichnungen*, p. 166.
5. Kalm, *Gorlice*, p. 34, and François, *Gorlice 1915*, p. 34.
6. Germany, Reichsarchiv, *Der Weltkrieg 1914 bis 1918*, Vol. 7, p. 405. Foerster, ed., *Mackensen: Briefe und Aufzeichnungen*, p. 153 and KTB/Bavarian 11th Infantry Division, May 6, 1915, BH-KA File 11/4/1. Born February 12, 1856, Böhm-Ermolli followed his father's footsteps with a career in the army. Having graduated from the Theresa Military Academy in 1875, Böhm-Ermolli enjoyed a successful series of tours with various cavalry units in the Austro–Hungarian Army. After a serving several assignments on the general staff, in 1911 he was promoted General der Kavallerie and appointed commander of the I Corps. By 1914 Böhm-Ermolli was commander of the Austro–Hungarian Second Army, which he led through the campaigns of 1914 and 1915 until, on September 19, 1915, when he was given command of an army group. After successes in eastern Galicia and Romania, Böhm-Ermolli was promoted General-alfeldmarschall on January 31, 1918. He was in charge of the Austro–Hungarian sector of the occupied territories when disagreements with his German counterparts led to his removal and the end of his active service. Böhm-Ermolli died on December 9, 1941. Herwig and Heyman, *Biographical Dictionary of World War I*, pp. 89–90.
7. Falkenhayn to Conrad, May 6, 1915, AOK Operations Bureau, Conrad–Falkenhayn correspondence, Russia, ÖSA-KA R512, Foerster, ed., *Mackensen: Briefe und Aufzeichnungen*, p. 155, Meier-Welcker, *Seeckt*, p. 53, Tappen Diary, May 7–8, 1915, BA-MA W 10/50661, Plessen diary, May 8, 1915, BA-MA W 10/50656 and Falkenhayn to Conrad, May 9, 1915, AOK Operations Bureau, Conrad–Falkenhayn correspondence, Russia, ÖSA-KA R512.

8. Conrad to Falkenhayn, May 9, 1915, AOK Operations Bureau, Conrad–Falkenhayn correspondence, Russia, ÖSA-KA R512.

9. The Anglo-French attack made limited gains. Ironically, Joffre kept the French part of the offensive going through mid-May because of his concern over Mackensen's breakthrough. Doughty, *Pyrrhic Victory*, p. 161.

10. Falkenhayn to Conrad, May 10, 1915, BA-MA W 10/51380. The message was sent at 10:30 A.M.

11. Conrad to Falkenhayn, May 10, 1915, AOK Operations Bureau, Conrad–Falkenhayn correspondence, Russia, ÖSA-KA R512 and Wendt, *Der italienische Kriegschauplatz in europäischen Konflikten*, p. 434.

12. Falkenhayn to Cramon, May 11, 1915 and Falkenhayn to Eleventh Army, May 12, 1915, BA-MA W 10/51388.

13. Falkenhayn to Cramon, May 11, 1915, and Cramon to Falkenhayn, May 11, 1915, BA-MA W 10/51388.

14. Wilhelm II to Mackensen, May 10, 1915, *Nachlass* Seeckt, BA-MA N 247/24, and Conrad to Bolfras, May 10, 1915, ÖSA-KA MKSM 78.

15. Germany, Reichsarchiv, *Der Weltkrieg 1914 bis 1918*, Vol. 7, p. 409, Bavarian 11th Infantry Division/May 7, 1915 BH-KA File 11/4/1, Kraft, *Der Anteil der 11. Bayer. Inf. Div. an der Durchbruchsschlacht von Gorlice-Tarnow*, pp. 50–51, Austro–Hungarian VI Corps, "Verfolgungskampfe nach der Schlacht bei Gorlice-Tarnow," BA-MA W 10/51393, Prince Frederick of Prussia, *Das Erste Garderegiment zu Fuss im Weltkrieg 1914–1918*, p. 93, and Rosenberg-Lipinsky, *Das Königin Elisabeth Garde-Grenadier-Regiment Nr. 3 im Weltkriege 1914–1918*, p. 160.

16. Austria, Bundesministerium, *Österreich-Ungarns Letzter Krieg 1914–1918*, Vol. 2, p. 337, and Danilov, *Russland im Weltkriege 1914–1915*, pp. 492–493. Kornilov was able to escape from captivity in 1916, being the first Russian general to perform such a feat. After making a triumphant return to Russia, Kornilov was given command of a corps and later the Russian 8th Army. Although very conservative politically, Kornilov was able to accept the toppling of the Romanov dynasty and was appointed commander of the Petrograd Military District by the provisional government. Disenchanted with the provisional government of Alexandr Kerensky, Kornilov launched an abortive coup in September 1917. After his arrest and subsequent release, Kornilov fled south following the Bolshevik coup in November 1917. He quickly established himself as one of the leaders of the anti-Bolshevik White forces but was killed in action near Ekaterinodar on April 13, 1918. Herwig and Heyman, *Biographical Dictionary of World War I*, pp. 210–211.

17. Meier-Welcker, *Seeckt*, p. 53, Plessen diary, May 12, 1915, BA-MA W 10/50656, Tappen diary, May 12, 1915, BA-MA W 10/50661, and Germany, Reichsarchiv, *Der Weltkrieg 1914 bis 1918*, Vol. 7, p. 426.

18. Foerster, ed., *Mackensen: Briefe und Aufzeichnungen*, p. 157, German, Reichsarchiv, *Der Weltkrieg 1914 bis 1918*, Vol. 7, p. 423, and Cramon, *Unser Österreich-Ungarischer Bundesgenosse im Weltkriege*, p. 17.

19. Germany, Reichsarchiv, *Der Weltkrieg 1914 bis 1918*, Vol. 7, p. 426, and Foerster, ed., *Mackensen: Briefe und Aufzeichnungen*, p. 158.

20. François, *Gorlice 1915*, p. 106, and Germany, Reichsarchiv, *Der Weltkrieg 1914 bis 1918* (Berlin: E. S. Mittler und Sohn; 1932), Vol. 8, p. 151.

21. François, *Gorlice 1915*, p. 106 and Foerster, ed., *Mackensen: Briefe und Aufzeichnungen*, p. 158.

22. François, *Gorlice 1915*, p. 106, German Eleventh Army, Special Order Nr. 28, May 15, 1915, BH-KA File 11/43/4, Corps Emmich, Special Orders, May 12, 1915, BH-KA File 11/44/10 and Germany, Reichsarchiv, *Der Weltkrieg 1914 bis 1918*, Vol. 7, p. 428.

23. Kneussl Diary, May 14, 1915, *Nachlass* Kneussl, BH-KA NL 3, François, *Gorlice 1915*, p. 109, Austro–Hungarian VI Corps, "Schlacht bei Jaroslau," BA-MA W 10/51393, Germany, Reichsarchiv, *Der Weltkrieg 1914 bis 1918*, Vol. 7, p. 427, and Rosenberg-Lipinsky, *Das Königin Elisabeth Garde-Grenadier-Regiment Nr. 3 im Weltkriege 1914–1918*, p. 168.

24. Prince Frederick of Prussia, *Das Erste Garderegiment zu Fuss im Weltkrieg 1914–18*, p. 95.

25. Seeckt, *Aus meinem Leben 1866–1917*, p. 135, Foerster, ed., *Mackensen: Briefe und Aufzeichnungn*, p. 159, Cramon, *Unser Österreich-Ungarischer undesgenosse im Weltkriege*, p. 17, and Austro–Hungarian VI Corps, "Schlacht bei Jaroslau," BA-MA W 10/51393.

26. Bavarian 11th Infantry Division KTB/May 14, 1915, BH-KA File 11/4/1 and François, *Gorlice 1915*, p. 110.

27. Rosenberg-Lipinsky, *Das Königin Elisabeth Garde-Grenadier-Regiment Nr. 3 im Weltkriege 1914–1918*, p. 169, Bose, *Das Kaiser Alexander Garde-Grenadier-Regiment Nr. 1 im Weltkriege 1914–1918*, p. 178, Erwin Berghaus, *Vier Monate mit Mackensen: Von Tarnow-Gorlice bis Brest-Litowsk* (Stuttgart: Verlag von Julius Hoffmann, 1916), pp. 25–26, Seeckt, *Aus meinem Leben 1966–1917*, p. 135 and Germany, Reichsarchiv, *Der Weltkrieg 1914 bis 1918*, Vol. 8, p. 141.

28. François, *Gorlice 1915*, p. 112, and Bose, *Das Kaiser Alexander Garde-Grenadier-Regiment Nr. 1 im Weltkriege 1914–1918*, p. 178.

29. François, *Gorlice 1915*, p. 114, and Germany, Reichsarchiv, *Der Weltkrieg 1914 bis 1918*, Vol. 8, p. 143.

30. Austro–Hungarian VI Corps, "Schlacht bei Jaroslau," BA-MA W 10/51393, Germany, Reichsarchiv, *Der Weltkrieg 1914 bis 1918*, Vol. 8, p. 144, Luyken, *Das 2. Garde-Feldartillerie-Regiment im Weltkriege*, p. 82, Bose, *Das Kaiser Alexander Garde-Grenadier-Regiment Nr. 1 im Weltkriege 1914–1918*, p. 179, Rosenberg-Lipinsky, *Das Königin Elisabeth Garde-Grenadier-Regiment Nr. 3 im Weltkriege 1914–1918*, p. 170, Prince Friedrich of Prussia, *Das Erste Garderegiment zu Fuss im Weltkrieg 1914–1918*, p. 98, and Unger, *Das Königin Augusta Garde-Grenadier-Regiment Nr. 4 im Weltkriege 1914–1919*, p. 102.

31. Prince Friedrich of Prussia, *Das Erste Garderegiment zu Fuss im Weltkrieg 1914–1918*, p. 99, Rosenberg-Lipinsky, *Das Königin Elisabeth Garde-Grenadier-Regiment Nr. 3 im Weltkriege 1914–1918*, p. 172, and Luyken, *Das 2. Garde-Feldartillerie-Regiment im Weltkriege*, p. 82.

32. Germany, Reichsarchiv, *Der Weltkrieg 1914 bis 1918*, Vol. 8, pp. 144, Foerster, ed., *Wir Kämpfer im Weltkrieg*, p. 189, and Paul Heinrici, ed., *Das Ehrenbuch der deutschen Pionere* (Berlin: Verlag Tradition Wilhelm Kolk, 1932), p. 203.

33. Germany, Reichsarchiv, *Der Weltkrieg 1914 bis 1918*, Vol. 8, p. 146, François, *Gorlice 1915*, p. 115, and Austro–Hungarian VI Corps, "Schlacht bei Jaroslau," BA-MA W 10/51393.

34. Germany, Reichsarchiv, *Der Weltkrieg 1914 bis 1918*, Vol. 8, p. 147, and Heinrici, ed., *Das Ehrenbuch der deutschen Pionere*, p. 205.

35. Germany, Reichsarchiv, *Der Weltkrieg 1914 bis 1918,* Vol. 8, p. 146, and Bose, *Das Kaiser Alexander Garde-Grenadier-Regiment Nr. 1 im Weltkriege 1914–1918,* p. 181.

36. Rosenberg-Lipinsky, *Das Königin Elisabeth Garde-Grenadier-Regiment Nr. 3 im Weltkriege 1914–1918,* pp. 173–174, Bose, *Das Kaiser Alexander Garde-Grenadier-Regiment Nr. 1 im Weltkriege 1914–1918,* p. 182, and Germany, Reichsarchiv, *Der Weltkrieg 1914 bis 1918,* Vol. 8, p. 146.

37. Prince Friedrich of Prussia, *Das Erste Garderegiment zu Fuss im Weltkrieg 1914–1918,* p. 99, Germany, Reichsarchiv, *Der Weltkrieg 1914 bis 1918,* Vol. 8, pp. 148–149, Austro–Hungarian VI Corps, "Schlacht bei Jaroslau," BA-MA W 10/51393, and François, *Gorlice 1915,* p. 119.

38. German Eleventh Army, Special Order Nr. 28, May 15, 1915, BH-KA, File 11/43/4, Foerster, ed., *Mackensen: Briefe und Aufzeichnungen,* p. 161, Germany, Reichsarchiv, *Der Weltkrieg 1914 bis 1918,* Vol. 8, p. 148, François, *Gorlice 1915,* p. 122, Luyken, *Das 2. Garde-Feldartillerie-Regiment im Weltkriege,* p. 82, and Plessen diary, May 17, 1915, BA-MA W 10/50656.

39. François, *Gorlice 1915,* p. 121.

40. Afflerbach, *Falkenhayn,* pp. 266–267, Sondhaus, *Franz Conrad von Hötzendorf,* p. 176, Conrad to Falkenhayn, May 18, 1915, BA-MA W 10/50683, and Conrad to Bolfras, May 21, 1915, ÖSA-KA MKSM 78.

41. Memorandum of General von Falkenhayn, May 16, 1915, Conrad to Falkenhayn, May 17, 1915, Falkenhayn to Conrad, May 17, 1915, BA-MA W 10/50683, Notes of General von Falkenhayn on the Result of the Conference in Teschen on May 18, 1915, BA-MA W 10/50683, and Rudolf Kundmann diary, May 8, 1915, Conrad Archive, ÖSA-KA B/13.

42. Germany, Reichsarchiv, *Der Weltkrieg 1914 bis 1918,* Vol. 7, p. 426, Meier-Welcker, *Seeckt,* p. 53, and Austria, Bundesministerium, *Österreich-Ungarns Letzter Krieg 1914–1918,* Vol. 2, p. 372.

43. Germany, Reichsarchiv, *Der Weltkrieg 1914 bis 1918,* Vol. 8, p. 149, and Austria, Bundesministerium, *Österreich-Ungarns Letzter Krieg 1914–1918,* Vol. 2, p. 397.

44. Falkenhayn to Eleventh Army, May 18, 1915, Eleventh Army to OHL, 18 May 1915, Falkenhayn to Eleventh Army. May 18, 1915, Eleventh Army to Falkenhayn, May 18, 1915 and Eleventh Army to Falkenhayn, May 19, 1915, BA-MA W 10/51388.

45. François, *Gorlice 1915,* p. 126, and Rosenberg-Lipinsky, *Das Königin Elisabeth Garde-Grenadier Regiment Nr. 3 im Weltkriege 1914–1918,* pp. 153 and 178. See also Bose, *Das Kaiser Alexander Garde-Grenadier-Regiment Nr. 1 im Weltkriege 1914–1918,* p. 184.

46. Cramon to OHL Operations Section at Pless, May 20, 1915, BA-MA W 10/51388, Austro–Hungarian VI Corps, "Durchbruch bei Jaroslau," BA-MA W 10/51393, Germany, Reichsarchiv, *Der Weltkrieg 1914 bis 1918,* Vol. 8, p. 190, Brusilov, *A Soldier's Notebook,* p. 146, and Danilov, *Russland im Weltkriege 1914–1915,* p. 505.

47. Germany, Reichsarchiv, *Der Weltkrieg 1914 bis 1918,* Vol. 8, p. 161, Conrad to Falkenhayn, May 24, 1915, BA-MA W 10/51388, and Foerster, ed., *Mackensen: Briefe und Aufzeichnungen,* p. 162.

48. François, *Gorlice 1915,* p. 127, and Germany, Reichsarchiv, *Der Weltkrieg 1914 bis 1918,* Vol. 8, p. 161.

49. Germany, Reichsarchiv, *Der Weltkrieg 1914 bis 1918,* Vol. 8, p. 168.

50. Luyken, *Das 2. Garde-Feldartillerie-Regiment im Weltkriege*, p. 86, Bose, *Das Kaiser Alexander Garde-Grenadier-Regiment Nr. 1 im Weltkriege 1914-1918*, pp. 184–185, Unger, *Das Königin Augusta Garde-Grenadier-Regiment Nr. 4 im Weltkriege 1914–1919*, p. 107, Rosenberg-Lipinsky, *Das Königin Elisabeth Garde-Grenadier Regiment Nr. 3 im Weltkriege 1914–1918*, p. 181, Prince Friedrich of Prussia, *Das Erste Garderegiment zu Fuss im Weltkrieg 1914–18*, p. 100, Austria, Bundesministerium, *Österreich-Ungarns Letzter Krieg 1914–1918*, Vol. 2, p. 424, and Austro–Hungarian VI Corps, "Offensive östlich des San, Kampfe bei Wietlin–Wysocko," BA-MA W 10/51393.

51. François, *Gorlice 1915*, pp. 139–142, Eder, *Das Preussische Reserve-Infanterie-Regiment 269*, p. 60, Germany, Reichsarchiv, *Der Weltkrieg 1914 bis 1918*, Vol. 8, p. 166, and Stengel, *Das K.B. 3. Infanterie-Regiment Prinz Karl von Bayern 1914–1918*, p. 20.

52. Germany, Reichsarchiv, *Der Weltkrieg 1914 bis 1918*, Vol 8, p. 173 and François, *Gorlice 1915*, p. 153.

53. Austria, Bundesministerium, *Österreich–Ungarns Letzter Krieg 1914–1918*, Vol. 2, pp. 426–429, Germany, *Der Weltkrieg 1914 bis 1918*, Vol. 8, p. 176, and Foerster, ed., *Mackensen: Briefe und Aufzeichnungen*, p. 164.

54. Cramon to Falkenhayn, May 29, 1915, BA-MA W 10/51388.

55. Cramon to OHL Operations Section, Pless, May 26, 1915, Falkenhayn to Ober Ost, May 28, 1915, and Ober Ost to Falkenhayn, May 28, 1915, BA-MA W 10/51388.

56. Tappen diary, May 30–31, 1915, BA-MA W 10/50661 and Seeckt, *Aus meinem Leben 1866-1917*, p. 142.

57. Germany, Reichsarchiv, *Der Weltkrieg 1914 bis 1918*, Vol. 8, p. 177, Bose, *Das Kaiser Alexander Garde-Grenadier-Regiment im Weltkriege 1914–1918*, p. 186, Austro–Hungarian VI Corps, "May 28–June 12, 1915. Ausgestaltung des Brückenkopfes und Vorbereitung weitern Offensive," BA-MA W 10/51393, and François, *Gorlice 1915*, p. 162.

58. Germany, Reichsarchiv, *Der Weltkrieg 1914 bis 1918*, Vol. 8, p. 178, and François, *Gorlice 1915*, p. 163.

59. German Eleventh Army, Report on the Fall of Przemysl, June 1915, *Nachlass* Seeckt, BA-MA N 247/24, François, *Gorlice 1915*, p. 155, and Seeckt, *Aus meinem Leben 1866-1917*, p. 142.

60. Brusilov, *A Soldier's Notebook*, p. 145, Danilov, *Russland im Weltkriege*, p. 508, and Cramon to OHL Operations Section, Pless, May 29, 1915, BA-MA W 10/51388,

61. François, *Gorlice 1915*, p. 163, Germany, Reichsarchiv, *Der Weltkrieg 1914 bis 1918*, p. 179, Bavarian 11th Infantry Division KTB/May 29, 1915, BH-KA File 11/4/1, and Unger, *Das Königin Augusta Garde-Grenadier-Regiment Nr. 4 im Weltkriege 1914–1919*, p 108.

62. German Eleventh Army, Report on the Fall of Przemysl, June 1915, *Nachlass* Seeckt, BA-MA N 247/24, François, *Gorlice 1915*, pp. 163–165, Stengel, *Das K.B. 3. Infanterie-Regiment Prinz Karl von Bayern 1914–1918*, p. 21, and Conrad to Falkenhayn, May 30, 1915, AOK Operations Bureau, Conrad–Falkenhayn correspondence, Russia, ÖSA-KA R512.

63. Germany, Reichsarchiv, *Der Weltkrieg 1914 bis 1918*, Vol. 8, pp. 181–182, Stengel, *Das K.B. 3. Infanterie-Regiment Prinz Karl von Bayern 1914–1918*, p. 22 and Unger, *Das Königin Augusta Garde-Grenadier-Regiment Nr. 4 im Weltkriege 1914–1919*, p. 108.

64. German Eleventh Army, Report on the Fall of Przemysl, June 1915, *Nachlass* Seeckt, BA-MA N 247/24, Fleck to OHL Operations Section, Pless, June 2, 1915,

BA-MA W 10/51388, and Stengel, *Das K.B. 3. Infanterie-Regiment Prinz Karl von Bayern 1914–1918*, p. 23.

65. German Eleventh Army, Report on the Fall of Przemysl, June 1915, *Nachlass* Seeckt, BA-MA N 247/24 and Kneussl Diary, June 6, 1915, *Nachlass* Kneussl, BH-KA NL 3.

66. François, *Gorlice 1915*, p. 166, and Kneussl Diary, June 6, 1915, *Nachlass* Kneussl, BH-KA NL 3.

67. Palmer and Wallis, eds., *Intimate Voices from the First World War*, pp. 91–92, and François, *Gorlice 1915*, p. 174.

68. Kundmann Diary, June 3,1915, Conrad Archive, ÖSA-KA B/13, and Cramon, *Unser Österreich–Ungarischer Bundesgenosse im Weltkriege*, p. 18.

69. François, *Gorlice 1915*, p. 128, Tappen diary, June 3, 1915, BA-MA W 10/50661, Bavarian 11th Infantry Division KTB/June 3, 1915, BH-KA 11/4/1, and Foerster, ed., *Mackensen: Briefe und Aufzeichnungen*, p. 167.

70. See, for examples, Conrad to Bolfras, May 21, 1915, ÖSA-KA MKSM 78, Conrad to Falkenhayn, May 17, 1915, Operations Bureau, Conrad–Falkenhayn correspondence, ÖSA-KA AOK R512, Conrad to Falkenhayn, May 18, 1915, BA-MA W 10/50683, and Falkenhayn to Conrad, May 19, 1915, BA-MA W 10/50683, Tappen diary, May 19, 1915, BA-MA W 10/50661, and Görlitz, ed., *The Kaiser and His Court*, p. 79.

71. Hamilton and Herwig, *Decisions for War, 1914–1917*, p. 176, and Danilov, *Russland im Weltkriege 1914–1915*, p. 510.

72. German Eleventh Army, Special Order Nr. 28, May 15, 1915, BH-KA File 11/43/4.

73. François, *Gorlice 1915*, p. 174.

74. Austria, Bundesministerium, *Österreich–Umgarns Letzter Krieg 1914–1918*, Vol. 2, p. 451, and Falkenhayn to Conrad, May 17, 1915, BA-MA W 10/50683.

75. Danilov, *Russland im Weltkriege 1914–1915*, p. 508, and Brusilov, *A Soldier's Notebook 1914–1918*, pp. 136–137.

CHAPTER SIX

1. Quoted in Pares, *Day by Day with the Russian Army 1914–15*, p. 22. Bobrinski (a lieutenant general) was the Russian governor general of Galicia. Brusilov, *A Soldier's Notebook 1914–1918*, p. 68.

2. Quoted in Brandt, *Mackensen*, p. 39.

3. Falkenhayn to Conrad, May 10, 1915, BA-MA W 10/51380, and Doughty, *Pyrrhic Victory*, p. 165.

4. Herwig, *The First World War*, p. 157, and Falkenhayn, *The German General Staff and Its Decisions, 1914–1916*, pp. 117–119.

5. Afflerbach, *Falkenhayn*, p. 232, Afflerbach, "Wilhelm II as Supreme Warlord," *The Kaiser*, p. 207, and Hoffman, *War Diaries and Other Papers*, Vol. I, p. 60.

6. Sondhaus, *Franz Conrad von Hötzendorf*, pp. 175–176. For some of the hurdles that had to be passed, see Conrad to Bolfras, June 27, 1915, and Bolfras to Conrad, June 30, 1915, ÖSA-KA MKSM 78.

7. Stone, *The Eastern Front 1914–1917*, p. 139, Conrad to Falkenhayn, May 9, 1915, BA-MA W 10/51380, Conrad to Falkenhayn, May 10, 1915, AOK Operations

Bureau, Conrad–Falkenhayn correspondence, Russia, ÖSA-KA R512, and Falkenhayn to Conrad, May 10, 1915, BA-MA W 10/51380.

8. Cramon, *Unser Österreich–Ungarischer Bundesgenosse im Weltkriege*, p. 19, Afflerbach, *Falkenhayn*, pp. 267–270, Sondhaus, *Franz Conrad von Hötzendorf*, p. 176, and Shanafelt, *The Secret Enemy*, p. 62.

9. Rauchensteiner, *Der Tod des Doppeladlers*, p. 215, and Conrad to Bolfras, May 19,1915, and Conrad to Bolfras, May 21, 1915, ÖSA-KA MKSM 78.

10. Conrad to Falkenhayn, May 17, 1915, BA-MA W 10/50683.

11. Hamilton and Herwig, *Decisions for War, 1914–1917*, pp. 199–200, Falkenhayn, *The German General Staff and Its Decisions, 1914–1916*, p. 103, Sondhaus, *Franz Conrad von Hötzendorf*, p. 177, and Falkenhayn to Conrad, June 13, 1915, BA-MA W 10/51388.

12. Falkenhayn, *The German General Staff and Its Decisions, 1914–1916*, p. 112, and Groener diary extract, *Nachlass* Groener, BA-MA N 46/41.

13. Seeckt, *Aus meinem Leben 1866–1917*, p. 145, Foerster, ed., *Mackensen: Briefe und Aufzeichnungen*, p. 171, Tappen diary, May 30, 1915, BA-MA W 10/50661, and Conrad to Falkenhayn, June 2, 1915, AOK Operations Bureau, Conrad–Falkenhayn correspondence, Russia, ÖSA-KA R512.

14. German Eleventh Army to OHL, June 3, 1915, BA-MA W 10/51388, and Kundmann diary, June 4, 1915, Conrad archive, ÖSA-KA B/13.

15. Falkenhayn to Conrad, June 2, 1915, AOK Operations Bureau, Conrad–Falkenhayn correspondence, Russia, ÖSA-KA R512, Falkenhayn to Eleventh Army, June 3, 1915, and AOK to All Armies, June 4, 1915, BA-MA W 10/51388. See also Meier-Welcker, *Seeckt*, p. 54, and Foerster, ed. *Mackensen: Briefe und Aufzeichnungen*, p. 171.

16. John R. Schindler, *Isonzo: The Forgotten Sacrifice of the Great War* (Westport, Conn.: Praeger, 2001), pp. 46–47, Austria, Bundesministerium, *Österreich–Ungarns Letzter Krieg 1914–1918*, Vol. 2, p. 449, and Sondhaus, *Franz Conrad von Hötzendorf*, p. 177.

17. Leonhard Graf von Rothkirch Freiherr von Trach, *Gorlice–Tarnow* (Oldenburg, Germany: Verlag von Gerhard Stalling, 1918), p. 86, Austro–Hungarian VI Corps, "May 28–June 12 1915. Ausgestaltung des Brückenkopfes und Vorbereitung der weiteren Offensive," BA-MA W 10/51393, François, *Gorlice 1915*, p. 189, Eder, *Das Preussische Reserve-Infanterie-Regiment 269*, p. 74, and Helmut Viereck, *Das Heideregiment Königlich Preussisches 2. Hannoversches Infanterie-Regiment Nr. 77 im Weltkriege 1914–1918*, p. 194.

18. Tappen diary, May 31, 1915, BA-MA W 10/50661, Groener diary, June 2, 1915, *Nachlass* Groener, BA-MA N 46/41, Falkenhayn to Eleventh Army, June 2, 1915, BA-MA W 10/51388, and Bavarian 8th Reserve Division KTB/June 2, 1915, BH-KA File 8R/1/3. Born September 4, 1953, Eugen von Falkenhayn was commissioned lieutenant on December 8, 1870. After completing an assignment with the Great General Staff, Falkenhayn spent almost a decade with the cavalry. After his promotion to Generalleutnant on April 14, 1906, Falkenhayn commanded the 11th Infantry Division and then took over the XXII Reserve Corps on September 10, 1914. He was promoted General der Kavallerie on September 24, 1914. Falkenhayn retired on June 30, 1919, and died in Berlin on January 3, 1934. Short Biographical Chronology, BA-MA MSg 109/10858. Herman Freiherr von Stein was born on February 11, 1859, and entered the Bavarian Army in 1879. Stein spent his career in the field artillery, ultimately com-

manding the Bavarian 1st Artillery Brigade. He was promoted to Generalleutnant on 10 September 10, 1914, and took command of the Bavarian 8th Reserve Division in December 1914. Having commanded a division successfully, Stein later commanded the Bavarian III Corps. He retired on December 29, 1918, and died on February 26, 1928. Short Biographical Chronology, BA-MA MSg 109/10871.

19. Eder, *Das Preussische Reserve-Infanterie-Regiment 269,* p. 68.

20. Bose, *Das Kaiser Alexander Garde-Grenadier-Regiment Nr. 1 im Weltkriege 1914–1918,* p. 187, and Rosenberg-Lipinsky, *Das Königin Elisabeth Garde-Grenadier-Regiment Nr. 3 im Weltkriege 1914–1918,* p. 183.

21. Austria, Bundesministerium, *Österreich-Ungarns Letzter Krieg 1914–1918,* Vol. 2, p. 470.

22. Germany, Reichsarchiv, *Der Weltkrieg 1914 bis 1918,* Vol. 8, p. 217. Unfortunately, details on this and other logistical matters are often lacking. Official histories, for example, are normally more concerned with operational and tactical events and thus give only short shrift to logistics.

23. Luyken, *Das 2. Garde-Feldartillerie-Regiment im Weltkriege,* p. 88, and Bavarian 8th Reserve Division, Billeting, Supply and Road Conditions in Galicia, April 10, 1916, BH-KA File 8R/1/3.

24. German Eleventh Army, Special Orders Nr. 28, May 15, 1915, and German Eleventh Army, Special Orders Nr. 53, June 10, 1915, BH-KA File 11/43/4.

25. Luyken, *Das 2. Garde-Feldartillerie-Regiment im Weltkriege,* p. 88.

26. Falkenhayn to Cramon, May 11, 1915, and Cramon to Falkenhayn, May 11, 1915, BA-MA W 10/51388.

27. Under the German imperial constitution, Bavaria maintained its own military establishment, including a war ministry.

28. Cramon to Falkenhayn, June 5, 1915, and Falkenhayn to Cramon and Eleventh Army, June 6, 1915, BA-MA W 10/51388.

29. François, *Gorlice 1915,* pp. 189–190, Germany, Reichsarchiv, *Der Weltkrieg 1914 bis 1918,* Vol. 8, p. 218, Archduke Joseph Ferdinand to AOK, June 22, 1915, and Archduke Friedrich to Mackensen, July 3, 1915, AOK Operations Bureau, Conrad–Falkenhayn correspondence, Russia, ÖSA-KA R512.

30. Eleventh Army, Situation Report to OHL, June 9, 1915, BA-MA W 10/51388, extract from disposition of the Fourth Army, AOK Operations Bureau, Conrad–Falkenhayn correspondence, Russia, ÖSA-KA R512 and Germany, Reichsministerium, *Der Weltkrieg 1914 bis 1918,* Vol. 8, p. 218.

31. Eleventh Army, Special Orders Nr. 57, June 14, 1915, BH-KA File 11/43/4.

32. Eleventh Army, order for aerial reconnaissance, June 6, 1915, and Bavarian 8th Reserve Division, extract from the campaign experiences of the German Eastern Army, June 1915, BH-KA File 8R/11/1.

33. Bavarian 8th Reserve Division, uniforms and rank insignia of the Austro–Hungarian Army, June 9, 1915, BH-KA File 8R/11/1.

34. Falkenhayn to Conrad, June 12, 1915 and Conrad to Falkenhayn, June 12, 1915, AOK Operations Bureau, Conrad–Falkenhayn correspondence, Russia, ÖSA-KA R512.

35. François, *Gorlice 1915,* p. 195.

36. Germany, Reichsarchiv, *Der Weltkrieg 1914 bis 1918,* Vol. 8, p. 219, and François, *Gorlice 1915,* p. 196.

37. The 11th Army had been withdrawn to the Dniestr. Germany, Reichsarchiv, *Der Weltkrieg 1914 bis 1918*, Vol. 8, p. 261, Danilov, *Russland im Weltkriege 1914–1915*, p. 509, and Brusilov, *A Soldier's Notebook*, p. 160.

38. Germany, Reichsarchiv, *Der Weltkrieg 1914 bis 1918*, Vol 8, p. 221, and Austria, Bundesministerium, *Österreich–Ungarns Letzter Krieg 1914–1918*, Vol. 2, pp. 469–470.

39. François, *Gorlice 1915*, p. 205, and Eder, *Das Preussische Reserve-Infanterie-Regiment 269*, p. 77.

40. Engelberg, *Das Reserve-Infanterie-Regiment Nr. 270 im Weltkriege 1914-1918*, p. 47.

41. François, *Gorlice 1915*, p. 205, and Germany, Reichsarchiv, *Der Weltkrieg 1914 bis 1918*, Vol. 8, p. 222.

42. Germany, Reichsarchiv, *Der Weltkrieg 1914 bis 1918*, Vol. 8, p. 222.

43. Prince Friedrich of Prussia, *Das Erste Garderegiment zu Fuss im Weltkrieg 1914–18*, pp. 102–103, and Germany, Reichsarchiv, *Der Weltkrieg 1914 bis 1918*, Vol. 8, p. 222.

44. Bose, *Das Kaiser Alexander Garde-Grenadier-Regiment Nr. 1 im Weltkriege 1914–1918*, pp. 188–189, Unger, *Das Königin Augusta Garde-Grenadier-Regiment Nr. 4 im Weltkriege 1914–1919*, pp. 111–112, Rosenberg, *Das Königin Elisabeth Garde-Grenadier-Regiment Nr. 3 im Weltkriege 1914–1918*, pp. 185–186, and Germany, Reichsarchiv, *Der Weltkrieg 1914 bis 1918*, Vol. 8, p. 222.

45. Rosenberg-Lipinsky, *Das Königin Elisabeth Garde-Grenadier-Regiment Nr. 3 im Weltkriege 1914–1918*, p. 186, and Germany, Reichsarchiv, *Der Weltkrieg 1914 bis 1918*, Vol. 8, p. 222.

46. Viereck, *Das Heideregiment Königlich Preussisches 2. Hannoversches Infanterie-Regiment Nr. 77 im Weltkriege 1914–1918*, pp. 195–196, and Germany, Reichsarchiv, *Der Weltkrieg 1914 bis 1918*, Vol. 8, p. 223.

47. Austria, Bundesministerium, *Österreich-Ungarns Letzter Krieg 1914–1918*, Vol. 2, p. 471, Germany, Reichsarchiv, *Der Weltkrieg 1914 bis 1918*, Vol. 8, p. 223, and Bavarian 8th Reserve Division KTB/June 13, 1915, BH-KA File 8R/1/3.

48. Austria, Bundesministerium, *Österreich-Ungarns Letzter Krieg 1914–1918*, Vol. 2, p. 472.

49. Foerster, ed., *Mackensen: Briefe und Aufzeichnungen*, p. 174, Germany, Reichsarchiv, *Der Weltkrieg 1914 bis 1918*, Vol. 8, p. 223, and François, *Gorlice 1915*, pp. 208–209.

50. Austria, Bundesministerium, *Österreich-Ungarns Letzter Krieg 1914–1918*, Vol. 2, p. 473, and Germany, Reichsarchiv, *Der Weltkrieg 1914 bis 1918*, Vol. 8, p. 224.

51. François, *Gorlice 1915*, p. 206.

52. Germany, Reichsarchiv, *Der Weltkrieg 1914 bis 1918*, Vol. 8, p. 224, and François, *Gorlice 1915*, pp. 206–207.

53. Austria, Bundesministerium, *Österreich-Ungarns Letzter Krieg 1914–1918*, Vol. 2, p. 477, and Germany, Reichsarchiv, *Der Weltkrieg 1914 bis 1918*, Vol. 8, p. 224.

54. Rosenberg-Lipinsky, *Das Königin Elisabeth Garde-Grenadier-Reguiment Nr. 3 im Weltkriege 1914–1918*, p. 188, Germany, Reichsarchiv, *Der Weltkrieg 1914 bis 1918*, Vol. 8, p. 224, Bose, *Das Kaiser Alexander Garde-Grenadier-Regiment Nr. 1 im Weltkriege 1914–1918*, p. 190, Unger, *Das Königin Augusta Garde-Grenadier-Regiment Nr. 4*

im Weltkriege 1914–1919, p. 113, and Prince Friedrich of Prussia, *Das Erste Garderegiment zu Fuss im Weltkrieg 1914–1918,* p. 103.

55. Austria, Bundesministerium, *Österreich-Ungarns Letzter Krieg 1914–1918,* Vol. 2, p. 478, and Germany, Reichsarchiv, *Der Weltkrieg 1914 bis 1918,* Vol. 8, pp. 224–225.

56. Austria, Bundesministerium, *Österreich-Ungarns Letzter Krieg 1914–1918,* Vol. 2, p. 478, Viereck, *Das Heideregiment Königlich Preussisches 2. Hannoversches Infanterie-Regiment Nr. 77 im Weltkriege 1914–1918,* pp. 196–197, and Germany, Reichsarchiv, *Der Weltkrieg 1914 bis 1918,* Vol. 8, p. 225.

57. Austria, Bundesministerium, *Österreich–Ungarns Letzter Krieg 1914–1918,* Vol. 2, p. 479, Germany, Reichsarchiv, *Der Weltkrieg 1914 bis 1918,* Vol. 8, p. 225, and François, *Gorlice 1915,* p. 211.

58. Germany, *Der Weltkrieg 1914 bis 1918,* Vol. 8, pp. 225–226, Austria, Bundesministerium, *Österreich–Ungarns Letzter Krieg 1914–1918,* Vol. 2, pp. 479–480, Bose, *Das Kaiser Alexander Garde-Grenadier-Regiment Nr. 1 im Weltkriege 1914–1918,* p. 190, Unger, *Das Königin Augusta Garde-Grenadier-Regiment Nr. 4 im Weltkriege 1914–1919,* p. 113, Engelberg, *Das Reserve-Infanterie-Regiment Nr. 270 im Weltkriege 1914/1918,* p. 48, Eder, *Das Preussische Reserve-Infanterie-Regiment 269,* p. 77, and Viereck, *Das Heideregiment Königlich Preussisches 2. Hannoverersches Infanterie-Regiment Nr. 77 im Weltkriege 1914–1918,* pp. 197–198.

59. The corps in question were the VIII, XII, XVII, XXIII, XXVIII, II Caucasian, and V Caucasian Corps, plus the IV Cavalry Corps. François, *Gorlice 1915,* p. 213.

60. Foerster, ed., *Mackensen: Briefe und Aufzeichnungen,* p. 175. Ever critical of Mackensen, Plessen regarded these totals as meager. Plessen diary, June 15, 1915, BA-MA W 10/50656.

61. Foerster, ed., *Mackensen: Briefe und Aufzeichnungen,* pp. 174–175, and Conrad to Falkenhayn, June 14, 1915, AOK Operations Bureau, Conrad–Falkenhayn correspondence, Russia, ÖSA-KA R512.

62. Falkenhayn to Conrad, June 13, 1915, Conrad to Falkenhayn, June 14, 1915, AOK Operations Bureau, Conrad–Falkenhayn correspondence, ÖSA-KA R512, German Eleventh Army, estimate of the situation of the Eleventh Army as of noon, June 15, 1915, BA-MA W 10/51388, and Seeckt, *Aus meinem Leben 1866–1917,* p. 150.

63. Danilov, *Russland im Weltkriege 1914–1915,* p. 511, B.H. Liddell Hart, *History of the First World War,* p. 143, François, *Gorlice 1915,* p.213, and German Eleventh Army, estimate of the situation of the Eleventh Army as of noon, June 15, 1915, BA-MA W 10/51388.

64. Stone, *The Eastern Front 1914–1917,* p. 142, and Brusilov, *A Soldier's Notebook,* p. 152.

65. Danilov, *Russland im Welrtriege 1914–1915,* p. 505, Austria, Bundesministerium, *Österreich–Ungarns Letzter Krieg 1914–1918,* Vol. 2, pp. 481–482, and François, *Gorlice 1915,* pp. 219–219.

66. Germany, Reichsarchiv, *Der Weltkrieg 1914 bis 1918,* Vol. 8, pp. 227–229, Bavarian 8th Reserve Division, division battles on the army flank in the breakthrough battle in Galicia, June 1915, BH-KA File 8R/11/2, Bose, *Das Kaiser Alexander Garde-Grenadier-Regiment Nr. 1 im Weltkriege 1914–1918,* pp. 190–191, and Austria, Bundesministerium, *Österreich–Ungarns Letzter Krieg 1914–1918,* Vol. 2, pp. 483–484.

67. Douglas Wilson Johnson, *Topography and Strategy in the War* (New York: Henry Holt, 1917), p. 103, and François, *Gorlice 1915,* p. 220.

68. W. Bruce Lincoln, *Passage through Armageddon: The Russians in War and Revolution 1914–1918* (New York: Simon and Schuster, 1986), pp. 128–129.

69. Cramon to OHL, June 18, 1915, BA-MA W 10/51388, Germany, Reichsarchiv, *Der Weltkrieg 1814 bis 1918,* Vol. 8, p. 230, Bose, *Das Kaiser Alexander Garde-Grenadier-Regiment Nr. 1 im Weltkriege 1914–1918,* p. 192, and German Eleventh Army, Special Orders Nr. 57, June 14, 1915, BH-KA File 11/43/4.

70. Johnson, *Topography and Strategy in the War,* p. 103, and François, *Gorlice 1915,* p. 220.

71. Germany, Reichsarchiv, *Der Weltkrieg 1914 bis 1918,* Vol. 8, p. 231, François, *Gorlice 1915,* pp. 222–225, Eder, *Das Preussische Reserve-Infanterie-Regiment 269,* pp. 80–82, and Engelberg, *Das Reserve-Infanterie-Regiment Nr. 270 im Weltkriege 1914/1918,* p. 49.

72. Austria, Bundesministerium, *Österreich-Ungarns Letzter Krieg 1914–1918,* Vol. 2, p. 489, and Germany, Reichsarchiv, *Der Weltkrieg 1914 bis 1918,* Vol. 8, p. 231.

73. Austria, Bundesministerium, *Österreich-Ungarns Letzter Krieg 1914–1918,* Vol. 2, p. 490, Germany, *Der Weltkrieg 1914 bis 1918,* Vol. 8, p. 231, Foerster, ed., *Wir Kämpfer im Weltkrieg,* p. 191, Bose, *Das Kaiser Alexander Garde-Grenadier-Regiment Nr. 1 im Weltkrieg 1914–1918,* p. 193, Rosenberg-Lipinsky, *Das Königin Elisabeth Garde-Grenadier-Regiment Nr. 3 im Weltkrieg 1914-1918,* pp. 192–193, Unger, *Das Königin Augusta Garde-Grenadier-Regiment Nr. 4 im Weltkriege 1914–1919,* p. 117, and Prince Friedrich of Prussia, *Das Erste Garderegiment zu Fuss im Weltkrieg 1914–1918,* p. 106.

74. Germany, Reichsarchiv, *Der Weltkrieg 1914 bis 1918,* Vol. 8, p. 232.

75. François, *Gorlice 1915,* p. 228, Viereck, *Das Heideregiment Königlich Preussisches 2. Hannoversches Infanterie-Regiment Nr. 77 im Weltkriege 1914–1918,* pp. 200–201, and Austria, Bundesministerium, *Österreich-Ungarns Letzter Krieg 1914–1918,* Vol. 2, p. 491.

76. Görlitz, ed., *The Kaiser and His Court,* p. 86, Plessen diary, June 19, 1915, BA-MA W 10/50656, Tappen diary, June 20, 1915, BA-MA W 10/50661, Seeckt, *Aus meinem Leben,* p. 153, and Foerster, ed., *Mackensen: Briefe und Aufzeichnungen,* p. 176.

77. Tappen diary, June 20, 1915, BA-MA W 10/50661, and Kundmann diary, June 20, 1915, Conrad archive, ÖSA-KA B/13.

78. Cramon to OHL, June 19, 1915, BA-MA W 10/51388, Foerster, ed., *Mackensen: Briefe und Aufzeichnungen,* p. 176, and Stone, *The Eastern Front, 1914–1917,* p. 142.

79. Germany, Reichsarchiv, *Der Weltkrieg 1914 bis 1918,* Vol. 8, p. 233, and François, *Gorlice 1915,* p. 231.

80. Germany, Reichsarchiv, *Der Weltkrieg 1914 bis 1918,* Vol. 8, p. 233, Prince Friedrich of Prussia, *Das Erste Garderegiment zu Fuss im Weltkrieg 1914–18,* p. 106, Bose, *Das Kaiser Alexander Garde-Grenadier-Regiment Nr. 1 im Weltkriege 1914–1918,* p. 195, and Luyken, *Das 2. Garde-Feldartillerie-Regiment im Weltkriege,* p. 92.

81. Austria, Bundesministerium, *Österreich-Ungarns Letzter Krieg 1914–1918,* Vol. 2, p. 499, Germany, Reichsarchiv, *Der Weltkrieg 1914 bis 1918,* Vol. 8, p. 233, and Viereck, *Das Heideregiment Königlich Preussisches 2. Hannoversches Infanterie-Regiment Nr. 77 im Weltkriege 1914–1918,* p. 201.

82. François, *Gorlice 1915,* pp. 231–232, and Germany, Reichsarchiv, *Der Weltkrieg 1914 bis 1918,* p. 234.

83. Danilov, *Russland im Weltkriege 1914–1915*, pp. 512–513, Brusilov, *A Soldier's Notebook*, pp. 152–153, Lincoln, *Passage through Armageddon*, p. 129, and Stone, *The Eastern Front, 1914–1917*, p. 142. Born November 15, 1857, the son of an officer, Alexeyev graduated from the Moscow Infantry Cadet School in 1876. After seeing action in the Russo-Turkish War of 1877, Alexeyev attended the General Staff Academy. After graduating in 1890, Alexeyev filled a variety of command and staff assignments, including 3rd Army deputy chief of staff in Manchuria during the Russo-Japanese War. At the onset of war, Alexeyev served as Ivanov's chief of staff. Appointed commander of the northwest front in March 1915, Alexeyev proved jealous of his prerogatives as a front commander, especially when it came to sending reinforcements to the hard-pressed southwest front. After the assumption of command of Russian field forces by Tsar Nicholas II, Alexeyev was named as his chief of staff. After suffering a heart attack in late 1916, Alexeyev returned to duty in February 1917. Confronted by the reality of the March revolution, Alexeyev arranged for the abdication of Nicholas II. Although supportive of the Kerensky government, Alexeyev was supplanted by Brusilov. After the Bolshevik coup, Alexeyev sided with the White forces. He did not live to fight much in the Russian Civil War, dying in Ekaterinodar on October 8, 1918. Herwig and Heyman, *Biographical Dictionary of World War I*, pp. 66–67.

84. Austria, Bundesministerium, *Österreich-Ungarns Letzter Krieg 1914–1918*, Vol. 2 p. 503, Cramon to OHL, June 22, 1915, Conrad to Falkenhayn, June 22, 1915, BA-MA W 10/51388, and Rauchensteiner, *Der Tod des Doppeladlers*, p. 283.

85. Germany, Reichsarchiv, *Der Weltkrieg 1914 bis 1918*, Vol. 8, p. 234, and Bavarian 8th Reserve Division, KTB/June 23, 1915, BH-KA File 8R/1/3.

86. Germany, Reichsarchiv, *Der Weltkrieg 1914 bis 1918*, Vol. 8 p. 236, Witkop, ed., *German Students' War Letters*, pp. 100 and 114, François, *Gorlice 1915*, p. 154, and Bose, *Das Kaiser Alexander Garde-Grenadier-Regiment Nr. 1 im Weltkriege 1914–1918*, p. 189.

87. François, *Gorlice 1915*, p. 208, Rosenberg-Lipinsky, *Das Königin Elisabeth Garde-Grenadier-Regiment Nr. 3 im Weltkriege 1914–1918*, pp. 153 and 178, and Stengel, *Das K.B. 3. Infanterie-Regiment Prinz Karl von Bayern 1914–1918*, pp. 25–26.

88. Stone, *The Eastern Front, 1914–1917*, p. 143, Meier-Welcker, *Seeckt*, p. 56, Golovine, *The Russian Army in the World War*, p. 97, Danilov, *Russland im Weltkriege 1914–1915*, p. 517, and François, *Gorlice 1915*, p. 228. For a brief discussion on the question of the number prisoners taken and concomitant issues, see Reinhard Nachtigal, "Die Kriegsgefangenen—Verlust an der Ostfront. Eine Übersicht zur Statistik und zu Problemen der Heimatfronten 1914/15," *Die vergessene Front*, pp. 201–215.

89. Cramon, *Unser Österreich-Ungarischer Bundesgenosse im Weltkriege*, p. 19, and Frank, *Oil Empire*, p. 188. For two brief discussions of the Russian occupation of Galicia, see Hagen, *War in a European Borderland*, pp. 23–28, and Piotr Szlanta, "Der Erste Weltkrieg von 1914 bis 1915 als identitätsstiftender Faktor für die moderne polnische Nation," *Die vergessene Front*, pp. 159–160.

90. Kundmann diary, June 23, 1915, Conrad archive, ÖSA-KA B/13 Conrad, *Aus meiner Dienstzeit 1906–1918*, Vol. 4, p. 774, Conrad to Bolfras, June 27, 1915, ÖSA-KA MKSM 78, Rauchensteiner, *Der Tod des Doppeladlers*, p. 283, and Sondhaus, *Franz Conrad von Hötzendorf*, p. 175.

91. Tappen diary, June 22, 1915, BA-MA W 10/50661, and Falkenhayn, *The German General Staff and Its Decisions, 1914–1916*, p. 111.

92. Görlitz, ed., *The Kaiser and His Court,* p. 86, Plessen diary, June 22, 1915, BA-MA W 10/50656, Meier-Welcker, *Seeckt,* p. 55, Seeckt to wife, June 28, 1915, *Nachlass* Seeckt, BA-MA N 247/57, Nowak, ed., *Die Aufzeichnungen des Generalmajors Max Hoffman,* Vol. I, p. 71, and Ludendorff to Moltke, June 18, 1915, *Nachlass* Ludendorff, BA-MA N 77/2.

93. Danilov, *Russland im Weltkriege 1914–1915,* p. 507.

94. Hindenburg, *Aus meinem Leben,* p. 127.

95. Germany, Reichsarchiv, *Der Weltkrieg 1914 bis 1918,* Vol. 8, p. 229, Bavarian 8th Reserve Division, excerpt from the campaign experiences of the German Eastern Army, June 1915, BH-KA File 8R/11/1, and German Eleventh Army, Special Orders Nr. 57, June 14, 1915, BH-KA File 11/43/4.

96. See, for example, Germany, Reichsarchiv, *Der Weltkrieg 1914 bis 1918,* Vol. 8, p. 228. For communications issues, see Colonel Erich Fellgiebel, "Aus grosser Zeit vor zwanzig Jahren. Verwendung von Nachrichtenmitteln im ersten Kriegsjahr und Lehren daraus für Heute," *Militär Wochenblatt* Vol. 119, Nr. 35 (18 March 1935): pp. 1371–1374.

97. François, *Gorlice 1915,* pp. 208–209, Bavarian 8th Reserve Division, excerpt from the campaign experiences of the German Eastern Army, June 1915, BH-KA File 8R/11/1, and Foerster, ed., *Mackensen: Briefe und Aufzeichnungen,* p. 176.

98. Jones, "Imperial Russia's Forces at War," *Military Effectiveness,* Vol. I, pp. 310–311, and Bavarian 8th Reserve Division, excerpt from the campaign experiences of the German Eastern Army, June 1915, BH-KA File 8R/11/1.

CHAPTER SEVEN

1. German Eleventh Army, Estimate of the situation of the Eleventh Army as of noon, June 15, 1915, BA-MA W 10/51388.

2. Ibid. The quote was Falkenhayn's marginalia on the memorandum.

3. AOK–OHL Directive for the conduct of operations, July 11, 1915, AOK, Operations Bureau, Conrad–Falkenhayn correspondence, Russia, ÖSA-KA R512.

4. Falkenhayn, *The German General Staff and Its Decisions, 1914–1916,* p. 115.

5. Wild, *Briefe und Tagebuchaufzeichnungen,* p. 70, Doughty, *Pyrrhic Victory,* p. 168, Falkenhayn, *The German General Staff and Its Decisions, 1914–1916,* p. 119, Tappen diary, June 20, 1915, BA-MA W 10/50661, and Falkenhayn to Mackensen, June 20, 1915, BA-MA W 10/51388.

6. Schindler, *Isonzo,* p. 53, and Conrad to Bolfras, June 2, 1915, ÖSA-KA MKSM 78.

7. Rothenberg, *The Army of Francis Joseph,* p. 190, Schindler, *Isonzo,* p. 59, and John Gooch, "Italy during the First World War," *Military Effectiveness,* Vol. I, p. 178.

8. Conrad to Falkenhayn, May 18, 1915, Conrad to Falkenhayn. May 19, 1915, Falkenhayn to Conrad, May 19, 1915, and Conrad to Falkenhayn, May 23, 1915, BA-MA W 10/50683, Conrad to Bolfras, May 19, 1915, and Conrad to Bolfras, May 21, 1915, ÖSA-KA MKSM 78, and Cramon, *Unser Österreich–Ungarischer Bundesgenosse im Weltkriege,* p. 19.

9. Falkenhayn, *The German General Staff and Its Decisions, 1914–1916,* pp. 106–107.

10. Afflerbach, *Falkenhayn*, p. 285.

11. Ludendorff to Moltke, May 17, 1915, *Nachlass* Ludendorff, BA-MA N 77/2, Falkenhayn to Conrad, May 16, 1915, BA-MA W 10/50683, and Rothenberg, *The Army of Francis Joseph*, p. 189.

12. Plessen Diary, July 1, 1915, BA-MA W 10/50656.

13. Hamilton and Herwig, *Decisions for War, 1914–1917*, pp. 173–174.

14. Notes of General von Falkenhayn on the Results of the Conference in Teschen, May 18, 1915, Conrad to Falkenhayn, May 19, 1915, Falkenhayn to Conrad, May 19, 1915, BA-MA W 10/50683, and Falkenhayn to Conrad, June 13, 1915, AOK Operations Bureau, Conrad–Falkenhayn correspondence, Russia, ÖSA-KA R512.

15. Herwig, *The First World War*, pp. 156–157, Shanafelt, *The Secret Enemy*, pp. 68–69, and Falkenhayn, *The German General Staff and Its Decisions, 1914–1916*, pp. 179–180.

16. Conrad to Bolfras, June 7, 1915, and Conrad to Bolfras, June 14, 1915, ÖSA-KA MKSM 78, and Shanafelt, *The Secret Enemy*, p. 69.

17. Falkenhayn to Conrad, May 16, 1915, AOK Operations Bureau, Conrad–Falkenhayn Correspondence, Russia, ÖSA-KA R512.

18. Falkenhayn to Mackensen, June 20, 1915, BA-MA W 10/51388, Austria, Bundesministerium, *Österreich–Ungarns Letzter Krieg 1914–1918*, Vol. 2, p. 550, Groener diary, June 23, 1915, *Nachlass* Groener, BA-MA N 46/41, Wild, *Briefe und Tagebuchaufzeichnungen*, p. 76, and Afflerbach, *Falkenhayn*, p. 299.

19. Danilov, *Russland im Weltkriege 1914–1915*, p. 513.

20. Falkenhayn to Conrad, June 13, 1915 and Conrad to Falkenhayn, June 14, 1915, AOK Operations Bureau, Conrad–Falkenhayn Correspondence, Russia, ÖSA-KA R512.

21. German Eleventh Army, Estimate of the situation of Eleventh Army as of noon, June 15, 1915, BA-MA W 10/51388.

22. Seeckt, *Aus meinem Leben 1866–1917*, p. 153, and Foerster, ed., *Mackensen: Briefe und Aufzeichnungen*, pp. 183–184.

23. Tappen diary, June 20, 1915, BA-MA W 10/50661, Kundmann diary, June 20, 1915, Conrad archive, ÖSA-KA B/13 and Meier-Welcker, *Seeckt*, p. 57.

24. Tappen diary, June 28, 1915, BA-MA W 10/50661, and Kundmann diary, June 28, 1915, Conrad archive, ÖSA-KA B/13.

25. Conrad to Bolfras, June 21, 1915, ÖSA-KA MKSM 78, Conrad to Falkenhayn, June 27, 1915, and Falkenhayn to Conrad, June 28, 1915, AOK Operations Bureau, Conrad–Falkenhayn correspondence, Russia, ÖSA-KA R512, Kundmann diary, July 2, 1915, Conrad archive, ÖSA-KA B/13, and Foley, *German Strategy and the Path to Verdun*, p. 146.

26. Plessen diary, June 28, 1915, BA-MA W 10/50656.

27. German Eleventh Army, estimate of the situation of the Eleventh Army as of noon, June 15, 1915, BA-MA W 10/51388.

28. Ludendorff, *Meine Kriegserinnerungen*, p. 114. The Nieman Army was created from part of the German Eighth Army on May 25, 1915. As its name indicates, the unit's area of responsibility included the Nieman River. Germany, Reichsarchiv, *Der Weltkrieg 1914 bis 1918*, Vol. 8, p. 124.

29. Born in Breslau on May 2, 1852, Max Gallwitz was a volunteer for the Franco-Prussian War in 1870. As a young officer, Gallwitz served in the artillery, and served

a tour on the Great General Staff. In 1890 he was promoted to major and then colonel in 1896. In the latter rank Gallwitz served as the chief of field artillery in the War Ministry. After his promotion to Generalmajor in 1902, he served another tour in the ministry, and was later promoted Generalleutnant. In 1913 Wilhelm II raised Gallwitz to the nobility. In 1914, Gallwitz led the Guard Reserve Corps in the opening campaign in the west. Transferred to the east in September 1914, Gallwitz participated in the battles on the eastern front in the autumn of 1914. Promoted to General der Artillerie, Gallwitz eventually ended up in command of an army sized unit called Army Group Gallwitz, which took part in the 1915 summer campaign that overran Poland. In September 1915 Gallwitz was appointed Eleventh Army commander and took part in the overrunning of Serbia. Transferred back to the west, Gallwitz held a series of army or army group commands until the end of the war. Gallwitz resigned on December 6, 1918. Later he dabbled in right-wing German politics, serving as a deputy in the Reichstag for the German National People's Party (DNVP) from 1920–1924. Gallwitz died in Naples on April 17, 1937. Herwig and Heyman, *Biographical Dictionary of World War I,* pp. 160–161. On August 7, 1915 Army Group Gallwitz was redesignated as German Twelfth Army. German, Reichsarchiv, *Der Weltkrieg 1914 bis 1918,* p. 351.

30. Foley, *German Strategy and the Path to Verdun,* p. 148. Born on February 9, 1846, Leopold had served a long and distinguished career in the Bavarian Army, culminating in his promotion to Generalfeldmarschall in 1905. Having retired in 1912, Leopold was called back to service in April 1915, and appointed to the command of the Ninth Army. In 1916, Leopold was named as Hindenburg's successor at Ober Ost, a post he held for the rest of the war. Leopold retired in January 1919 and died in Munich on September 28, 1930. Herwig and Heyman, *Biographical Dictionary of World War I,* pp. 223–224.

31. Kundmann Diary, July 2, 1915, Conrad archive, ÖSA-KA B/13, Plessen diary, July 2, 1915, BA-MA W 10/50656, Foerster, ed., *Mackensen: Briefe und Aufzeichnungen,* p. 186, Ludendorff, *Meine Kriegserinnerungen,* p. 117, Hoffmann, *War Diaries and Other Papers,* Vol. II, p. 108, and Hindenburg, *Aus meinem Leben,* p. 127.

32. Falkenhayn, *The German General Staff and Its Decisions, 1914–1916,* pp. 128–129, and Afflerbach, *Falkenhayn,* p. 307.

33. Tappen Diary, July 3, 1915, BA-MA W 10/50661, Falkenhayn, *The German General Staff and Its Decisions, 1914–1916,* p. 129, Cecil, *Wilhelm II,* Vol. II, p. 227, Afflerbach, *Falkenhayn,* pp. 309–310, and Hoffmann, *War Diaries and Other Papers,* Vol. I, p. 62.

34. Hoffmann, *War Diaries and Other Papers,* Vol. II, p. 108, and François, *Gorlice 1915,* p. 251.

35. Hoffmann, *war Diaries and Other Papers,* Vol. II, pp. 111–112, Ludendorff, *Meine Kriegserinnerungen,* p. 124, François, *Gorlice 1915,* p. 251, and Major Henoumont, "Eisenbahnwesen," *Die militärischen Lehren des Grossen Krieges* (Generalleutnant M. Schwarte, ed.) (Berlin: E. S. Mittler und Sohn, 1920), pp. 313–314.

36. François, *Gorlice 1915,* p. 252.

37. Falkenhayn, *The German General Staff and Its Decisions, 1914–1916,* pp. 129–130, and Stone, *The Eastern Front 1914–1917,* pp. 176–177.

38. Germany, Reichsarchiv, *Der Weltkrieg 1914 bis 1918,* Vol. 8, p. 258, Foerster, ed., *Mackensen: Briefe und Aufzeichnungen,* p. 187 and Stone, *The Eastern Front 1914–1917,* pp. 177–178.

39. Germany, Reichsarchiv, *Der Weltkrieg 1914 bis 1918,* Vol. 8, p. 260.

40. In the course of the operation, the Süd Army took 60,000 prisoners, over 100 machine guns and 24 artillery pieces. Germany, Reichsarchiv, *Der Weltkrieg 1914 bis 1918,* Vol. 8, p. 252, and Austria, Bundesministerium, *Österreich–Ungarns Letzter Krieg 1914–1918,* Vol. 2, pp. 559–560.

41. Germany, Reichsarchiv, *Der Weltkrieg 1914 bis 1918,* Vol. 8, p. 384, and Austria, Bundesministerium, *Österreich-Ungarns Letzter Krieg 1914–1918,* Vol. 2, pp. 583–587.

42. Germany, Reichsarchiv, *Der Weltkrieg 1914 bis 1918,* Vol. 8, p. 385.

43. Johnson, *Topography and Strategy in the War,* p. 107, Bose, *Das Kaiser Alexander Garde-Grenadier-Regiment Nr. 1 im Weltkriege 1914–1918,* p. 199, Luyken, *Das 2. Garde-Feldartillerie-Regiment im Weltkriege,* p. 94, and Viereck, *Das Heideregiment Königlich Preussisches 2. Hannoversches Infanterie-Regiment Nr. 77 im Weltkriege 1914–1918,* pp. 203–204.

44. Rosenberg-Lipinsky, *Das Königin Elisabeth Garde-Grenadier-Regiment Nr. 3 im Weltkriege 1914–1918,* p. 199, Berghaus, *Vier Monate mit Mackensen,* p. 56, and Austria, Bundesministerium, *Österreich–Ungarns Letzter Krieg 1914–1918,* Vol. 2, p. 588.

45. Bose, *Das Kaiser Alexander Garde-Grenadier-Regiment Nr. 1 im Weltkriege 1914–1918,* p. 200, Germany, Reichsarchiv, *Der Weltkrieg 1914 bis 1918,* Vol. 8, p. 382, and François, *Gorlice 1915,* p. 242.

46. Unger, *Das Königin Augusta Garde-Grenadier-Regiment Nr. 4 im Weltkriege 1914–1919,* pp. 120–121, Prince Friedrich of Prussia, *Das Erste Garderegiment zu Fuss im Weltkrieg 1914–18,* p. 110, Foerster, ed., *Mackensen: Briefe und Aufzeichnungen,* p. 187, and Germany, Reichsarchiv, *Der Weltkrieg 1914 bis 1918,* Vol. 8, pp. 383–384.

47. Falkenhayn to Conrad, July 5, 1915, AOK Operations Bureau, Conrad–Falkenhayn correspondence, Russia, ÖSA-KA R512, Foerster, ed., *Mackensen: Briefe und Aufzeichnungen,* p. 188, and Austria, Bundesministerium, *Österreich–Ungarns Letzter Krieg 1914–1918,* Vol. 2, p. 600. Born in 1859, Lüttwitz enjoyed a successful career in the army, holding a number high level command and staff positions. After the war Lüttwitz's most notable activity was his involvement in the abortive Kapp Putsch against the Weimar Republic. Craig, *Germany 1866–1945,* pp. 429–430.

48. Germany, Reichsarchiv, *Der Weltkrieg 1914 bis 1918,* Vol. 8, p. 382. Born December 10, 1852 in Munich, Bothmer entered the Bavarian Army on February 12, 1871. Over the ensuing 40 years, Bothmer served in the Bavarian Army, including a tour in the Bavarian War Ministry. He also spent time on the German General Staff in Berlin. Promoted General der Infanterie on May 4, 1910, Bothmer took command of the Bavarian II Reserve Corps late in 1914. After a short stint in the west, Bothmer was sent east to command a provisional corps in the Süd Army. On July 8, 1915, he was selected by Falkenhayn to command the Süd Army. Bothmer commanded the Süd Army until Russia's withdrawal from the war. In April 1918 he took command of the German Nineteenth Army in Lorraine, a position he held until just before the armistice. Immediately after the armistice, Bothmer retired from the army. He died in Munich on March 19, 1937. Herwig and Heyman, *Biographical Dictionary of World War I,* pp. 92–93, and Short Biographical Chronology, BA-MA MSg 109/10857.

49. Foerster, ed., *Mackensen: Briefe und Aufzeichnungen,* p. 187.

50. Austria, Bundesministerium, *Österreich–Ungarns Letzter Krieg 1914–1918,* Vol. 2, p. 600 and Conrad to Falkenhayn, July 4, 1915, AOK Operations Bureau, Conrad–Falkenhayn correspondence, Russia, ÖSA-KA R512.

51. Falkenhayn to Conrad, July 5, 1915, AOK Operations Bureau, Conrad–Falkenhayn correspondence, Russia, ÖSA-KA R512.

52. Conrad to Archduke Friedrich, July 7, 1915, AOK Operations Bureau, Conrad–Falkenhayn correspondence, Russia, ÖSA-KA R512.

53. Austria, Bundesministerium, *Österreich–Ungarns Letzter Krieg 1914–1918,* Vol. 2, pp. 602–605, Kundmann Diary, July 7, 1915, Conrad archive, ÖSA-KA B/13, and Tappen Diary, July 7, 1915, BA-MA W 10/50661.

54. Conrad to Falkenhayn, July 8, 1915, Falkenhayn to Conrad, July 8, 1915, Conrad to Falkenhayn, July 9, 1915, and Falkenhayn to Conrad, July 9, 1915, AOK Operations Bureau, Conrad–Falkenhayn correspondence, Russia, ÖSA-KA R512, and Tappen diary, July 8, 1915, BA-MA W 10/50661.

55. Bavarian 8th Reserve Division, Billeting, Supply and Road Conditions in Galicia, April 10, 1916, BH-KA File 8R/1/3, Rosenberg-Lipinsky, *Das Königin Elisabeth Garde-Grenadier-Regiment Nr. 3 im Weltkrieg 1914–1918,* p. 204, and Prince Friedrich of Prussia, *Das Erste Garderegiment zu Fuss im Weltkrieg 1914–18,* p. 110.

56. Bose, *Das Kaiser Alexander Garde-Grenadier-Regiment Nr. 1 im Weltkriege 1914–1918,* p. 202.

57. Liulevicius, *War Land on the Eastern Front,* p. 22, and François, *Gorlice 1915,* p. 201.

58. Bavarian 8th Reserve Division, Billeting, Supply and Road Conditions in Galicia, April 10, 1916, BH-KA File 8R/1/3, and German Eleventh Army, Special Orders Nr. 69, June 26, 1915, BH-KA File 11/43/4.

59. Liulevicius, *War Land on the Eastern Front,* p. 81, Cecil, *Wilhelm II,* Vol. II, p. 178, Hagen, *War in a European Borderland,* p. 61, Moltke, *Errinerungen-Briefe-Dokumente,* p. 374, and Conrad, *Aus Meiner Dienstzeit 1906–1918,* Vol. 3, pp. 146–147.

60. Liulevicius, *War Land on the Eastern Front,* p. 81, Plessen diary, August 19, 1915, BA-MA W 10/50656, and François, *Gorlice 1915,* p. 154.

61. Germany, Reichsarchiv, *Der Weltkrieg 1914 bis 1918,* Vol. 8, p. 281, Tappen diary, July 10, 1915, BA-MA W 10/50656, Hoffmann, *War Diaries and Other Papers,* Vol. I, p. 63, and Wheeler-Bennett, *Wooden Titan,* p. 59.

62. Tappen diary, July 11, 1915, W 10/50661, AOK, draft directive for conduct of operations in mid-July, July 11, 1915, and AOK–OHL, directive for conduct of operations, July 11, 1915, AOK Operations Bureau, Conrad–Falkenhayn correspondence, Russia, ÖSA-KA R512, and Foerster, ed., *Mackensen: Briefe und Aufzeichnungen,* p. 189.

63. François, *Gorlice 1915,* p. 248.

64. Afflerbach, *Falkenhayn,* p. 300, Uhle-Wettler, *Erich Ludendorff in seiner Zeit,* p. 184, and Wild, *Briefe und Tagebuchaufzeichnungen,* p. 90.

65. Citino, *The German Way of War,* p. 235, and Stone *The Eastern Front 1914–1917,* p. 178.

66. Conrad to Falkenhayn, June 27, 1915 and Falkenhayn to Conrad, June 28, 1915, AOK Operations Bureau, Conrad–Falkenhayn correspondence, Russia, ÖSA-KA R512, Plessen diary, June 28, 1915, BA-MA W 10/50656, and Tappen diary, July 2, 1915, BA-MA W 10/50661.

CHAPTER EIGHT

1. Foerster, ed., *Mackensen: Briefe und Aufzeichnungen,* p. 189.

2. Quoted in Stone, *The Eastern Front 1914–1917,* p. 177.

3. Frenzel, a common German soldier, was killed in Poland on August 13, 1915. Witkop, ed., *German Students' War Letters*, p. 154.

4. Foerster, ed., *Mackensen: Briefe und Aufzeichnungen*, p. 206. The two events referred to by Mackensen occurred during the Napoleonic Wars. The battle of Gross Görschen was fought between the Allied forces and Napoleon on May 2, 1813, while the battle of the Katzbach was fought between a French corps and a Prussian force on 26 August 26, 1813. In both battles Generalfeldmarschall Gebhard von Blücher, the person with whom Mackensen was compared most frequently, figured prominently.

5. See for example Danilov, *Russland im Weltkriege 1914–1915*, p. 412.

6. Stone, *The Eastern Front 1914–1917*, p. 174, Jones, "Imperial Russia's Forces at War," *Military Effectiveness*, Vol. I, p. 290, and Khavkin, "Russland gegen Deutschland," *Die vergessene Front*, p. 85.

7. Stone, *The Eastern Front 1914–1917*, pp. 30–31, V. A. Sukhomlinov, *Erinnerungen* (Berlin: Remar Hobbing, 1924), pp. 346–347, Danilov, *Russland im Weltkriege 1914–1915*, p. 525, Menning, "The Offensive Revisited," *Reforming the Tsar's Army*, p. 222, and William C. Fuller Jr., *Strategy and Power in Russia 1600–1914* (New York: The Free Press, 1992), pp. 432–433.

8. Generalleutnant Max Schwarte, "Festungskrieg, Feldbefestigung," *Die militärischen Lehren des Grossen Krieges*, p. 229.

9. Stone, *The Eastern Front 1914–1917*, pp. 174–175.

10. Germany, Reichsarchiv, *Der Weltkrieg 1914 bis 1918*, Vol. 8, p. 388, and Johnson, *Topography and Strategy in the War*, pp. 105–107.

11. Germany, Reichsarchiv, *Der Weltkrieg 1914 bis 1918*, Vol. 8, p. 389.

12. Groener diary extract, July 11, 1915, *Nachlass* Groener, BA-MA N 46/41.

13. Viereck, *Das Heideregiment Königlich Preussisches 2. Hannoversches Infanterie-Regiment Nr. 77*, p. 208, Unger, *Das Königin Augusta Garde-Grenadier-Regiment Nr. 4 im Weltkriege 1914–1919*, p. 121, Rosenberg-Lipinsky, *Das Königin Elisabeth Garde-Grenadier-Regiment Nr. 3 im Weltkriege 1914–1918*, p. 212. and Groener diary extract, *Nachlass* Groener, BA-MA N 46/41.

14. Foerster, ed., *Mackensen: Briefe und Aufzeichnungen*, p. 189.

15. Tappen diary, July 11, 1915, BA-MA W 10/50661, Kundmann diary, July 12, 1915, Conrad Archive, ÖSA-KA B/13, and Meier-Welcker, *Seeckt*, p. 58.

16. Germany, Reichsarchiv, *Der Weltkrieg 1914 bis 1918*, Vol. 8, p. 388.

17. Tappen diary, July 11, 1915, BA-MA W 10/50661, and Kundmann diary, July 12, 1915, Conrad archive, ÖSA-KA B/13.

18. AOK—OHL directive for the conduct of operations, July 11, 1915, AOK Operations Bureau, Conrad–Falkenhayn correspondence, Russia, ÖSA-KA R512, and Seeckt, *Aus meinem Leben 1866–1917*, p. 164.

19. Austria, Bundesministerium, *Österreich-Ungarns Letzter Krieg 1914–1918*, Vol. 2, p. 625, Foerster, ed., *Mackensen: Briefe und Aufzeichnungen*, p. 190, and Germany, Reicharchiv, *Der Weltkrieg 1914 bis 1918*, Vol. 8, p. 390.

20. Hoffmann, *War Diaries and Other Papers*, Vol. I, p. 64, and Germany, Reichsarchiv, *Der Weltkrieg 1914 bis 1918*, Vol. 8, pp. 283–284.

21. Hoffmann grossly inflated the number of prisoners taken. Hoffmann, *War Diaries and Other Papers*, Vol. I, p. 65, Hindenburg, *Aus meinem Leben*, p. 128, Germany, Reichsarchiv, *Der Weltkrieg 1914 bis 1918*, Vol. 8, p. 291, and Stone, *The Eastern Front 1914–1917*, p. 180.

22. Born on January 18, 1857, Otto von Below hailed from a distinguished military family. After attending the *Kriegsakademie* from 1884–1887, Below held the usual series of command and staff appointments for an officer in the German Army. When war broke out in 1914, Below was appointed to command of the I Reserve Corps. In that capacity he fought the early campaigns on the eastern front. In late 1914, Below was promoted to the command of the Eighth Army, which he successfully led though the Second Masurian Lakes campaign. Over the period 1915–1916, Below held a series of army-level commands. In 1917 he commanded the Fourteenth Army at Caporetto. He played an important role in the ultimately abortive 1918 offensives and resigned in June 1919. The Weimar government refused to turn Below over to the Allies, who wanted to prosecute him for war crimes. Below died on March 9, 1944. Herwig and Heyman, *Biographical Dictionary of World War I*, pp. 81–82.

23. Germany, Reichsarchiv, *Der Weltkrieg 1914 bis 1918*, Vol. 8, p. 289.

24. Stone, *The Eastern Front 1914–1917*, p. 180.

25. Carl Mönckeberg, *Bei Süd und Bug Armee 1915*, (Stuttgart: Deutsche Verlags Anstalt; 1917), p. 46, Germany, Reichsarchiv, *Der Weltkrieg 1914 bis 1918*, Vol. 8, p. 390, Norman Franks, Frank Bailey, and Rick Duiven, *Casualties of the German Air Service 1914–1920*, (London: Grub Street; 1999), p. 177, and Eder, *Das Preussische Reserve-Infanterie-Regiment 269*, p. 92.

26. Germany, Reichsarchiv, *Der Weltkrieg 1914 bis 1918*, Vol. 8, p. 390, Seeckt, *Aus meinem Leben 1866–1917*, p. 164, Foerster, ed., *Mackensen: Briefe und Aufzeichnungen*, p. 190, and Austria, Bundesministerium, *Österreich-Ungarns Letzter Krieg 1914–1918*, Vol. 2, p. 626.

27. Foerster, ed., *Mackensen: Briefe und Aufzeichnungen*, p. 190, Austria, Bundesministerium, *Österreich-Ungarns Letzter Krieg 1914–1918*, Vol. 2, pp. 627–628, and Germany, Reichsarchiv, *Der Weltkrieg 1914 bis 1918*, Vol. 8, p. 393.

28. Mönckeberg, *Bei Süd und Bug Armee 1915*, p. 47, Eder, *Das Preussische Reserve-Infanterie- Regiment 269*, p. 93, Germany, Reichsarchiv, *Der Weltkrieg 1914 bis 1918*, Vol. 8, p. 393, and Seeckt, *Aus meinem Leben 1866–1917*, p. 165.

29. Prince Friedrich of Prussia, *Das Erste Garderegiment zu Fuss im Weltkrieg 1914–18*, 112, Bose, *Das Kaiser Alexander Garde-Grenadier-Regiment Nr. 1 im Weltkriege 1914–1918*, p. 203, and Austria, Bundesministerium, *Österreich-Ungarns Letzter Krieg 1914–1918*, Vol. 2, p. 624.

30. Unger, *Das Königin Augusta Garde-Grenadier-Regiment Nr. 4 im Weltkriege 1914–1919*, p. 125, Rosenberg-Lipinsky, *Das Königin Elisabeth Garde-Grenadier-Regiment Nr. 3 im Weltkriege 1914–1918*, p. 213, and Prince Freidrich of Prussia, *Das Erste Garderegiment zu Fuss im Weltkrieg 1914–18*, pp. 111–112.

31. Unger, *Das Königin Augusta Garde-Grenadier-Regiment Nr. 4 im Weltkriege 1914–1919*, p. 127, Prince Friedrich of Prussia, *Das Erste Garderegiment zu Fuss im Weltkrieg 1914–18*, p. 113, and Austria, Bundesministerium, *Österreich-Ungarns Letzter Krieg 1914–1918*, Vol. 2, pp. 624–625.

32. Germany, Reichsarchiv, *Der Weltkrieg 1914 bis 1918*, Vol. 8, pp. 392–393, Luyken, *Das 2. Garde-Feldartillerie-Regiment im Weltkriege*, pp. 100–101, Viereck, *Das Heideregiment Königlich Preussisches 2. Hannoversches Infanterie-Regiment Nr. 77 im Weltkriege 1914–1918*, pp. 210–211, and Foerster, ed., *Wir Kämpfer im Weltkrieg*, p. 195.

33. Austria, Bundesministerium, *Österreich-Ungarns Letzter Krieg 1914–1918,* Vol. 2, pp. 628–629, Tappen diary, July 17, 1915, BA-MA W 10/50661, and Kundmann diary, July 17, 1915, Conrad archive, ÖSA-KA B/13.

34. Austria, Bundesministerium, *Osterreich-Ungarns Letzter Krieg 1914–1918,* Vol. 2, pp. 624–625, Prince Friedrich of Prussia, *Das Erste Garderegiment zu Fuss im Weltkrieg 1914–18,* p. 114, Foerster, ed., *Mackensen: Briefe und Aufzeichnungen,* p. 191, and Luyken, *Das 2. Garde-Feldartillerie-Regiment im Weltkriege,* p. 101.

35. Plessen diary, July 19, 1915, BA-MA W 10/50656, Tappen diary, July 19, 1915, BA-MA W 10/50661, and Hoffmann, *War Diaries and Other Papers,* Vol. I, p. 66.

36. Stone, *The Eastern Front 1914–1917,* p. 180, and Johnson, *Topography and Strategy in the War,* p. 109.

37. Bose, *Das Kaiser Alexander Garde-Grenadier-Regiment Nr. 1 im Weltkriege 1914–1918,* p. 207, Foerster, ed., *Wir Kämpfer im Weltkrieg,* p. 196, Rosenberg-Lipinsky, *Das Königin Elisabeth Garde-Grenadier-Regiment Nr. 3 im Weltkriege 1914–1918,* p. 217, and Viereck, *Das Heideregiment Königlich Preussisches 2. Hannoversches Infanterie-Regiment Nr. 77 im Weltkriege 1914–1918,* p. 213.

38. Prince Friedrich of Prussia, *Das Erste Garderegiment zu Fuss im Weltkrieg 1914–18,* p. 114, Meier-Welcker, *Seeckt,* p. 59, and Seeckt, *Aus meinem Leben 1866–1917,* p. 176.

39. Stone, *The Eastern Front 1914–1917,* p. 181, and Golovine, *The Russian Army in the World War,* p. 223.

40. Lincoln, *Passage through Armageddon,* pp. 152–153, Witkop, ed., *German Students' War Letters,* p. 154, Berghaus, *Vier Monate mit Mackensen,* p. 84, and Hoffmann, *War Diaries and Other Papers,* Vol. I, p. 66.

41. Franz Bettag, *Schlachten des Weltkrieges. Die Eroberung von Nowo Georgiewsk* (Berlin: Druck und Verlag Gerhard Stalling; 1926), pp. 36–37, Khavkin, "Russland gegen Deutschland," *Die vergessene Front,* p. 79, Cruttwell, *A History of the Great War 1914–1918,* p. 180, and Stone, *The Eastern Front 1914–1917,* pp. 181–182.

42. See for example Ludendorff, *Meine Kriegserrinerungen,* p. 120.

43. Falkenhayn to Conrad, July 21, 1915 and Conrad to Falkenhayn, July 15, 1915, AOK Operations Bureau, Conrad–Falkenhayn correspondence, Russia, ÖSA-KA R512, Ludendorff, *Meine Kriegserinnerungen,* p. 119, Plessen diary August 6, 1915, BA-MA W 10/50656, and Germany, Reichsarchiv, *Der Weltkrieg 1914 bis 1918,* Vol. 8, p. 410.

44. Falkenhayn to Conrad, July 23, 1915, AOK Operations Bureau, Conrad–Falkenhayn correspondence, Russia, ÖSA-KA R512, Falkenhayn, *The German General Staff and Its Decisions, 1914–1916,* p. 132, and Foley, *German Strategy and the Path to Verdun,* p. 169. After the collapse of the French offensive in May, Joffre planned to launch another offensive in the summer, but a series of delays forced Joffre, much to Russian irritation, to postpone the offensive repeatedly until late September. The British waited to launch their attack in conjunction with the French. Both ended with minimal gains and large losses. Doughty, *Pyrrhic Victory,* p. 188, Khavkin, "Russland gegen Deutschland," *Die vergessene Front,* p. 85, and Cruttwell, *A History of the Great War 1914–1918,* p. 165.

45. Conrad to Falkenhayn, July 23, 1915, AOK Operations Bureau, Conrad–Falkenhayn correspondence, Russia, ÖSA-KA R512.

46. Austria, Bundesministerium, *Österreich-Ungarns Letzter Krieg 1914–1918,* Vol. 2, p. 643, Johnson, *Topography and Strategy in the War,* p. 83, Germany, Reichsarchiv, *Der Weltkrieg 1914 bis 1918,* Vol. 8, p. 407, Heinrici, ed., *Das Ehrenbuch der deutschen Pionere,* p. 215, and Hoffmann, *War Diaries and Other Papers,* Vol. I, p. 69.

47. Ludendorff, *Meine Kriegserinnerungen,* p. 117, Conrad to Falkenhayn, July 25, 1915, Falkenhayn to Conrad, July 25, 1915, and Cramon to Falkenhayn, July 27, 1915, AOK Operations Bureau, Conrad–Falkenhayn correspondence, Russia, ÖSA-KA R512, and Falkenhayn, *The German General Staff and Its Decisions, 1914–1916,* p. 135.

48. Schindler, *Isonzo,* pp. 73–74, and Kundmann diary, July 25, 1915, Conrad archive, ÖSA-KA B/13.

49. Falkenhayn to Conrad, July 27, 1915, Conrad to Falkenhayn, July 27, 1915, and Falkenhayn to Conrad July 28, 1915, AOK Operations Bureau, Conrad–Falkenhayn correspondence, Russia, ÖSA-KA R512, Austria, Bundesministerium, *Österreich-Ungarns Letzter Krieg 1914–1918,* Vol. 2, p. 759, and Schindler, *Isonzo,* p. 75.

50. Germany, Reichsarchiv, *Der Weltkrieg 1914 bis 1918,* Vol. 8, p. 401. Born in 1859, Estorff spent much of his career in Germany's African colonies, serving in both the Herrero War and the Hottentot Rebellion. At the onset of the war, Estorff commanded and infantry brigade and was wounded in the Battle of the Frontiers. Returning to active duty in 1915, Estorff commanded the 103rd Infantry Division in both Poland and Serbia. After distinguished service as commander of the 42nd Infantry Division in Romania and the capture of Riga, Estorff commanded the 42nd Infantry Division during the landings in the Baltic Islands. He held division command early in the postwar period but was dismissed for his involvement in the Kapp Putsch. Estorff died in 1943. Michael B. Barrett, *Operation Albion: The German Conquest of the Baltic Islands* (Bloomington: Indiana University Press; 2008), pp. 100–101 and 237.

51. Germany, Reichsarchiv, *Der Weltkrieg 1914 bis 1918,* Vol. 8, p. 401, Foerster, ed., *Mackensen: Briefe und Aufzeichnungen,* p. 195, Seeckt, *Aus meinem Leben 1866–1917,* p. 178, and Luyken, *Das 2. Garde-Feldartillerie-Regiment im Weltkriege,* p. 102.

52. Austria, Bundesministerium, *Österreich-Ungarns Letzter Krieg 1914–1918,* Vol. 2, p. 645, and Stone, *The Eastern Front 1914–1917,* p. 177.

53. Germany, Reichsarchiv, *Der Weltkrieg 1914 bis 1918,* Vol. 8, pp. 402–403, Viereck, *Das Heideregiment Königlich Preussisches 2. Hannoversches Infanterie-Regiment Nr. 77 im Weltkriege 1914–1918,* p. 219, and Foerster, ed., *Mackensen: Briefe und Aufzeichnungen,* p. 195.

54. Germany, Reichsarchiv, *Der Weltkrieg 1914 bis 1918,* Vol. 8, p. 403 and Rosenberg-Lipinsky, *Das Königin Elisabeth Garde-Grenadier-Regiment Nr. 3 im Weltkriege 1914–1918,* p. 229.

55. Austria, Bundesministerium, *Österreich-Ungarns Letzter Krieg 1914–1918,* Vol. 2, pp. 645–646.

56. Foerster, ed., *Mackensen: Briefe und Aufzeichnungen,* p. 195, Austria, Bundesministerium, *Österreich-Ungarns Letzter Krieg 1914–1918,* Vol. 2, p. 646, Germany, Reichsarchiv, *Der Weltkrieg 1914 bis 1918,* Vol. 8, p. 404, Bose, *Das Kaiser Alexander Garde-Grenadier-Regiment Nr. 1 im Weltkriege 1914–1918,* p. 211, and Mönckeberg, *Bei Süd und Bug Armee 1915,* p. 49.

57. Golovine, *The Russian Army in the World War,* p. 223 and Khavkin, "Russland gegen Deutschland," *Die vergessene Front,* p. 81.

58. Falkenhayn to Conrad and Conrad to Falkenhayn, August 1, 1915, AOK Operations Bureau, Conrad–Falkenhayn correspondence, Russia, ÖSA-KA R512, and Plessen Diary, August 1, 1915, BA-MA W 10/50656.

59. Rauchensteiner, Der *Tod des Doppeladlers,* p. 285, Mönckeberg, *Bei Süd und Bug Armee 1915,* p. 50, Cramon, *Unser Österreich-Ungarischer Bundesgenosse im Weltkriege,* p. 25, and Germany, Reichsarchiv, *Der Weltkrieg 1914 bis 1918,* Vol. 2, p. 340.

60. Conrad to Falkenhayn, August 4, 1915, AOK Operations Bureau, Conrad–Falkenhayn correspondence, Russia, ÖSA-KA R512.

61. Falkenhayn to Conrad, August 4, 1915, and Conrad to Falkenhayn (copies to Burián and Bolfras), July 21, 1915, AOK Operations Bureau, Conrad–Falkenhayn correspondence, Russia, ÖSA-KA R512, Conrad to Bolfras, July 21, 1915, ÖSA-KA MKSM 78, Plessen diary, August 4, 1915, BA-MA W 10/50656, Afflerbach, *Falkenhayn,* pp. 304–305, and Herwig, *The First World War,* p. 144.

62. Groener diary extract, *Nachlass* Groener, BA-MA N 46/41, and Falkenhayn to Conrad, August 5, 1915, AOK Operations Bureau, Conrad–Falkenhayn correspondence, Russia, ÖSA-KA R512.

63. Foerster, ed., *Mackensen: Briefe und Aufzeichnungen,* p. 197, Conrad to Falkenhayn and Falkenhayn to Conrad, August 9, 1915, AOK Operations Bureau, Conrad–Falkenhayn correspondence, Russia, ÖSA-KA R512, Seeckt, *Aus meinem Leben 1866-1917,* p. 183, and Tappen diary, August 10, 1915, BA-MA W 10/50661.

64. Foerster, ed., *Mackensen: Briefe und Aufzeichnungen,* p. 199, and Tappen diary, August 11–12, 1915, BA-MA W 10/50661.

65. Germany, Reichsarchiv, *Der Weltkrieg 1914 bis 1918,* Vol. 8, p. 417, and Falkenhayn to Conrad, August 9, 1915, AOK Operations Bureau, Conrad–Falkenhayn correspondence, Russia, ÖSA-KA R512.

66. Foerster, ed., *Mackensen: Briefe und Aufzeichnungen,* p. 198, Meier-Welcker, *Seeckt,* p. 60, and Austria, Bundesministerium, *Österreich-Ungarns Letzter Krieg 1914-1918,* Vol. 2, p. 687.

67. Bose, *Das Kaiser Alexander Garde-Grenadier-Regiment Nr. 1 im Weltkriege 1914-1918,* p. 213, Luyken, *Das 2. Garde-Feldartillerie-Regiment im Weltkriege,* p. 105, and Eder, *Das Preussische Reserve-Infanterie-Regiment 269,* p. 107.

68. Unger, *Das Königin Augusta Garde-Grenadier-Regiment Nr. 4 im Weltkriege 1914-1919,* p. 131, Bose, *Das Kaiser Alexander Garde-Grenadier-Regiment Nr. 1 im Weltkriege 1914-1918,* pp. 214–215, Prince Friedrich of Prussia, *Das Erste Garderegiment zu Fuss im Weltkrieg 1914-18,* p. 116, and Rosenberg-Lipinsky, *Das Königin Elisabeth Garde-Grenadier-Regiment Nr. 3 im Weltkriege 1914-1918,* pp. 235–236.

69. Foerster, ed., *Mackensen: Briefe und Aufzeichnungen,* p. 200.

70. Bose, *Das Kaiser Alexander Garde-Grenadier-Regiment Nr. 1 im Weltkriege 1914-1918,* p. 215, Austria, Bundesministerium, *Österreich-Ungarns Letzter Krieg 1914-1918,* Vol. 2, p. 689, Unger, *Das Königin Augusta Garde-Grenadier-Regiment Nr. 4 im Weltkriege 1914-1919,* p. 131, Germany, Reichsarchiv, *Der Weltkrieg 1914 bis 1918,* Vol. 8, pp. 422–423, and Seeckt, *Aus meinem Leben 1866-1917,* p. 193.

71. Bose, *Das Kaiser Alexander Garde-Grenadier-Regiment Nr. 1 im Weltkriege 1914-1918,* pp. 218–219.

72. Eder, *Das Preussische Reserve-Infanterie-Regiment 269,* p. 108, Germany, Reichsarchiv, *Der Weltkrieg 1914 bis 1918,* Vol. 8, pp. 424–425, and Mönckeberg, *Bei Süd und Bug Armee 1915,* pp. 50–51.

73. Foerster, ed., *Mackensen: Briefe und Aufzeichnungen,* pp. 204–205, Germany, Reichsarchiv, *Der Weltkrieg 1914 bis 1918,* Vol. 8, pp. 427–428, and Rosenberg-Lipinsky, *Das Königin Elisabeth Garde-Grenadier-Regiment Nr. 3 im Weltkriege 1914–1918,* p, 242

74. Germany, Reichsarchiv, *Der Weltkrieg 1914 bis 1918,* Vol. 8, p. 430, Seeckt, *Aus meinem Leben 1866–1917,* p. 195, Unger, *Das Königin Augusta Garde-Grenadier-Regiment Nr. 4 im Weltkriege 1914–1919,* p. 132, Austria, Bundesministerium, *Österreich-Ungarns Letzter Krieg 1914–1918,* Vol. 2, p. 722, and Cramon *Unser Österreich-Ungarischer Bundesgenosse im Weltkriege,* p. 24.

75. Stone, *The Eastern Front 1914–1917,* p. 181, Rauchensteiner, *Der Tod des Doppeladlers,* pp. 289–290 Austria, Bundesministerium, *Österreich-Ungarns Letzter Krieg 1914–1918,* Vol. 2, p. 705 Germany, Reichsarchiv, *Der Weltkrieg 1914 bis 1918,* Vol. 8, p. 430, and Meier-Welcker, *Seeckt,* p. 60.

76. Bettag, *Die Eroberung von Nowo Georgiewsk,* pp. 30–32. Born in 1850 Beseler, after a long and distinguished career, had retired with the rank General der Infanterie in 1910. Recalled to active duty as commander of the III Reserve Corps, he served in the opening campaign in the west. In the fall of 1914 he was entrusted with the siege of Antwerp, which was successfully concluded on October 10, 1914. Sent east with the III Reserve Corps in early 1915, Beseler was part of Gallwitz's German Twelfth Army. In August he was sent to command the siege of Novogeorgievsk. After its fall, Beseler was appointed military governor of Poland by Falkenhayn. In that capacity he ran afoul of various German political interest groups who regarded his ideas on Poland as too pro-Polish. Beseler retired just after the armistice in 1918, but his failure to make or publish a farewell address to his soldiers was a major violation of etiquette. Tried for that and his "pro-Polish policies," Beseler was acquitted by the III Corps court. He died on December 20, 1921. Herwig and Heyman, *Biographical Dictionary of World War I,* pp. 85–86.

77. Stone, *The Eastern Front 1914–1917,* p. 181, Bettag, *Die Eroberung von Nowo Georgiewsk,* p. 37, and Germany, Reichsarchiv, *Der Weltkrieg 1914 bis 1918,* Vol. 8, p. 377.

78. Stone, *The Eastern Front 1914–1917,* p. 182, Germany, Reichsarchiv, *Der Weltkrieg 1914 bis 1918,* Vol. 8, pp. 378–379, and Bettag, *Die Eroberung von Nowo Georgiewsk,* p. 108.

79. Born on February 13, 1848, Eichhorn entered the Prussian Army just prior to the Austro-Prussian War. He received his first commission on September 6, 1866. After seeing action in the Franco-Prussian War, Eichhorn was promoted to captain on August 6, 1878. Over the next two decades, he filled the normal variety of command and staff positions; he was promoted to Generalmajor on July 20, 1897. After holding brigade and division commands, Eichhorn was promoted to Generaloberst on January 1, 1913. He was slated to command the German Fifth Army in 1914, but a serious injury from a fall while riding kept him out of the opening campaigns. Appointed commander of the German Tenth Army on January 28, 1915, Eichhorn led it with distinction in the Second Masurian Lakes operation. His force captured Kovno and Vilna in August and September 1915, respectively. Given army group command on July 30, 1916, Eichhorn was promoted to Generalfeldmarschall on December 18, 1917. After the Brest–Litovsk treaty, Eichhorn became the German mili-

tary governor of Ukraine. On July 30, 1918, both Eichhorn and his adjutant were assassinated by a bomb thrown by a Left Socialist Revolutionary. Short Biographical Chronology, BA-MA MSg 109/10859, Herwig and Heyman, *Biographical Dictionary of World War I*, pp. 138–139 and Hagen, *War in a European Borderland*, pp. 96–97.

80. Ludendorff to Moltke, August 15, 1915, *Nachlass* Ludendorff, BA-MA N 77/2, Hoffmann, *War Diaries and Other Papers*, Vol. I, p. 75, Stone, *The Eastern Front 1914–1917*, pp. 186–187, and Germany, Reichsarchiv, *Der Weltkrieg 1914 bis 1918*, Vol. 8, p. 480.

81. On the debate concerning the virtues and defects of Grand Duke Nicholas as a commander, see Ludendorff, *Meine Kriegserinnerungen*, p.120, Hoffmann, *War Diaries and Other Papers*, Vol. II, p. 121, and Hindenburg, *Aus meinem Leben*, pp. 107–108. The grand duke's reputation remained high among early students of the war. More recent scholarship had taken a more critical view. See, for examples, Cruttwell, *A History of the Great War 1914–1918*, p. 39, and Jones, "Imperial Russia's Forces at War," *Military Effectiveness*, Vol. I, p. 300. For the political impact of the tsar's personal assumption of command, see Lincoln, *Passage through Armageddon*, pp. 164–167, and Herwig, *The First World War*, p. 145.

82. Herwig, *The First World War*, p. 147, Kundmann diary, September 13, 1915, Conrad archive, ÖSA-KA B/13, Rauchensteiner, *Der Tod des Doppeladlers*, p. 295, and Seeckt to wife, August 14, 1915, *Nachlass* Seeckt, BA-MA N 247/58.

83. Rosenberg-Lipinsky, *Das Königin Elisabeth Garde-Grenadier-Regiment Nr. 3 im Weltkriege 1914–1918*, p. 250, Unger, *Das Königin Augusta Garde-Grenadier-Regiment Nr. 4 im Weltkriege 1914–1919*, p. 139, Viereck, *Das Heideregiment Königlich Preussisches 2. Hannoversches Infanterie-Regiment Nr. 77 im Weltkriege 1914–1918*, p. 228, Foerster, ed., *Mackensen: Briefe und Aufzeichnungen*, p. 208, Germany, Reichsarchiv, *Der Weltkrieg 1914 bis 1918*, Vol. 8, p. 561, and Meier-Welcker, *Seeckt*, p. 65.

84. Falkenhayn, *The German General Staff and Its Decisions, 1914–1916*, p. 115, Shanafelt, *The Secret Enemy*, p. 69, and Stone, *The Eastern Front 1914–1917*, p. 191.

85. Groener diary extract, *Nachlass* Groener, BA-MA N 46/41, and Falkenhayn to Conrad, August 5, 1915, AOK Operations Bureau, Conrad–Falkenhayn correspondence, Russia, ÖSA-KA R512.

86. Bulgaria signed a military convention with the Central Powers on September 6, 1915. Rauchensteiner, *Der Tod des Doppeladlers*, p. 298, and Hamilton and Herwig, *Decisions for War, 1914–1917*, p. 174.

87. See, for examples, Ritter, *The Sword and the Scepter*, Vol. 3, pp. 72–74, Afflerbach, *Falkenhayn*, p. 310, Uhle-Wettler, *Erich Ludendorff in seiner Zeit*, p. 186, and Fritz Fischer, *Germany's Aims in the First World War* (New York: W.W. Norton; 1967), pp. 198–200.

88. For some various perspectives on this issue, see Shanafelt, *The Secret Enemy*, pp. 69–71, Ritter, *The Sword and the Scepter*, Vol. 3, pp. 100–106, and Fischer, *Germany's Aims in the First World War*, pp. 138–141.

89. Herwig, *The First World War*, p. 145, Hoffmann, *War Diaries and Other Papers*, Vol. I, p. 58, and Schwarzmüller, *Generalfeldmarschall August von Mackensen*, p. 117.

90. For Ober Ost's occupation policy in Lithuania, see Liulevicius, *War Land on the Eastern Front*, pp. 54–81. For an introductory essay on the subject, see Vejas Gabriel Liulevicius, "Besatzung (Osten)," *Enzyklopädie Erster Weltkrieg* (Gerhard Hirschfeld, Gerd Krumeich, Irina Renz eds.) (Paderborn, Germany: Ferdinand Schöningh; 2004), pp. 379–381.

91. Mönckeberg, *Bei Süd und Bug Armee 1915*, p. 50, Trach, *Gorlice-Tarnow*, p. 86, Bavarian 11th Infantry Division, compilation of booty captured by the Bavarian 11th Infantry Division, December 19, 1917, BH-KA File 11/97/2, and Golovine, *The Russian Army in the World War*, p. 186.

92. Hoffmann, *War Diaries and Other Papers*, Vol. I, p. 76 and Wild, *Briefe und Tagebuchaufzeichnungen*, p. 84.

93. Meier-Welcker, *Seeckt*, p. 64, and Eder, *Das Preussische Reserve-Infanterie-Regiment 269*, p. 107.

94. Hindenburg, *Aus meinem Leben*, p. 127, Danilov, *Russland im Weltkriege 1914–1915*, p. 505, Höbelt, "Österreich-Ungarns Nordfront 1914/15," *Die vergessene Front*, p. 110, Herwig, *The First World War*, p. 172, Seeckt, *Aus meinem Leben 1866–1917*, p. 199 and Golovine, *The Russian Army in the World War*, p. 98.

CHAPTER NINE

1. Seeckt, *Aus meinem Leben 1866–1917*, p. 202.

2. Unsigned, "Die Führung Falkenhayn," p. 22, BA-MA W 10/50704.

3. Lieutenant Colonel Schirmer, "Schwere Artillerie," *Die militärischen Lehren des Grossen Krieges*, p. 118.

4. François, *Gorlice 1915*, p. 243.

5. Danilov, *Russland im Weltkriege 1914–1915*, p. 510, Herwig, *The First World War*, p. 157 and Falkenhayn, *The German General Staff and Its Decisions, 1914–1916*, pp. 117–119.

6. Hamilton and Herwig, *Decisions for War, 1914–1917*, p. 174.

7. Danilov, *Russland im Weltkriege 1914–1915*, p. 518, Doughty, *Pyrrhic Victory*, p. 188 and Khavkin, "Russland gegen Deutschland," *Die vergessene Front*, p. 85.

8. Doughty, *Pyrrhic Victory*, p. 166.

9. Lincoln, *Passage Through Armageddon*, pp. 160–163 and Lindsey Hughes, *The Romanovs: Ruling Russia 1613–1917* (London: Hambledon; 2008), p. 230.

10. See especially William C. Fuller, Jr., *The Foe Within: Fantasies of Treason and the End of Imperial Russia* (Ithaca, N.Y.: Cornell University Press; 2006), pp. 150–183 and Lohr, "The Russian Army and the Jews," p. 415.

11. Cramon, *Unser Österreich–Ungarischer Bundesgenosse im Weltkriege*, p. 10, Kundmann Diary, June 23, 1915, Conrad Archive, ÖSA-KA B/13, and Rauchensteiner, *Der Tod des Doppeladlers*, p. 283.

12. Schwarzmüller, *Generalfeldmarschall August von Mackensen*, p. 110, and Afflerbach, *Falkenhayn*, p. 313. For details on the dispute between Delbrück and the general staff over the wisdom of Frederick the Great's strategy, see Echevarria, *After Clausewitz*, pp. 183–188.

13. Falkenhayn to Conrad, May 9, 1915, BA-MA W 10/51380 and Tappen diary, June 22, 1915, BA-MA W 10/50661.

14. Plessen Diary, June 28, 1915, BA-MA W 10/50656, Tappen diary, July 2, 1915, BA-MA W 10/50661, Hoffmann, *War Diaries and Other Papers*, Vol. I, p. 62, and Foley, *German Strategy and the Path to Verdun*, p. 154.

15. Bose, *Das Kaiser Alexander Garde-Grenadier-Regiment Nr. 1 im Weltkriege 1914–1918*, p. 198, and Rosenberg-Lipinsky, *Das Königin Elisabeth Garde-Grenadier-Regiment Nr. 3 im Weltkriege 1914–1918*, pp. 234 and 240.

16. Rothenberg, *The Army of Francis Joseph*, p. 187.

17. Germany, Reichsarchiv, *Der Weltkrieg 1914 bis 1918*, Vol. 7, p. 131 and Cramon to Falkenhayn, April 6, 1915, BA-MA W 10/51388.

18. Schwarzmüller, *Generalfeldmarschall August von Mackensen*, p. 104, Germany, Reichsarchiv, *Der Weltkrieg 1914 bis 1918*, Vol. 7, p. 369, Afflerbach, *Falkenhayn*, p. 291, and Falkenhayn to Conrad, July 5, 1915, AOK Operations Bureau, Conrad–Falkenhayn correspondence, Russia, ÖSA-KA R512.

19. Günther Kronenbitter, "Von 'Schweinehunden' und 'Waffenbrüdern.' Der Koalitionskrieg der Mittelmächte 1914/15 zwischen Sachzwang und Ressentiment," *Die vergessene Front*, p. 137, Rothenberg, *The Army of Francis Joseph*, p. 186, and Sondhaus, *Franz Conrad von Hötzendorf*, p. 176.

20. Urbanski, *Conrad von Hötzendorf*, p. 310, and Conrad, *Mein Leben mit Conrad von Hötzendorf*, pp. 132–133.

21. Kuhl, *Der Weltkrieg 1914–1918*, Vol. I, p. 19, and Liddell Hart, *History of the First World War*, p. 147.

22. Rauchensteiner, *Der Tod des Doppeladlers*, p. 203, Herwig, *The First World War*, p. 89, and Rothenberg, *The Army of Francis Joseph*, p. 184.

23. Kuhl, *Der Weltkrieg 1914–1918*, Vol. I, p. 121. For a contrary view see Cramon, *Unser Österreich-Ungarischer Bundesgenosse im Weltkriege*, p. 13.

24. See, for example, unsigned, "Die Führung Falkenhayn," p. 22, BA-MA W 10/50704.

25. General Erich Ludendorff, *Tannenberg: Geschichtliche Wahrheit uber die Schlacht* (Munich: Ludendorffs Verlag; 1939), p. 142, General Hans Knoerzer, "Hannibal und Hindenburg, ein zeitgemasser Vergleich," *Militär Wochenblatt*, Vol. 106, No. 13 (September 24, 1921): pp. 265–268, Showalter, *Tannenberg*, p. 351, and Craig, *Germany 1866–1945*, pp. 511 and 522.

26. Foerster, ed., *Mackensen: Briefe und Aufzeichnungen*, p. 178.

27. Meier-Welcker, *Seeckt*, p. 84, Cramon, *Unser Österreich-Ungarischer Bundesgenosse im Weltkriege*, p. 14, and Gehard Tappen to Wolfgang Foerster, October 22, 1935, *Nachlass* Tappen, BA-MA N 56/5.

28. Seeckt to wife, June 15, 1915, *Nachlass* Seeckt, BA-MA N 247/57.

29. Seeckt to wife, July 27, 1915, *Nachlass* Seeckt, BA-MA N 247/58, Seeckt to mother, July 11, 1916, *Nachlass* Seeckt, BA-MA N 247/66, and Seeckt, *Aus meinem Leben*, pp. 373–374.

30. Herwig and Heyman, *Biographical Dictionary of World War I*, pp. 71 and 244, and Short Biographical Chronologies of Emmich and Fabarius, BA-MA MSg 109/10859.

31. Germany, Reichsarchiv, *Der Weltkrieg 1914 bis 1918*, Vol. 8, p. 146, and François, *Gorlice 1915*, p. 243.

32. Citino, *The German Way of War*, p. 308, and Peter Hart, *The Somme: The Darkest Hour on the Western Front* (New York: Pegasus Books; 2008), p. 329.

33. Kalm, *Gorlice,* p. 27, Hoeppner, *Germany's War in the Air,* p. 44, and Eleventh Army, Special Orders Nr. 57, June 14, 1915, BH-KA File 11/43/4.

34. Cramon to OHL, June 18, 1915, BA-MA W 10/51388, and Bavarian 8th Reserve Division, excerpt from the campaign experiences of the German Eastern Army, June 1915, BH-KA File 8R/11/1.

35. Cramon to OHL Operations Section at Pless, May 20, 1915, BA-MA W 10/51388, and Eleventh Army, order for aerial reconnaissance, June 6, 1915, BH-KA File 8R/11/1.

36. Germany, Reichsarchiv, *Der Weltkrieg 1914 bis 1918,* Vol. 7, p. 379, Kalm, *Gorlice,* p. 44, Kraft, *Der Anteil der 11. Bayer. Inf. Div. an der Durchbruchsschlacht von Gorlice-Tarnow,* p. 23, François, *Gorlice 1915,* p. 127, and Germany, Reichsarchiv, *Der Weltkrieg 1914 bis 1918,* Vol. 8, p. 161.

37. Eleventh Army, Special Orders Nr. 57. 14 June 1915, BH-KA File 11/43/4, François, *Gorlice 1915,* p. 174 and Golovine, *The Russian Army in the World War,* p. 227.

38. François, *Gorlice 1915,* pp. 56–57, and Eder, *Das Preussusche Reserve-Infantry-Regiment 269,* p. 38.

39. Kalm, *Gorlice,* pp. 84–85, François, *Gorlice 1915,* p. 53, and Engelberg, *Das Reserve-Infanterie-Regiment Nr. 270 im Weltkriege 1914/1918,* pp. 36–38.

40. See for example François, *Gorlice 1915,* p. 90.

41. Hart, *The Somme,* p. 272, François, *Gorlice 1915,* p. 44, Fellgiebel, "Verwendung und Nachrichtenmitteln im ersten Kriegsjahr und Lehren daraus für heute," p. 1371, Captain Schering, "Nachrichtenwesen," *Die militärischen Lehren des Grossen Krieges,* pp. 359–360, and Eleventh Army, order for aerial reconnaissance, June 6, 1915, BH-KA File 8R/11/1.

42. Foerster, ed., *Mackensen: Briefe und Aufzeihnungen,* pp. 146–147, François, *Gorlice 1915,* p. 106

43. Hart, *The Somme,* pp. 414–415 and Paul Kennedy, "Britain in the First World War," *Military Effectiveness,* Vol. I, p. 55. To be sure, Ober Ost did employ cavalry in a mounted role operationally in the campaign in Lithuania during 1915, with some success if conditions were favorable. Captain von Ammon, *Die militärischen Lehren des Grossen Krieges,* p. 71.

44. Quoted in Herwig, *The First World War,* p. 392.

45. Showalter, *Tannenberg,* p. 344.

46. Germany, Reichsarchiv, *Der Weltkrieg 1914 bis 1918,* Vol. 7, p. 409, Eleventh Army to Falkenhayn, May 19, 1915 and Eleventh Army to OHL, June 3, 1915, BA-MA W 10/51388, and Kundmann diary, 4 June 4, 1915, Conrad Archive, ÖSA-KA B/13.

47. François, *Gorlice 1915,* pp. 208–209, and Foerster, ed., *Mackensen: Briefe und Aufzeichnungen,* p. 176.

48. Brusilov, *A Soldier's Notebook 1914–1918,* pp. 148–150, Jones, "Imperial Russia's Forces at War," *Military Effectiveness,* Vol. I, p. 310, and Danilov, *Russland im Weltkriege 1914–1915,* p. 505.

49. Stone, *The Eastern Front 1914–1917,* pp. 174–175 and Golovine, *The Russian Army in the World War,* p. 186.

50. Stone, *The Eastern Front 1914–1917,* p. 177, Jones, "Imperial Russia's Forces at War," *Military Effectiveness,* Vol. I, pp. 310–311, and François, *Gorlice 1915,* pp. 70–71.

51. Doughty, *Pyrrhic Victory*, pp. 153–154, Herwig, *The First World War*, p. 141, Germany, Reichsarchiv, *Der Weltkrieg 1914 bis 1918*, Vol. 7, p. 374, and Novikov, "Der russissche Nachrichtendienst vor den Gorlice-Durchbruch," p. 1671.

52. Herwig, *The First World War*, pp. 410–411.

53. Doughty, *Pyrrhic Victory*, pp. 478–479, Greenhalgh, *Victory Through Coalition*, p. 254, and Herwig, *The First World War*, p. 409.

Bibliography

ARCHIVAL MATERIALS

Austria

Österreichisches Staatsarchiv–Kriegsarchiv, Vienna

78—Military Chancery of His Majesty.
512—AOK Operations Bureau, Conrad-Falkenhayn Correspondence, Russia.
B/13—Rudolf Kundmann Diary, Conrad Archive.

Germany

Bayerisches Hauptstaatsarchiv–Kriegsarchiv, Munich

Nachlass Paul von Kneussl
NL 3
NL 4
Bavarian 8th Reserve Division
File 8R, Bund 1, Akt 3
File 8R, Bund 11, Akt 1
File 8R, Bund 11, Akt 2
Bavarian 11th Division
File 11, Bund 4, Akt 1
File 11, Bund 4, Akt 2
File 11, Bund 43, Akt 4
File 11, Bund 52, Akt 2
File 11, Bund 97, Akt 2

Bundesarchiv–Militärarchiv, Freiburg-im-Breisgau

MSg 1/1914—Karl von Kaganeck Diary
MSg 1/2514—Karl von Kaganeck Diary
MSg 109—Short Biographical Chronologies
N 39—*Nachlass* Mackensen
N 46—*Nachlass* Groener
N 56—*Nachlass* Tappen
N 77—*Nachlass* Ludendorff
N 247—*Nachlass* Seeckt
RM 28/53—German Admiralty Correspondence
W 10/50656—Plessen Diary
W 10/50661—Tappen Diary and Unpublished Memoir
W 10/50683—Conrad–Falkenhayn Correspondence, May 1915
W 10/50704—"Die Führung Falkenhayn, 1934"
W 10/50755—Training Documents, 1914–1918
W 10/51373—Beurteilung der Feindliche Lage (Ost) Jan.–Mar. 1915
W 10/51380—"Die Urheberschaft am Entschluss" (Gorlice)
W 10/51388—OHL, Ost Operationen, 18 Mai–Okt. 1915
W 10/51393—Austro–Hungarian VI Corps, May 1915
W 10/51443—"Ninth Army from January 1–February 5, 1915," 1927

PUBLISHED WORKS

Afflerbach, Holger. *Falkenhayn: Politisches Denken und Handeln im Kaiserreich*. Munich: R. Oldenbourg; 1996.

Austria, Bundesministerium für Landesverteidigung. *Österreich-Ungarns Letzter Krieg 1914–1918*. 7 Vols. Vienna: Verlag der Militärwissenschaftlichen Mitteilungen; 1931–1938.

Barnett, Correlli. *The Swordbearers: Supreme Command in the First World War*. Reprinted edition. Bloomington: Indiana University Press; 1975.

Barrett, Michael B. *Operation Albion: The German Conquest of the Baltic Islands*. Bloomington: Indiana University Press; 2008.

Berghaus, Erwin. *Vier Monate mit Mackensen: Von Tarnow–Gorlice bis Brest–Litovsk*. Stuttgart: Verlag von Julius Hoffmann; 1916.

Bettag, Franz. *Schlachten des Weltkrieges. Die Eroberung von Nowo Georgiewsk*. Berlin: Druck und Verlag von Gerhard Stalling; 1926.

Blumenthal, Generalfeldmarschall Carl Constantine Graf von. *Tagebucher des Generalfeldmarschalls Graf von Blumenthal aus den Jahren 1866 und 1870/71*. Albrecht Graf von Blumenthal ed. Berlin: Gotta'sche Buchhandlung Nachfolger; 1902.

Bose, Thilo von. *Das Kaiser Alexander Garde-Grenadier-Regiment Nr. 1 im Weltkriege 1914–1918*. Zeulenroda, Germany: Bernhard Sporn; 1932.

Brandt, Karsten. *Mackensen: Leben, Wesen und Wirken des deutschen Feldherrn*. Leipzig: Gustav Schloessmanns Verlagbuchhandlung; 1916.

Broadberry, Stephen, and Mark Harrison, eds. *The Economics of World War I*. New York: Cambridge University Press; 2005.

Brusilov, General Alexei A. *A Soldier's Notebook 1914–1918*. Reprinted edition. Westport, Conn.: Greenwood Press; 1970.

Bucholz, Arden. *Moltke, Schlieffen and Prussian War Planning*. Oxford: Berg Publishers; 1993.

Cecil, Lamar. *Wilhelm II.* 2 Vols. Chapel Hill: University of North Carolina Press; 1994–1996.

Churchill, Winston. *The Unknown War: The Eastern Front.* New York: Charles Scribner's Sons; 1931.

Citino, Robert M. *The German Way of War: From the Thirty Years' War to the Third Reich.* Lawrence: University Press of Kansas; 2005.

Citino, Robert M. *Quest for Decisive Victory: From Stalemate to Blitzkrieg in Europe, 1899–1940.* Lawrence: University Press of Kansas; 2002.

Conrad von Hötzendorf, Franz Baron. *Aus Meiner Dienstzeit 1906–1918.* 5 Vols. 6th ed. Vienna: Rikola Verlag; 1921–1925.

Conrad von Hötzendorf, Gina Grafin. *Mein Leben mit Conrad von Hötzendorf; Sein geistiges Vermächtnis.* Leipzig: Grathlein; 1935.

Craig, Gordon A. *Germany 1866–1945.* New York: Oxford University Press; 1978.

Cramon, August von. *Unser Österreich-Ungarischer Bundesgenosse im Weltkriege. Errinerungen aus meiner vierjährigen Tätigkeit als bevollmächtiger deutsche General beim K.u.K. Armeeoberkommando.* Berlin: E. S. Mittler und Sohn; 1920.

Cramon, August von, and Paul Fleck. *Deutschlands Schicksalsbund mit Österreich–Ungarn: Von Conrad von Hötzendorf zu Kaiser Carl.* Berlin: Verlag für Kulturpolitik; 1932.

Creveld, Martin van. *Supplying War: Logistics from Wallenstein to Patton.* 2nd ed. Cambridge: Cambridge University Press; 2005.

Cruttwell, C.R.M.F. *A History of the Great War 1914–1918.* Oxford: Oxford University Press; 1934.

Danilov, Yuri. *Russland im Weltkriege 1914–1915.* Jena, Germany: Frommannsche Buchhandlung; 1925.

Deák, István. *Beyond Nationalism: A Social and Political History of the Habsburg Officer Corps, 1848–1918.* New York: Oxford University Press; 1990.

DeGroot, Gerard. *Douglas Haig, 1861–1928.* London: Unwin and Hyman; 1988.

Deutsch, Harold C. "Sidelights on the Redl Case: Russian Intelligence on the Eve of the Great War," *Intelligence and National Security.* Vol. 4, No. 4 (October 1989): pp. 827–828.

Deutsche Gesellschaft für Wehrpolitik und Wehrwissenschaften. *Heerführer des Weltkrieges.* Berlin: E. S. Mittler und Sohn; 1939.

DiNardo, Richard L. "Huns with Web-Feet: Operation Albion, 1917," *War in History.* Vol. 12, No. 4 (November 2005): pp. 396–417.

DiNardo, Richard L. *Germany and the Axis Powers: From Coalition to Collapse.* Lawrence: University Press of Kansas; 2005.

DiNardo, Richard L., and Daniel J. Hughes. "Germany and Coalition Warfare in the World Wars: A Comparison," *War in History.* Vol. 8, No. 2 (April 2001): pp. 166–190.

Doughty, Robert A. *Pyrrhic Victory: French Strategy and Operations in the Great War.* Cambridge, Mass.: Harvard University Press; 2005.

Echevarria, II, Antulio J. *After Clausewitz: German Military Thought before the Great War.* Lawrence: University Press of Kansas; 2000.

Eder, Max. *Das Preussische Reserve-Infanterie-Regiment 269.* Zeulenroda, Germany: Bernhard Sporn Verlag; 1937.

Engelberg, Walther. *Das Reserve-Infanterie-Regiment Nr. 270 im Weltkriege 1914/1918.* Berlin: Verlag Bernard und Graefe; 1934.

Erfurth, General Waldemar. "Die Verteidigung im Landkrieg," Part II, *Militärwissenschaftliche Rundschau.* Vol. 1, No. 5 (August 1936): pp. 565–591.

Falkenhayn, General Erich von. *The German General Staff and Its Decisions, 1914–1916.* New York: Dodd, Mead; 1920.

Farmborough, Florence. *With the Armies of the Tsar: A Nurse at the Russian Front 1914–18.* New York: Stein and Day; 1975.

Fellgiebel, Colonel Erich. "Aus grosser Zeit vor zwanzig Jahren. Verwendung von Nachrichtenmitteln im ersten Kriegsjahr und Lehren für heute," *Militär Wochenblatt.* Vol. 119, Nr. 35 (18 March 1935): pp. 1371–1374.

Fischer, Fritz. *Germany's War Aims in the First World War.* New York: W. W. Norton; 1967.

Foerster, Roland G. ed. *Die Wehrpflicht: Entstehung, Erscheinungsformen und Politisch-militärische Wirkung.* Munich: R. Oldenbourg; 1994.

Foerster, Wolfgang. ed. *Mackensen: Briefe und Aufzeichnungen des Generalfeldmarschalls aus Krieg und Frieden.* Leipzig: Bibliographisches Institut; 1938.

Foerster, Wolfgang. ed. *Wir Kämpfer im Weltkrieg: Feldzugbriefe und Kriegstagebücher von Frontkämpfen aus dem Material des Reichsarchivs.* Berlin: Neufeld und Henius Verlag; 1929.

Foley, Robert T. *German Strategy and the Path to Verdun: Erich von Falkenhayn and the Development of Attrition; 1870–1916.* Cambridge: Cambridge University Press; 2005.

François, Hermann von. *Gorlice 1915. Der Karpathendurchbruch und die Befreiung von Galizien.* Leipzig: Verlag von K. F. Koehler; 1922.

Frank, Alison Fleig. *Oil Empire: Visions of Prosperity in Austrian Galicia.* Cambridge, Mass.: Harvard University Press; 2005.

Franks, Norman, Frank Bailey, and Rick Duivan. *Casualties of the German Air Service 1914–1920.* London: Grub Street; 1999.

Friedrich III, Kaiser. *Das Kriegstagebuch von 1870/71.* Heinrich Otto Meissner, ed. Berlin: Verlag von K. S. Koehler; 1926.

Friedrich, Prince of Prussia. *Das Erste Garderegiment zu Fuss im Weltkrieg 1914–1918.* Berlin: Junker und Dünnhaupt; 1934.

Fuller, William C. Jr. *The Foe Within: Fantasies of Treason and the End of Imperial Russia.* Ithaca, N.Y.: Cornell University Press; 2006.

Fuller, William C. Jr. *Strategy and Power in Russia 1600–1914.* New York: The Free Press; 1992.

Germany, Reichsarchiv, *Der Weltkrieg 1914 bis 1918.* 14 Vols. Berlin: E. S. Mittler und Sohn; 1925–1944.

Golovine, Lieutenant General Nicholas N. *The Russian Army in the World War,* New Haven, Conn.: Yale University Press; 1931.

Görlitz, Walter, ed. *The Kaiser and His Court: The Diaries, Notebooks and Letters of Admiral Georg Alexander von Müller, Chief of the Naval Cabinet 1914–1918.* New York: Harcourt, Brace and World; 1961.

Greenhalgh, Elizabeth. *Victory through Coalition: Britain and France During the First World War.* Cambridge: Cambridge University Press; 2005.

Gross, Gerhard P., ed. *Die vergessene Front. Der Osten 1914/15: Ereignis, Wirkung, Nachwirkung.* Paderborn, Germany: Ferdinand Schöningh; 2006.

Gudmundsson, Bruce I. *Stormtroop Tactics: Innovation in the German Army, 1914–1918.* Reprinted edition. Westport, Conn.: Praeger; 1995.

Hagen, Mark von. *War in a European Borderland: Occupations and Occupation Plans in Galicia and Ukraine, 1914–1918.* Seattle: University of Washington Press; 2007.

Hamilton, Richard F., and Holger H. Herwig. *Decisions for War, 1914–1917.* Cambridge: Cambridge University Press; 2004.

Hart, Peter. *The Somme: The Darkest Hour on the Western Front.* New York: Pegasus Books; 2008.

Healy, Maureen. *Vienna and the Fall of the Habsburg Empire: Total War and Everyday Life in World War I.* New York: Cambridge University Press; 2004.

Heinrici, Paul, ed. *Das Ehrenbuch der deutschen Pionere.* Berlin: Verlag Tradition Wilhelm Kolk; 1932.

Herwig, Holger H. *The First World War: Germany and Austria–Hungary 1914–1918.* London: Arnold; 1997.

Herwig, Holger H., and Richard F. Hamilton, eds. *The Origins of World War I.* Cambridge: Cambridge University Press; 2003.

Herwig, Holger H., and Neil M. Heyman. *Biographical Dictionary of World War I.* Westport, Conn.: Greenwood Press; 1982.

Hindenburg, Paul von. *Aus meinem Leben.* Leipzig: Verlag von S. Hirzel; 1920.

Hirschfeld, Gerhard, Gerd Krumeich, and Irina Renz, eds. *Enzyklopädia Erster Weltkrieg.* Paderborn, Germany: Ferdinand Schöningh; 2004.

Höbelt, Lothar. "Schlieffen, Potiorek und das Ende der gemeinsam deutschösterreichisch-ungarischen Aufmarschpläne im Osten." *Militärgeschichtlichen Mitteilungen.* No. 36 (1984): pp. 7–30.

Hoeppner, General of Cavalry Ernest von. *Germany's War in the Air: The Development and Operations of German Military Aviation in the World War.* Nashville, Tenn.: The Battery Press; 1994.

Hoffmann, Major General Max. *War Diaries and Other Papers.* 2 Vols. Eric Sutton trans. London: Martin Secker; 1929.

Hughes, Daniel J. *The Kings Finest: A Social and Bureaucratic Profile of Prussia's General Officers, 1871–1914.* Westport, Conn.: Praeger; 1987.

Hughes, Lindsey. *The Romanovs: Ruling Russia 1613–1917.* London: Hambledon; 2008.

Hull, Isabel V. *The Entourage of Kaiser Wilhelm II 1888–1918.* Cambridge: Cambridge University Press; 1982.

Jäger, Herbert. *German Artillery of World War One.* Baydon, U.K.: The Crowood Press; 2001.

Johnson, Douglas Wilson. *Topography and Strategy in the War.* New York: Henry Holt; 1917.

Kalm, Oskar Tile von. *Schlachten des Weltkrieges. Gorlice.* Berlin: Oldenbourg; 1930.

Kessel, Eberhard. *Moltke.* Stuttgart: K. F. Koehler; 1957.

Kihntopf, Michael P. *Handcuffed to a Corpse: German Intervention in the Balkans and the Galician Front, 1914–1917.* Shippensburg, Penn.: White Mane Books; 2002.

Knoerzer, General Hans. "Hannibal und Hindenberg, ein zeitgemasser Vergleich." *Militär Wochenblatt.* Vol. 106, No. 13 (24 September 1921): pp. 265–268.

Kolshorn, Otto. *Unser Mackensen: Ein Leben und Charakterbild.* Berlin: E. S. Mittler und Sohn; 1916.

Kraft, Heinrich. *Der Anteil der 11. Bayer. Inf. Div. an der Durchbruchsschlacht von Gorlice–Tarnow.* Munich: C. H. Beck'sche Verlagsbuchhandlung; 1934.

Kronenbitter, Günther. "Die Macht der Illusionen: Juli Krise und Kriegsausbruch 1914 aus der Sicht des deutschen Militärattachés in Wien." *Militärgeschichtliche Mitteilungen.* Vol. 57, No. 2 (1998): pp. 519–550.

Kuhl, General of Infantry Hermann von. *Der Weltkrieg 1914–1918.* 2 Vols. Berlin: Verlag Tradition Wilhelm Kolk; 1929.

Liddell Hart, B. H. *Through the Fog of War.* New York: Random House; 1938.

Liddell Hart, B. H. *History of the First World War.* Reprinted edition. London: Cassell; 1970.

Lincoln, W. Bruce. *Passage through Armageddon: The Russians in War and Revolution 1914–1918.* New York: Simon and Schuster; 1986.

Liulevicius, Vejas Gabriel. *War Land on the Eastern Front: Culture, National Identity and German Occupation in World War I.* Cambridge: Cambridge University Press; 2000.

Lohr, Eric. "The Russian Army and the Jews: Mass Deportations, Hostages and Violence during World War I." *The Russian Review*. Vol. 60, No. 3 (July 2001): pp. 404–419.

Ludendorff, Erich. *Meine Kriegserinnerungen 1914–1918*. Berlin: E. S. Mittler und Sohn; 1919.

Ludendorff, Erich. *Tannenberg: Geschichtliche Wahrheit über die Schlacht*. Munich: Ludendorffs Verlag; 1939.

Luyken, Walter. *Das 2. Garde-Feldartillerie-Regiment im Weltkriege*. Berlin: Verlag Tradition Wilhelm Kolk; 1929.

Markus, Georg. *Der Fall Redl*. Vienna: Amalthea Verlag; 1984.

Meier-Welcker, Hans. *Seeckt*. Frankfurt-am-Main: Bernard und Graefe Verlagfür Wehrwesen; 1967.

Millett, Allan R. and Williamson Murray, eds. *Military Effectiveness*. 3 Vols. Boston: Allen and Unwin; 1988.

Mohr, Eike. *Heeres- und Truppengeschichte des Deutschen Reiches und Seiner Länder 1806 bis 1918: eine Bibliographie*. Osnabrück: Biblio Verlag; 1989.

Moltke, Colonel General Helmuth von. *Erinnerungen–Briefe–Dokumente*. Eliza von Moltke, ed. Stuttgart: Der Kommende Tag; 1922.

Mombauer, Annika. *Helmuth von Moltke and the Origins of the First World War*. Cambridge: Cambridge University Press; 2001.

Mombauer, Annika, and Wilhelm Deist, eds. *The Kaiser: New Research on Wilhelm II's Role in Imperial Germany*. Cambridge: Cambridge University Press; 2003.

Mönckeberg, Carl. *Bei Süd und Bug Armee 1915*. Stuttgart: Deutsche Verlags Anstalt; 1917.

Neiberg, Michael S. *Foch: Supreme Allied Commander in the Great War*. Washington, D.C.: Brassey's; 2003.

Novikov, General A. A. "Der russische Nachrichtendienst vor der Gorlice-Durchbruch." *Militär Wochenblatt*. Vol. 119, No. 2 (May 11, 1935): pp. 1670–1671.

Oye, David Schimmelpennick van der, and Bruce W Menning, eds. *Reforming the Tsar's Army: Military Innovation in Imperial Russia from Peter the Great to the Revolution*. Cambridge: Cambridge University Press; 2004.

Palmer, Svetlana, and Sarah Wallis, eds. *Intimate Voices from the First World War*. New York: William Morrow; 2003.

Pares, Bernard. *Day by Day With the Russian Army 1914–1915*. Boston: Houghton Mifflin; 1915.

Paret, Peter, ed. *Makers of Modern Strategy*. Princeton, N.J.: Princeton University Press; 1986.

Parkinson, Roger. *Tormented Warrior: Ludendorff and the Supreme Command*. New York: Stein and Day; 1979.

Passingham, Ian. *Pillars of Fire: The Battle of Messines Ridge June 1917*. Stroud, U.K.: Sutton Publishing; 1998.

Petrovsky-Shtern, Yohanan. *Jews in the Russian Army, 1827–1917: Drafted into Modernity*. New York: Cambridge University Press; 2009.

Prior, Robin, and Trevor Wilson. *Command on the Western Front*. Oxford: Blackwell; 1992.

Prior, Robin, and Trevor Wilson. *Passchendaele: The Untold Story*. New Haven, Conn.: Yale University Press; 1996.

Rauchensteiner, Manfred. *Der Tod des Doppeladlers: Österreich–Ungarn und der Erste Weltkrieg*. Vienna: Verlag Styria; 1993.

Ritter, Gerhard. *The Schlieffen Plan: Critique of a Myth*. New York: Praeger; 1958.

Ritter, Gerhard. *The Sword and the Scepter: The Problem of Militarism in Germany.* 4 Vols. Coral Gables, Fla.: University of Miami Press; 1970.

Rosenberg-Lipinsky, Hans-Oskar von. *Das Königin Elisabeth Garde-Grenadier-Regiment Nr. 3 im Weltkreige 1914–1918.* Zeulenroda, Germany: Verlag Bernhard Sporn; 1935.

Rothenberg, Gunther E. *The Army of Francis Joseph.* West Lafayette, Ind.: Purdue University Press; 1976.

Schindler, John R. *Isonzo: The Forgotten Sacrifice of the Great War.* Westport, Conn.: Praeger; 2001.

Schmidt-Pauli, Edgar von. *General von Seeckt: Lebensbild eines Deutschen Soldaten.* Berlin: Verlag Reinar Hobbing; 1937.

Schwarzmüller, Theo. *Zwischen Kaiser und Führer. Generalfeldmarschall August von Mackensen: Eine politische Biographie.* Paderborn, Germany: Ferdinand Schöningh; 1996.

Seeckt, Hans von. *Aus meinem Leben 1866–1917.* Leipzig: Von Hase und Koehler Verlag; 1938.

Seyfert, Gerhard. *Die militärischen Beziehungen und Vereinbarungen zwischen dem deutschen und österreichischen Generalstab vor und bei Beginn des Weltkrieges.* Leipzig: J. Moltzen; 1934.

Shanafelt, Gary W. *The Secret Enemy: Austria-Hungary and the German Alliance, 1914–1918.* Boulder, Colo.: East European Monographs; 1985.

Showalter, Dennis E. *Tannenberg: Clash of Empires, 1914.* Reprinted edition. Dulles, Va.: Brassey's; 2004.

Smith, Leonard V., Stephane Audoin-Rouzeau, and Annette Becker. *France and the Great War 1914–1918.* Cambridge: Cambridge University Press; 2003.

Sondhaus, Lawrence. *Franz Conrad von Hötzendorf: Architect of the Apocalypse.* Boston: Humanities Press; 2000.

Stengal, Franz Freiherr von. *Das K.B. 3. Infanterie-Regiment Prinz Karl von Bayern 1914–1918.* Munich: Verlag Bayerisches Kriegsarchiv; 1924.

Stone, Norman. *The Eastern Front 1914–1917.* New York: Charles Scribner's Sons; 1975.

Strachan, Hew. *The First World War.* Vol. I. *To Arms.* New York: Oxford University Press; 2001.

Stürgkh, Count Josef. *Im Deutschen Grossen Hauptquartier.* Leipzig: Paul List Verlag; 1921.

Sukhomlinov, V. A. *Erinnerungen.* Berlin: Reimar Hobbing; 1924.

Trach, Leonhard Graf von Rothkirch Freiherr von. *Gorlice–Tarnow.* Oldenburg, Germany: Verlag von Gerhard Stalling; 1918.

Travers, Tim. *The Killing Ground: The British Army, the Western Front and the Emergence of Modern Warfare, 1900–1918.* London: Routledge; 1987.

Tunstall, Graydon A. Jr. *Planning For War Against Russia and Serbia: Austro–Hungarian and German Military Strategies, 1871–1914.* Boulder, Colo.: East European Monographs; 1993.

Überegger, Oswald. "Auf der Flucht vor dem Krieg. Trentiner und Tirolen Deserteure im Ersten Weltkrieg." *Militärgeschichtliche Zeitschrift.* Vol. 62, No. 2 (2007): pp. 355–393.

Uhle-Wettler, Franz. *Erich Ludendorff in Seiner Zeit: Soldat—Stratege—Revolutionär: Eine Neubewertung.* Augsburg, Germany: Kurt Vowinckel Verlag; 1996.

Unger, Fritz von. *Das Königin Augusta Garde-Grenadier-Regiment Nr. 4 im Weltkriege 1914–1919.* Berlin: Gebr Ohst Verlag; 1922.

Urbanski von Ostrymiecz, August. *Conrad von Hötzendorf: Soldat und Mensch.* Vienna: Ulrich Mosers Verlag; 1938.

Viereck, Helmut. *Das Heideregiment Königlich Preussisches 2. Hannoversches Infanterie-Regiment Nr. 77 im Weltkriege 1914–1918.* Celle, Germany: Druck und Verlag August Pohl; 1934.

Vitarbo, Gregory. "Nationality Policy and the Russian Imperial Officer Corps, 1905–1914." *Slavic Review.* Vol. 66, No. 4 (Winter 2007): pp. 682–701.

Wallach, Jehuda. *The Dogma of the Battle of Annihilation: The Theories of Clausewitz and Schlieffen and Their Impact on the German Conduct of Two World Wars.* Westport Conn.: Greenwood Press; 1986.

Wendt, Hermann. *Der italienische Kriegsschauplatz in europäischen Konflikten. Seine Bedeutung für die Kriegführungen an Frankreichs Nordostgrenze.* Berlin: Dunnhaupt Verlag; 1936.

Wetzell, General Georg. *Der Bündniskrieg: Eine militärpolitisch operative Studie des Weltkrieges.* Berlin: E. S. Mittler und Sohn; 1937.

Wheeler-Bennett, John. *Wooden Titan: Hindenburg in Twenty Years of German History 1914–1934.* New York: William Morrow; 1936.

Wiest, Andrew A. *Haig: The Evolution of a Commander.* Washington, D.C.: Potomac Books; 2005.

Wild von Hohenborn, Adolf. *Briefe und Tagebuchaufzeichnungen des preussischen Generals als Kriegsminister und Truppenführer im Ersten Weltkrieg.* Helmut Reinhold, ed. Boppard-am-Rhein: Harald Boldt Verlag; 1986.

Winter, Denis. *Haig's Command: A Reassessment.* New York: Viking; 1991.

Witkop, Philipp, ed. *German Students' War Letters.* Reprinted edition. Philadelphia: Pine Street Books; 2002.

Ziethen, General Alfred. "Aus grosser Zeit vor zwanzig Jahren. Die Durchbruchsschlacht von Gorlice." *Militär Wochenblatt.* Vol. 119, No. 41 (4 May 1935): pp. 1627–1632.

Ziethen, General Alfred. "Aus grosser Zeit vor zwanzig Jahren. Die Durchbruchsschlacht von Gorlice." *Militär Wochenblatt.* Vol. 119, No. 42 (11 May 1935): pp. 1667–1670.

Zuber, Terence. *Inventing the Schlieffen Plan: German War Planning, 1871–1914.* Oxford: Oxford University Press; 2002.

Index

Hofmann, Generalleutnant Max, 8, 16, 18, 92
Hohensalza, 39
Hranilovic, Colonel Oskar, 23

Isonzo River, 87, 103, 125, 143
Italy, 20, 26, 27, 61, 76, 82, 83, 84, 85, 86, 99, 100, 103, 104, 105, 107, 115, 125, 143
Ivangorod, 11, 12, 108, 117, 121, 124, 125, 126
Ivanov, General Nicholas, 10, 27, 52, 90, 94, 101, 106, 142; commander of southwest front, 10; reaction to German breakthrough at Gorlice, 77, 83

Jablonska, Helena, 24, 25, 82
Jagow, Gottlieb von, 113
Jaroslau, 72, 73, 74, 75, 80, 83, 88, 94, 97, 107, 109, 111
Jasiolka River, 63
Jaslo, 61, 64, 65, 66, 71
Joffre, Marshal Joseph, 5, 49, 135
Josefowka, 88, 89, 92
Joseph Ferdinand, Archduke, 42, 43, 60, 94, 113; commander of Austro-Hungarian Fourth Army, 30, 42, 87

Kaganeck, Karl von, 7; German military attaché in Vienna, 7, 23; views of behavior at AOK, 20
Kamieniec Forest, 58
Karl, Emperor of Austria Hungary, 19
Kestranek, Feldmarschalleutnant Paul, 46, 58, 65
Kirchbach auf Lauterbach, General der Infanterie Karl Freiherr von, 121
Kneussl, Generalmajor Paul Ritter von, 44, 45, 56, 60, 61, 62, 63, 75, 76, 80, 81, 82, 88, 99
Kornilov, General Lavr, 71
Kosch, Generalleutnant Robert, 125
Kotowka Forest, 91
Kovel, 119, 128, 129, 141
Krakowiec Lake, 93
Kovno, 107, 108, 109, 115, 117, 125, 127, 130, 132, 142

Kralicek, Feldmarschalleutnant Rudolf, 60
Krasnik, 112, 113, 118
Kressenstein, Generaloberst Otto Freiherr Kress von, 45
Kritek, General der Infanterie Karl, 89
Kuhl, Hermann von, 2, 40, 49
Kundmann, Lieutenant Colonel Rudolf, 13, 19
Kusmanek von Burgneustädten, Hermann, 24, 25

Leeb, Captain Wilhelm Ritter von, 45
Lemberg, 3, 10, 20, 35, 83, 84, 86, 89, 91, 92, 94, 95, 97, 98, 99, 102, 105, 106, 109, 110, 112, 113, 119, 136, 141
Leopold, Generalfeldmarschall Prince of Bavaria, 108, 120, 121, 124
Lesh, General Leonid, 77, 94, 97, 98, 106, 118, 125
Liddell Hart, B.H., 137
Limanowa-Lapanow, 13, 46
Liman von Sanders, Generalleutnant Otto, 104
Linsingen, General der Infanterie Alexander von, 22, 24, 34, 110, 112, 114, 119, 121, 126, 129, 132; commander of the Süd Army, 22; appointed commander of the Bug Army, 111
Lithuania, 105, 117, 130
Litvinov, General A.I., 120
Lodz, 14, 37, 38, 39, 106
Lötzen, 108
Longstreet, James, 38
Lubaczowka River, 78, 91, 92, 93
Lublin, 106, 117, 118, 119, 122, 125, 126, 127, 128
Ludendorff, Generalmajor Erich, 1, 2, 3, 8, 9, 11, 13, 15, 16, 21, 22, 23, 26, 32, 39, 40, 103, 108, 109, 114, 115, 124, 125, 130, 132, 136, 137, 138, 141, 143; opinion of Austro-Hungarians, 37, 100; opinion of Falkenhayn, 37; opinion of Mackensen, 41
Ludwig III, King of Bavaria, 45
Lüttwitz, Generalleutnant Walter Freiherr von, 111

About the Author

RICHARD L. DINARDO is professor for national security affairs at the Marine Corps Command and Staff College in Quantico, Virginia. He is the author of a number of books and articles on a wide variety of topics in military history. His most recent book on German military history, *Germany and the Axis Powers: From Coalition to Collapse,* appeared in 2005. Among his other books are *Germany's Panzer Arm* and *Mechanized Juggernaut or Military Anachronism?: Horses and the German Army in World War II.*